LANIN A.
GYURKO

SPELLBOUND

ALFRED HITCHCOCK
AND
CARLOS FUENTES

UNIVERSITY PRESS
OF THE SOUTH

2021

Published in the United States by The University Press of the South. Printed in France by Monbeaulivre.fr
E-mails: unprsouth@aol.com; universitypresssouth@gmail.com
Visit our award-winning web pages: www.unprsouth.com
www.punouveaumonde.com

Lanin A. Gyurko.
Spellbound. Alfred Hitchcock and Carlos Fuentes.
Second Edition in English.
xii + 418 pages. Cinema Studies Series, 10. Latin American Studies Series, 32.
Front Cover Art by Carlos Mal Pacheco: 'Alfred Hitchcock Meets Aztec Mexico.'
Front Cover Design by Ector Sandoval.
1. Alfred Hitchcock. 2. Carlos Fuentes. 3. Vertigo. 4. Rear Window. 5. The Birds.
6. Aura. 7. Double Theme. 8. Vampirism. 9. Obsession. 10. Supernatural.

ISBN: 978-1-937030-08-7 (First Edition: USA, 2012)
ISBN: 978-1-952799-35-8 (Second Edition: Europe, 2021)

To the memory of Dr. Gustavo Correa, eminent Professor of Spanish, Yale University, in honor of his masterful teaching, superb scholarship, and unremitting dedication to his students.

To the memory of the inimitable, highly versatile actor Warner Baxter (1889-1951). His greatest role, as Julian Marsh, the hard-biting, driven yet compassionate stage director in *42nd Street* (1933)—one of the most sparkling of Hollywood musicals—is parallelled by his flamboyant performance in the starring role of *In Old Arizona* (1929) and *The Cisco Kid* (1931).

CONTENTS

VII

“Jean Harlow was very soft about her toughness.” GEORGE CUKOR

“Everybody wants to be Cary Grant. Even *I* want to be Cary Grant.” CARY GRANT

“Joan Crawford was the perfect image of the movie star, and, as such, was largely the creation of her own indomitable will.” GEORGE CUKOR

“With all the unrest in the world, I don’t think anybody should have a yacht that sleeps more than twelve.” JOE/JOSEPHINE IN BILLY WILDER’S *SOME LIKE IT HOT*

“Man’s main task is to give birth to himself.” ERICH FROMM, PSYCHOLOGIST AND SOCIOLOGIST

“To fulfill a dream, to be allowed to sweat over lonely labor, to be given the chance to create, is the meat and potatoes of life.” BETTE DAVIS, HOLLYWOOD SUPERSTAR

“Make visible what, without you, might perhaps never have been seen.” ROBERT BRESSON, FRENCH FILM DIRECTOR

The ten commandments of a film director, by BILLY WILDER: Commandments one through nine: Never be boring. Tenth commandment: Always leave the final cut for yourself.

“We know that people like legends. I think people like legends more than they like truth. I think there is a fascination with the western hero, because the West is a great myth.” LINDSAY

ANDERSON, BRITISH FILMMAKER

"When legend becomes fact, print the legend"
THE MAN WHO SHOT LIBERTY VALENCE, 1962

"If we were a primitive society, movie stars would be gods." SYDNEY POLLACK, HOLLYWOOD DIRECTOR

"No more goddamn shop girls. " JOAN CRAWFORD TO LOUIS B. MAYER, HEAD OF METRO-GOLDWYN-MAYER

"My movies have always been more devious, or, if you prefer a more devious word, sinister." ALFRED HITCHCOCK, MOTION PICTURE DIRECTOR

"It is the way our sympathy flows and recoils that really determines our lives. And here lies the importance of the novel, properly handled: it can lead the sympathetic consciousness into new places, and away in recoil from things gone dead." D.H. LAWRENCE, *LADY CHATTERLEY'S LOVER*

IX

"They were different from those coming along now, and they were conscious of it. They had a dignity and straightforwardness about them from the fact that they had worked in pictures before pictures were bathed in a golden haze of success. They were still rather humble before their amazing triumph, and thus, unlike the new generation, who took it all for granted, they were constantly in touch with reality. Half a dozen or so of the women were especially aware of being unique. No one had come along to fill their places; here and there a pretty face had caught the public imagination for a year, but those of the old crowd were already legends, ageless and disembodied. With all this, they were still young enough to believe that they would go on forever."

F. SCOTT FITZGERALD, "MAGNETISM" (1928)

ACKNOWLEDGEMENTS

To Malcolm A. Compitello, *suaviter in modo, fortiter in re*, dynamic and innovative Head of the Department of Spanish and Portuguese, for his exemplary leadership and for his strong support of this project throughout all of its stages. To Mary Wildner-Basett, Dean of the College of Humanities at the University of Arizona for her generous support of this endeavor. To Eric Wheeler for his great computer expertise and dedication. To Ainsley M. Lloyd, for her outstanding technical mastery and genius work at the computer. To Mary Portillo, Administrative Associate in the Department of Spanish and Portuguese, for her outstanding dedication and expertise. To Dr. Alberto Chamorro, Professor at Drury University, for his generosity and expert knowledge of Latin American Film. To the many brilliant graduate students at the University of Arizona in my seminars on Mexican Literature and Film Studies and the Latin American Literature of the Fantastic, and especially to Nathan Mehr, Claudia Cruz, Maritza Maldonado,Thalia Martinez, Elsa Velasquez, Edgard Ore-Giron, Jose Ninawanka, Crescencio Lopez, Wasilia Yapur, Eva Romero, Luis Anchondo, Teresa Lorenz and Gilbert Gutierrez. To Professor Guadalupe Cruikshank, Director of the Department of Modern Languages at Pima College, for her outstanding teaching, research, and administrative expertise. To Dr. Alain Saint-Saens, distinguished Editor, Scholar, Teacher and Administrator, for his unflagging dedication to the Humanities. And to the always inspiring, extraordinarily creative and scholarly masters Professor Miguel Leon Portilla of the Universidad Nacional Autonoma de Mexico, and Manuel Duran, Professor at Yale University. To Dottie, Harrison, and Elaine Mildred Gyurko, as Always, and to my good friends and colleagues in the English Department at the University of Arizona, Professors Gerald Monsman, Edgar Dryden, Jerry Hogle, Charles Scruggs, Ken McAllister, Peter Medine, Roger Dahood, Roseann Gonzalez, Robert Houston, Suresh Raval, and to the Memory of the inimitable and wonderful poets Peter Wild and Steve Orlen.

INTRODUCTION: TWO MASTERS OF PSYCHOLOGICAL REALISM AND THE FANTASTIC

Why a book on Alfred Hitchcock and Carlos Fuentes? Since the 1980s, when the estate of Hitchcock re-released after a hiatus of twenty years major films like *Rear Window* and *Vertigo* and *Rope* which had been kept out of public circulation after the death of Hitchcock, the critical bibliography of the Hollywood master has rapidly expanded—testifying not only to the extraordinary impact of the superb, iconic director in Great Britain, the United States, and the world, but also to the depth and passion and power of his cinematic brilliance. At one point in his lengthy career, which spanned both Silent and Sound films, as Hitchcock began his film career in Great Britain as a titler in Silent Film, Hitchcock was regarded primarily as a gigantic commercial success—a fabulator of murder mysteries with a penchant for never-before screened violence and horror. It is only in the last twenty years that his art is being analyzed and interpreted—and enormously appreciated—as high art, and as the cornerstone of the development of the feature film industry. Similarly, the critical bibliography on the Mexican novelist, short story writer, dramatist and essayist Carlos Fuentes, the founder and leading exponent of the titanic Latin American Novel of the Boom—whose primary exponents also include two writers who have received the Nobel Prize in Literature—Gabriel García Márquez, the Colombian master of magical realism, whose most famous works are *Cien años de soledad* (*One Hundred Years of Solitude)* and *El amor en los tiempos de cólera (Love in the Time of Cholera*) and, in 2011, Mario Vargas Llosa, the great Realist author from Peru, among whose novels are *La ciudad y los perros*, *La casa verde, Conversación en la catedral* and *La tía Julia y el escribidor*, as well as the late Julio Cortázar, one of the most important short story writers of the twentieth century and the successor of Edgar Allan Poe and Franz Kafka. Cortázar's narrative masterpiece *Rayuela* (*Hopscotch*) thrust the Argentine expatriate, who for much of his life resided in Saignon, France, near to his beloved Paris, into the limelight as a fitting successor to the Irish novelist who so brilliantly experimented with language and myth—James Joyce—in his masterful *Ulysses.* And Carlos Fuentes himself—a literary dynamo, still restlessly active in his eighties, the author of vast epic novels like *La región más transparente* and *La muerte de Artemio Cruz* and *Cambio de piel* and *Terra nostra*, has many times been among finalists for the coveted Nobel Prize in Literature, which thus far has eluded him but which he most assuredly deserves.

Fuentes through his outstanding literary art and through his relentless publicity and his success at attracting North American agents to promote his works in the United States, opened the doors for countless Latin American authors, like, in the 1960s and 1970s, the Chilean José Donoso, who in his seminal work *Historia personal del Boom (A Personal History of the Boom)* renders extensive homage to Fuentes's inspiring leadership as well as to many Mexican novelists, particularly those of a literary movement called La Onda including Gustavo Sainz and José Agustín. Similarly, the impact of Alfred Hitchcock on Hollywood directors is enormous—films, now regarded as cinematic classics, like *Psycho* and *Vertigo*and *To Catch a Thief* and *Dial M for Murder* and *North by Northwest* and *The Birds* and *Marnie* have had a decisive impact on leading contemporary Hollywood directors like Brian De Palma and on Latin American film directors like González Iñarritu in his brilliant film *Amores perros.*

What factors can join Hitchcock and Fuentes? Major cinematic currents which have deeply impacted both Hitchcock and Fuentes are the films of German Expressionism—*M* and *Dr. Mabuse der Spieler* of the inimitable Fritz Lang, *Das Kabinett des Doktor Caligari* of Robert Wiene, *Der blaue Engel* of Eric Von Sternberg as well as the dark, tragic Hollywood *film noir* of the 1940s. Literarily, the spellbinding short stories and poems of the master of the stunning depiction of Gothic horror, Edgar Allan Poe, from *The Fall of the House of Usher* to poems of dark and beauty and death and the supernatural like "The Raven" and "Annabel Lee" have exerted a powerful influence on the art of the psychological and the supernatural of both Carlos Fuentes and Alfred Hitchcock. Both outstanding Hollywood director and Latin

American narrative master are perfectionists, both are masters of the intricate interplay of darkness and light, death and new life, suffering and redemption. Both firmly believe in the art of illusion—the conjurer's art—that casts a spell over its beholder.

Carlos Fuentes, the outstanding and chameleonic contemporary Mexican novelist, short story writer, essayist, and dramatist, is an extraordinarily eclectic writer, one who blends the worlds of painting, dance, sculpture, architecture, and film, both explicitly and implicitly, into his literary art. Indeed, Fuentes is one of the most visual of Latin American and world authors, and the dynamism, intensity, and depth of his creative vision owe much to the world of the Visual Arts.

In an interview with Fuentes conducted by the author of this study, the distinguished writer and dynamic, forceful public speaker commented on the great power which the cinematic image in particular exerts on the literary artist, and then added, somewhat apprehensively, that perhaps it was too powerful. One of the basic reasons for Fuentes's skillful incorporation of themes, techniques and structures from the cinema into his literary vision may very well be an attempt to harness that power, and in the process to demonstrate the unity of the verbal and the visual modes of expression.

Fuentes's masterful art is one of continual synthesis: of literary genres, historical epochs and humanistic disciplines. Indeed, he is the maximum exponent of the *novela totalizante* or all-encompassing novel in Latin America—a dazzling, experimental fusion of reality and fantasy, history and philosophy, architecture, sociology and psychology, linguistic innovations and anthropological themes, music, painting, theatre, and cinema. Cinema, the only original art form of the twentieth and twenty-first centuries, can be seen as the culmination of all the arts—and so too is the highly eclective universe elaborated by Carlos Fuentes. Fuentes's works have markedly expanded the scope of the Mexican novel, as they stunningly evoke the Pre-Columbian, Aztec and Mayan era and world, and the sanguinary Conquest of Aztec Mexico by Hernán Cortés and Pedro de Alvarado to the Juárez Reform era in the nineteenth century and the French Intervention that led to the imposition of a monarchy under the ill-fated Emperor Maximilian and his consort Carlotta, and from the

Mexican Revolution of 1910 to the depiction of the massacre of the student protesters in the Plaza of Nonoalco-Tlatelolco in 1968. And, in vatic novels such as *Cristóbal nonato* (1987), Fuentes prophetically envisions the Mexico City of the year 1992, just as *Terra nostra* (1978) focuses prophetically on the world of 2000, which Fuentes evokes dramatically, in terms of the Apocalypse. And much of what Fuentes foresees as afflicting his country years in advance, comes tragically to occur, like his grim ecological predictions in *Cristóbal nonato.*

Fuentes's art is one of dynamic and extensive intertexuality, as he constantly builds literature out of literature, expertly weaving into mammoth creative novels, such as *Terra nostra*, themes and characters from the most important works of the literature of Spain in the Golden Age: characters such as Celestina, Don Juan, Don Quixote and Sancho Panza. Paralleling this complex intertexuality, in which authors such as Miguel de Cervantes, Alexandre Dumas, Franz Kafka, James Joyce, and Ramón López Velarde are all re-created in Fuentes's own works, to emphasize the art of literary creation as a communal and democratic process, is a phenomenon which can be termed "intervisuality"—Fuentes's incessant incorporation of characters, settings, themes and plots, as well as a plethora of cinematic techniques such as closeups and crosscutting, pan shots and dissolves, distant shots and forward and reverse zoom shots, as well as allusions to directors, actors, and actresses from myriad Hollywood, Mexican, European, and Asian films. Through this dexterous and highly imaginative employment of visual influences, Fuentes convincingly brings to fruition his theory of what the new novel in Latin America should be—a narrative of openness: "El lenguaje ... de la ambigüedad, de la pluralidad de significados, de la constelación de alusiones: de la apertura." ["The language of ambiguity, of the plurality of meanings, of the constellation of allusions: of openness."] [1]

In an interview, Fuentes has referred to himself as a "putter-inner, not a taker-outer," as he characterizes the vast scope of the many five and six-hundred page novels that he has written.[2]

---

[1] See Carlos Fuentes, *La nueva novela hispanoamericana* (México: Joaquín Mortiz, 1969), p. 32. Translation by L.G.

[2] Consult the interview between Fuentes and Emir Rodríguez Monegal, included

In this regard, the definition of cinema as an all-encompassing art given by Canudo *(L'Usine aux images)* as "a fusion of the three arts of space—painting, architecture and dance, and of the three arts of time—music, theatre, and literature" helps to explain why Fuentes is so fascinated by the world of the cinema. Emphasizing the great importance of film for him, he states:

> Plato defined time as the moving image of eternity. When eternity moves, it's called time. Well, I think the film has given us that. The greatest heartbreak of our personal lives can finally be inscribed in the permanent memory of film today. It gives an eternity as it moves. It gives us a chance to be present in time. The photograph gave us an identity in the 19th-century. The movie gives us our identity today.[3]

It is the intensely mythic nature of film as well as its constant emphasis on motion—indeed *Kino* in Greek signifies movement, giving us *cinema* and in English, movies—that so often inspires Fuentes. In an extensive interview with James Fortson, in response to the journalist's inquiry about what constitutes the fundamental significance of film for him, Fuentes replies eloquently:

> Its mythologizing capacity. What finally matters to me about film is the structuring of a modern pantheon, the construction of a whole contemporary mythology . . . Film has created all the contemporary myths: those shadows move across the screen as Apollo and Venus and all of the gods of Olympus could have passed through the mind of an ancient Greek: the movie stars are the ghosts of the gods.[4]

---

in *Homenaje a Carlos Fuentes*, edited by Helmy Giacoman (New York: Las Américas, 1971), p. 43.

[3] See Carlos Fuentes, interview conducted by Claudia Dreifus, *Film Comment*, XXII, 3 (May-June, 1986), p. 52.

[4] Consult James R. Fortson, *Perspectivas mexicanas desde París: Un diálogo con Carlos Fuentes*, Supplement to *Él* (México: Corporación Editorial, 1973), p. 84. The translation is by L.G.

Orson Welles's cinematic masterpiece, *Citizen Kane* (1941), which was initially titled *The American*, and which from multiple and constantly changing perspectives evokes the career of the impetuous and titanic newspaper tycoon, banker, and industrialist Charles Foster Kane, and demonstrates how the conniving and easily corruptible Kane betrayed his initial idealism for social reform by becoming a ruthless exploiter and power monger, has exerted a profound thematic, structural, and stylistic influence on Fuentes's greatest novel, *La muerte de Artemio Cruz* (*The Death of Artemio Cruz;* 1962), a penetrating examination of the former revolutionary turned *hacendado* and industrial magnate, who like Kane also ends his life in virtual isolation, attempting to find in his tenacious embrace of material possessions a substitute for the idealism and the capacity to love which he has thoroughly suppressed.[5] *Das Kabinett des Dr. Caligari*, the landmark German expressionist film directed by Robert Wiene (1919), piles dreams and nightmares on hallucinations, delusions, and megalomania, permeating the problematic world created by Fuentes in his novel *Cambio de piel*, whose very title reflects the world of *Caligari*, a silent horror film where identities suddenly shift and change, and the august, imperious director of an insane asylum is suddenly placed in a strait jacket by his fellow doctors and becomes one of its inmates. In this topsy turvy world, the very narrator of the film, Franz, at the end is revealed to be a rebellious inmate in the asylum, and his whole previous testimony, which has been accepted as the product of a concerned and rational mind, suddenly becomes that of a madman, unreliable and capricious. In *Cambio de piel* (*A Change of Skin;* 1968) Fuentes re-creates the demonic Dr. Caligari in the form of the monstrous Herr Urs, an egomaniacal painter and restorer of dolls, and Caligari's automaton-like servant Cesare is also brought back to life and permeates the highly

---

[5] For an extensive examination of the thematic, stylistic, and structural influences of Welles's intricate and dynamic cinematic art on Fuentes, consult my study "Fuentes's *La muerte de Artemio Cruz* and Welles's *Citizen Kane*: A Comparative Analysis," in *Carlos Fuentes: A Critical View*, edited by Robert Brody and Charles Rossman (Austin: University of Texas Press, 1982), pp. 64-94.

convoluted, expansive narrative. Similar to *Das Kabinett des Dr. Caligari*, *Cambio de piel* is plagued by violence from beginning to end—the savage violence of the Conquest of indigenous Mexico, such as the massacre in the sacred city of Cholula, consecrated to the Aztec deity Quetzalcóatl, the Plumed Serpent, where more than three thousand perished at the command of the wily and brutal Cortés, to the holocaust perpetuated by Nazi Germany in the twentieth century in which millions were imprisoned and perished. And just as the murder of the sensitive Alan in *Caligari* is shockingly predicted the night before by the somnambulist Cesare, so too does the enigmatic and highly manipulative narrator in *Cambio de piel*, Freddy Lambert, predict the death of Franz at the very outset of the novel, a death that the highly elusive and sinister Freddy conspires with another of the characters, Isabel, to bring about, just as Dr. Caligari conspires with Cesare to conduct mayhem and murder.

The multiple, contradictory endings of *Caligari* are paralleled by the many different endings of *Cambio de piel*, in one of which both Freddy Lambert and one of the central characters of his narrative, Elizabeth, are incarcerated in an insane asylum, just as are Franz and Jane, who walks in hallucination and madness, in *Caligari.* The backdrops to the scenes and action in Wiene's remarkable film of demonic possession—the possession of the twentieth century scientist by the terrifying spirit of a eleventh century mountebank named Caligari—are not realistic but instead composed of Expressionist paintings that dramatically and powerfully symbolize the inner states of the characters, their anxieties, murderous impulses, and self-ensnarement. Indeed, in this brilliant film, the lights and shadows were painted right onto the sets. This bizarre, grotesque world, designed to exteriorize the delusions of a madman, who in this case is both Franz and Dr. Caligari, has strongly influenced Fuentes's somber, expressionistic vision, as in *Cambio de piel* the backdrops to various scenes are fantastic ones—either a painting brought to life or a series of sculptures, or an entire city, in this case a fog-enshrouded Prague—the setting for the romantic yet fated interlude between Hanna and Franz—the architect who will later collaborate with the Nazis and refuse to aid Hanna when he later finds her in a concentration camp, imprisoned for being a Jew. The medieval

Czech capital city created by Fuentes is a fantasy Prague, the hallucinatory Prague of an Expressionist film such as *Der Student von Prague*, combined with the shadowy world of the medieval, shadow-drenched town in *Das Kabinett des Doktor Caligari.* In both *Das Kabinett.* and *Cambio de piel*, inner worlds, those of dream, nightmare, hallucination, revery and premonition, combine to create a highly unstable and disintegrating universe in which nothing is clear, in which the characters struggle through twisted labyrinths that symbolize the demented and anguished consciousness.

Fuentes has stated that filmic images often have greater meaning for him than do literary ones. He himself is a treasure house of filmic knowledge and indeed has written a novel entitled *Zona sagrada* (*Holy Place*; 1967), which is inspired by the career of one of the greatest of Mexican film stars and cinematic legends, the incomparable, relentlessly dynamic María Félix, the equivalent in Mexico to the Hollywood superstar who played so many roles as strong and independent and unconquerable woman, and who also appears in Fuentes's works, both *The Death of Artemio Cruz* and *A Change of Skin:* Joan Crawford. In the convoluted, highly complex novel that is *Zona sagrada,* written initially as a filmscript, cinematic myth is expertly blended with myths drawn from classical Greek and Roman sources such as the *Odyssey* and the *Telegonia*, as well as Egyptian and ancient Aztec myths.

Claudia Nervo, the *persona* of María Félix, is evoked mystically as *fascinatrix* and *femina saga.* She is stunningly portrayed as a combination of the deadly Circe from Homer's *The Odyssey* and Tlazoltéotl, the ancient Aztec goddess of filth and of carnal love. Just as Tlazoltéotl, evoked as both cruel and redeeming, demanded the sacrifice of women, and prostitutes were beheaded to propitiate her, so too does Claudia surround herself with a court of models who are forced to sacrifice their individuality and integrity to become her mincing puppets. And Fuentes's third drama, *Orquídeas a la luz de la luna* (*Orchids in the Moonlight*; 1982), constitutes an ironic but eloquent homage to three of the finest of Mexican actresses—María Félix, Dolores Del Río and Lupe Vélez—all of whom starred in films both in Mexico and in other countries, including the United States and France, and whose international careers and "celebrity status" reflect that of

Fuentes himself, who stated in an interview with the author of this study that he aspired to be a film actor, on the model of Sydney Greenstreet and Conrad Veidt. Fuentes in *Orquídeas a la luz de la luna* pays homage to the beautiful and extremely versatile Dolores Del Río, who began her film career in Hollywood in the silent era, starring in films such as Raoul Walsh's *What Price Glory?* (1926), and then made the important transition to sound films, a transition that some silent screen stars like Constance Talmadge publicly refuted and that they refused to make, and a transition that many leading stars of the silent screen attempted to make like the great John Gilbert but whose high-pitched voice made the *Cambio de piel* impossible. The highly versatile Dolores Del Río starred in Hollywood musicals such as *Flying Down to Rio* (1933), in which she dances a tango with Fred Astaire, the lilting "Orchids in the Moonlight," that Fuentes takes as the title of his drama. Directed by Orson Welles in the film *Journey into Fear* (1942), Del Río after her breakup with Welles returned to her native Mexico to inaugurate what is now regarded as the Golden Age of Mexican cinema. She starred in films directed by Emilio Fernández which are now regarded as classics: *María Candelaria* (1942), *Flor Silvestre* (1943), and *Las abandonadas* (1944), films whose plots and characters Fuentes repeatedly alludes to in *Orquídeas*, a drama built up of incessant cinematic roles and scenes.

The dazzling but ill-fated Hollywood actress Lupe Vélez is also alluded to in *Orquídeas.* Like Del Río, Guadalupe Vélez de Villalobos began her film career in the silent era in films such as *Lady of the Pavements*, and *Tiger Rose* (1929) and also became a Hollywood star, appearing in an enormously popular series entitled *Mexican Spitfire* (1942), before her untimely death by suicide at age thirty-four—a death that is paralleled in that of the vivacious yet death-haunted María in *Orquídeas.* Third, Fuentes re-creates the dynamic and irrepressible film star and national legend María Félix, the ravishing and imperious star of such films as Fernando de Fuentes's *Doña Bárbara* (1943) and Emilio Fernández's *Enamorada* (1948) and *Río escondido* (1947). In many of his works, such as *Diana,* o *la cazadora solitaria (Diana, or The Goddess Who Hunts Alone;* 1994), film is evoked explicitly, as Fuentes skillfully incorporates personalities and scenes as well as emotional milieu and psychic states from silent films such as Carl

Theodore Dreyer's classic silent film *The Passion of Joan of Arc,* Otto Preminger's modern version *Saint Joan,* starring the *ingenué* Jean Seberg as the titanic French Patriot and martyr, as well as cinematic techniques such as *chiaroscuro* and zoom shots and panoramic shots. Film is a commanding presence in *Zona sagrada*, with its allusion to the films of the great German director Fritz Lang like *Metropolis* (1927), the many films of María Félix like *El peñón de las ánimas*, *Río escondido*, *Enamorada, La monja Alférez,* even to the extent that the cast-off son Guillermo/Guillermito/Mito in *Holy Place* becomes both audience to the hypnotizing films of his mother Claudia Nervo, the imperious *persona* of María Félix and even director, as in his febrile imagination Mito attempts to film himself into the life of Claudia, to consumate vicariously an incestuous impulse, also conveyed through his secret donning of Claudia's cashmere sweater.

But in other works of this Latin American master, film is implicit as it is in one of Fuentes's most abstract and temporarily challenging works. *El instinto de Inez (Inez;* 2001) in which film is never mentioned but through which creation runs a deep and penetrating influence of one of the foremost films of the great Swedish director Ingmar Bergman, the enchanting and nightmare-suffused film classic *Wild Strawberries* (1957) and in the enigmatic *novela Aura* which is *per se* an extraordinarily visual work there is an implicit impact of the greatest of the films of Alfred Hitchcock, *Vertigo* (1955) which like *Aura* occurs half in reality but most of all in dream—in illusions and delusion, in nightmare and daytime recovery, in behavior that is obsessive-compulsive and paranoid and at times, megalomaniac.

It is significant that like Fuentes's all-encompassing, epic, brilliantly synthesizing work, Hollywood too throughout its turbulent, scandal-ridden, yet always fascinating history has constituted a remarkably open universe—giving immediate opportunity to the many emegré directors like Eric von Stroheim and Fritz Lang and Ernest Lubitsch and Billy Wilder and providing myriad acting opportunities to minority groups—Afro-Americans

Figure 1. Scottie to Madeleine: "There's nothing you must do." But what she does is ambivalent: assist in a murder or attempt to save victim?

Figure 2. Auburn-tressed, Judy has no meaning for Scottie as Judy Barton; Scottie is entranced by a revenant Madeleine.

and Native Americans and Hispanic Americans and Asian Americans, welcoming talented and versatile artists, technicians, products and directors from around the world. Indeed, it is this openness of Hollywood, as well as its perpetually magical quality that seems to draw Fuentes to Hollywood film. and to the cinematic triumphs of Alfred Hitchcock. Just as Alfred Hitchcock, unlike most film directors, who seem to shun the limelight, constantly drew attention to himself, carefully re-creating himself as a Hollywood celebrity, so too is Fuentes one of the most publicity seeking and image-creating of world writers. Just as Hitchcock relentlessly appeared before photographers and motion picture concerns and constantly inverted himself as a character in his films—giving himself a usual signature, Fuentes is a debonair, endlessly photographed fashion plate and intellectual eminence. One of the great differences between the two creators is Hitchcock's self-parody—having himself photographed with his enormous stomach wrapped in sausages to make fun of his expansive girth, or posing before a huge pie stuffed with black birds that he is about to consume, to publicize *The Birds*, or even appearing as a living scarecrow—symbolizing his love of frightening his audiences and his great sense of humor in mocking his own excesses. Fuentes is a dashing crowd-pleaser, a parallel to the tremendous public acclaim received in both England and the United States by the great author who also has inspired the highly eclectic Fuentes: Charles Dickens, who like the irrepressible Fuentes drew vast, appreciative crowds on both sides of the Atlantic.

Figure 3. Vertigo is crammed with ghostly labyrinths, signifying mystery, entrapment, and despair.

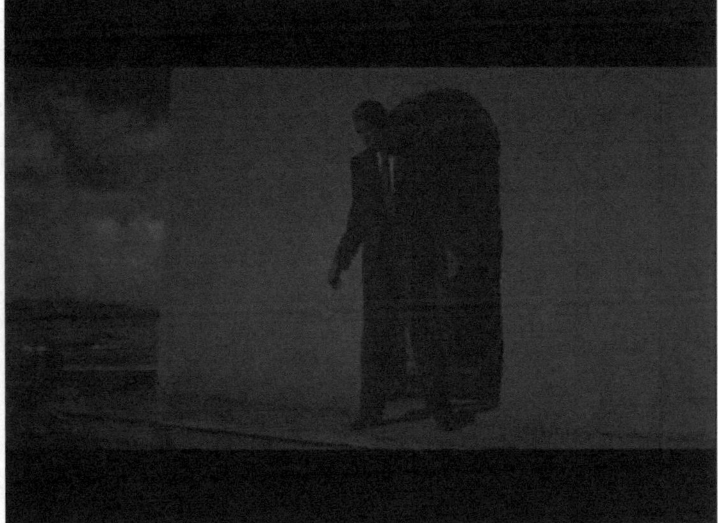

Figure 4. From beginning to end of Vertigo the hapless Scottie is a man dangling over an abyss.

CHAPTER I:

THE DEAD AMONG US:

HITCHCOCK'S *VERTIGO* AND FUENTES'S *AURA*

God helps those who invent what they need.

LILLIAN HELLMAN

I go but I return:

I would I were

The pilot of the darkness and the dream.

ALFRED LORD TENNYSON

Aura, a short novel by Fuentes published in 1962, shows an extensive incorporation of cinematic techniques. The fluid and hypnotic style of this work parallels and no doubt has been influenced by the movement of a travelling camera. Not only on the stylistic but also on the thematic level, *Aura* has been significantly influenced by Hollywood film, both by the now classic film *Sunset Boulevard* (1950) directed by the vibrant and inmitable Billy Wilder, and by the masterwork of Alfred Hitchcock, which many film critics now regard as Hitchcock's greatest achievement, *Vertigo* (1958). Like *Vertigo*, *Aura* from start to finish is a work of great hypnotic power. Indeed, both novel and film could very easily have been re-titled "Possession." The theme of possession functions on several levels in both Fuentes and Hitchcock: the physical, the psychological, and the supernatural. Both *Vertigo* and *Aura* are remarkable works of synthesis that constantly blend present, recent past, and remote, nineteenth century past; both expertly fuse reality and illusion, and both are populated by the living who obsessively intermingle with the spirits of the dead. According to the spurious account given by Gavin Elster, his disturbed wife Madeleine is possessed by the revenant spirit of her great grandmother, Carlotta. Together Gavin and his lover Judy Barton, brilliantly played by Kim Novak in what is her finest Hollywood role, conspire to kill Madeleine so that Gavin can inherit her vast fortune. To make it seem as if the actual murder were instead a suicide, Gavin hires a dupe—Scottie Ferguson—a former detective who suffers from vertigo, to follow his seemingly demented wife in order to protect her. When Scottie subsequently sees her fall from the top of the tower at the Mission of San Juan Bautista, he mistakenly believes that it is his own illness which is to blame for her death, since a spell of vertigo prevents him from climbing to the very top of the tower to rescue her from her apparently devastating *thanatos* impulses.

In order to lure Scottie to the scene of the murder, Gavin Elster concocts an elaborate scheme whereby Judy is patiently but exactingly coached to play the role of his presumably mentally disturbed wife Madeleine and to inveigle Scottie to bring her to the colonial mission of San Juan Bautista, where the crime against Elster's real wife is to be committed. Ironically, the only living person in *Vertigo* who is really mentally afflicted is the tortured and self-tortured Scottie. Thus Judy/Madeleine pretends to be highly distraught as she speaks as if she were possessed by the spirit of Carlotta risen from her tomb to drive her twentieth century descendant to madness and self-destruction, just as the original Carlotta took her life at an early age. Midway through the film the anguished Scottie, masterfully played by James Stewart, believes that Judy/Madeleine, with whom he has now fallen in love, has succumbed to this bizarre possession and hurled herself from the tower. Ironically, although Elster is the real murderer, at the coroner's hearing he is not suspected at all, as the extremely biased and even sadistic coroner blames the innocent yet guilt-stricken Scottie for failing to fulfill his assignment, which was to protect Madeleine from all harm.

At first Judy merely pretends that she is haunted by visions of a Spanish settlement and a dangerously high bell tower where as a child she had been forbidden to play—in order to attempt to convince an ever-more vulnerable Scottie that she has been possessed by a supernatural Other, the death-haunted spirit of her mad ancestor Carlotta. Scottie, at first highly rational and skeptical, scoffs at Elster's elaborate story of his wife's being possessed by a revenant spirit. Yet in both Hitchcock and Fuentes, fantasies suddenly and monstrously become real. At the end of the film, Judy actually does become possessed psychologically, by her marked feelings of guilt over having been an accomplice in the murder of the real Madeleine. Thus, when Scottie, in the brutal conclusion of *Vertigo* drags Judy Barton, now once more exquisitely playing the role of Madeleine, this time to gratify her new lover and dominator, her replacement for Gavin Elster, Scottie Ferguson. Judy at the end is desperate to please the very man she has worked to destroy. Indeed Scottie, who now forcefully and unremittingly replaces Elster in Judy's life, literally drags Judy up the stairs of the tower in an attempt to repeat the circumstances of the original crime but this time to climb to the very top of the fated tower and master his vertigo. At the very moment when Scottie and Judy again embrace one another and seem to be reconciled, the masterful Hitchcock provides a shocking *cambio de piel*, as Judy suddenly sees a strange form issuing from the darkness and in her terror she steps back and accidentally plunges from the tower, through an open window to her death. Judy's sudden death is one more example of the fatalistic gloom that saturates *Vertigo*, just as it does Fuentes's elusive masterwork *Aura* which *Vertigo* has extensively influenced. Judy's startling plunge to her death thus duplicates that of the real Madeleine, thrown from the tower by Elster after her neck was broken, and also duplicates the death of Carlotta, who had thrown herself from the very same tower. Is Judy/Madeleine under the delusion that what she perceives as a ghostly presence coming toward her is the spirit of Carlotta or the ghost of a vengeful Madeleine? In any case, while Scottie remains unperturbed at the sudden intrusion, Judy is terrified of the seemingly sinister apparition that in reality is one of the nuns of San Juan Bautista. It is extremely ironic that the nun at the end orders the ringing of the bell tower—an echo of the ominous ringing of a mission bell at the very beginning of *Vertigo*, as a bewitched Scottie gazes on the tombstone of Carlotta Valdés in the magically filmed garden which appears as an island of dream, a pocket of delusion, of the Mission Dolores in downtown San Francisco.

Possession operates on the psychological level with Scottie Ferguson as well. From the very first moment that he sights the enigmatic Judy/Madeleine in the luxurious, romantic setting of *Ernie's Restaurant* in downtown San Francisco, Scottie is awestruck, and he immediately begins to fall in love with her. Although he has been hired by Elster to trail his supposedly suicidal wife and report back to him on her strange behavior, so that a seemingly protective Elster can have his wife committed to an insane asylum, Scottie, imbued with a combination of paternalism and erotic attraction, seeks to cure Judy/Madeleine himself. But when he sees her apparently attempting to drown herself by suddenly leaping into the turbulent waters of San Francisco Bay near the Golden Gate Bridge, Scottie perceives her as a "damsel in distress" and claims her as his prize. And, after apparently witnessing his adored Madeleine's plunge from the tower of San Juan Bautista, Scottie suffers from excruciating grief and shock over the loss of his beloved. After being committed to a mental institution and subsequently released but not cured, Scottie is compelled by his feelings of guilt and desire to "resurrect" his beloved Madeleine, as he imposes her identity on many women who resemble her in their manner of dress, hair color and style, features, or bodily motion. When he meets the beautiful but commonplace Judy Barton, not realizing that she was the very Madeleine with whom he had fallen in love, he refuses to accept her as Judy but instead, rapidly and relentlessly, forces her to assume the identity of the dead Madeleine so that he can make love to her and at the same time free himself of his corrosive feelings of inadequacy and guilt. Although Judy, whose exaggerated makeup is cheap and even garish in contrast to the shimmering perfection of the makeup of the poised, stylish Madeleine, seeks to be loved for herself, she quickly submits to his game playing, just as she has remolded herself from a lower middle class girl from Salina, Kansas, into the reserved, demure upper class Madeleine, to please

Figure 5. Made it! But is Scottie's relentless Vertigo cured or exacerbated at the top of the tower?

Figure 6. Judy in profile; shadows derealize her as prelude to transformation into a ghost.

her former lover, Gavin Elster.

In *Vertigo*—as well as in *Aura*—a hypnotic mood is established from the outset, in the very credits of the film, masterfully done by Saul Bass who also collaborated in the production of the bewitching *Psycho*. Multicolored spirals emanate from the eyes of the bewitching Judy/Madeleine and thereby underscore her hypnotic and destructive power, as Kim Novak becomes the most deadly of Hitchcock's famed ice princesses, roles stunningly played by blonde actresses like Grace Kelly—*Rear Window* (1954), *Dial M for Murder, To Catch a Thief* (1955)—and Tippi Hedren (*The Birds*, 1963; *Marnie*, 1964). This spellbinding quality is also seen in *Aura*, as the gullible Felipe is soon entranced by the alluring green eyes of the beauteous Aura and rapidly falls under her spell. Hitchcock unfolds his compelling story in San Francisco, one of the most beautiful and the most haunting of American cities, with its fog-enshrouded bay, its sweeping, dramatic vistas of land and ocean, and its forests of giant and majestic sequoias. Indeed, San Francisco still contains traces of its romantic and adventurous past as part of the Barbary Coast laced with roving pirates. With its gleaming bay and its sinuous streets, its Golden Gate Bridge and its majestic, intricately designed Victorian houses, San Francisco is the North American city closest to dream. Although decked in realist trappings, *Vertigo* is essentially a film of myth and enchantment, of mystery and revelation, so very similar to the atmosphere of the uncanny and the supernatural established and masterfully sustained by Fuentes in *Aura,* which *Vertigo* has so strikingly and profoundly influenced. The enigmatic Madeleine, whose identity Scottie first patiently, then ruthlessly imposes on Judy Barton, can be seen as the working out of Scottie's obsession with reincarnation as leading to his personal redemption. This same fanatic desire to bring back the dead can be seen in Fuentes's magical work *Aura*, in Consuelo's persistent, even fanatic efforts to revive her husband Llorente, a vauntingly ambitious general in the imperial army of the doomed Emperor Maximilian and now dead for sixty years. The vessel of reincarnation is the body of the young historian Felipe Montero, whom Consuelo hires not merely, as she states, to revise and edit the dusty memoirs of Llorente, but to become the General reborn.

It is highly significant that the French novel which influenced Hitchcock's *Vertigo* is entitled *D'entre les morts* (The Living and the Dead; 1954). Both Scottie Ferguson and Consuelo are necrophilic; both insistently reject the living in their obsession with dead lovers who must be reborn body and soul in the form of the victimized Other. The ethereal young Aura is as ambiguous as is Madeleine in *Vertigo*—and as destructive to the male protagonist.

Just as Judy/Madeleine tricks Scottie into taking her to the colonial Spanish mission at San Juan Bautista, and despite her professed love for him, never tells him anything concerning her role as willing tool of Gavin Elster, so too is Aura, whom Felipe perceives as the victim kept imprisoned in her lair by the tyrannous Consuelo, actually a spirit, expertly controlled by Consuelo, sustained by the fierce mind and indomitable will of the aged woman—a sorceress who receives her power from the Devil. But *Aura* is a complex narrative that can also be interpreted on the psychological level. According to this perspective, Aura becomes a product of the highly unstable mind of Felipe, who under the influence of the drugs administered to him by Consuelo in the wine that he drinks, laced with the herbs that Consuelo cultivates in her secret garden like bella donna, suffers hallucinations and acts on suggestions of the one-hundred nine year old crone and falls readily under her hypnotic spell. The theme of psychological possession is reinforced by the very style of *Aura*, which is narrated in the second person singular—the very person that a hypnotist uses to entrance his subject, "You are getting drowsy, you are falling asleep…"

It is also significant that a person cannot be hypnotized unless he or she is willing. Felipe is a weak and malleable character, one literally without an "I," bereft of a strong ego. Indeed, from start to finish he is totally the "you," the Other. Felipe is thus very similar to the character of Scottie Ferguson, who is extremely frustrated and existentially adrift, and also parallels many of the indecisive, fantasy-prone male characters created by Fuentes in his other works. For example, the withdrawn and spineless, even masochistic youth Guillermo Nervo in *Zona sagrada* retreats into a defensive solitude and dedicates himself to looking for ways to take vengeance on his highly controlling mother Claudia, who first kidnaps him from his irresolute father and then abandons him, paying for his apartment but sadistically withdrawing attention and love from him. Guillermo finally goes insane as the result of the severe alienation he has suffered. The highly insecure Javier Ortega, the frustrated, even paranoid writer in *Cambio de piel*, is another weak-willed male who is both extremely dependent on a strong female, his wife Elizabeth, a mother-substitute, and yet resents that dependency and seeks above all the fantasy female, the one whom he can summon up and suppress at will, the woman whom he can thoroughly control. The obsessed Javier is afflicted by severe ulcers and has terrifying nightmares of drowning in the sea, a vision that expresses his deep feelings of helplessness and perhaps also his subconscious longings to suppress the independent self in a more powerful Other. The spineless and hypocritical Jaime Ceballos, the young protagonist of Fuentes's novel, a *Bildungsroman* entitled *Las buenas conciencias* (*The Good Conscience*; 1959), initially makes feeble efforts to assert an independent, morally righteous self, to define himself as different from the vacillating and cowardly father Rodolfo, who allows himself to be pressured by his overbearing sister Asunción into permanently driving his own wife Adelita from the house.

Yet the vacillating Jaime cannot sustain his rebellion. His acts of defiance of his bourgeois family, as he shelters and aids the oppressed, protecting the indigenous boy Ezequiel Zuno, a fugitive who is being persecuted for his attempts to unionize the disadvantaged, quickly cede to accommodation to his wealthy aunt and sanctimonious uncle, and the suppression of his true conscience, as he adopts the posturing and self-righteousness and embraces the comfortable life of the uncle, Balcárcel, his very name signifying his oppressiveness—the extremely hypocritical, zealot uncle whom previously the self-righteous Jaime had loathed. *Las buenas conciencias* is another narrative significantly influenced by film, in this case by the savage film from the Mexican period of Luis Buñuel, the mentor and friend of Carlos Fuentes, the great Spanish (Aragonese) director. In one of his most brutal and violent films, *Los olvidados* (*The Young and the Damned*; 1950) a youth savagely kills his companion by beating him over the head with a boulder. This scene has impacted the violent, sadistic ending of *Las buenas conciencas*, in which Jaime suddenly and pitilessly kills the cat of his aunt Asunción by smashing a rock over the skull of the trusting animal—an act symbolizing a final, ironic rebellion against the tyrannous aunt to whom he finally will succumb. Angel Fagoaga, the protagonist of Fuentes's *Cristóbal nonato*, is another vacillating male in the process of self-definition who allows himself to be carried away by his libido and temporarily sacrifices the love of the devoted Angeles to pursue the meretricious Penny López after whom he slavers, in what is Fuentes's parody of the egotistic and irresponsible male whose self-satisfaction takes precedence over his familial responsibility, as the pregnant Angeles carrying the foetus significantly named after the Discoverer of the New World, Christopher, is left alone and vulnerable and finally is kidnapped while Angel is indulging in his affairs.

Underscoring the complexity of both *Vertigo* and *Aura* is that the relentless quest of Scottie for Madeleine and that of Felipe to rescue Aura are but external manifestations of internal quests—the desperate search for an identity, for self-actualization and self-transcendence, on the part of these highly unstable, and in many senses self-loathing and extremely self-destructive protagonists. Yet the fundamental irony of both of these masterworks is that the nebulous Self, incarnated not only in Scottie but also in Judy Barton and in Felipe Montero, can find itself, assert itself, indeed, redeem itself, only in the spectral Other. Scottie is an extremely ambitious person who has longed to be police chief but whose ambitions crumble after he suffers his first devastating attack of vertigo while futilely chasing a criminal across the San Francisco rooftops. After his crippling attack, rather than accommodating to a routine and stifling desk job, the chagrined and, seemingly, stubbornly independent Scottie retires from the force all together. He is not only adrift professionally but emotionally as well. Scottie is unable to make a definite commitment to the ever comforting, consoling Midge, who loves him. She herself breaks off their engagement, yet Scottie, who is basically indifferent to her sexually, still clings to the highly protective Midge for her unremitting motherly support. Similar to the rootless Scottie, Felipe in *Aura* never mentions family or friends; he has no attachments in the outside world, a social vacuum that is quickly filled by his experiences in the gloomy but often soothing and increasingly sensual realm of Consuelo. Like the dreaming Scottie, Felipe too is consumed by ambition. He is bored by his temporary position as secondary school history teacher and dreams of writing his thesis, one which will synthesize all of the diverse chronicles of the Conquest of the New World. Yet his already prolonged dissertation will never be finished, for once Felipe enters the realm of Consuelo, he will never re-emerge into reality.

At the end, the hapless Felipe has no identity other than that of the spectral Other, Llorente. Both Felipe and Scottie become similar to Orpheus in his descent into the land of the dead, in quest of his lost lover, Eurydice. Orpheus is reunited by Pluto, Lord of the Dead, with his cherished bride, yet he can bring her back into the realm of the living only if he fulfills the condition of never turning around to see if she is still following him out of the Underworld. But the deep insecurity of Orpheus, his desperate desire to confirm the presence of his beloved, compels him to turn around, and he loses his bride forever, as she fades back into the Land of the Dead.

Like the Orpheus myth, one of the excruciating and permanent loss of the beloved made all the more heart-rendering because that beloved has once been at least temporarily recovered from death, both *Vertigo* and *Aura* depict the desperate soul questing for the dead—or, as at the core of *Aura*—constantly disappearing lover. Indeed, in the Boileau/Narcejac novel in which *Vertigo* is based, there appears a Eurydice lighter—an allusion to the ghostly, lost love found in classical Greek and Roman mythology. Felipe's identity rapidly becomes an inextricable from that of Aura. The youth in the twentieth century repeats the servility of Llorente in the nineteenth, as the naïve and vulnerable Felipe readily consecrates himself to Consuelo/Aura. So too is Scottie in *Vertigo* unable to define himself independently of Judy/Madeleine. At the end of the rivetting film, the violent death of Judy again relegates Scottie to an existential limbo if not again to a full blown delirium and mental collapse. And even if Scottie recovers, he is permanently entrapped; he will immediately begin the quest for Madeleine all over again—and only in what has for the fated protagonist become a suffocating yet consecrated space—the confines of San Francisco. And Judy Barton too is a person who almost without resistance allows herself to be molded—first by the iron will of Gavin Elster and then by an equally disciplined, even more fanatic Scottie. Although Judy is extremely attractive and personable, she is extraordinarily insecure about her identity. Ironically, she gains the poise and self-assertion and self-expression only as the consequence of appropriating the identity of the Other, of the ill-fated but sophisticated, aristocratic Madeleine Elster, a role that the coarse Judy Barton seems to relish playing. In what constitutes just one of the multiple mirrorings found in *Vertigo* the insecurity of Judy Barton mirrors the uncertainty and apprehensiveness of Kim Novak herself under the direction of the exacting and dictatorial Alfred Hitchcock. In both Hitchcock and Fuentes, the Other most always is a negative force, initially offering fulfillment but finally crushing the initial Self, just as Felipe's fragile identity is completely overwhelmed by that of Llorente, and Judy Barton is compelled to suffer a fate similar to that of the real Madeleine.

In both *Vertigo* and *Aura*, the physical self again and again becomes symbolic of the metaphysical. Fuentes has defined his literary style as one of Symbolic Realism. He creates a world in which apparently realistic structures, objects, characters and settings symbolize the fantastic. For example, the weird labyrinthine castle in which the sadistic, thirteenth century heretic Siger de Brabant dwells in Fuentes's brief, dense, metaphysical novel *Cumpleaños* (*Birthday*; 1970), symbolizes the rancorous, self-divided personality of the supercilious Siger himself. The passageways of the strange, demonic structure constrict and entrap the protagonist, the twentieth century English architect George—an allusion to the distinguished Argentine poet, short story writer, and essayist Jorge Luis Borges, called Georgie by his Anglophilic family. The architect George symbolizes a positive, creative, constructive impulse. The contemporary figure George is a contrast figure with the repressive, constrictive, ever tyrannous machinations of Siger. The hapless George, paralleling the victimized Felipe in *Aura*, suddenly finds himself imprisoned in this house which is also a tomb—a symbol of Siger as voracious demiurge seeking victims of sacrifice throughout the centuries.

Figure 7. Scottie views not a flesh and blood reality but a mirror image that captures essence of Madeleine.

Figure 8. Kim Novak, as Madeleine naked in her "rescuer's" bed, projects animal sensuality with which Midge cannot compete.

And, like the doomed Felipe, George never wakes up from his supernatural experience, never escapes the dungeon of Siger's castle.

In Fuentes's *Cambio de piel,* the gigantic pyramid at Cholula into which descend the two middle-aged couples—Elizabeth and her effete husband Javier, the guilt-ridden Franz and his sensuous, fickle lover Isabel—is both a concrete structure and a symbol of the tormented consciousness, of inner anxieties and the relentless but ultimately frustrated quest for self-exploration and self-actualization that the protagonists undertake. This immense pyramid, the largest edifice in the Pre-Columbian world, is evoked as an anti-Manichean structure, as a place where opposites, good and evil, present and ancient past, cowardice and fearlessness, are terrifyingly fused. In the depths of the pyramid are the ancient idols of the dread locust gods of the ancient Aztecs, highly ambivalent deities, both the protectors and the destroyers of the harvest, both worshipped and feared by their human subjects. The pyramid thus symbolizes the duality of the male protagonists, the capacity for good and evil present in both Javier Ortega and Franz Jellinek, evoked as Self and Double, as artists and criminals—paralleling the castration by the rabidly jealous Franz of the lover of Hanna Werner in the concentration camp and the apparent strangulation by the highly paranoid Javier of his young and voluptuous lover Isabel—using the very same shawl that Javier's seemingly forgiving wife Elizabeth has presented to her rival Isabel as a gift—which now experiences its own *Change of Skin*, this time into a murder weapon.

That the darkened house of Consuelo in *Aura* in the very center of Mexico center is built of *tezontle* symbolizes Consuelo's realm as a mysterious house of Time. *Tezontle* is a volcanic stone, material that was originally part of the Aztec pyramids that had been destroyed by the *conquistadores* and the stones used again to erect their new colonial palaces. The allusion to *tezontle*, to the ancient Aztec past and the mythic time of the Aztec gods who inexorably demanded blood sacrifice, presages the functioning of Consuelo as a twentieth century equivalent of the ancient Aztec goddess Coatlicue, symbolic of the Earth as duality, as both nurturing womb and receptively fatalistic tomb. Consuelo/Coatlicue is both the generator of a new Felipe, bringing to fruition an identity that was always present within him but previously suppressed, and the monstrous force that inexorably demands the surrender of his original identity as Felipe Montero. Consuelo's highly paradoxical functioning is indicated from the very start of the narrative, in the epigraph, a quotation from the work of Jules Michelet, *La Sorcière*:

> Man hunts and struggles. Woman intrigues and dreams; she is the mother of fantasy, the mother of the gods. She has second sight, the wings that enable her to fly to the infinite of desire and the imagination . . . The gods are like men: they are born and they die on a woman's breast . . .

And the twisting, labyrinthine nature of the gloomy mansion of Consuelo also symbolizes the struggle of Felipe to differentiate and to assert his identity independently of Consuelo, his desperate attempts to move out of physical—and existential—darkness into the light. But this *novella*, like *Vertigo*, is a work of fatalistic, cyclical time, and Felipe is as doomed as was Llorente in a previous century and as doomed as is Scottie Ferguson in *Vertigo*. The highly impressionable Llorente in the nineteenth century— like Felipe in the present—was infused with grandiose ambitions that collapsed forever with the sudden fall and the execution at Querétaro, at the fated Cerro de las Campanas, The Hill of the Bells, of his patron, the Emperor Maximilian, executed along with two of his generals, Miramón and Mejía, by a firing squad at the orders of the implacable Benito Juárez.

In both *Vertigo* and *Aura*, journeys that begin through a concrete, definable space—Scottie's dogged pursuit of Madeleine through the sinuous streets of San Francisco, or his travels down the Peninsula to the Jesuit mission at San Juan Bautista, are symbolic of a journey through Time—to the highly constrictive past that suffuses and even dominates both of these works. Again and again the modern, commercialized San Francisco fades, and Scottie enters zones of an eery quietude, such as the Mission Dolores, a pocket of suspended, apparently redemptive time in the midst of twentieth century San Francisco. Another house of deadening silence and past time eerily suspended in the present is the majestic Hotel McKittrick, which once was the lavishly ornate

Great House where Carlotta was brought by her husband, who took her away from her dance hall life imperiously to fashion her into a "Great Lady" before he suddenly and capriciously threw her away, forcing her to wander the streets—again adumbrating the behavior of the deracinated Judy Barton in contemporary San Francisco.

Though the process of cyclical time, which is so important in both *Vertigo* and *Aura*, this elaborate process of refashioning, of remaking a socioeconomically marginalized woman into a Grande Dame, is precisely what Gavin Elster will do after he one day by chance meets Judy, who is working as a waitress, and is struck by her resemblance to his wife, adumbrating, in this work spiralling with cyclical time, the chance encounter of a forlorn Scottie with Judy Barton—and Scottie like Gavin Elster before him, is struck by the seemingly uncanny resemblance between Judy Barton and Madeleine Elster. Like the nineteenth century potentate before him, Gavin Elster takes a very willing Judy Barton out of her marginal, drifter existence and installs her in a lavish apartment on Nob Hill. It is highly significant that we never see the inside of this love nest, just as we never see the inside of Felipe's own apartment in *Aura*, so tightly constructed are both of these masterpieces. And, similar to the fated trajectory of the life of Carlotta, Judy too will be discarded, first by Elster, who after the coroner's hearing permanently abandons Judy and flees to Europe, and then by the second person who re-creates her, the well-to-do Scottie. It is most significant that in the course of this extensive chase scene in *Vertigo*, in which a befuddled but increasingly infatuated Scottie pursues Madeleine through the streets of the city, the personage of Judy/Madeleine is never evoked—all attention is focussed only on Scottie as befuddled but maniacal pursuer—thus both her essential ambiguity and her elusiveness as well as the fact that she is but an intricate aparition of Scottie's dreamworld are underscored. Instead of the traditional focus, first on the ardent pursuer, then on the desperate pursuer, for more than fifteen minutes Hitchcock's ever probing camera as fixated only on a mesmerized Scottie, underscoring both his attraction to Judy/Madeleine and the obsessiveness of that desire. Similarly, the radiantly evil figure of Aura may be but an elaborate concoction of the febrile, drug-suffused mind of Felipe. Like the transfixed Scottie in *Vertigo*, who moves from contemporary time to past centuries and back again, Felipe in *Aura* moves from the 1950s cosmopolitan and extremely traffic-congested Mexico City, to absorption into a sacred zone, a *zona sagrada* that is Consuelo's mansion, a house that like so many of the structures in *Vertigo* is suspended between reality and fantasy. Paralleling the increasingly befuddled Scottie Ferguson as he gazes at the second story of the McKittrick Hotel and spies Madeleine at one of the windows for a few seconds before she suddenly disappears, is the befuddled Felipe as he gazes not merely at the second floor of the nineteenth century Porfirista mansion in which Consuelo dwells alone, but also another world—suffused by a treacherous calm. Here is evidenced a seeming escapism that is but an elaborate, baroque mask over a hellworld. For Felipe, the mansion itself begins to hypnotize him, it is both eery and inviting, like the mansion where Carlotta once dwelled in *Vertigo*:

> You look up at the second stories. Up there, everything is the same as it was. The jukeboxes don't disturb them. The mercury streetlights don't shine in. The cheap merchandise on sale along the street doesn't have any effect on that upper level; on the baroque harmony of the carved stones; on the battered stone saints with pigeons clustering on their shoulders; on the latticed balconies, the copper gutters, the sandstone gargoyles; on the greenish curtains that darken the long windows; on that window from which someone draws back when you look at it. (A, 9-11)[6]

The movements of the beleaguered Scottie throughout the entire film are cyclical and fatalistic. The futile trajectory of his existence is symbolized early on, as he relentlessly follows Madeleine through the narrow, labyrinthine streets of San Francisco only to find that she has led him back to his own residence near the landmark Coit Tower. And at the end of *Vertigo,* an obsessed Scottie is impelled to return with

[6] Consult Carlos Fuentes, *Aura* (México, D.F.: Ediciones Era, 1962). Subsequent references are to the bilingual English-Spanish translation *Aura*, translated by Lysander Kemp (New York: Farrar, Straus and Giroux, 1963) and are included parenthetically in the text, preceded by A.

Judy/Madeleine, whom he forces to be by his side, to the colonial mission of San Juan Bautista and to re-enact the past with the hopes thereby of conquering his vertigo and freeing himself from the stranglehold of that past. An essential part of the vertigo movement seen throughout Hitchcock's masterpiece is the fatalistic operation of cyclic time. The spectre of Carlotta Valdés, imposed by a guileful Gavin Elster over his wife, seemingly transhabits Judy/Madeleine and finally is transmuted into an apparition that circumscribes Judy's life—and her manner of death. Scottie's compelling Judy/Madeleine to return to San Juan Bautistia is a repetition of his first journey there—a romantic interlude that marked a sincere but thoroughly misguided attempt to free Madeleine from her obsessing—to prove to her that there is no ghost, that Madeleine's obsession with her great-grandmother can be explained—and expunged—rationally. Ironically, the movement of *Vertigo*, like that of *Aura,* is deeper and deeper into fantasy, delusion and madness. This is exactly how Scottie initially had desired to liberate Judy/Madeleine from her obsession with Carlotta, by bringing her to the Mission to prove to her that her visions are based not on the invasion of her being by a supernatural or demonic spirit of Carlotta but by real-life memories of a past visit to the monastery and carriage house at San Juan Bautista.

Similarly, *Aura* too is characterized by a monstrously cyclical time. At the end, Felipe and Consuelo and the ghost of Llorente are all united, in their abject devotion to Aura. Significantly, Aura can remain in the realm of Consuelo for only three days at a time. The first time Felipe sees her she is a young, virginal girl; the second time a hardened middle-aged woman, and the third time she has fused entirely with the decrepit Consuelo. In order for Aura to be reborn again, a new victim, a new Llorente must be found, and we can imagine the sequence to the ending of *Aura* being the placing by Consuelo of still another advertisement in the newspaper, as she again desperately seeks a replacement for Felipe. Similarly, at the end of *Vertigo*, now that for the third time the forlorn Scottie has been witness to a death, now that he again has lost his beloved Madeleine, we can imagine Scottie beginning the search anew for a replacement, for another hapless—and willing—Judy Barton whom he will painstakingly transform into Madeleine, just as Consuelo, at the very end of Fuentes's chilling and masterful work, will transform Felipe's replacement again into the lost but cyclically returning Llorente.

In both *Vertigo* and *Aura*, the primacy of the past—threatening, fatalistic, inescapable—is emphasized. This is similar to other films of Hitchcock such as *Psycho*, in which the strange, warped devotion of Norman Bates to his mother and Norman's extreme jealousy of her lover both of whom Norman in his insane rage murders—is transferred to the fugitive Marion Crane, whom he murders while she is taking a shower, in one of the most shocking and brutal sequences in the cinema world. Indeed, the wanton Mother, whom the innocent appearing but in reality psychotic and murderous Norman Bates both fears and loathes as he becomes the demonic Other; is the most important character in the bizarre film. The dutiful yet rebellious son repeatedly stabs the innocent Marion while dressed as his mother, whose dead body he keeps in the cellar of his forbidding Gothic mansion. Norman utilizes his craft of taxidermy not only in stuffing and mounting birds—and it is no accident that his victim is named Marion Crane—but also on the mother whom he both reveres and despises for her wantonness—the mother whom he first kills then monstrously assumes her identity to kill again. The crazed Norman Bates, like the increasingly demented Scottie Ferguson, is dominated by the past. Fuentes too in other novels such as *La región más transparente* emphasizes the past as a negative force. Here the ancient Aztec past is revivified as a monstrous force relentlessly at work in contemporary Mexico. The malefic narrator, Ixca Cienfuegos, is a reincarnation of the dread ancient Aztec god of war and death Huitzilopochtli. The commercial and technological Mexico of the twentieth century is portrayed as but a fragile and flimsy mask over its indelible ancient core of violence and blood sacrifice to propitiate the wrath of the Aztec gods.

At the beginning of *Vertigo*, the past is evoked romantically, as Scottie meets his old college friend Gavin Elster at the latter's lavish office on the Embarcadero and gazes at the romantic paintings that line the walls—paintings that evoke San Francisco's nineteenth century, seafaring past as colorful, adventurous and exciting. Throughout *Vertigo* as in *Aura*, the background to the episodes is not merely decorative or even secondary, it is often the key to what is transpiring in the

Figure 9. A stricken Scottie suspended in space, afflicted with incurable vertigo.

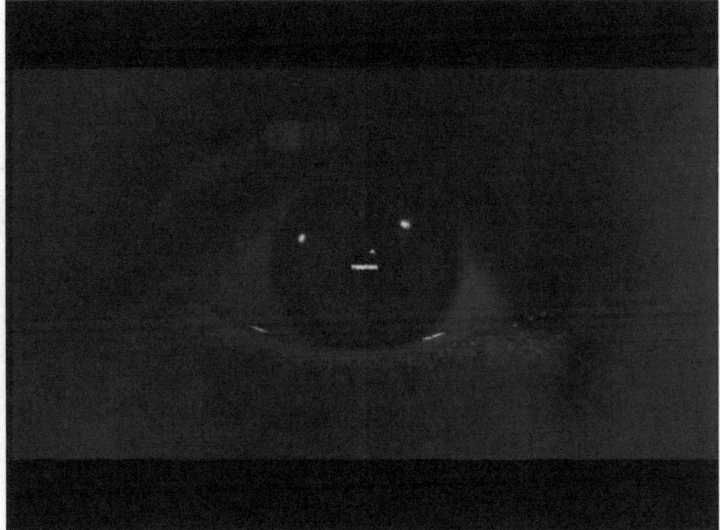

Figure 10. Titles radiate from nervous, frightened eyes of Madeleine—both cause and cure for Scottie's affliction.

foreground. Scottie for the first time in his career has no present and no future and thus wistfully embraces this romantic past. He is a dangling man—first literally, then professionally, and finally psychologically and even metaphysically. And once suspended in the bizarre world of Judy/Madeleine, one linked irremediably with the disconsolate Carlotta, even though Scottie consciously attempts to scoff at or to escape from or to triumph over the past, he, ironically, becomes bound more inextricably to it. He is impelled to play again the role of the wealthy, nameless nineteenth century magnate who transformed the highly malleable Carlotta into mistress of the manor only subsequently to throw her into the street. Ultimately in both *Vertigo* and *Aura*, the past is neither romantic nor nostalgic but terrifying. The constant attempts by the commonsensical girlfriend Midge to puncture Scottie's illusions, to bring him back to reality, as she paints a duplicate of the portrait of Carlotta by which both Madeleine and Scottie are so entranced, and inserts her own down-to-earth features, complete with prominent eye-glasses, that so contrast with the graceful, enigmatic features complete with prominent eye-glasses instead of Carlotta, arouses only the ire of Scottie, who breaks off his tenuous relationship with Midge. She has dared to desecrate an icon, for the painting of Carlotta in Scottie's mind is fused with the idealized—and increasingly idolized—image of Judy/Madeleine.

In Fuentes's *Aura*, Felipe too throughout his career has envisioned history in a romantic light and indeed, he seems to fashion himself as a *conquistador intelectual.* Yet over and over again in Fuentes's dark vision the *conquistador* is *conquistado*—the arrogant Cruz in *La muerte de Artemio Cruz*, who in his dream exalts himself as a twentieth century Hernán Cortés superciliously striding down the nave of a huge church, but at the end of his dream is silently mocked by the statues, seemingly of the Christian saints but designed by the Indian artesans as masks that cover the Aztec idols that they have placed within, idols that mock the supercilious Cruz and that signify his ultimate defeat and destruction. Similarly, in *Cristóbal nonato*, the plutocrat and politician Ulysses López and his haughty wife, who treat the *paracaidistas* who have occupied their lands with savagery, burning their houses, become themselves the objects of vengeance by the mob, as their lavish mansion is invaded and sacked and both are killed. And in *Una familia lejana* (*Distant Relations*; 1980), the arrogant youth ironically named Víctor, the son of the eminent archaeologist Hugo Heredia, damages an exquisite Indian artifact, and thereby provokes the wrath of the ancient deities who through the supernatural presence of the diabolic André Heredia bring about the destruction of the willful Víctor.

Both *Vertigo* and *Aura* are highly intricate works that trace the desperate attempts of the male protagonists to exorcise themselves of their private demons, ironically at the same time that part of them cultivates these very demons. Scottie suffers excruciating guilt and shame the first time he is at San Juan Bautista, as he sees what he believes is his beloved Madeleine committing suicide while he is paralyzed by his vertigo and unable to save her. The sensitive Scottie thoroughly blames himself, believing that he is responsible for Madeleine's death, because he had failed to protect her. His guilt feelings are exacerbated because the death awakens memories of the first time that Scottie suffered from devastating vertigo, and the self-sacrificing policeman who attempted to rescue him and died in the attempt.

It is highly significant that instead of rushing to Madeleine's side to determine the extent of her injuries and to attempt to save her if she is still alive, Scottie, who concludes that his beloved must have committed suicide under the supernatural power of the revenant Carlotta, slinks away—not even informing the nuns at San Juan Bautista or summoning the police. Thus, if Scottie is guilty of any offense, it is of abandoning the scene of a crime. What can account for his actions—quickly and quietly disappearing, even though he had served as a detective—a law enforcer—and thus is well experienced regarding crime including violent death and even murder? We can assume that Scottie is so dazed, so traumatized, not only by the sudden death of his beloved but also by his own paralyzing feelings of guilt over having failed to carry out the role of hero/rescuer/savior that he has fashioned for himself after his corrosive attack of vertigo, that instead of the normal responses not only of a would-be lover to the falling from a tower of his or her beloved but every moral person in such a dilemma would at very least have summoned help for his beloved, and would have remained at the scene of the devastating incident either to attempt to rescue his romantic idol or to console the dying

Madeleine. That Scottie is interested only in quietly slinking away—and not even reporting the death—provides a strong indication of his inveterate self-absorption, even narcissism, which finds a parallel in the egomania of Fuentes's domineering Consuelo. The highly presumptuous Scottie seems to equate Madeleine's fall with the fall to his death of the heroic, self-sacrificing policeman at the outset. It is significant that both of Hitchcock's masterpieces—*Vertigo* and *Psycho*—are titles of ravaging and irremediable mental illnesses.

At the end of *Vertigo*, Scottie's compelling Judy to return a second time to San Juan Bautista is not merely to wreak vengeance on her because Judy has been a highly willing accomplice in the murder of Madeleine, but to prove to himself that he can master his vertigo. Yet the very beginning of the film is its outcome—just as Scottie fails to reach the top of the stepstool in Midge's apartment, at the end he will reach the top of the tower but only as a prelude to the probable jump off the tower to join Judy/Madeleine in death. One of the reasons why Scottie is so attracted to Judy/ Madeleine is her vulnerability, which in many aspects reflects his own susceptible, victimized state. Scottie cannot relate to the poised and apparently self-sufficient and economically independent Midge, because he compulsively needs to play the role of protector and comforter. Ironically, he believes that he has saved the life of Judy/Madeleine once when she apparently attempts to commit suicide by jumping into San Francisco Bay. This is why Scottie's rage is so great at the end, when he realizes that he has been duped not only in the matter of Madeleine's death but also sinuously led into believing that he was a hero when in fact the conniving Judy/Madeleine—an expert swimmer—has only perpetrated a cruel hoax on him, basely toying with him—just as Consuelo does with Felipe.

Scottie's experiences with Judy/Madeleine are for him life-defining—they initially represent his psychological, social, and even spiritual rebirth. Similarly, the vapid, colorless Felipe's entering into the bizarre world of Consuelo initially brings about his existential regeneration. Instead of drifting existentially, he has now found a purpose for his life, paralleling the way in which the drifter Scottie, dangling not only literally, from the rooftop at the very start of *Vertigo*, but also existentially, is imbued with renewed vigor and purpose. The febrile imagination of Felipe even envisions Aura as a princess, kept enthralled by a harridan aunt, and Felipe himself becomes the noble prince who will gallantly rescue his beloved. Yet his desire to assert himself is countered and finally defeated by another impulse, a willessness, a strong desire to obey the rules of Consuelo, and not even turn on a light in her gloomy, sinister mansion but rather meekly to conform to the darkness. Only at the very end of *Aura* does Felipe realize what is happening to him, as he feels his features being torn away as the result of a horrendous supernatural force. Only at the end, when it is now too late, does he desperately attempt to cling to and to affirm his original identity.

Both of these intense, highly concentrated works are saturated with irony. This irony is present even in the very name Aura, which on one level signifies "dawn," the new light that is the aurora, and, symbolically, the new life for both Consuelo and Felipe—and for the revenant spirit of Llorente. Yet a variant of "aura" has another, more sinister meaning. As Callan has pointed out, Aura also means "vulture."[7] The very person whom Felipe sees as needing his protection is actually one who will entrap and betray him and feast symbolically on his remains—paralleling the way in which the seemingly agitated and death-haunted Judy/Madeleine is really the extremely glamorous, very seductive bait that Gavin Elster uses to ensnare the highly gullible Scottie. In both *Vertigo* and *Aura*, true, selfless love is impossible. The love of Consuelo for Llorente is but a façade; the egomaniacal Consuelo is capable of loving only herself —her elaborate worship before a wall of icons is really a self-adoration. Her extreme frustration over her inability to have children, which she attributes to the infertility of Llorente, is due to her excruciating need to perpetuate her beauty, not because she wants to assume what for her would be a constrictive maternal role.

It is highly significant that both Scottie and Felipe are connoisseurs of the past. As a historian, Felipe is drawn to the

---

[7] See Richard J. Callan, "The Jungian Basis of Carlos Fuentes's *Aura,*" *Kentucky Romance Quarterly*, XVIII, 1 (1971), p. 70.

ancient Pre-Columbian and colonial past of Latin America, similar to the eminent United States historian William H. Prescott, who actually carried out the project that Felipe will be permanently stalled on—that of making a grand synthesis of all the various accounts by the Chroniclers of the Discovery and Conquest of the New World in his monumental works *The History of the Conquest of Mexico* (1843) and *A History of the Conquest of Peru* (1847). Indeed Prescott in his romanticized account of epic history looms as a spectral predecessor of Felipe Montero, the historian manqué. Yet for the hapless Felipe, the historical past will be much more than an academic or intellectual phenomenon; it becomes converted into a monstrous living reality, brutally imposing itself upon him. Scottie too is drawn, both intellectually and aesthetically, to the past; he is an avid collector of antiques, and indeed, responds to Judy Barton when he meets her after his internment in the asylum as but one more of his prized possessions.

One of the primary reasons why Fuentes is so much attracted to and influenced by *Vertigo* is that this film magnificently fuses two of the major themes of Fuentes's own art: the dread power of illusion—the weak and inchoate male self that is invaded and easily conquered by the fantasy Other—and the preoccupation with death and resurrection, the ultimate *cambio de piel* evoked in so many of Fuentes's works. For example, the stricken Cruz in the now classic narrative *The Death of Artemio Cruz* on his deathbed attempts egomaniacally to bargain with God, as the ever-wily Cruz offers to believe in Him in exchange for being granted terrestrial immortality. And it is immortality that the demonic Siger in *Cumpleaños* seeks, a prolongation of his life throughout the centuries which is possible only through the continued blood sacrifices of myriad victims, the latest of whom will be the hapless English architect George whose lack of a last name indicates his status as an identity *manqué*, just as are those of Felipe Montero and Scottie Ferguson. Similarly, the goal of Consuelo is not love but immortality; she senses that she is near death and that the only way she can prolong her existence is by giving birth to herself, in the form of the tantalizing Aura. Similarly, to conquer time, to be eternally young and beautiful, is the goal of the dazzling Claudia Nervo in *Zona sagrada*, who attempts to cheat time by emulating the model of Proteus and incessantly changing—appearance, roles, costumes, and lovers, renewing herself by denying her own son and by constantly keeping him out of public view, the son who is rapidly maturing and whose changing age indicates Claudia's own irremediably advancing age and the relentless withering of her beauty and her desireability.

Both Scottie and Consuelo become perverted creators, inverse Pygmalions. In the ancient Greek myth, Pygmalion was a master sculptor who fell in love with the statue that he had created of a woman—Galatea—and so fiercely adored the marble beauty that the goddess Venus—the goddess of erotic love whose ardent devotee is Pygmalion—brought it to life for him—a divine operation wondrously captured in the series of paintings of Pygmalion and Galatea of the eminent Pre-Raphaelite master, Sir Edward Bulwer-Lytton. In contrast, both Scottie and Consuelo take human beings and seek to reduce them to zombies. Although the Judy Barton whom Scottie meets when he leaves the asylum is radiantly beautiful and is falling in love with him, Scottie is repulsed even at kissing her. Indeed, he can accept her only for the Madeleine within her, and thus sets about painstakingly to restoring that Madeleine, first by having Judy dress like the dead woman, then by compelling her to change her makeup and hair style, and even the manner in which she moves, from the trudging gait of the working girl to the graceful movements of a royal princess. Similarly, although Consuelo apparently is seeking someone to revise her husband's memoirs, that someone must be handsome, young and male, and must immediately become her lover/worshipper.

Fuentes also develops this inverse Pygmalion theme elaborately in *Cambio de piel.* The highly insecure protagonist Javier Ortega cannot accept a woman of flesh and blood because he fears to be dominated by that woman, as he was controlled at crucial times in his life by his dominant and ever prying mother, Ophelia. Thus Javier seeks to reduce his wife Elizabeth to an *objet d'art*, as he compares her to the restraint found in a Greek *stele*. He plays dehumanizing games with her, as he sends her ahead of him to a party so that he can arrive and pretend that she is the eternally New Woman, the woman whom he has never met and thus who exerts no control over him. The highly manipulative Javier exploits

Figure 11. Vertigo: attraction and repulsion, fear of falling and desire for death.

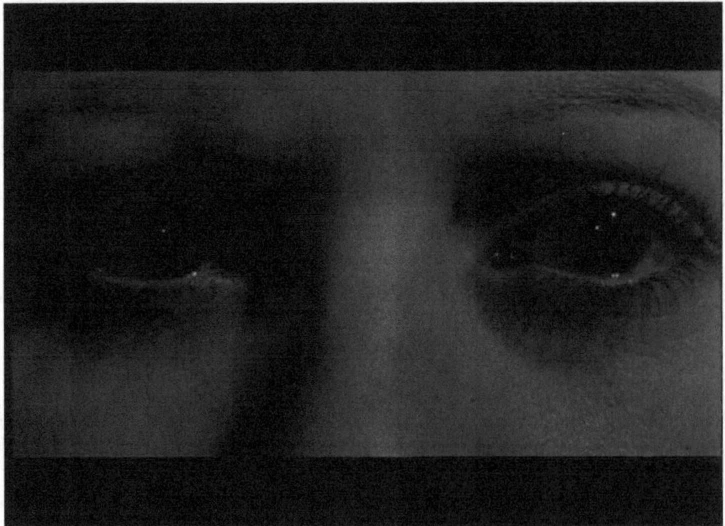

Figure 12. Eyes of Madeleine, that signify allure, deception, and terror.

his vivacious mistress Isabel, perceiving her as a younger, less intimidating version of Elizabeth, and even compels Isabel to repeat the past, as she dresses in the manner that Elizabeth was attired when Javier had his first romantic encounter with her. Yet when Isabel, who herself experiences a *cambio de piel,* becomes too dominating and wants to make their relationship permanent instead of a continual free love affair, Javier strangles her. Pathologically insecure, the highly controlling Javier, a deviant Pygmalion, seeks to reduce Isabel to a mere memory that he can summon up or suppress at will. Javier's ideal woman is always the distant one, the one who blends into a painting, such as the mysterious, dark-haired woman across the way whom he sees framed by a window, as if she were a living portrait. Javier frequents museums, just like Scottie does, and gazes rapturously at the women painted by the great Italian painter Modigliani.

Just as the artistic Midge through duplicating the mysterious portrait of Carlotta, by which Scottie remains spellbound, attempts to penetrate this private world of the person she loves, the sphere from which she feels herself increasingly shut out, so too does the tenacious Elizabeth, unwilling to give up Javier, follow her husband to the museums. Elizabeth, emulating the superficially poised but actually highly insecure Midge in *Vertigo*, even dresses in the style of Modigliani's women in order to indulge her husband's fantasies, so that he can turn from the mere image to behold the painting brought to life by his complacent wife. Although these activities require Elizabeth constantly to suppress her individual identity and forfeit her integrity, just as Judy is forced to suppress her unique identity to become once again the Other—the creation Madeleine—both women endure the humiliation in a vain attempt to keep and hold the love of males who can never accept or even deal with complex, ever-changing human beings, but instead transform them into zombielike, fantasy beings. Paralleling the neurotic and ultimately psychotic Javier in *A Change of Skin*, a *Cambio de piel*, that signifies a physical and spiritual renewal that Elizabeth, Javier and Franz all obsessively seek to attain but which they fail to actualize—who systematically destroys the living woman in order to perpetuate the mere image, who lives in an extremely solipsistic world and who accepts and loves Elizabeth only to the extent that she dutifully performs her role, are the increasingly unhinged actions of the narcissistic and dehumanizing Scottie in *Vertigo*. The very name of Javier's apparently rebellious and insouciant lover, Isabel, the Spanish version of Elizabeth, indicates her inseparability from Javier's wife, and her function as a *simulacrum*—younger, less threatening, and thus more desirable, than the original. It is gruesomely ironic that Javier strangles Isabel with the very same shawl that Elizbeth had presented to Isabel as a gift—a present that falls over Isabel like a cloak of doom.

There are many indications of the insubstantiality of Aura, for example, the way in which she appears before Felipe out of nowhere and then suddenly disappears. Although she is at first demure and remote, she appears naked to Felipe at night—as if she were a succubus. Aura seems to have no independent will of Consuelo; as she dines with her aunt, her movements duplicate exactly those of Consuelo. Aura moves like a ghost through the domain of Consuelo and seems to be a combination of somnambulist and automaton. Similarly, the ghostliness of Judy/Madeleine is emphasized by Rothman, as he analyzes the scene in which Judy/Madeleine suddenly appears toward dawn at the doorway of Scottie's apartment:

> The filming of the woman at Scottie's door in silhouette, by contrast, intimates that she is not real, or not exactly, real, as though we are seeing not a woman of flesh and blood but a ghost. Indeed, this silhouette prefigures, among other moments, the ghostly apparition that rises into Judy's view at the climax of the film, precipitating her death. Hitchcock understands that in the face of the camera, the future as well as the past may haunt the present. And it is one of his abiding insights that there is an aspect of the supernatural, a ghostliness, in all human beings on film, all subjects of the camera.[8]

[8] Consult William Rothman, *The "I" of the Camera: Essays in Film Criticism, History and Aesthetics* (Cambridge and New York: Cambridge University Press, 1988), p. 154. Subsequent references are included in text, preceded by IC.

This haunting of the present by both the past and the future is powerfully expressed in *Aura* through the use of the second person singular point of view in the *future* tense. Felipe's behavior is controlled by the past, is a repetition of the past, and may even have already occurred in the past, and yet it is paradoxically expressed in a ghostly future, indicative not so much of things to come as of what must inevitably occur again exactly as it has transpired in the past. Paralleling the movement of the camera in Hitchcock, Fuentes's compelling use of the second-person narrative also parallels the tense and time utilized in the *tú*-narrative in *La muerte de Artemio Cruz*—the metaphysical voice as opposed to the apocalyptic, sonorously eloquent, highly emotional, extremely fragmented and incessantly repetitious first-person account of Cruz's physical self, of his disease-stricken and deteriorating body:

> And if you become one thing, rather than another, that will be because in spite of everything you will have to choose. Your choices will not negate the possibilities remaining to you, or anything that you will leave behind by the act of choice: but these possibilities will be weakened, attenuated to the degree that today your choice and your destiny will become the same: the coin will no longer have two faces: desire and destiny will be one. Will you die? It will not be your first death: you will have lived enough dead life, enough moments of mere gesticulation, to assure that.[9]

Both *Vertigo* and *Aura* portray existence as enigma. As Fuentes states in an interview with Harss:

> "every story is written with a ghost at your shoulder." The ghost is Woman, "the keeper of secret knowledge,

[9] Consult Carlos Fuentes, *La muerte de Artemio Cruz* (México, D.F.: Fondo de Cultura Económica, 1962). The translation is from *The Death of Artemio Cruz* translated by Sam Hileman (New York: Farrar, Straus, and Giroux, 1964) pp. 29-30.

which is true knowledge, general knowledge, universal knowledge."[10]

Yet in *Aura,* woman as sacred keepers of Knowledge are accompanied by the pathetic, emasculated male finally reduced to a nonthinking, nonacting, zombielike *tabula rasa*. It is ironic that although the search of Felipe is both an epistemological and an ontological quest, one for both knowledge and for Being, he fails on both counts. Instead Felipe at the end is immersed in ignorance and deceit and self-deception; his initial identity is at the end erased. At the end he believes that he is making love to his beloved Aura, whereas in reality he has become the paramour of the wizened Consuelo. Ironically, the light of the moon that falls upon Felipe at the end is one that does not illuminate the situation for him but instead further bewitches him. He is now totally the Other—the ill-fated Llorente, his destiny embedded in his very name, "The Crying One."

Both Hitchcock's film and Fuentes's novel are characterized by a profound ambiguity. Is Felipe redeemed from a life of tedium and insignificance in the real world, one which he at the outset has been very eager to leave behind as he enters and is rapidly absorbed into the languorous, comforting but deadly realm of Consuelo, or is he permanently destroyed as the result of his contact with Aura and Consuelo? At times Felipe's sensation of himself as the Other, as releasing hidden potentialities and desires within him, is even experienced as pleasurable:

> You sit down in Aura's chair, stretch your legs, and light a cigarette, feeling a pleasure you've never felt before, one that you knew was part of you but that only now you're experiencing fully, setting it free, bringing it out because this time you know it'll be answered and won't be lost (A, 45)

Yet, at the very end, the Other is not fulfilling but degrading and monstrously destructive:

---

[10] See Luis Harss and Barbara Dohmann, *Into the Mainstream: Conversations with Latin-American Writers* (New York: Harper and Row, 1967), p. 302.

> you fall exhausted on the bed, touching your cheeks, your eyes, your nose, as if you were afraid that some invisible hand had ripped off the mask that you've been wearing for twenty-seven years, the cardboard features that hid your true face, your real appearance, the appearance you once had but then forgot. (A, 137)

Similarly, after the death of Judy, as a tormented Scottie is seen at the very top of the tower at San Juan Bautista, the film abruptly ends, leaving a dazed Scottie in literal and emotional suspension. Scottie at the end as at the beginning is but a desperately suspended entity. After clinging for his life to a gutter about to collapse and send him hurtling to the ground, this traumatic initial scene abruptly terminates, leaving the would-be hero suspended in space. At the very end, is Scottie finally fulfilled, has he regained his health and stamina by conquering his vertigo? Or is he about to plunge from the tower, emulating the manner of death of his beloved Madeleine, and actualizing his recurrent nightmare of falling from the tower, the nightmare in which he envisions an open grave which seems to be not only that of Madeleine but that of the morbidly obsessed Scottie himself. Is Scottie at the end finally freed of the curse of the past, as he has obsessively struggled to free himself, or is he now permanently mired in his feelings of inadequacy and guilt and frustration? It is significant that Hitchcock had filmed a realistic and unambiguous ending to the film, one which evoked a contented Scottie, once again reunited with Midge in her expensive apartment overlooking Russian Hill, calming himself with a drink and intently listening to the news of Gavin Elster's capture in Switzerland. This "happily ever-after" ending with its pronouncement of poetic justice—the criminal, Gavin Elster, is brought to justice, was one developed with the Hollywood censors in mind, since in the fifties the Hayes Code, set into motion to curb the lewdness and immorality of Hollywood films of the 1920s, was still in effect, although its power had markedly lessened. But a defiant Hitchcock who like Billy Wilder was savvy in dealing with the increasingly ineffectual censors, scrapped this ending, choosing instead to leave everything unresolved, perhaps because he wanted to stimulate what he referred to as "icebox talk." This now quaint term refers to the conversations held around the refrigerator—in the 1930s and 1940s equipped with a block of ice—by puzzled moviegoers after they had seen the film, as they attempt to clarify its meanings.

Is Scottie victor or victim? His anguished posture at the very end of *Vertigo*, arms outstretched, as if he were a stricken Christ-figure, an image used repeatedly by Fuentes in *Aura*, indicates that Scottie may be merely on the verge of hurling himself from the tower, joining the second Madeleine in death. It is very likely that Scottie feels his guilt again multiplied, for now he has witnessed the deaths of three persons whom he could have rescued—the self-sacrificing, heroic policeman at the very beginning, the real Madeleine Elster, and now the terror-stricken Judy. As opposed to the first two deaths, for which Scottie feels responsible, but in reality deaths that he could do nothing to stop, his monstrous, brutal actions at the end have brought Judy to the tower and thus at least indirectly occasion her death.

A moral ambiguity characterizes both Scottie and Judy, as it does both Consuelo and Felipe. For whatever motive, genuine love for Gavin Elster or desire rapidly to attain socioeconomic status as the next Mrs. Gavin Elster, Judy Barton thoroughly and successfully carries out Elster's criminal desires. Yet, at the end, Judy seems to gain in integrity as Scottie loses his. Although the merciless Scottie has compelled Judy to climb to the top of the tower, at times so furious at being an object of repeated deceit that he has dragged her by the throat up the steep wooden steps, Judy makes a deep, sincere, and moving plea to Scottie to begin their relationship again and to be accepted for herself. The couple embrace and kiss, and it seems for a moment as if a conventional, romantic, happily-ever-after ending will be imposed upon the film, a supposed ending that initially delighted early viewers of *Vertigo* who were moments later stunned by Hitchcock's swift *cambio de piel*. It is then that Judy suddenly glimpses, emerging from the shadows of the tower, the spectral form that so terrifies her, the form that turns out to be a black-robed nun who has climbed to the top of the tower to investigate the strange noises that she has heard.

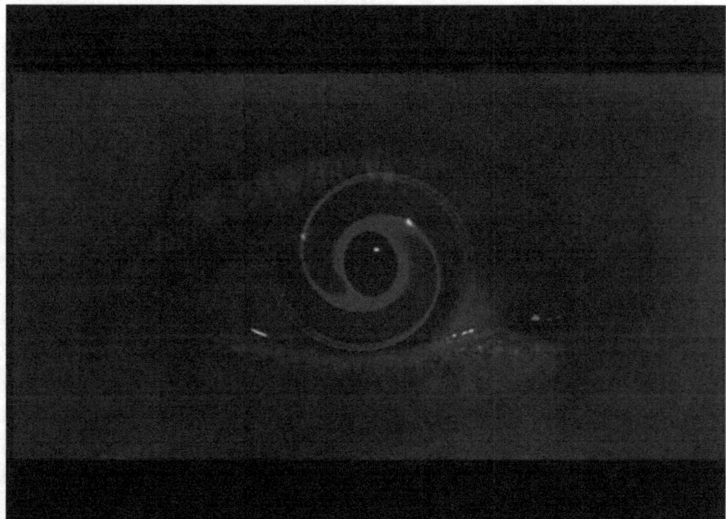

Figure 13. Purple spirals at outset reflected at end in Judy's purple dress, symbolizing vertiginous abyss.

Figure 14. Mahogany walls of Elster's plush office lined with romantic seafaring images of high adventure. What Scottie longs for.

Does Judy, thoroughly traumatized by Scottie, see what she believes is the real Madeleine Elster come back to life in order to take vengeance upon her? Or does Judy descry the revenant spirit of Carlotta? If so, the story that Gavin Elster initially has concocted about his wife being possessed by the mad Carlotta at the end seems to become monstrously true. And the words of the nun, "I heard voices," could easily have been uttered either by Carlotta or by the real Madeleine from within her madness if indeed Gavin Elster's story to an initially skeptical Scottie about his wife's madness is true. Yet as we have seen, Gavin Elster, like so many of Fuentes's killer narrators—Artemio Cruz, Siger de Brabante, Andrés Heredia, the Director General in *La cabeza de la hidra* (*Hydra Head*; 1978), is an extremely unreliable, Machiavellian narrator, and we never see the real Madeleine Elster alive—hers is never a moving, articulating presence in the film, so there is no one to corroborate what may be Elster's spiderlike, web-enveloping machinations.

Even the final, desperate protestations of her love to Scottie by Judy are suspect; the artful Judy may be humoring a madman in an attempt to extricate herself from the traumatic situation and save her life. And so enmeshed in his own delusions is Scottie that he once again reverts to calling Judy by the name "Madeleine," addressing her as a dead woman: "Oh Madeleine, I loved you so." The past tense utilized by a stricken Scottie indicates the impossibility of his ever loving, even repentant Judy Barton. The highly problematic nature not only of *Vertigo* but of Hitchcock's entire art is stressed by Rothman, in an analysis that can apply equally as well to the conundrum that is *Aura:*

> To read a Hitchcock film is to understand that Hitchcock is the most unknown as well as the most popular of filmmakers. His films are meditation on unknownness, emerging from and addressed to a condition of unknownness. *Vertigo* envisions no transcendence, no ideal community or marriage or fulfilled human existence on earth; within every salvation there is a damnation (IC, 173)

In both *Vertigo* and *Aura*, the initial ambiguities, rather than being resolved, continue to multiply to the very end of both of these works. The complexity and the ambiguousness of Scottie, for example, are evident in that he moves slowly but inexorably from the role of victim to that of monstrous victimizer, just as Consuelo goes from that of victim, as she caustically inveighs against the ruthless commercial forces that have attempted to evict her from her home and seems at the beginning to be the defenseless and solitary old woman exploited by an insensitive, even oppressive society, to that of relentless and highly efficient victimizer, as she in effect imprisons Felipe in her realm and keeps him there until he surrenders his soul, in exchange for the return of the soul of the lost Llorente.

Like Consuelo in *Aura*, Scottie Ferguson inexorably moves from victim to sadistic and brutal victimizer. Scottie in the first half of *Vertigo* is the pawn of his seemingly jovial, eloquent college friend Elster, who takes advantage of their friendship to ask for Scottie's help, when all along he is counting on Scottie's vertigo to make it impossible for him to be more than a helpless witness to Madeleine's death. Scottie is also the unsuspecting victim of the very woman whom he protects and loves, Judy/Madeleine. And he is mercilessly browbeaten by the sadistic coroner at the inquest, the coroner who holds Scottie responsible for the deaths of both Madeleine and the policeman, even though Scottie is not indicted and is totally innocent. And yet, in the second half of the film, Scottie becomes as inhuman as those who had deceived and exploited him. His prototype is found in the past, not only in the cunning and ruthless Gavin Elster but more significantly in that of the nameless power baron who took Carlotta away from her previous existence and remade her only to abandon her, to throw her away when he grew tired of her. Depriving her even of her child, reducing her to a lost soul wandering the streets crying out for her lost child, Carlotta's powerful, expolitative husband is indirectly responsible for her death, just as Scottie is to be blamed for the seemingly accidental death of Judy Barton at the end of the film. The second time that Judy is at the top of the tower, it is because Scottie, as the new Gavin Elster, has almost strangled her by grabbing her by the throat to force her up the final stairs to the top.

Paralleling the ambiguity that saturates *Vertigo*, Hitchcock's most complex and metaphysical film, is the all-pervading ambiguity in *Aura*, present even in the names of the characters. We have seen how even Aura's name is infused with a dual meaning. Consuelo is the counterpart to Llorente, "cada dolor tiene su consuelo," and yet the consolation that she gives to the devastated Felipe at the end, as she promises him that his beloved Aura will return, is a false one, since Felipe's love for Aura is consummated only at the cost of the destruction of his independent mind and will and the permanent claiming of his soul. Felipe's last name, Montero, alludes to his role as the hunter, as he hunts both for the key to the understanding of the bizarre situation in which he finds himself and for the way to free Aura from the control of Consuelo. Yet he is rapidly reduced from hunter to hunted. Felipe never understands that Aura is not tyrannized as Felipe in his delusions believes, but in fact is sustained by the implacable will of the imperious Consuelo, just as Scottie does not understand until the very end that Judy/Madeleine is not constantly fleeing from but in fact is in criminal league with Gavin Elster.

Consuelo too has multiple and ever-changing identities. She is linked with the mad Empress Carlotta, who desperately and almost single-handedly attempted to save the doomed Mexican monarchy led by her beloved husband Maximilian, as she traveled to France to implore the Emperor Napoleon III not to abandon his New World enterprise and even was granted an audience with the Pope—and was the first woman ever allowed to stay overnight at the Vatican. Paralleling the childless marriage of Consuelo and Llorente is that of the Empress Carlotta and Maximilian. According to some sources, the Emperor was sterile as the result of a venereal disease, contracted as the result of his numerous affairs in Mexico with Indian concubines, yet according to others, Carlotta was barren—reflected in the inability of Consuelo to conceive. The Austrian Archduke and his beauteous Belgian princess adopted a son—the scion of the first Emperor of Mexico, Agustín Iturbide, in a vain attempt to ensure royal succession. Carlotta died in 1927, sixty years after the execution of Maximilian at Querétaro in 1867. She wore a crown of madness, at times still believing that she was reigning over Mexico and crying out desperately for "Maxl." Similarly, Consuelo is one-hundred-nine years old; she has survived Llorente by more than sixty years, and like the Empress imprisoned in her castle at Bouchot, Consuelo dwells alone in her madness with which she rapidly infects Felipe.

Paralleling Aura, Judy Barton in *Vertigo* is linked both with the present, with Madeleine Elster, the wealthy and sophisticated socialite whom the socioeconomically marginal Judy longs to become for the rest of her life, and with the remote past, with another mad Carlotta from the nineteenth century. And just as Aura may be an independent being, if we interpret the story from a psychological rather than a supernatural standpoint, or may be but a projection of the disturbed mind of Consuelo—a spectral presence that the dominating Consuelo summons up—so too is Judy Barton both a living being and, from the dislocated perspective of the dazed Scottie, a painstaking fabrication of his own consciousness. Just as the mind of the pseudo-heroic Felipe needs to find a vulnerable but enticing girl whom he can protect, so too does the tormented Scottie Ferguson need a glamorous female, vulnerable and submissive, one who will imbue Scottie's empty existence with meaning, one before whom he can play the hero even though in reality he feels himself to be a coward and a guilt-stricken invalid. Both Scottie and Felipe exemplify self-loathing—a self-hatred that seems to impel them into the destructive Other.

Another one of the myriad ambiguities of *Vertigo* is the nature of the real Madeleine Elster, whom we never see alive. When she does appear it is as a mere image within the consciousness of the guilt-stricken memory as evoked by a highly disconcerted Judy in a key flashback. Has the real Madeleine Elster really gone mad, is she really possessed by the spirit of Carlotta, or is this demented personality ascribed to her but one more concoction of the arch-fabulator Gavin Elster? Is Judy the ravishing blonde victimizer and exploiter of Scottie or at the end, as she too plunges to her death, his victim? Similarly, in *Aura,* can the wizened Consuelo be regarded as a *mater terribilis*, similar to the fanatic Claudia Nervo in *Zona sagrada*, who like Consuelo also sustains her myth and attains her agelessness by the continual sacrifice of the young with whom she surrounds herself as living mirrors of the eternal youth that so obsesses her? Or can Consuelo be seen as a heroine, as a stalwart person with an indomitable will whose deep love for her husband succeeds in transcending the boundaries of time, age, and even death itself? In both cases, the reader/spectator must decide—both *Vertigo* and *Aura* are paradoxically, both closed and fated yet at the same time highly ambiguous and remarkably open creations which have resulted in myriad critical interpretations of both film and *novella.*

In *Vertigo*, the ambiguity and the mystery that constitute the essence of Judy/Madeleine and that explain why the enervated Scottie is so attracted to her are underscored visually, both through the indeterminate gray suit that Judy/Madeleine wears and also through her black and white ensembles, the white coat with an elaborate black scarf that Judy/Madeleine stunningly wears in one of the key scenes in *Vertigo*—the submergence of both Judy/Madeleine and Scottie into the ageless yet threatening world of the giant, ominously towering sequoias, like everything else in *Vertigo* ambivalent symbols, signifying both life—immortality—and in the gigantic sequoia that has been cut down and whose rings signify the passing of centuries—death. Judy acts ambivalently, both leading Scottie on toward a rendezvous with death and at the same time, since she has departed from Elster's script and fallen in love with Scottie, attempting, still within the confines of her role as the tormented Madeleine, to warn him away from her—to save him even if she has to lose him.

Judy/Madeleine is enticing and elusive, beguiling and admonitory, precisely as is the spectral Aura with Felipe. At times, such as when Judy/Madeleine leads Scottie to the grove of immense sequoia trees then wanders off into the depths of the forest, she seems not to want to continue with her deception, as she implores Scottie not to persist in his questions: "Please don't ask me, please don't ask me . . . Promise me something, you won't ask me again, please promise me that." Similarly, Aura is a divided creation. At times she appears with a warning bell, ringing it as if she were warning lepers to get out of the way. The person who is marked by inoperable contagion is Felipe. His affliction is exteriorized in the weird, voodoolike doll that he one day finds at his dinner plate, poorly sewn and with its stuffing coming out. Felipe alternately caresses the doll and then drops it, behavior that exteriorizes his paradoxical response to Consuelo/Aura as both being drawn to them and feeling the urgency to escape. Yet just as Scottie continues blindly in his devotion to Judy/Madeleine, sacrificing his relationship with the ever-consoling, ever-protective

Midge, consecrating himself instead to the very person who is ensnaring and destroying him, so too does Felipe become a willing pawn of the destructive Consuelo and her minion, the mesmeric Aura.

Just as *Vertigo* provides a seething critique of twentieth century society, as it repeatedly depicts the power of the *macho* and the exploitation of the female, all of whose resistance is futile, the enthronement of the male who as in the nineteenth century controls the female economically and can twist her to his whim, as both Gavin Elster and Scottie do with Judy, Elster "paying off" Judy for her services by giving her the necklace of Carlotta, so too can *Aura* be interpreted not only as a story of the supernatural but one that provides an indirect indictment of several aspects of Mexican society. The vibrant and beautiful Consuelo is extremely frustrated at not being able to have children. In traditional Hispanic society, the maternal role is one that is deemed paramount for women—paralleling the traditional German role-model for the woman as signifying "Kinder, Kirche, Küchen" ("Children, Church, and Kitchen")—and when she is unable to fulfill it, like the frustrated Yerma in the tragedy *Yerma* by Federico García Lorca, the third play after *Bodas de sangre* (*Blood Wedding*) and *La casa de Bernarda Alba* (*The House of Bernarda Alba*) all of which have significantly influenced Fuentes's fatalistic vision of love and power she goes insane. Although Consuelo does not go to the drastic extreme of Yerma, who kills her presumably sterile husband, Fuentes's heroine succumbs to insanity and begins her worship of the devil. Consuelo even resorts to monstrous rituals of torturing and killing of cats in an attempt to restore the fertility of the increasingly agitated and helpless Llorente, who sees his vivacious wife slipping away from him. And through its linking of Consuelo with the domineering Empress Carlotta, Fuentes's work provides a critique of vaunting ambition and unbridled power, as it alludes to the circumstance that the apparently overly ambitious and willful Carlotta had pressured her vacillating husband to accept the Mexican throne. Once the imperial couple had established themselves in Mexico, even though they discovered that the liberal leader and President of Mexico Benito Juárez and his forces were an insistent and a growing threat, Carlotta was determined to retain her power, exactly as the physically enfeebled

Figure 15. Smooth, manipulative Gavin Elster against backdrop that strikingly confirms his money and power.

Figure 16. Back photography and graceful mid-shot accentuate Madeleine's mystery and allure. Note shimmering green cape and stole.

Consuelo vows to remain in her domicile which the forces of urban renewal are threatening to demolish. Maximilian was counseled over and over again by members of his imperial court to give up his increasingly perilous venture and return to the safety of Europe. After the withdrawal of the French forces under Marshall Bazine, Maximilian is left with only a few staunch loyalists and is extremely vulnerable yet refuses to abandon his throne, presumably under the controlling influence of the dominant Carlotta.

The dangers of fanaticism, of surrendering oneself to a fantasy existence, are underscored through the downfall of the protagonists of both *Aura* and *Vertigo.* Despite all of the efforts of the maniacal Consuelo, at the end as at the very beginning of *Aura*, the always elusive girl has once again disappeared. Similarly, despite all of his planning and his fanatic remolding of Judy into Madeleine, Scottie at the end, as at the very beginning, is once more alone, distressed, and helpless.And this time, the motherly Midge is no longer there to comfort him.

Another one of the major structural parallels between *Vertigo* and *Aura* is the space that is deliberately left throughout both creations for the reader/viewer to fill. Both stories are punctured by many holes—gaps in meaning that must be filled in by the reader/viewer, who thereby becomes an attentive collaborator with the director/writer in creating the work.

In *Aura*, the true nature of the spectral Aura is never made clear. Is she but an emanation of the delirious mind of Consuelo? And why can she remain for only three days at a time in the domain of Consuelo? Is this an allusion to the death and resurrection of Christ on the Third Day? One critic has interpreted all of the action of *Aura* as occurring within the deluded consciousness of Consuelo as she lies near death.[11] From this point of view, not only Aura but Felipe himself becomes a ghostly presence, a creation of the desperate old woman. Yet another, equally valid interpretation would be that Aura is the creation of the unbalanced, delusion-prone mind of Felipe, under the effects of

---

[11] See Santiago Rojas, "Modalidad narrativa en *Aura:* realidad y enajenación," *Revista iberoamericana*, 112-113 (julio-diciembre 1980), p. 491.

the drugs that Consuelo grows in her patio and which she has slipped into his wine.

In contemporary Latin American literature, this space of ambiguity is a hallmark of the Latin American Boom Novel of the 1960s. Fuentes is the acknowledged founder and may also be considered the maximum exponent of the Novel of the Boom, which is also represented by masterful works such as the intricate metaphysical meta–narrative *Rayuela* by the late Argentine novelist and short story writer Julio Cortázar; *El obsceno pájaro de la noche* and *El lugar sin límites* by the late Chilean author José Donoso; and *La ciudad y los perros* and *La Casa Verde* by the Peruvian novelist Mario Vargas Llosa, who in 2010 was the second Boom novelist, after Gabriel García Márquez, to be awarded the Nobel Prize for Literature, as well as novels such as *La región más transparente* and *Cambio de piel*, *Aura* and *Cumpleaños*, by Fuentes himself. And Carlos Fuentes, the third still living member of the stellar Boom Generation, is a frequently touted candidate for this coveted international prize. In all of these superlative works, the reader must actively create the work along with the author, entering the zones of indecision and ambiguity and deciding, for example, whether the outcome of the life of Horacio Oliveira, the ever-doubting, always questioning and self-questioning, Hamlet-like protagonist of *Rayuela* is a positive one, with Oliveira attaining the self-transcendence–the highly elusive Center to his existence—after which he has so persistently quested, or whether the depressed and exceedingly alienated protagonist permanently bereft of his beloved La Maga, commits suicide or succumbs to madness. Fuentes masterfully continues this structure of co-creation in *Cristóbal nonato* (*Cristopher Unborn;* 1987), a work in which pages are deliberately left blank for the reader to fill in, and some scenes are deliberately and self-consciously left open-ended for the reader, whom Fuentes refers to as the Elector, underscoring the option that the reader has to continue the work or end it, to shape the fate of the character creations who are literally incomplete, such as the foetal narrator *Cristóbal nonato*, or existentially indeterminate, such as the quixotic father of Cristóbal, Angel Fagoaga, who vacillates among several women, partly because of his Don Juan fixation, partly because of his rampant immaturity. In many aspects of his life and career, Angel is directionless. His protean identity is underscored through his many costume changes. At times, playing the role of the acerbic social critic, he dresses as a twentieth century Francisco de Quevedo, a renowned Spanish novelist-author of the picaresque novel *El Buscón* (The Searcher; 1626), and poet of the seventeenth century; at other times the highly protean Angel emulates the provincial life style and the mannerisms of Ramón López Velarde, the famous contemporary Mexican poet of "Suave patria," which is re-created by Fuentes in *Christopher Unborn*, one of the many examples of the significant intertextuality that characterizes this open, indeterminate, highly porous and demanding work.

As we have seen, in both *Vertigo* and *Aura*, the sacred is combined with the demonic as it is in *Psycho* and *The Birds*, an occurrence which also is found in many other works of Fuentes, including *Terra nostra*, *Una familia lejana*, and most explicitly and extensively, the bizarre *Cumpleaños*, in which Fuentes re-creates the thirteenth century theologian and heretic Siger de Brabante as a monstrous figure of egolatry, one who defies the laws of creation as he disdains birth through the female womb and glorifies himself as the Arch Creator, usurping the role of God, and finally being linked with the devil in his fragmentation and dispersion, as opposed to the unifying power of God. In *Aura*, when the naive Felipe first sees Consuelo before her wall of icons and in prayer, she seems to be the archetypal Mexican *beata*, humbly devoted to her prayers, votive lamps ablaze. Aura too initially appears as a spiritual force. She carries a candelabra, and lights the way for Felipe through the darkened and highly treacherous domain of Consuelo. Yet this is a false illumination, unlike the role that the classical heroine Ariadne plays in providing the thread—the means by which Theseus can re-emerge from the darkened labyrinth after he has slain the Minotaur. Aura lights the way only to Felipe's destruction, as she leads him to a table where there are four places set, although only three and in reality two—Felipe and Consuelo—will dine. It is at this table that Felipe encounters the poorly sewn doll, its stuffing coming out, that symbolizes his own ragdoll nature as well as his imminent destruction.

Similarly, in *Vertigo* as well, illumination is deceptive. Hitchcock masterfully illuminates Judy/Madeleine, the first time Scottie sees her at *Ernie's*, with a sudden, radiant backlighting that imbues her with a celestial quality, as if she were a divine presence. As she leaves *Ernie's*, the faux but enticingly beautiful Madeleine pauses, and the camera catches her in profile, face regally uplifted, as if she were a twentieth century incarnation of the classical Roman goddess of Love, Venus or a cameo of the Greek goddess Aphrodite—Hitchcock alluding to the Pygmalion-Galatea myth of a marble statue of a breathtakingly beautiful woman brought to life for pleasure and love. The lighting is designed to make the audience of the film experience the same mesmerizing effect that the ethereally beautiful Madeleine is exerting on the initially highly skeptical but now thoroughly entranced Scottie. It imbues Judy/Madeleine with a radiant, halo effect, in contrast with the conventional lighting used in the evocation of the witty but pedestrian Midge, who is most often evoked in comfortable mid-shots. Judy/Madeleine is thus evoked as an ethereal being, very similar to the way that the magical Aura initially appears.

There are many centers of ambiguity in *Aura.* Although the proliferation of rats in the bedroom of Consuelo indicates that there have been no cats in her domicile for many years, Felipe experiences a horrifying vision of screeching and smoldering cats. These seem to be the hellish memory, perpetuated through time and space, of the cats which Consuelo had tortured as part of a bizarre fertility rite, in a vain attempt to restore the fertility of Llorente, whom she deeply resents for his incapacity to give her children. Once when the rabbit, a familiar of Consuelo the sorceress, disappears, Consuelo states that it will come back, but instead of the rabbit reappearing, it is Aura. It is significant that the rabbit is named Saga, related to sagacity and indicative of the arcane knowledge that Consuelo possesses:

> "Saga. Saga. Where are you? Ici, Saga!"
> "Who?"
> "My companion."
> "The rabbit?"
> "Yes. She'll come back." (A, 21-23)
>
> "I told you that she'd come back."
> "Who?"

"Aura. My companion. My niece."
"Good afternoon."(A, 25)

The rabbit is a fertility symbol, one that represents Consuelo's fanatic desire for self-perpetuation, but its glowing red eyes indicate that this fertility is a demonic one, and that Consuelo has succeeded in giving birth to herself, only as a result of consorting with the Devil. Ironically, after the weird Black Mass in which Felipe participates, he feels as if something had been engendered during the night. It is he himself who has been reborn, or rather the spirit of Llorente who has been reborn through him.

Aura, similar to Hitchcock's masterpiece, constitutes a vision that is psychedelic, that is constantly changing. It is a narrative in which style and theme coincide perfectly to give the reader the exact sensations of doubt, bewilderment and consternation that the hapless Felipe experiences. Hitchcock does the same through his expert use of the camera, which fastens itself relentlessly upon Scottie as he follows Madeleine through the sinuous, labyrinthine streets of San Francisco. Indeed, *Vertigo* achieves a purity and an intensity of form as Hitchcock in evoking the pursuit of the ever-elusive Madeleine by an increasingly absorbed Scottie, eliminates all dialogue, creating for an extended period of time what is essentially a silent movie like those which the venerable Hitchcock created at the beginning of his superlative career including *The White Shadow* (1923), *The Pleasure Garden* (1925) and *The Lodger* (1926), and powerfully conveying the moods of Scottie, similar to those of Felipe—bafflement, anticipation, anxiety, enchantment—as he pursues his beloved Madeleine through seemingly modern San Francisco that at every point sheers off a spectral past—like the dreamlike episode entirely without dialogue, of a rapt Scottie stealthily spying on Judy/Madeleine in the secluded, misty and mystifying garden of the closed sacred space of the Mission Dolores. In *Vertigo* as in *Aura*, reality is like an immense Swiss cheese, with many gaps that are never explained. For example, at the very beginning, the climax to the scene of Scottie's chasing the criminal, slipping and nearly falling to his death, as he hangs on to a dangerously bent and close to collapsing eves trough, suddenly fades out, and Scottie is left dangling. The scene suddenly shifts to Midge's comfortable apartment—a substitute womb for the physically crippled—he loathes carrying a cane—but most significantly, mentally warped Scottie, some time after this traumatic occurrence. How Scottie was rescued, his subsequent hospitalization, his dealings with the police force, are never treated, as Hitchcock presents a story with multiple excisions and mere allusions at key moments exactly as Fuentes through allusion and condensing develops his masterpiece, *Aura*.

Similarly, the youth of the mad Carlotta in the nineteenth century and her aimless wandering as a beggar woman through the streets of San Francisco, are never explicitly evoked by Hitchcock—only symbolically, through the endless and duplicitous "wanderings" of Judy/Madeleine. And, at the very end, Scottie once more is left as a dangling man, at the top of another tower, just as he was at the beginning, reeling after still another death for which he feels responsible. In *Aura*, constant ambiguity is also evident, for example in Consuelo's statement that a servant is going to bring Felipe's belongings, so that he may reside with Consuelo until he finishes revising the tedious memoirs of the deceased Llorente. Yet no servant is ever seen. And just as Scottie is suspended at the end of *Vertigo*, so also are the fates of both Aura and Felipe left unclear and in abeyance. At the end, is Felipe totally the Other, Llorente, or is he a hybrid form, a Dr. Jekyll/Mr. Hyde type of creation? Will he remain forever within the realm of Consuelo, is his only function now to worship her as the slavish Llorente doted on Consuelo? What will happen to him as he inevitably grows old and weak? And when will the ever elusive, ever beguiling Aura return again to cast her Madeleine-like spell over inchoate males? All these ambiguities are left unanswered.

At the end of *Vertigo*, a dazed Scottie gives the impression that he will once again lapse into a catatonic state, similar to the one that the benumbed Felipe is in at the end of *Aura*, where there is now no hope whatsoever of his regaining an autonomous identity, if indeed he was ever a truly independent self.

All of the hesitancies that Felipe experiences, his instinct for self-preservation that warns him to leave Consuelo's house, are overcome as Consuelo immediately summons up the presence of the alluring Aura to hold him:

> "My conditions are that you have to live here. There isn't much time left."
> "I don't know if . . ."
> "Aura . . ." (A, 25)

As a critic has pointed out, in *Vertigo* Madeleine seems to glide not walk across the floor. This is paralleled by the unreal, somnambulistic way in which Aura moves through space:

> You look around and a girl is standing there, a girl whose whole body you can't see because she's standing so close to you and her arrival was so unexpected, without the slightest sound . . . (A, 25)

All of Felipe's initial doubts about Aura rapidly vanish as in a trancelike state, he promises that he will remain with Consuelo. Similarly, immediately after he has glimpsed Madeleine, Scottie immediately falls in love with her, and all of his reservations about accepting Elster's assignment vanish. Both of these nebulous males have suddenly found intense purpose to what were previously inchoate existences. Here, in *Aura*, is the equivalent to the hypnotic credit sequence in *Vertigo* with its sustained focus on the eyes of Judy/Madeleine. Here Fuentes provides a masterful close-up and also conveys the essence of cinema—insistent and mesmerizing movement:

> Finally you can see that those eyes are sea green and that they surge again like a wave. You look into them and tell yourself it isn't true, because they're beautiful green eyes just like all the beautiful green eyes you've ever known. But you can't deceive yourself: those eyes do surge, do change, as if offering you a landscape that only you can see and desire. (A, 27)

The exclusivity of Aura's mesmerizing glance parallels the exclusivity of the advertisement cunningly placed by Consuelo in the newspaper—an advertisment that the vulnerable but narcissistic Felipe believes is directed to him alone. Yet in both *Vertigo* and *Aura*, promised exclusivity is but a fraud. The advertisement that Felipe feels is directed personally to him, as well as the glance of Aura, that he naively interprets as designed for himself alone, are but Consuelo's shrewd attempts to play on Felipe's vanity. And in *Vertigo* as well, Scottie's entering into a world in which he and Madeleine are the only two occupants, in which Gavin Elster is quickly disregarded and Midge is nonexistent, is another false paradise that will end in tragedy, in the physical destruction of Judy and the mental and spiritual demise of Scottie.

Many of the lines which Judy/Madeleine speaks with such apparent sincerity to Scottie have multiple meanings, depending on which of her three identities is uttering them. As Wood insightfully points out:

> Her behaviour before the "suicide" is full of obvious ambiguities. ("It wasn't supposed to happen this way. . . If you love me, you'll know I loved you and wanted to go on loving you")—the remarks mean something quite different depending on whether we think of them as spoken by Madeleine or by Judy, and if we look further we shall see that in fact every moment of the relationship is ambiguous, it is impossible to distinguish pretense from reality. Is her nervousness during the car journey to San Juan Bautista real or feigned—Judy pretending to be Madeleine becoming distraught, or Judy becoming distraught as she gets nearer to what she has agreed to do?[12]

Immediately prior to the murder scene of the real Madeleine Elster at the top of the dread tower, Judy states enigmatically, "There's something I must do." Is she referring to her part in the crime, that of luring Scottie to the top of the tower, or is she stating that she has changed her mind, is now intending to disavow Gavin Elster and has decided to rush to the top of the tower in order to prevent the murder because she has now fallen in love with Scottie, the very person she was supposed to ensnare? At the last minute, does Judy scream in order to attempt to halt the murder, to stop Elster from hurling his wife's body from the top of the tower, or does she

[12] Consult Wood, *Hitchcock's Films Revisited*, p. 122.

Figure 17. Derealization of Madeleine Elster: mirror reflection of a glamorous ghost. Note plush, blood red wallpaper and shimmering gold mirror frame.

Figure 18. More Pillars of the Past: Luxurious Brocklebank Apartments where Madeleine does and does not dwell.

cry out as part of a pre-arranged scheme in order to draw Scottie's attention to the window so that he will see the falling body and later testify to the "suicide" of Madeleine? Similarly, the words of Aura to Felipe have multiple meanings, depending on whether they are spoken as Consuelo to Llorente or as Aura to the benumbed Felipe. After an amorous tryst with Felipe, Aura states: "Eres mi esposo" (A, 36), and an extremely compliant Felipe agrees, believing that Aura has now totally accepted him, not realizing that what he is agreeing to is his permanently and totally becoming Llorente, the person whom Aura/Consuelo is really addressing.

When Judy, on the couple's first trip down the Peninsula to the mission at San Juan Bautista, seeks to break away from Scottie's embrace and rush to the top of the tower, she makes another cryptic yet highly poetic remark to the person whom she regards as both beloved and object of her deception: "And if you lose me, then you'll know I loved you and wanted to go on loving you." Are these highly poetic words the ones that Judy has been exactingly trained to say, as part of her role as the possessed Madeleine, speaking as the mad Carlotta, desperately attempting reconciliation with her husband before she commits suicide? Are these apparently deeply felt words the confession of Judy to Scottie of genuine love or are they designed and very convincingly uttered by a shrewd, well-trained Judy to ensure that a love-stricken Scottie will fall into her trap and attempt desperately to follow her to the top of the tower? Or are these words—a confession of deep, abiding yet thwarted love—Judy's recognition that even though she loves Scottie, she will follow and eventually hope to marry Gavin Elster? The intensely lyrical quality of the utterance coincides with the master of lyricism, the poetic manner in which Gavin Elster at the outset has evoked the lost, endlessly wandering Madeleine, in a script that Judy has thoroughly memorized and artfully, even passionately, delivered. Or are these the words of the frantic, even dismayed Judy herself, in love with Scottie but compelled to fulfill her iron pact with Gavin Elster? It is highly significant that despite her love for Scottie, Judy never confesses to him her role in the plot, either at this point, or when she encounters Scottie months after the murder or when she is compelled to return to San Juan Bautista by the now cold-blooded and extremely callous and vengeful Scottie. The letter of confession and of self exculpation that Judy initially writes, depicting herself as the mere instrument of the will of Elster, she subsequently tears up, perhaps fearful that Scottie will not believe her and that she will lose him again. Ironically, the words that Judy utters to Scottie immediately prior to the death of Madeleine Elster, "Too late," words that refer both to the futility of her attempting to stop the crime and to the possibility that she and Scottie could have established a meaningful, redemptive relationship, are echoed by the broken Scottie at the very end of the film, when their original roles are reversed, and it is the anguished Judy who is now attempting to bring Scottie back to reality, to hold him with her kiss while he slips into madness, which this time may be permanent. It is significant that when Scottie by chance encounters a working class Judy Barton on the street, Judy is all set to leave San Francisco, to flee what she recognizes is for her a highly dangerous situation, since Scottie may discover her role as Gavin Elster's shrewd accomplice. Does Judy change her travel/escape plans out of deep love for Scottie? Out of unremitting guilt for her role in the crime that killed one innocent person and severely devastated a second innocent bystander?

The marked ambiguity of *Vertigo* continues until the very end. In what is a masterpiece of cinematic photography, the nun who climbs to the top of the tower is photographed indistinctly, as a dark shadow suddenly rising up, as if she were the revenant spirit of Madeleine Elster come to exact vengeance on her murderer and his accomplice. In this meticulously structured film, the emergence from the murky darkness of what Judy perceives as a vengeful, phantom presence, provides the grim counterpoint to the emergence of a radiantly transformed Judy Barton enveloped in an eery, phantasmagorical green light, into a resuscitated Madeleine, anticipated both with extreme pleasure and marked apprehensiveness by an impatient Scottie in Judy's modestly furnished apartment at the Empire Hotel—the fatalistic setting that marks her fatal rebirth as the imprisoned Other.

Judy speaks as three persons: at times as the distraught Madeleine Elster, supposedly under the iron control of the spirit of Carlotta, but in reality masterfully carrying out the elaborate instructions of Gavin Elster, at other times, as a demented Carlotta Valdés speaking through Madeleine, and at still other moments as a bewildered and insecure Judy Barton attempting to break out of both of these other roles and begin a genuine relationship with Scottie. Similarly, Aura speaks as three persons: as herself, as the highly frustrated Consuelo, and as the mad Empress Carlotta, endlessly grieving over the death of her beloved Maximilian, shot to death by a firing squad.

Like Judy/Madeleine, Aura is constantly surrounded by light. This light is a markedly ambiguous one, symbolic both of Aura's celestial nature and of her capacity for duplicity. Felipe is blinded by the radiant light, indicating how much he is under the control of the stunningly beautiful young girl, so that he blindly promises his very soul to her, and thus ensures the triumph of Consuelo in bringing Llorente back to life:

> Sitting on the bed, you try to make out the source of that diffuse, opaline light that hardly lets you distinguish the objects in the room, and the presence of Aura, from the golden atmosphere that surrounds them. She sees you looking up, trying to find where it comes from. You can tell from her voice that she's kneeling down in front of you.
> "The sky is neither high nor low. It's over us and under us at the same time." (A, 105)

Just as it does from Madeleine from the very first moment that a transfixed Scottie views her, light seems to emanate from Aura, imbuing her with a transcendental, spiritual quality. The light is present even in her name, signifying in one of its meanings the light of the dawn, as allusions both to the classical Roman goddess Aurora and to the light of Resurrection, the miraculous rebirth of Christ at Easter and the light of the halos that surround Christ and the Virgin Mary and the Saints, in countless paintings—medieval, Renaissance, modern. Yet, ironically, new life for Aura/Consuelo is possible only as the result of the existential and spiritual sacrifices of victims such as the hapless Felipe.

The utterances of Aura to Felipe are characterized by the same cryptic quality as are the enigmatic words of Madeleine to Scottie. Aura refers to the sky as both a physical entity and as heaven. If heaven is above them, they are in a type of hellworld. If it is below them, then they exist in a limbo realm. The circumstance that heaven is simultaneously above and beneath them indicates the highly paradoxical nature of their existence—redemptive for Aura/Consuelo, condemnatory for Felipe. Indeed, both Felipe and Scottie Ferguson are ultimately mired in damnation. Paralleling the *macho* Scottie, who immediately adopts a protective attitude toward Madeleine, one which is reinforced after he mistakenly believes that he has rescued his beloved from her suicide attempt after she tears apart the Carlotta bouquet and unexpectedly throws herself into the San Francisco Bay, Felipe also fashions himself as Aura's insistent and heroic rescuer from the tyrannous power of Consuelo:

> "She's trying to bury you alive. You've got to be reborn, Aura."
> "You have to die to be reborn . . . No, you don't understand. Forget about it, Felipe. Just have faith in me." (A, 123)

Aura's reply to the imploration by Felipe is also ambiguous. It alludes not to Aura, who already is a renascent force, but to Felipe, who must die spiritually in order that the shadow of Llorente can return to life. Aura's plea to Felipe to forget his thoughts and place complete confidence in her parallels the pleas made by Judy/Madeleine to Scottie in the sequoia forest at Big Basin Redwoods south of San Francisco for him not to delve any further into the Carlotta enigma in which she ostensibly is enmeshed.

The extremely puzzling nature of *Vertigo* is again evident in a key confrontation between Scottie and Judy/Madeleine toward the end of the film. Why does Judy, once she has successfully completed the transformation back into Madeleine, deliberately don the incriminating necklace of Carlotta, right in front of Scottie, thus making the hitherto rather dense detective realize immediately that Judy has been Madeleine all along and that he has been hideously duped both by Judy and Gavin Elster? Is Judy so caught up in the pretense and so enamoured of her role, that her vanity impels her to make the role complete by adding the necklace? Is this but a continuation of an almost servile desire by an ever willing Judy to cater to Scottie's every whim, as she makes her portrayal of the lost Madeleine even more authentic? Is it an act done unthinkingly, so sure has Judy now become of Scottie's love? Or does Judy unconsciously desire to be caught, in order to have her complicity in the crime revealed to Scottie, from whom she now expects total forgiveness because she has ceded to his every demand? Judy Barton is sensitive and intelligent enough to remember that Scottie had seen, indeed, had been mesmerized by the portrat of Carlotta that he had beheld in the San Francisco museum. She also on some level must know that her making the phantom of Carlotta/Madeleine "perfect" by donning the necklace is an extremely perilous act. Is this an act of supreme carelessness, or does it reflect the subconscious desire of the guilt-stricken Judy to be caught and punished and finally to rid herself of the Other, of the comfortable but stultifying and ultimately sterile role in which she has become mired? Does the self-destructive act adumbrate the final plea of Judy Barton to a stunned Scottie at the very end to start anew and to be loved for herself, not as a ghost? It is for the spectator to decide, just as Fuentes throughout his prolific work leaves it up to the imaginative reader to collaborate with him. Indeed, the active, collaborative reader is converted by Fuentes into a veritable co-creator is called upon to provide an ending to *Aura*, one that either damns or redeems Felipe, a finale that either glorifies Consuelo as an intransigent, ultimately victorious superwoman or which condemns her as the epitome of evil and deceit.

Both *Vertigo* and *Aura* finally exemplify but futile, involuted relationships, ones that are forced into repetitive and fatalistic patternings. The sterility of Llorente is both literal and symbolic. It symbolizes not only the probable sterility of the Emperor Maximilian, but also the essential sterility of Llorente's own distorted relationship with the egomaniacal Consuelo. The proud but demented recluse directs her fierce will and energy toward sustaining a mere phantom. Nothing productive is ever achieved from the relationship between Aura and Felipe, since Aura is a sterile creation, incapable of bearing children, bereft of a true future.

Similarly, in *Vertigo* the relationship between Scottie and the re-transformed Madeleine goes nowhere. At the end, Judy at Scottie's command but now thoroughly accepting the Madeleine role, has donned the same elegant black dress that she wore the first time Scottie saw her, and she suggests that they return once more to dine at *Ernie's*, which looms as a type of shrine to which the lovers must repeatedly pilgrimage—or else the relationship will cease to exist. Like the relationship between Felipe and Aura, that between Scottie and Judy/Madeleine is tragically circumscribed by the past, since Scottie is incapable of responding to Judy as other than a ghost. Scottie sits contentedly in Judy's apartment, and yet he is in a type of stupor—reminiscent of his catatonic state in the mental asylum and far worse than his seemingly relaxed but nervous interchange with Midge right after his devastating attack of vertigo at the outset of the film. Scottie merely watches approvingly as Judy expertly performs for him; he is a benumbed, blithely contented puppetmaster—unlike the ever alert, ever tense Gavin Elster. It is significant that Scottie has not even brought an ever-willing-to-please Judy back to his own, more spacious and comfortable apartment, as if that zone were off limits to a person whom he still regards as but a somehow tarnished or inadequate copy of his beloved, regal Madeleine. He and Judy have not married; they have no friends; they are both doomed to a repetition of the past, exactly as are Consuelo and Felipe. The latter, narcotized, stupefied, permanently incarcerated in Consuelo's domain, is similar to Judy Barton, playing forever the role of a dead person, catering to the necrophilic desires of the person who now utterly controls him, weak-willed and inchoate.

Both *Vertigo* and *Aura* contain monstrously cyclical visions, in which both the recent and the remote past plays itself out over and over again in the vaporous present. Indeed, in *Vertigo*, one wonders whether anything that was not a part of the original relationship between Scottie and Madeleine could ever be tolerated by the outwardly calm but increasingly rigid and even ossified Scottie. Perhaps it is the natural desire for something new that motivates Judy to don the necklace—but here again the New that can only be the constrictive, even strangling Old.

At the end of *Vertigo*, Scottie discovers, just as does Consuelo in *Aura*, the impossibility of resurrecting and permanently sustaining an illusion. Yet, like the adamant Consuelo, he is doomed to keep trying. Even at the very end, despite his vow to Judy that he will boldly confront the past, re-experience the climb to the top of the tower, and this time master his vertigo, Scottie states to an increasingly terrified Judy, whom he once again reverts to calling "Madeleine": "It's too late . . . there's no bringing her back." But to which Madeleine is the anguished Scottie referring, to the real Madeleine Elster, the one whom he never knew, or to the delectable illusion of Madeleine, the one whom he himself created, first in his delirium-stricken imagination and then in reality—the clinging, apparently helpless Madeleine, disturbed and fragile and in desperate need of Scottie's continued protection? Ironically, as if to contravene Scottie's declaration, a moment later "Madeleine" does indeed seem to come back, to rise up from the dead and appear at the top of the tower.

In both *Vertigo* and *Aura* we see women—Judy/Madeleine and Consuelo/Aura—who are but tantalizing masks. Like the treacherous Gavin Elster, Consuelo is a master of deceit, pretending abjectness when she is in fact ruthless:

> Excuse me . . . Excuse me, Señor Montero. Old ladies have nothing left but . . . the pleasures of devotion . . . (A, 49)

Like the eloquent but shifty Elster, Consuelo is articulate but cagey; even her glance is a hooded one. Here again the highly cinematic Fuentes presents a striking film technique—an extreme close-up on Consuelo's eyes, reminiscent of the close-up by Hitchcock on the mesmeric eyes of Judy/Madeleine at the stunning outset of *Vertigo*:

> When you look at her again you see that her eyes have opened very wide, and that they're clear, liquid, enormous, almost the same color as the yellowish whites around them, so that only the black dots of the pupils mar that clarity. It's lost a moment later in the heavy folds of her lowered eyelids, as if she wanted to protect that glance which is now hiding at the back of its dry cave. (A, 23)

The befuddled Felipe, throughout his stay in the domain of the sorceress, remains half in light, half in shadow. He is always attentive only to the foreground of what he perceives, remaining oblivious to the significance of the background. Although Felipe concentrates on the fragile, seemingly penitent figure of Consuelo in the foreground he is blinded by the array of votive lights. The perplexed Felipe sees but fails to understand that the center of the wall of icons marks the triumph not of the saints and Christ but of the gleeful demons who are tormenting the souls in hell. Indeed, here is the first revelation to Felipe of his future destiny as tormented victim of Consuelo. Felipe remains fascinated by the hellish vision, as Consuelo, despite her decrepit state, furiously battles against the saints and the Archangel Michael himself on behalf of her demonic master. In a masterful evocation, Fuentes utilizes a forward zoom to concentrate intensely on what initially are background images. It is here that Felipe sees but is tragically unable to comprehend his future fate, paralleling the detective who cannot detect—Scottie Ferguson in *Vertigo*:

> . . . she suddenly raises her fists and strikes feebly at the air, as if she were doing battle against the images you can make out as you tiptoe closer: Christ, the Virgin, St. Sebastian, St. Lucia, the Archangel Michael, and the grinning demons in an old print, the only happy figures in that iconography of sorrow and wrath, happy because they're jabbing their pitchforks into the flesh of the damned, pouring cauldrons of boiling water on them, violating the women, getting drunk, enjoying all the liberties forbidden to the saints. You approach that central image, which is surrounded by the tears of Our Lady of Sorrows, the blood of Our Crucified Lord, the delight of Lucifer, the anger of the Archangel . . . (A, 47-49)

The demons are ecstatically celebrating their capturing of the souls of the innocent—symbolizing the permanent entrapment of and damnification of Felipe himself. Felipe will experience many other visions, and yet his shortsightedness will prevent him from understanding their true and deadly significance. For example, he one day views his beloved, ethereal Aura engaged in a grisly task, skinning a goat, her clothes splattered with blood. The goat symbolizes Felipe himself; at the end he senses that his features, his unique identity, is being stripped from him, just as the goat has suffered *desollamiento* which will now be horrifyingly experienced by Felipe himself. Felipe's stupefied reaction before the wall of icons parallels that of Scottie Ferguson as he watches Madeleine gazing on and transfixed by the museum portrait of Carlotta, reflecting Scottie's own deep, mesmerized link to Madeleine.

Felipe has interrupted Consuelo's demon worship. But, aware that he is spying on her, she confuses him by placing herself squarely on the side of the angels and thus immediately allays his suspicions:

> "Come, City of God! Gabriel, sound your trumpet! Ah, how long the world takes to die!" (A, 49)

Dialogue in *Aura* is as convoluted and as maddeningly deceptive as is dialogue in *Vertigo*. Even the seemingly hard-headed Midge is perfused with delusions—first that her love and constant attention, even devotion to Scottie can redeem him, and second that she can puncture Scottie's infatuation with the alluring—and highly sensuous—Madeleine. The task that Consuelo assigns Felipe—to edit and reconstruct her husband's memoirs for publication—is but a ruse to keep him with her until he can be totally possessed, paralleling the temptress Judy/Madeleine, who slowly but inexorably entraps the now very pliable Scottie. Like Scottie under the subtle control of Gavin Elster, Felipe is quickly reduced to a mere instrument of his crafty and sinister employer.

Although Scottie is given repeated warnings by his subconsciousness of the destructive nature of Judy/Madeleine, he systematically suppresses all of these admonitions and pursues her fanatically. So too does Felipe receive many warnings, on both the conscious and subconscious levels, of the true nature of his beloved Aura, of her essence as but a mask for the demonic Consuelo, and thus of her tantalizing but lethal nature. Yet so spellbound is Felipe by Aura's beauty and so fulfilled is she by his new found role of romantic lover and knight-errant that he repeatedly ignores all of these many warnings.

After Scottie's traumatic experience at the coroner's harsh and even punishing inquest into the circumstances surrounding

Madeleine's bizarre death, he experiences a devastating nightmare, in which he envisions the disintegration of huge, cartoonlike flowers. These garish and fake flowers represent Scottie's mental transformation of the real flowers that Judy/Madeleine at the very beginning has purchased at the Podesta/Baldocchi florist—elegant flowers that in turn duplicate those in the portrait of Carlotta. On the unconscious level, Scottie is beginning to realize that the woman with whom he has fallen in love is an elaborate—and even menacing—fraud. And a distraught Scottie at the inquest of Madeleine Elster also experiences a vision of Carlotta, alive and in the company of Gavin Elster, linked conspiratorially with Elster. Here both Gavin Elster and a rapt Carlotta are bathed in an eery red filter light, to symbolize both as conspiratorial figures of menance. And, after his subsequent, excruciatingly laborious transformation of the coarse Judy into the refined and elegant Madeleine is complete, when Scottie for the first time is able to respond to Judy erotically, as he takes her into his arms and kisses her, he experiences another intuition that something is wrong. Instead of experiencing happiness, his countenance registers disbelief and apprehension, even fraud. Kissing Judy makes him sense that it is not a reconstructed Madeleine whom he holds in his arms, but the original fake Madeleine for whose suicide Scottie holds himself responsible. Yet Scottie and Felipe are parallel figures in that all their suspicions—up until the very end—are thoroughly suppressed. As in *Aura*, everything that occurs in the present in the conundrum that is *Vertigo* is but a flimsy mask over the ineradicable past. The camera in *Vertigo* itself now becomes a source of vertiginous illusion, as it swirls around the couple as they embrace, its movement making the audience experience the vertigo that Scottie too is experiencing. This time, however, the dizziness that Scottie experiences is highly pleasureable, yet at the same time extremely discomforting. Scottie now hallucinates back to the climactic moment at San Juan Bautista when he embraced and kissed Madeleine in the livery stable. Once again a key moment in the present is but a veil torn away to uncover an ineradicable past —exactly as occurs again and again in Aura.

For the bereaved and guilt-stricken Scottie as for Fuentes's Consuelo, the only meaningful experience is the Past made

Figure 19. *From Among the Dead.* Distant past looms inexorably over both Scottie and Madeleine.

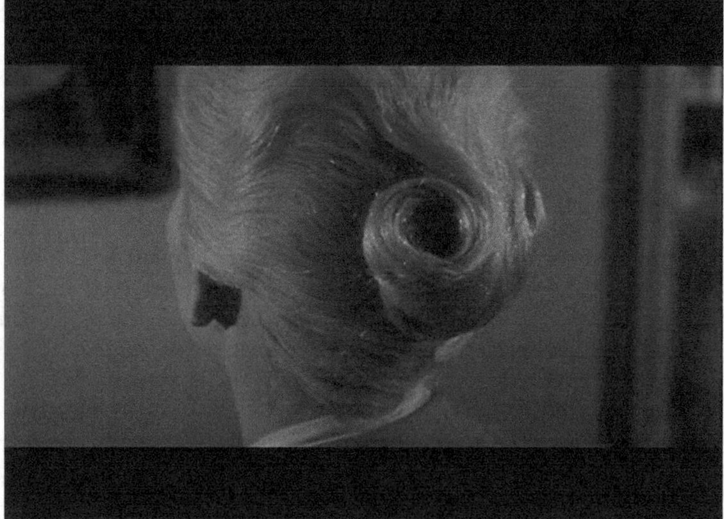

Figure 20. Tight whorl symbolizes beauty, restraint, engulfment and destruction for fated Scottie.

present. The actions of Aura in seducing Felipe, as she begins to dance a waltz with him, are but the duplication of the waltzes that Consuelo danced with Llorente years earlier in a dazzling imperial court of Maximilian in Mexico City in the monumental castle of Chapultepec that the monarchs constructed as their new, regal dwelling in their adopted homeland. Indeed, it was Maximilian who introduced the waltz—made glamorous and all the rage in Hapsburg Vienna by Johann Straus—into faroff Mexico—the waltz that seemed daring and delightful for dancers accustomed to the stiff, formal movement of the courtly minuet. Consuelo dances, tenaciously grasping the empty tunic of Llorente, while Aura convokes this distant past by her behavior with Felipe. Fuentes masterfully captures this vertiginous movement that emphasizes how rapidly Felipe is being sucked into the past through the cascading movement of his images, which pile up on one another. Here the style becomes incantatory, through an expert combination of the phrasing, the hallucinatory repetition and the insistent intensification. Swept away by the movement of the style, the reader once more is made to feel reality as Felipe experiences it, as he is swept away by the seductive Aura. Again there is a warning to Felipe that once more he will ignore, as Aura bathes his feet. As Aura gazes nervously at the crucifix, the reader understands that Felipe does not—that he is the victim of sacrifice and that this sacrifice is imminent. One of the many roles that the extremely protean Aura plays is now Mary Magdalene, the prostitute and sinner who washed the feet of Christ. Here again Felipe becomes aroused and active sexually; from an initial, naive *doncel* he rapidly is transformed into an eager lover.

But in determining the ultimate fate of Felipe, we recall the chilling final words of the fanatic fans of the famed cinematic actress Glenda Garson in Julio Cortázar's ironically titled short story "Queremos tanto a Glenda" ("We Love Glenda So Much") who are so devoted to her that in order to make perfect her image, purchase copies of all of her films and remake them, and finally even murder the actress in order to prevent an aging and increasingly maladroit Glenda Garson from returning to the screen to mar the perfect image that they have laboriously crafted of her: "No se baja vivo de una cruz" "No one comes down from the

Cross alive." Once more Fuentes's style is extraordinarily cinematic:

> You feel the warm water that bathes the soles of your feet, while she washes them with a heavy cloth, now and then casting furtive glances at that Christ carved from black wood. Then she dries your feet, takes you by the hand, fastens a few violets in her loose hair, and begins to hum a melody, a waltz, to which you dance with her, held by the murmur of her voice, gliding around to the slow, solemn rhythm she's setting, very different from the light movements of her hands, which unbutton your shirt, caress your chest, reach around to your back and grasp it. You also murmur that wordless song, that melody rising naturally from your throat: you glide around together, each time closer to the bed, until you muffle the song with your hungry kisses on Aura's mouth, until you stop the dance with your crushing kisses on her shoulders and breasts. (A, 107)

Here again, the emphasis on incessant movement emphasizes the cinematic nature of Fuentes's brilliant work. In Hitchcock, the whirling camera itself becomes a silent and ghostly character in the film. This is paralleled in *Aura* by the mesmeric effect of the second-person narrative, which underscores the atmosphere of the dislocated, of the uncanny, and the unreal. Like the climatic scene of sexual fulfillment in Judy´s room at the Empire Hotel, a scene that radiates back to San Juan Bautista and to an enigmatic, sinister past, the erotic encounter between Aura and Felipe resonates back to biblical times—to Mary Magdalene washing the feet of Christ, and underscores Felipe´s erotic possession as an ironic crucifixion.

Scottie in *Vertigo* quickly suppresses his intuitions, his doubts and suspicions and even his dread, and in the very next scene after his total remake of Judy, is evoked as a narcotized being, submerged in a comfortable lethargy. This parallels the sonambulistic state of Felipe at the very end of *Aura*, as he embraces the wizened and cadaverous Consuelo, heedless of the fact that she is not his young and beauteous Aura, because he himself has been permanently transformed into Llorente. At the end, neither Consuelo nor Scottie needs to provide cues for their "mates," who have now been reduced to automatonlike servants, performing their roles to perfection:

> You bring your lips close to the head that's lying next to yours. You stroke Aura's long black hair. You grasp that fragile woman by the shoulders, ignoring her sharp complaint. You tear off her taffeta robe, embrace her . . . kissing her face without thinking, without distinguishing . . (A, 143-145)

According to Samuel Taylor, who collaborated with Hitchcock on the filmscript of *Vertigo*: "*Vertigo* is a film about the most horrible practical joke ever played on a man." Indeed, the same can be said of the duping of the naive and innocent Felipe Montero, who once he enters the lugubrious, mausoleumlike realm of Consuelo, will never re-emerge, and who at the end is as psychically destroyed as is Scottie Ferguson. Yet these works by Hitchcock and Fuentes are both fatalistic and existential. Although Scottie Ferguson seems to be a protagonist manqué and a doomed one, much in his behavior is self-induced. He is extremely stubborn; out of vanity he disdains the well paid desk job that is immediately offered to him after his disaster on the rooftop. Just as Scottie's blindness is evident in that initially he has no suspicions whatsoever that the sophisticated, elegantly dressed and eloquently spoken Elster is just the opposite—a brutal con man and a cold-blooded killer. Yet Judy Barton is voluntarily if plaintively enmasked in self-fabrication as the Other, as the impeccably dressed and coifed Madeleine, and Scottie too allows himself over and over again to slip into delusion, and to a self creation that ironically, is ultimately and overwhelmingly destructive.

Paralleling the zombielike behavior of Judy/Madeleine, her trancelike state, is the automatonlike behavior of Aura. And just as Scottie in his mind repeatedly fuses distant past and present, age and youth, the features of Carlotta with those of Judy/Madeleine, Felipe does the same with the images of Aura and those of Consuelo. Yet the benighted Felipe mistakenly believes that Aura is rendered mute with fear and is totally subordinate to her malefic

Aunt, when in fact it is the mind and tenacious will of Consuelo that are vivifying the wraithlike and evanescent young girl:

> You're going to ask about him but you're suddenly surprised to realize that up to this moment Aura hasn't said a word and is eating with a sort of mechanical fatality, as if she were waiting for some outside impulse before picking up her knife and fork, cutting a piece of liver—yes, it's liver again, apparently the favorite dish in the house—and carrying it to her mouth. You glance quickly from the aunt to the niece, but at that moment the Señora becomes motionless, and at the same moment Aura puts her knife on her plate and also becomes motionless, and you remember that the Señora put down her knife only a fraction of a second earlier. (A, 69)

The liver, an aphrodisiac, demonstrates how thorough Consuelo is in resorting to myriad strategies—drugs, wine, hypnosis, enchantment—to trap and destroy her prey. In this Consuelo is very similar to the arch plotter, Gavin Elster, who tricks not only his wife but his loyal mistress Judy Barton and his former friend, Scottie, and yet, like Consuelo, gets off scot free. At the end of *Aura*, the aged sorceress will regain the strength necessary once again to begin her elaborate—and highly successful—machinations.

Yet, from the start, both Judy/Madeleine and Aura are highly ambivalent, paradoxical presences. Indeed, although she appears most of the time as the tool of Consuelo, Aura does seem at certain moments to be an independent being, and even one at cross purposes with her aunt. Felipe one day sees Aura ringing a bell, one compared to the bell used to warn people out of the way of lepers:

> She turns away, ringing her bell like the lepers who use a bell to announce their approach, telling the unwary: "Out of the way, out of the way." You put on your shirt and coat and follow the sound of the bell calling you to the dining room. (A, 125)

Here is another clear warning to flee the domain of Consuelo, that the mesmerized Felipe ignores, as he does all the others. Instead of running away in terror, a dutiful and increasingly stupefied Felipe follows Aura—the bell warning away lepers is converted by the highly vulnerable Felipe into a pleasant dinner ball. The vacillation of Aura, her ambivalent response to Felipe, beguiling him then later seeking to warn him away from Consuelo's lair, is paralleled by Judy/Madeleine's ambivalence toward Scottie—at the same time luring him and yet warning him away—dramatically caught in the forward shot/reverse zoom expertly utilized by Hitchcock as a bold, original technique to make his audience vividly experience the very same vertigo that Scottie is repeatedly suffering.

It is significant that once again reality in *Aura*, as in *Vertigo*, follows and is subservient to dream; action is but the repetition of illusion. Earlier in his stay with Consuelo, Felipe has experienced a nightmare in which a fleshless hand with a warning bell looms up before him and a skeletonlike face approaches. Felipe seemingly awakens from his terrifying nightmare, but again paralleling Scottie in *Vertigo*, not to reality but merely to another level of delusion. Now Aura appears naked before him—the succubus sent by Consuelo to obliterate the negative warnings that Felipe's subconsciousness has attempted to send him. The function of Aura as tranquilizer, as alluring "bait," parallels that of Judy/Madeleine. After Scottie has "rescued" her from San Francisco Bay, Judy/Madeleine, expertly feigning unconsciousness, allows him to take her back to his apartment and seductively permits him to undress her—Madeleine's nakedness, by which Scottie is entranced, is paralleled by and perhaps even inspires the sudden appearance of the nude Aura to Felipe. Both film and *novella* emphasize sensuous allure and seeming vulnerability as the mere mask over destructive and deadly purpose. Here again the marked ambiguity of *Vertigo* is evident. Does Judy allow herself to be completely exposed as part of Elster's plan to seduce him, or is her willingness an indication that she is rapidly falling in love with her only self-styled rescuer?

Paralleling Scottie's monstrous nightmares are those of Felipe, whose whole existence in the tenebrous realm of Consuelo is a fantasy one—combining illusion, delusion, daydreams, hallucinations, transports, and nightmares:

> When you're bored with them you undress slowly, get into bed, and fall asleep at once, and for the first time in years you dream, dream of only one thing, of a fleshless hand that comes toward you with a bell, screaming that you should go away; and when that face with its empty eye-sockets comes close to yours, you wake up with a muffled cry, sweating, and feel those lips murmuring in a low voice, consoling and asking you for affection. You reach out your hands to find that other body, that naked body with a key dangling from its neck, and when you recognize the key you recognize the woman who is lying over you, kissing you, kissing your whole body. (A, 75-77)

In both *Aura* and *Vertigo*, there is an incessant interplay of illusion and reality, reflection and substance, that continually befuddles the reader/spectator. It is significant that when a bemused Scottie follows Judy/Madeleine as she enters a flower shop through the back door, passing through a darkened store room, when the door to the shop itself is finally opened, he sees her not as a carnal reality, but only as an elusive reflection in a mirror. This encountering by the detective Scottie of mere illusion —to underscore the unreality of Madeleine—is a repetition of the way she had been reflected in the mirrors at *Ernie's* and will itself be repeated after the death of the real Madeleine Elster, when a disconsolate Scottie turns from contemplating flowers in a shop window, similar to the ones that Madeleine had purchased, to behold Judy, this time not in disguise. An even more complex interplay of fantasy and reality is analyzed by Gould, who interprets one of the key scenes toward the end of *Vertigo*, as Scottie suddenly realizes how he has been tricked by Judy:

> The view is subjective as Hitchcock cuts from the necklace seen in close-up, as reflected in a vanity mirror, to a match-cut of the necklace in the Valdés painting. The camera then tracks back to reveal the empty art gallery, with Madeleine again sitting immobile, the bouquet at her side, studying the painting. Illusion and reality are here so richly entwined that description becomes difficult. Hitchcock has tied

together the past elements and emotions of longing after the dream (Madeleine-Death) and the present reality of Judy. Not only does Scottie see her necklace and *imagine* the one in the painting, but the necklace is seen reflected in a mirror (a further level of illusion). We cut from reality (Judy's prop necklace, which was also part of a big hoax) reflected in a mirror to a painting; then track to see Madeleine studying the painting, knowing that this is not Madeleine but Judy. This is Scottie's realization and moment of truth, and although the viewer had this fact revealed to him earlier, this graphic confrontation of the many-leveled reality serves to astound the spectator as intensely as it does the protagonist.[13]

Once he has encountered Judy on the downtown San Francisco avenue, Scottie is as inflexible in his insistence on remolding her into his lost Madeleine as is the fanatic Consuelo in molding Felipe into her lost Llorente. So callous is Scottie toward the sensitive and highly vulnerable Judy that at the very moment when she is confessing her love to him, Scottie is attentive only to her hair, determining that it must be dyed blonde, to duplicate Madeleine's upswept, tightly coiled, stylish hairdo. Scottie insists that Judy wear a gray dress—an exact copy of the one that Madeleine wore, and black shoes. It is but one more level of mystery in *Vertigo* to speculate on why Judy has kept the original gray dress that she wore as Madeleine. Surely Judy would realize that the dress is incriminating, yet the economically lower-middle class Judy apparently keeps the garment as a symbol of her continuing ambitions for wealth and social status through the insistent bartering of her striking beauty. Yet Scottie, as he dines with Judy, stunningly beautiful in her own right, is much more preoccupied with the women who enter the restaurant who bear some resemblance to Madeleine. It is only when they are back at Judy's apartment and in the semidarkness Scottie sees Judy in profile—the profile that so provocatively matches Madeleine's—that he begins to respond to her sexually. Just as Scottie accepts

[13] See Michael Gould, *Surrealism and the Cinema* (Cranbury, New Jersey: A.J. Barnes and Company, 1977), p. 81.

Judy only to the extent that she reincarnates a ghost, so too is Consuelo interested in Felipe only as a simulacrum, as the dead past brought back to life. Thus when Felipe appears before her in response to her advertisement, Consuelo is interested not in his intellectual qualifications but in his physical appearance. Like Scottie Ferguson, Consuelo—a Mexican Pygmalion—is also is preoccupied with profiles:

> "That's all right. Don't worry about it."
> "Good. Please let me see your profile. No, I can't see it well enough. Turn toward the light. That's right. Excellent." (A, 17)

> "I can tell you everything. You'll learn to write in my husband's own style. You'll only have to arrange and read his manuscripts to become fascinated by his style . . . his clarity . . . his . . ." (A, 21)

The same unearthly appearance characterizes both Aura and Judy/Madeleine. It is significant that the first time she is evoked, Madeleine is brought into view as the result of a slow and languorous pan left by the camera across the wide, luxurious expanse of *Ernie's*, and that the alluring—and elusive—Judy/Madeleine is first seen in a mystifying distant shot—and from the back. For the audience as for Scottie, Madeleine is not seen but rather revealed, as if she were a sacred presence, in contrast with the far more conventional, direct manner in which the far more pedestrian Midge is presented, in midshot and directly from the front. As the seemingly gracious Madeleine, who for more than one half hour of *Vertigo* never utters a word to anyone, her first words an incoherent mumble as she lies naked in Scottie's bed, sweeps silently out of *Ernie's*, she is reflected briefly in the imposing mirror in the entranceway, again an indication that she is a double—and a duplicitous—identity. Unlike Midge, Madeleine does not simply appear; rather she is slowly and enticingly unveiled to both Scottie and the viewer of the film, to emphasize her spectral quality, her essence for Scottie as ethereal being, not as a flesh and blood woman such as the extremely talkative and

Figure 21. Portrait of Carlotta: for Scottie, an ironically sacred icon. Note huge pillar and agitated sky, as well as enigmatic expression.

Figure 22. Madeleine sits for hours before commanding, gold-framed portrait but Scottie is the one truly mesmerized by painting.

down to earth Midge, with whom the erstwhile detective cannot relate either romantically or carnally.

Even in the scenes toward the end of *Vertigo*, in Judy's apartment in the Empire Hotel, she is repeatedly evoked looking at herself in a mirror—one more underscoring of her intrinsic duality and her intriguing complexity as well as her illusory nature. These incessant reflections symbolize both what Judy is for Scottie—a boring, asexual unreality, as he quests for the exciting Madeleine—and for Judy herself, who has a self-loathing that seems to parallel Scottie's own self-hatred. Indeed, Judy, who has very low self-esteem—paralleling Scottie's diminished self-estimation after his crippling vertigo—is more and more of an illusory presence—a mirror reflection—for her own self—an indication of how ripe she is to again be transformed into the elegant and self-possessed Other. Indeed, and extremely ironically, the essence, the reality of Judy Barton for both the fanatic Scottie *and* for the extremely insecure Judy Barton herself—is the tantalizing, aristocratic, but doomed Madeleine Elster. Ironically, even though Judy makes repeated protestations about being loved by Scottie for herself alone, Judy like Scottie exemplifies a self-hatred and a self-disdain. Like Scottie, Judy is much happier playing the Other, actualizing herself through the Other, through the sophisticated and goddesslike Madeleine. Even Judy's calculated projection of herself as coarse and vulgar and even unsavory, as she alludes to having been picked up by a series of unknown men, are all designed to discourage Scottie's maneuvers, at least initially. Yet, significantly, Judy's deliberate accentuation of her streetwise nature is but another act—Judy pretending to be a facile pickup not to entice but to discourage the refined Scottie—maneuvers that fail to dissuade an obsessed Scottie and that Judy subsequently abandons.

Similar to Scottie with Madeleine, the unstable Felipe first takes possession of Aura in his mind. And, like Scottie, Fuentes's protagonist adopts both a protective and a proprietary attitude toward the strange girl. The fertile imagination of Felipe imbues Aura with a fairytale-like existence, as he envisions her as the beautiful princess kept enslaved by the wicked witch, while he becomes the handsome and noble prince who will valiantly conquer the dark forces and rescue her:

> . . . you wrinkle your brow and ask yourself if the Señora doesn't have some secret power over her niece: if the girl, your beautiful Aura in her green dress, isn't kept in this dark old house against her will. But it would be so easy for her to escape while the Señora was asleep in her shadowy room. You tell yourself that her hold over the girl must be terrible. And you consider the way out that occurs to your imagination: perhaps Aura is waiting for you to release her from the chains in which the perverse, insane old lady, for some unknown reason, has bound her. You remember Aura as she was a few moments ago, spiritless, hypnotized by her terror, incapable of speaking in front of the tyrant, moving her lips in silence as if she were silently begging you to set her free; so enslaved that she imitated every gesture of the Señora, as if she were permitted to do only what the Señora did. (A, 71-73)

Similarly, Scottie concocts a lifelong bond with Judy/Madeleine, as he quotes to her an ancient Chinese proverb whereby the person who saves another's life—as he self-deludedly believes he has saved that of Madeleine—becomes responsible for her forever. Here is indicated Scottie's intense desire for a permanent relationship with a person—Madeleine/Judy—who is continually elusive and who has become as cold-blooded as Gavin Elster in exploiting Scottie. Or is the very changeable, extremely vulnerable Judy at the key moment at Cypress Point, near the roiled ocean, whose vertiginous waters themselves symbolize the conflicting desires of both Judy/Madeleine and Scottie Ferguson, beginning genuinely to fall in love with Scottie? It is ironic that the scene of intense romance, as Judy/Madeleine and Scottie kiss, with the waves of the Pacific Ocean crashing in the background, is itself but a back projection by Hitchcock, thus technically adding fakery—the spellbinding illusion that is the cinema—to the mere *simulacrum* of a love affair. Back projection, a favorite technique of Hitchcock, although rarely used by most contemporary directors, serves masterfully to heighten the essential unreality of the scene—in this case the passionate but doomed—utterly futile—romance between Scottie and Madeleine, paralleled by the malevolent romance between the spectral Aura and the inchoate Felipe.

One of the greatest psychological differences between Judy/Madeleine and Scottie is that although their relationship seems to Scottie to be a genuine one and to Judy, on the contrary, it is—at least initially—but part of an elaborate hoax, Judy is capable of loving another—first Gavin, then Scottie, while the essentially cold, even frigid Scottie is basically incapable of corresponding to the genuine love offered to him repeatedly by both Midge and later, by an initially rejecting but then thoroughly trusting Judy Barton. Unlike Gavin Elster, unlike Judy Barton, unlike the increasingly perplexed and frustrated and finally forlorn Midge, the inhuman Scottie is capable of loving only a phantom that his own stricken, deluded consciousness has created and fanatically sustained. And Scottie's incapacity to love mirrors the calculating coldness and cruelty of both Gavin Elster, who apparently never loved his beautiful wife, only her vast fortune, and behind Gavin Elster, the spectral, unnamed husband who destroyed Carlotta Valdés by abruptly abandoning her and driving her to an early grave.

Both Hitchcock and Fuentes, through the magic and power and intensity of their poetic vision, are masters at making an almost totally unbelievable situation believable, as the spectator of *Vertigo* and the reader of *Aura* are inexorably drawn into the bizarre, circuitous plot of each work and come to identify—at least at first—with the determined Felipe and the obsessed Scottie, in their laborious and even obsessive quests. A similar transformation of a realistically impossible situation—the ferocious attacks on humans by united forces, species of ordinary, gentle birds—occurs in *The Birds*. The haunting words of Gavin Elster, who expresses his frustration as he pretends to lament his beautiful wife slipping away from him, becoming devoured by her madness, are echoed in the words of the plaintive Llorente in *Aura,* as he too suffers the excruciating loss of his beloved Consuelo, who also has become enshrouded in madness. As Elster states poetically, artfully concealing his brutalness, so unlike the killer actors who rapidly display their savagery, like James Cagney in *White Heat* and *The Public Enemy* and Lee Marvin in *The Big Heat*:

> Suddenly the words fade into silence. A cloud comes into her eyes and they go blank. . . . She's someone else . . . away from me . . . Someone I don't know . . . She even walked a different way . . .

Indeed the lyric resonance of Gavin Elster's words contrasts tremendously with his cruel reality—his monstrousness. The major difference is that although Felipe at the end of *Aura* is left in a stupor regarding Consuelo/Aura and the precise nature of the relationship between the elaborate subterfuge of Aunt and Niece and, while the depiction by Elster of his tormented wife is probably a phoney one, indeed, we never know what type of person the real Madeleine Elster is—we are certain that the real Madeleine is very wealthy and strikingly beautiful and totally innocent. In contrast to the Machiavellian Elster, who like Scottie can really love no one, the stricken Llorente in *Aura* is genuinely in love with Consuelo, mesmerized by her. The distraught Llorente also expresses himself in a highly poetic style to express his deepening sense of loss and helplessness:

> "Early this morning I found her walking barefooted through the hallways. I wanted to stop her. She went by without looking at me, but her words were directed to me. 'Don't stop me,' she said. 'I'm going toward my youth, and my youth is coming toward me. It's coming in, it's in the garden, it's come back . . .' Consuelo, my poor Consuelo! Even the devil was an angel once." (A, 133-135)

Indeed, the evocation of Consuelo as a lost soul, consumed by delusions and even madness, constitutes a remarkable parallel with the delusion-enshrouded Madeleine Elster. In both *Vertigo* and *Aura*, great emphasis is placed on color symbolism. *Vertigo* would be a vastly different picture had it been filmed in black and white, just as Hitchcock's NeoGothic thriller *Psycho* would have established an entirely different mood had it been filmed in color. For an example, Madeleine often appears in a gray suit, expressive on the surface level of her coolness, of her restraint and classic elegance. On another level, the color gray with which she is linked symbolizes Madeleine's existential vagueness or indeterminacy.

The dominant color associated with Madeleine, however, is green—a color of key importance in *The Birds*, *Vertigo,* and *Aura.*

In the twenty-first century, a film in color is generally regarded as more realistic than one made in black and white, for one reason because of the familiarity factor—most all films are now made in color. Thus viewing a film in black and white, or sequences in a color film that suddenly change to black and white, produce an atmosphere of strangeness, of mystery, even of otherwordliness – exemplified by the haunting film *The White Ribbon* (2010), directed by Michael Haneke. But in the mid 1950s when *Vertigo* was produced, color was still relatively new, and the striking use of intense color throughout the film, in the new technique heralded as Vista Vision, does much to reinforce its hallucinatory atmosphere. In a film such as *The Wizard of Oz* (1939, directed by the great Victor Fleming), sepia tones characterized the realistic opening, set in rural Kansas prone to tornadoes that result in Judy's being catapulted into the magical Land of Oz. But the entering of the characters into the wondrous Land of Oz is portrayed in brilliant, even dazzling—and unforgettable—color. In the fifties, Hitchcock masterfully continues this unreal use of color, yet since his background and training were in silent films, he also presents an incessant contrast between light and darkness that is characteristic of films made in black and white—both the masterful and highly innovative German Expressionist films of the twenties and American *film noir* of the forties, and which is found in films from Hitchcock's English period like *The Lodger* (1928), *The 39 Steps* (1935), *Blackmail* (1929), *The Lady Vanishes* (1938).

The color green is used in a similar fashion in both Hitchcock's eery film and Fuentes's ghostly *novella*—to underscore the illusory, the supernatural, and the bewitching. In both works it is linked with the female characters. Green on one level is the color of hope. Madeleine, who represents new hope and new life for the dessicated Scottie, drives a green Jaguar which belongs to Elster as Judy herself does. Later, when Scottie first catches sight of Judy on the streets of San Francisco, she is wearing a green dress. Scottie's perceiving her as a surrogate Madeleine Elster is facilitated when he sees her bathed in an eery green light, the glow of a huge neon sign outside the Empire Hotel where she lives. A key scene in *Vertigo* is when the physical transformation of Judy into Madeleine is finally complete, and Scottie gazes at her, spellbound, as she emerges into the bedroom with her hair, makeup, clothing, walk and total demeanor now precisely duplicating both that of the dead Madeleine and, more importantly that of Judy playing Madeleine. At this precise moment of emergence, Judy seems to be enveloped in an eery green mist, that underscores the way in which the demented Scottie is perceiving her, as a ghost brought back to life.

This parallels the way in which Aura is evoked, as a spectral presence that gradually achieves corporeality:

> You'd like to fix the girl's features in your mind. Every time you look away you forget them again, and an irresistible urge forces you to look at her once more. (A, 41)

Indeed, Felipe's utter fascination with the volatile and illusory Aura exactly parallels the enchantment of the previously highly skeptical Scottie Ferguson with the bewitching Madeleine. Yet in *Vertigo* and *Aura*, the color green has a dual significance. On the one hand, it seems to be positive, as it signifies new life—the greening of the Earth, in spring, the resurrection of the identity, and new life for both the rootless Scottie and especially for the stunted and alienated Felipe. Yet green is also the color of the demonic, signifying the green costumes worn by witches in medieval times. And indeed, both Judy/Madeleine and Aura are linked from start to finish with bewitchment. Ostensibly, Judy/Madeleine is transhabited by the spirit of the dead Carlotta, just as Aura is the zombielike creation of the sorceress Consuelo. Judy/Madeleine is first seen by the lovestruck Scottie dressed in a black gown with a shimmering green cape. Similarly, Aura first appears before Felipe dressed in green. And the hypnotic effect of the eyes of Judy/Madeleine on the dazed Scottie is paralleled by the enchanting effect of the liquid green eyes of Aura upon Felipe. The manner in which Fuentes evokes the eyes of Aura is highly cinematic. It is paralleled by the way in which the huge, expressive eyes of the somnambulist Cesare suddenly flutter open wide in *Das Kabinett des Doktor Caligari* (1919), signifying a transition not merely between sleep and wakefulness but even between suspended animation—a type of death—and new, hideous life, and also the opening of the eyes of the cadaver that will become the intended mate of Frankenstein in the horror film *Bride of Frankenstein* (1935, directed by James Whale), starring the inimitable Elsa Lanchester as the monster's reluctant and finally dismissive mate. Indeed, in all three cases, the opening of the eyes signifies much more than a mechanical act—it is an emergence from death to new and demonic life:

> You move a few steps so that the light from the candles won't blind you. The girl keeps her eyes closed, her hands at her sides. She doesn't look at you at first, then little by little she opens her eyes as if she were afraid of the light. Finally you can see that those eyes are sea green and that they surge, break to foam, grow calm again, then surge again like a wave. You look into them and tell yourself it isn't true, because they're beautiful green eyes just like all the beautiful green eyes you've ever known. But you can't deceive yourself: those eyes do surge, do change, as if offering you a landscape that only you can see and desire. (A, 27)

Aura fears the light because like Consuelo, she thrives in darkness and fears being exposed. Indeed, the emphasis on Aura's mesmerizing eyes that are compared to the surging of the waves of the ocean, duplicate the stunning initial sequence of *Vertigo*, in which the eyes of Judy/Madeleine are not fixed but evoked in anxious motion, both nervous and hypnotic. The phrase "but you can't deceive yourself" is extremely ironic, because Felipe is being deceived, indeed he is constantly deceiving himself, exactly paralleling the proud, naïve, endlessly deceived and insistently self-deceptive Scottie Ferguson.

Both Hitchcock and Fuentes are masters of Symbolic Realism, of creating atmospheres that gradually shear off from the apparently real to the monstrously phantasmagoric. Both Aura and Madeleine are living dreams, and excruciating nightmares. And Felipe is for Consuelo what Judy Barton is for the demented Scottie—the mere vessel that is used to summon up the dead. As

Hitchcock states in his interview with the eminent French director François Truffaut, emphasizing the unreal quality with which Judy/Madeleine is imbued:

> At the beginning of the picture, when James Stewart follows Madeleine to the cemetery, we gave her a dreamlike, mysterious quality by shooting through a fog filter. That gave us a green effect, like fog over a bright sunshine. Then, later on, when Stewart first meets Judy, I decided to make her live at the Empire Hotel in Post Street because it has a green neon sign flashing continually outside the window. So when the girl emerges from the bathroom, that green light gives her the same subtle, ghostlike quality. After focusing on Stewart, who's staring at her, we go back to the girl, but now we slip that shot effect away to indicate that Stewart's come back to reality.[14]

Both Hitchcock and Fuentes are masters of the gradual derealization of the real, and the corresponding incarnation of the illusory. Madeleine, and later Judy turned into Madeleine, are never really human beings for Scottie; both are incarnations of his desires, both are living dreams and that the silent and regal Madeleine herself is a fake adds still another vertiginous level of fantasy to Hitchcock's spellbinding film. After the numbed and shaken Scottie meets Judy Barton on the streets of San Francisco, he insistently, even fanatically attempts to convert her from a flesh and blood reality back into dream, just as Consuelo takes the human Felipe and rapidly turns him into a zombie presence. And yet, ironically, the dead—Carlotta Valdés and Madeleine Elster in *Vertigo*, Llorente in *Aura*—are brought back to life only at the expense of the living, who must die—physically, as in the case of Judy Barton, who dies to exemplify the workings of a bizarre curse from the past, who dies to fulfill the words initially uttered by Gavin Elster to Scottie as part of Elster's elaborate ruse, that his

[14] Consult *Hitchcock*, by François Truffaut, with the collaboration of Helen G. Scott, revised edition (New York: Simon and Schuster, 1984), pp. 244-245.

Figure 23. Iron gate in front of Portman Mansion signifying closed, menacing space.

Figure 24. Imposing windows in Vertigo and Rear Window are transformed into silent characters residing in nebulous worlds.

wife is being pursued by "someone dead," and who dies horribly transfixed by her guilt for the murder of the real Madeleine. The phantom presences that so haunt and afflict the mind of Scottie at the end plague the conscience of Judy Barton. Similar to these tormented characters, Consuelo, Llorente, and finally the hapless Felipe, all surrender their beings to a phantom; all three become fascinated by and finally paralyzed by the mystifying presence of Aura.

In both *Aura* and *Vertigo*, both women appear as both victims and victimizers. Both Aura and Judy/Madeleine initially pretend to be victims, but both ultimately are victimizers—Aura of the hapless Felipe, and Judy/Madeleine to entrap Scottie Ferguson in order to shift the blame from the real murderer, her lover whom she hopes will marry her *and convert her* into Madeleine Elster—a dead woman—just as Scottie later converts the coarse Judy Barton into the elegant, reserved, aristocratic dead woman—Madeleine Elster. Judy seeks in Scottie what she had sought in Gavin Elster—wealth, social prominence, escape from the tedium and marginal existence of Salina, Kansas, where she lost her father and became disaffected after her mother remarried.

It is significant that the brightly colored whorls signifying the maelstrom of vertigo emerge at the very beginning of *Vertigo* from the eyes of Judy/Madeleine even though Scottie's vertigo, at least initially, has nothing to do with Judy/Madeleine except for the fact that the diabolic Gavin Elster takes advantage of Scottie's well known vertigo savagely to manipulate him. The delicate and seductively whirling spirals both eminate from and recede back into the eyes of Judy/Madeleine at the very start of Hitchcock's mesmeric film, indicating her bewitching nature that so inspires Fuentes's most beguiling creation, *Aura*.

Both *Aura* and *Vertigo* are creations the demonstrate constant reversals. Although for much of their relationship it is the conniving Judy/Madeleine who cruelly exploits and frames Scottie Ferguson and drives him insane because of her elaborate machinations, at the end it is the cruel, even sadistic and very vengeful Scottie Ferguson who exploits Judy Barton, forcibly dragging her up to the top of the tower by her neck—a terrifying scene that echoes Gavin Elster's breaking the neck of the first Madeleine Elster. It seems as if Scottie seeks by torturing Judy

Barton to cure himself of the vertigo that her actions had exacerbated. But Judy/Madeleine ultimately is not therapeutic but a force that ultimately aggravates Scottie's dementia, precisely paralleled by Aura's ambivalent role in the life of Felipe Montero.

The irony that permeates *Vertigo* is accentuated at the end, as Scottie promises to Judy that once both climb again to the top of the tower they will both be free. Clearly Scottie believes that he will be free of his vertigo, but how will Judy gain the promised freedom? Ironically, instead of transcending the past—past illness, past crime, past love—Scottie at the end is still shackled with his vertigo even though he has triumphed over Judy by proving to her and, most importantly, to himself that he can reach the top, and instead of freedom from the stranglehold of the past, Judy finds only horror and death at the top of the tower—exactly as did the person she wanted to become, the real Madeleine Elster exactly as did Judy's phony, psychologically crippled and crippling "ancestor" Carlotta.

Both *Aura* and *Vertigo* are extremely fatalistic creations. The deterministic cyclical time that operates in *Aura* also suffuses *Vertigo*. The eyes of Judy/Madeleine that at the outset of the film suddenly open in terror adumbrate the ending, when a terrified Judy breaks away from the embrace with Scottie and plunges from the tower to her death.

Hitchcock's consummate and constantly shifting film, converting Judy/Madeleine from victimizer to victim and Scottie Ferguson from victim to, at the end, ruthless victimizer, defies strict feminist analysis that views Scottie as a symbol of patriarchal authority and an increasingly helpless Judy as Scottie's puppet, the fulfillment of his morbid, fetishistic desires. Judy is not forced but enticed by the velvet-voiced Gavin Elster to become his expert accomplice, and we can assume that none of the wheedling, prodding and commanding by Scottie as he rapidly converts Judy Barton into Madeleine was part of Judy's initial relationship as a very apt pupil and, indeed, totally co-operating and even submissive to Gavin Elster. Similarly, in Fuentes's condensed, elaborate *novella Aura*, Felipe Montero is both fulfilled, actualized, granted an identity, and at the same time destroyed, paralleling the fated course of the lives of both Judy Barton and Scottie Ferguson.

Both Hitchcock's *Vertigo* and Fuentes's *Aura* present extremely complex situations and relationships with very few answers. Thus the seemingly rational, overconfident and paternal Scottie seeks to convince Madeleine that her delusions of being the Other—Carlotta—can be instantly cured because they do not reflect a supernatural transhabitation of her identity by the spirit of Carlotta come back from the dead relentlessly seeking vengeance but are mere delusions based on a reality at San Juan Bautista that Madeleine herself experienced in the past and is now distorting. As Scottie, assuming the role of protector that he never could play with Midge, who needs no protection, states confidently to a seemingly distraught Judy/Madeleine: "You see, there's an answer for everything." What both *Vertigo* and *Aura* demonstrate is that there are no rational explanations—either to Scottie's *Vertigo* or to the rapid envelopment of Felipe Montero into the schemes of Fuentes's equivalent to Gavin Elster—Consuelo. There is no rational explanation to Scottie's insistence on re-creating Judy as Madeleine Elster instead of being willing to love Judy for herself, as she repeatedly pleads with him to do—Scottie, who parallels the egotistical L.B. Jefferies, the protagonist of Hitchcock's masterpiece *Rear Window* who refuses to love Lisa for herself—ironically in all of her perfections *not* imperfections—perfections that Jefferies finds intolerable, and who can accept a relationship with Lisa only if she becomes the Other—only if she becomes a female L.B. Jefferies, which at the end of *Rear Window* she pretends to become but rapidly abandons the pretense to return to her true love—the glamorous fashion world.

Judy's love for Scottie—like Aura's love for Felipe—is always suspect. When Judy/Madeleine warns Scottie not to follow her into the mission at San Juan Bautista, is she attempting to warn him away from the crime she knows has already been committed, or is she telling him not to follow knowing intuitively that this will exacerbate Scottie's fierce desire to watch over her, to protect her? And, at the end, how would Judy Barton continue to be in love with Scottie, a man whose maniacal fury is on the brink of killing her? One interpretation of the highly ambiguous ending of *Vertigo* is that a shrewd Judy is playing for time, once more artfully playing the role of a repentant, vulnerable needing-to-be protected innocent, to beguile once more a Scottie ever-willing to suppress his misgivings, in order to get herself down from the tower and forever out from under his outraged control.

And does an anguished Scottie, as he at the end once more embraces Judy/Madeleine really willing to give her a second chance, forgive her participation in the crime of Madeleine Elster's death, and instead of turning her in to the police forgive her and even desire to marry her—as Judy Barton, as true self not phantasmal Other? Here is but one more in an endless concatenation of ambiguities that make *Vertigo* Hitchcock's most profound work. Does the "hard headed Scot" as Gavin Elster condescendingly refers to Scottie Ferguson finally relent and accept Judy Barton only for himself, thus freeing her from the role of a dead woman? In contrast, Felipe Montero is doomed from the start to be only the Other, permanently repeated in the Other, in the identity of yet another dead person. Unlike the combination of existentialism and fatalism that permeates Fuentes's now classic epic narrative of the Mexican Revolution of 1910 *The Death of Artemio Cruz* with its emphasis on the continued betrayal of the Revolutionary ideals of land, labor, and educational reform, *Aura* is bereft of choice in regard to the future of the male protagonist—Montero's future is only the recapitulation of the ninteenth century, of the past which signifies not nostalgic revery, but an iron fatalism over both Felipe's present existence and his future.

Some critics interpret the ending of *Vertigo* as Judy's deliberate jumping from the tower to escape from the terrifying presence of the black-robed figure whom Judy presumably views as the ghost of Madeleine Elster reborn to take vengeance on her. According to this interpretation, Judy Barton is the one who at the end is guilt-stricken, although for much of the film it is Scottie who is obsessed over his failure to rescue his beloved and who is condemned by his guilt-stricken conscience.

At the end of *Vertigo*, there is no redemption for either Scottie or Judy, no renewal of life or love or hope. Scottie is desolate and emerges as a stricken Christ-figure—exactly as Felipe is evoked in *Aura*, as the beguiling ectoplasm that is Aura bathes his feet just as Mary Magdalene washed the feet of Christ.

"Well, San Francisco's changed. The things that spell San Francisco to me are disappearing fast." The words of the master con-man Gavin Elster to a vacillating Scottie, who initially wants nothing to do with the surveillance of Elster's despondent wife but for some reason immediately changes his mind and takes on the assignment, are both poetic and extremely ironic. In fact Gavin Elster cares little or nothing for San Francisco. It is to entice Scottie to enter his lair of deception—a parallel to Consuelo's enticement of an initially vacillating Felipe to enter her spiderweb, that Gavin savily appeals to the romantic within Scottie Ferguson, holding up before him in the prints that line the maghony walls of his luxurious office and that once more demonstrate the lack of intuition of Midge, who had exclaimed to Scottie that Gavin Elster wants to bum him for the price of a drink, evoking Gavin Elster as downtrodden and on Skid Row, whereas in fact Elster is prosperous and greedy, not content with administering his wife's vast fortune but fanatic about controlling all of it.

Just as Felipe Montero is not a seasoned man of action but an extremely weak-willed, vacillating protagonist, struggling on his doctoral dissertation and suspended—as is Scottie—in his professional career, so too is Scottie far from being an expert detective. The first time that Scottie views Madeleine at *Ernie's*, he puts all his suspicious about her aside—exactly as does the naïve, extremely vulnerable Felipe with the dazzingly beautiful Aura—because Scottie is spellbound by her. Scottie fails to realize that the guilt-possessed, serene blonde goddess that he sees is just the opposite of the agitated, depressed mental case—the gloomy way that the eloquent but murderous Gavin Elster evokes his tormented wife. The discrepancy between Gavin Elster's evocation of Madeleine as tormented and Madeleine's appearance at *Ernie's* as serene—and self-possessed far from distressed and dislocated—means nothing to a benumbed thoroughly entranced Scottie.

It is significant that the wily Judy/Madeleine initially projects herself to a highly vulnerable Scottie, with his career ambitions shattered, his love life nonexistent and even friends and family—with the sole exception of the ever loyal and ever attentive Midge—never mentioned—as graceful, sophisticated but also affable and even available. It is only when Judy/Madeleine is certain that she has Scottie under her spell that she plays the role of an impassioned, demented, Thanatos dominated woman, following the exact instructions of Gavin Elster. Indeed, in the key scene in which she lies naked in Scottie's bed after he supposedly rescues her from the supposed suicidal plunge at Fort Point achieving what he failed to do with the precariously-positioned policeman at the outset of *Vertigo*, she is calm, demure, highly seductive and projecting an availability that for a seemingly married woman Scottie does not find at all suspicious—in fact he gains satisfaction that a beautiful, desirable woman is spending time with him, in a scene in which a natural attraction between a Judy dressed in Scottie's bath robe and playing expertly to his male vanity—what the irreverent Midge is incapable of doing. The meticulousness, the enormous attention to deatil of Hitchcock is legendary. Kraft and Leventhal in their spellbinding book *Footsteps in the Fog* comment that Hitchcock took twelve hours to film the scene, at the beginning of *Vertigo* when Judy/Madeleine purchases the Carlotta bouquet at the exclusive florist shop *Podesta Baldocchi*—and used only one minute of the lengthy filming in the final cut of *Vertigo.* And Kim Novak herself remembers returning to *Podesta Baldocchi* because of the marvellous fragrance of the flowers—and, undoubtedly to retrace her footsteps in the fog—just as Madeleine Elster and Scottie Ferguson did, over and over again, in a dreamlike repetition that underscores the trancelike state of these two twin protagonists—for Judy/Madeleine a deceptive past, but for the increasingly agitated and attacked Scottie, a state of mental delirium that he never really recovers from—precipitated by the sudden death of his beloved, ghostly perfect dream girl Madeleine.

CHAPTER II:

HITCHCOCK'S CINEMATIC TECHNIQUES AND THEIR IMPACT ON FUENTES

Aura has been significantly impacted by *Vertigo* not only thematically, as we have demonstrated, but technically as well. *Aura,* a brilliant *novella* and one of Fuentes's finest works, along with *La región más transparente*, *La muerte de Artemio Cruz* and *Cambio de piel,* all written in the late 1950s and 1960s and constituting the cuadrivium of Fuentes's masterpieces, is an extraordinarily visual work, one in which a multitude of cinematic techniques—close-ups, extreme close-ups and traveling shots, deep focus shots in which the background scene or action acquires an importance equal to the characters and action in the foreground, and a marvelous *chiaroscuro*—an emphasis on the interplay of light and unrelenting darkness—are expertly utilized. On the thematic level as well as on the structural one, there are many parallels between *Aura* and Alfred Hitchcock's masterpiece. In both *novella* and film, the quest by the insecure and vacillating male protagonist to find and to assert the self is paralleled by an equally strong desire by that vapid or stunted Self for existential annulment and ironically redemptive oblivion.

Indeed, the identity that is tragically *manqué* and that quests for fulfillment in the more powerful Other constitutes a dominant theme in both *Vertigo* and *Aura.* In both creations, the present is fragile and precarious; it is finally dominated by an iron past that imposes itself ceaselessly and fatalistically on the characters, rendering their actions and movements ultimately futile, since they are all controlled by negative patterns established in remote epochs. Above all, both *Aura* and *Vertigo* focus on the return of the spirits of the dead to invade the identities and destroy the wills of the living. The male protagonists, the ex-detective Scottie Ferguson in *Vertigo* and the school teacher and would-be doctoral candidate Felipe Montero in *Aura,* are inchoate beings, nebulous personalities who are both constantly being absorbed into the fantasy world—into dreams and daydreams, hallucinations and nightmares.

Fuentes has characterized his artistic vision as neither realistic nor totally fantastic but as a combination of the two, as he refers to his technique as one of "Symbolic Realism." This is very similar to the complex, highly intriguing vision of Alfred Hitchcock, in which the physical—characters and settings, acts and events—many times symbolizes the metaphysical, as reality at every step fades into fantasy. Thus, in both *Vertigo* and *Aura,* the journeys by the protagonists through physical space symbolize a desperate inner quest for self-actualization, self-assertion, and genuine love. The obsessive quest by the oftentimes bewildered detective Scottie Ferguson for his beloved and ever-elusive Madeleine parallels the quest by an equally confounded Felipe for his dazzlingly beautiful but equally evasive and vaporous Aura. Yet in both works, this all-consuming, ideal love is rendered futile by the disappearance or death of the beloved.

Both *Vertigo* and *Aura* are stories of necrophilia—of the dominant characters, Scottie Ferguson in Hitchcock's film and the wizened Consuelo in *Aura*, who obsessively quest for the dead, as they both attempt to bring them back to life through the vessel of the Other. As we have seen, *Vertigo* is inspired by the French novel, written by Pierre Boileu and Thomas Narcejac, entitled *D'entre les morts* (1954), and throughout Hitchcock's mesmerizing film the dead control the living. Similarly, in *Aura,* the whole being of Consuelo, who seems to be on the verge of death, is oriented toward the past, toward sexual reunion with her dead husband Llorente, who passed away sixty years ago. Llorente, whose very name signifies his fate, dies of inconsolable grief after his beloved Consuelo rejects him because his sterility prevents them from having children. The egomaniacal Consuelo, who fanatically desires offspring not because of her maternal instinct but as a way of perpetuating her beauty, turns first to black magic, to the horrifying blood sacrifice of cats, as a means of restoring her husband's fertility. When this proves impossible, she succumbs to madness, and believes that she has given birth to herself, in the form of the spectral Aura. It is this wraithlike girl who is used by Consuelo, in pact with the devil, to lure and then permanently ensnare Felipe in her domain. The spiritual sacrifice of Felipe, his surrender of his soul to the demonic master of Consuelo, is necessary so that the spirit of Llorente can return to her from beyond the tomb. Felipe in the twentieth century duplicates the function of Llorente in the nineteenth; the would-be hero adores Aura just as the self-abasing and self-debasing Llorente has worshipped his beloved Consuelo.

Paralleling and perhaps also influencing the character of the fierce-willed Consuelo, who consecrates her entire existence to sustaining a phantom presence, is Scottie Ferguson in *Vertigo.* After he witnesses what he mistakenly believes is the suicide of the woman he loves—the beautiful and enigmatic Madeleine—Scottie, expertly played by James Stewart, one of Hollywood´s leading and most talented and versatile actors begins a frantic quest to bring her back to life. He feels responsible for her death, since he had been hired by Madeleine's scheming husband Gavin Elster to follow her and to protect her from her own increasingly powerful *thanatos* impulses. A major subtheme of *Vertigo* is the failure of Scottie—his professional failure as an aspiring police chief and, subsequently, his failure to achieve an enduring relationship with his beloved Madeleine, and thus Scottie's desperate need to prove himself and to redeem himself. But Scottie suffers from incurable *Vertigo*, a crippling psychological illness that prevents him from scaling heights. Indeed, the complex nature of vertigo, its paradoxical combination of a fear of heights and a strange compulsion to hurl oneself from these heights, symbolizes Scottie's highly ambivalent reaction toward the fascinating Madeleine—both the desire to protect her in a paternal way and an even stronger desire to make love to her. After the stricken Madeleine has rushed to the top of a bell tower at the Mission of San Juan Bautista, Scottie follows her, attempting to rescue her, but his *Vertigo* impedes him from reaching the top of the tower, and he cannot prevent her from committing suicide. After the sudden death, Scottie, suffering a combination of grief and intense guilt, falls into a full blown delirium and is interned—mute and extremely depressed to the point of being catatonic—in an asylum. Scottie already feels intense guilt for causing the death of the policeman whose hand, outstretched to rescue Scottie, who is clinging to a rickety gutter high above the San Francisco Street, is so paralyzed by his onslaught of vertigo that he cannot let go of the gutter to grasp the policeman's hand. As a consequence, Scottie's would-be rescuer has to lunge forward to aid a benumbed Scottie, and the policeman loses his own footing and falls screaming to his death. The very beginning of *Vertigo* thus adumbrates its tragic ending, in which despite his increasing insanity, Scottie is temporarily rescued by Madeleine's declaration of unshakeable love and kisses her—an initial promise of a happily-ever-after Hollywood ending—only to lose her again as Judy/Madeleine suddenly falls to her death from the fated tower, a structure of doom just as is the mansion of the delirium-enshrouded Consuelo.

After he is released from the sanitarium but definitely is not cured, the still dazed Scottie seeks to impose the identity of the dead Madeleine upon women who resemble her in their manner of dress or hair color and style. He seeks, like the mythic Orpheus, distraught after the death of his beloved Eurydice who is bitten by a poisonous serpent, to bring Madeleine back to life. Yet after Eurydice is released from the realm of the dead by Pluto, Lord of the Dead, on the condition that Orpheus, who is leading his beloved companion to the realm of the living, not turn back his head to look upon her, the extremely doubtful Orpheus, who needs to be reassured that his beloved is actually there, disobeys the command of the gods and turns back his head to be certain that Eurydice is following him—and thus loses his beloved forever. The myth of Orpheus is but one more fatalistic shadow over *Vertigo*, just as the ancient Aztec myth of blood sacrifice to redeem mankind by feeding the insatiably ravenous gods constitues a controlling, fatalistic motif behind *Aura*. Yet Scottie, like Consuelo in *Aura*, becomes a demented and perverted creator, as he selects a woman who resembles Madeleine physically, Judy Barton, and compels Judy to re-create herself totally as Madeleine. In order to retain the love of Scottie, Judy Barton must convert herself into a zombie, just as Felipe is transformed by the maniacal Consuelo into the replica of the dead Llorente.

In *Vertigo,* Scottie is repulsed by Judy, and is unable even to kiss her. He is ineluctably drawn to the unrefined at times even garish Judy only because of her physical resemblance to his lost Madeleine. There is a poigant contrast between the wistful Judy gazing at the recumbent couples in love in front of the Palace of the Legion of Honor and a distant, highly preoccupied and totally

Figure 25. Scottie dwarfed by imposing multistoried mansion: Great House from which Carlotta permanently banished.

Figure 26. Shadow-drenched labyrinth investigated by entranced, obsessed Scottie. Landlady is part of elaborate deception.

asensual Scottie, who adumbrates an equally unresponsive L.B. Jefferies in *Rear Window*, which also has significantly impacted Fuentes's highly visual art as we shall discover. Similarly, in *Aura*, Consuelo places an advertisement in the newspaper for a young male historian who knows French, and the first aspect of Felipe in which she is interested is his profile, which approximates that of her dead husband. Although Felipe ostensibly is hired by Consuelo to edit and revise the memoirs of her husband for publication, it is not merely to investigate history in an abstract, intellectual manner but to *become* history, to incarnate the past, that Felipe is hired. Both Felipe and Judy Barton become willing victims of master *titiriteros* whose facade of benevolence and consolation masks an intent to suffocate and in effect to destroy the respective identities of Felipe and Judy, so that the ghostly Other, the lost identity, can be reincarnated through them. Scottie becomes a Pygmalion in reverse, a person who takes a living being and reduces it to a statue, in opposition to what the ancient sculptor Pygmalion did in loving a statue, Galatea, so much that he brought his stony beloved creation to life with the aid of the goddess Aphrodite/Venus—Pygmalion's patronness. Indeed, the grim and increasingly fanatic Scottie painstakingly cajoles and threatens Judy into wearing the same style dress and shoes as Madeleine did, then changing her hair style and color and even her manner of walking and talking, until finally Scottie succeeds in transforming a living being into an enticing ghost. This is exactly what happens to the victimized Felipe in Fuentes's mesmerizing *Aura*. Consuelo goes many steps further than Scottie, as at the end, Felipe senses that he has been invaded by a supernatural force and suffers a Dr. Jekyll/ Mr. Hyde transformation. Consuelo, a sorceress, has received supernatural power from her demonic master the Devil to destroy the unique identity of Felipe Montero. At the end the benumbed Felipe makes love not to Aura but to the one-hundred-nine year old Consuelo. He, like Judy Barton, has become at the end totally the Other.

Both *Vertigo* and *Aura* are characterized by an ominous and fatalistic process of cyclical time, in which the destinies of the characters in the present are mere repetitions of the tragic fates of personages in the nineteenth century. In *Aura,* the aged Consuelo, engulfed in madness, desperately seeking reunion with the lost Llorente, who was a general in the army of the ill-fated Emperor of

Mexico Maximilian von Hapsburg, becomes a symbol of the mad Empress Carlotta. Some historians believe that it was the strong-willed and exceedingly ambitious Carlotta who impelled her weak-willed consort to accept the throne of Mexico from the imperialistic Napoleon III and who urged her beloved Maxl to remain in Mexico even when the forces of Benito Juárez, the duly elected President forced into exile, regained the offensive and the French forces under Mariscal Bazaine were withdrawn, in part because of the pressure exerted on Napoleon III by the United States after its own brutal internecine conflict, the Civil War had ended with the consolidation of the Union. After the capture and execution of Maximilian by Juárez, the Mexican Intervention was brought to an end, and yet Carlotta is portrayed by modern Mexican dramatists such as Rodolfo Usigli in *Corona de sombra* (*Crown of Shadow;* 1943) and by novelists such as Fernando del Paso in *Noticias del imperio* (*News of Empire*; 1998) as endlessly reliving in her stricken consciousness, extremely corroded by her insanity, the devastating experience in Mexico. The historical Carlotta, a recluse in her castle at Bouchot, Belgium, outlived her husband by sixty years; she died in 1927. Similarly, the venerable Consuelo has also outlived Llorente by sixty years. In *Aura*, the imperiousness of Consuelo, her life as a recluse, her hatred for the modern society that she accuses of having isolated her and threatened to destroy her house, all parallel the unremitting isolation and hatred of the doomed historical Carlotta. Similarly, *Vertigo* is an exceedingly fatalistic work in which revenant spirits from the nineteenth century invade the personalities of the twentieth century characters—first merely as part of an elaborate charade concocted by Gavin Elster, but finally as malefic, an irredeemable reality. And, significantly, Carlos Fuentes himself constitutes a parallel with Madeleine Elster, who is apparently the receptacle of a transmigration of souls, as Fuentes states that he was born the very year that the Empress Carlotta died, thus alluding to a supernatural process by which the identity of the Mexican artist is transhabited by the ghostly immortalized presence of the spellbinding Empress—a supernatural, phenomenon portrayed by Fuentes in one of his earliest short stories, "Tlactocatzine, del jardín de Flandes," from *Los días enmascarados*.

When Gavin Elster hires Scottie to keep watch over the activities of his wife, he states that Madeleine has gone mad, believing that she has been invaded by the revenant spirit of her great-grandmother—another woman named Carlotta. The latter, Carlotta Valdés, committed suicide at an early age, hurling herself from a bell tower at the Mission of San Juan Bautista. An impoverished, itinerant dance hall girl, she had been taken to San Francisco by her wealthy and powerful husband and installed in the Great House, but after she had born him a child was one day thrown out, condemned to wander the streets in search of her lost child. The reasons for this expulsion and degradation are, however, never explained in Hitchcock's film of relentless ellipsis. Hitchcock, like Fuentes, constantly leaves gaps or spaces that the viewer/reader must fill in to complete each of these highly complex and sinuous artistic creations. For example, in *Vertigo* we never see how Scottie at the outset got down from the top of the building, just as at the very end, as part of the fatalistic cyclistic time that dominates the film, we never know what will happen to Scottie now that he again has lost his beloved—the concluding images of *Vertigo* are of Scottie, alone and anguished, at the top of the forbidden and foreboding tower. At the traumatic beginning as at the devastating end, Scottie literally and psychically never has his feet on the ground. Similarly, in *Aura,* we never know the outcome of Felipe's Dr. Jekyll/Mr. Hyde transformation, even though the probability is that he, like the countless male lovers that Consuelo has taken throughout the years, will quickly be used up and then, like Judy Barton, the real Madeleine Elster and the nineteenth-century Carlotta, will be thrown away by his predatory employer. Gavin Elster is concerned that his wife, under the power of Carlotta's obsessively revenant spirit, may also take her own life. Yet, although Gavin suavely and eloquently projects the image of the preoccupied husband, he is plotting to murder his wife in order to inherit her vast, shipbuilding fortune.

Like Scottie—another diabolic Pygmalion—Gavin Elster painstakingly trains his lover, Judy Barton, to play the role of Madeleine, to lure Scottie down the California Peninsula to San Juan Bautista, then to rush to the top of the tower, knowing that Scottie's love for "Madeleine" will compel him to pursue her and his crippling illness will prevent him from reaching the top of the tower. Elster kills his real wife by breaking her neck, hurls her body from the top of the tower, and protects himself from being charged with the crime by having Scottie—at Madeleine's inquest—attest to the suicide. Thus although Scottie, like Felipe very susceptible to delusion, believes it is Judy/Madeleine who has died, the death is really of a person whom he has never met—the real wife of Gavin Elster.

Scottie is, at first, the innocent victim of a horrendous scheme of Elster. Similarly, the naive and highly impressionable—and essentially innocent—Felipe in *Aura* is constantly duped by the sinuous Consuelo. Although Felipe sees his beloved Madeleine in front of a whole wall of blazing icons, behind her sanctimoniousness is her deadly design, one which to succeed requires the destruction of Felipe's identity. The wizened Consuelo thus mirrors the velvet-voiced but insidious Gavin Elster in *Vertigo.*

It is ironic that an initially rational Scottie scoffs at Gavin Elster's story, believing it preposterous that a person could be haunted by the dead. Yet this is exactly what the increasingly demented Scottie will exemplify, as in the second half of the story Scottie himself wanders through San Francisco, captivated by a phantom presence. Another irony is that Judy Barton is molded into an alternate identity, into the image of the softspoken, aristocratic Madeleine Elster, twice. When Gavin Elster encounters Judy in a coffee shop where she is working as a waitress, he is struck by her resemblance to the real Madeleine and patiently but exactingly coaches her to assume the role of his wife.

Because of her love for Gavin Elster and because of her own desire for wealth and status, the unstable Judy dutifully conspires with Elster to murder the real Madeleine. Yet still another irony is added to *Vertigo* by the circumstance that although she is to deceive Scottie, and set him up as the gullible witness, Judy begins to fall in love with her intended victim. This is why when she encounters Scottie weeks after the death of the real Madeleine, she refuses to tell him that she was his "Madeleine" all along, but instead allows him to re-create her into what in essence is a walking cadaver. It is highly significant that after allowing an insistent Scottie into her room at the seedy Empire Hotel, where she lives alone, Judy at first writes a letter for Scottie telling him the truth about her relationship to Gavin Elster and her role in the murder of Madeleine Elster. Judy initially drags out her suitcase from the closet containing incriminating relics of her criminal past, like Madeleine's fashionable gray suit, intending to flee San Francisco forever. But she immediately tears up the confession, preferring to continue the charade—perhaps because she is still in love with Scottie, and in any case because she has been permanently ditched by Gavin Elster—just as Carlotta in the nineteenth century after serving her husband and even bearing him a child was cast out of her mansion and left to wander the streets, quickly succumbing to dementia and finally taking her own life. And, foreshadowing the escape of Gavin Elster, who is never caught or convicted or imprisoned for his crime, the vicious husband of Carlotta, significantly bereft of a name which would have underscored his human qualities and thereby imbued with a status of unvarnished power and malevolence, is never punished for his cruelty. Like so many of the characters of both *Vertigo* and *Aura*, this ninteenth-century potentate is one more figure left in suspension, for the spectator—and in the case of *Aura* the reader—to flesh out.

It seems clear that Judy tears up her confession because she is attracted to Scottie and knows that her revelation of her participation in the Madeleine crime will signify her instantly being abandonded by yet a third man—after both her stepfather, who deserted her family, and the wily Gavin Elster. Cyclic time is an all powerful, corrupting force in both *Vertigo* and *Aura* and may account for the fascination that Hitchcock's bizarre and wondrous film has for Fuentes.

Judy's cryptic remark to Scottie the first time the doomed couple is at San Juan Bautista "It wasn't supposed to happen this way," indicates her newfound desire—perhaps—to thwart the murder of the real Madeleine Elster in order to protect Scottie. Adding to the power and the fascination of both *Vertigo* and *Aura* is the way in which both film and *novella* expertly blend reality and fantasy, overweening ambition and intense frustration, desire and fulfillment, and, most importantly, Will and Fate. Consuelo in *Aura* is one of the strongest-willed of Fuentes's characters, paralleling the dynamic and domineering Claudia Nervo, the cinematic star and national legend in *Zona sagrada*, a *persona* of the captivating, irrepressible actress María Félix, by whom Fuentes, like Felipe with *Aura*, like Scottie with Madeleine, is entranced and to whom Fuentes has paid elaborate homage in his third, cinematic drama, *Orquídeas a la luz de la luna* (*Orchids in the Moonlight*; 1982) which reprises all of La Doña's cinematic roles and co-stars her with another icon of the Mexican film, Dolores Del Río[15]. Consuelo also is similar to the iron-willed and unforgiving Harriet Winslow in Fuentes's *Gringo viejo* (*The Old Gringo;* 1985), and parallels as well the titanic male characters created by Fuentes, in particular the demonic Siger de Brabant in Fuentes's enigmatic novel *Cumpleaños* (*Birthday;* 1969), and the imperious master of Time Andrés Heredia in still another novel of demonic possession, which, along with *Aura* and *Cumpleaños*, constitutes a trilogy of the fantastic, *Una familia lejana* (*Distant Relations;* 1982). All three works trace the sustaining of the Self by the titanic Will, the perpetuation of the identity across the centuries. Yet this immortality is gained only as a consequence of the reiterated blood sacrifice of the multiple victims claimed by these three insidious and terrifying supernatural presences: Consuelo, Siger, and Andrés Heredia.

Vertigo too is an extremely fatalistic work. Its fundamental theme of entrapment is sounded from the very start; in the striking closeup of the expression in the darting eyes of Kim Novak, or as one critic has maintained, of a woman *substituting* for Kim Novak—which would add still another dimension of duplicity and intrigue to *Vertigo,* of a trapped animal. To play a role is to be compelled to become that role. At the beginning, Judy Barton merely pretends to be the Other, Madeleine Elster, to gain the love, the social status and the wealth of Gavin Elster. Yet she will be forced to live the tragic role that she plays. At the end she too

[15] For an extensive examination of this facinating evocation of the two female superstars, and the significant thematic, structural and sylistic impact on *Orquídeas a la luz de la luna*—Fuentes's at once elegant and acerbic evocation of the leading actresses of the Mexican screen—of the great Hollywood director Billy Wilder in his Academy Award winning triumph *Sunset Boulevard*, consult Lanin A. Gyurko, *The Shattered Screen: Myth and Demythification in the Art of Carlos Fuentes and Billy Wilder* (New Orleans: University Press of the South, 2009). 450 pp.

Figure 27. Regal Palace of the Legion of Honor. Another labyrinth of intrigue and splendor. Note haunting fusion of sunshine and shadow.

Figure 28. Golden Gate Bridge looms as both reality and poetic fantasy: Scottie diminished, engulfed by darkness.

perishes, and in a manner that repeats the tragic way in which the ancestor of the real Madeleine Elster, Carlotta, took her life. *Vertigo* traces a series of tragic falls, both real and fantastic. It begins with the near death of Scottie, who suddenly slips on a rooftop as he is chasing a criminal and almost falls to his death. Although a policeman attempts to rescue him, the rescuer himself is doomed, as he suddenly falls to his death. At the end, there is but another deadly fall, as a startled Judy Barton accidentally loses her balance and falls from the very tower from which Carlotta had committed suicide, the very tower from which Madeleine Elster's body was hurled by the hidden Gavin Elster—never seen by Scottie at the scene of the crime yet strongly suspected by the former detective—who refuses to shake Elster's hand at the painful inquest of the tragic Madeleine Elster—of an ill-defined act of treachery. Although Scottie only falls once in reality—from the top of a stepstool in Midge's apartment into the consoling embrace of a stricken and sinuously concerned Midge—he suffers a frightening nightmare of an endless fall into an open grave. In his extremely traumatic nightmare, a tormented Scottie envisions himself hurtling to his death, falling into Madeleine's open grave —to join her in death. Even at the very end of *Vertigo*, in one of the possible endings of this highly ambiguous film—without a doubt Hitchcock's most complex, most elusive creation, Scottie seems ready to actualize his nightmare and hurl himself from the tower window, joining Judy/Madeleine in death. And once again, attesting to the insidious cyclic time of the film, Scottie is so traumatized and so certain that Judy/Madeleine has died that he fails to descend the tower to verify the tragedy. He becomes the epitome of hopelessness and helplessness, just like the willess Felipe in *Aura*. Felipe is but one of an endless series of young lovers whom Consuelo has lured to her domain, entranced, drugged with the herbs that she cultivates in her garden, and psychologically destroyed.

The fatalistic way in which the camera operates in *Vertigo* has been penetratingly analyzed by Rothman:

> In the Hitchcock thriller . . . the camera is an instrument of taxidermy, not transfiguration: the camera does violence to

its subjects, fixes them, and breathes back only the illusion of life into these ghosts.[16]

The central characters in both *Vertigo* and *Aura* quickly become submerged in a fatalistic past, partly because they have no strong identities in the present. Both Judy Barton and Felipe Montero are spongelike identities, quickly molding themselves to conform to the demands of their "employers." Judy comes to cosmopolitan San Francisco from a small rural town—Salina, Kansas, seeking socioeconomic advancement through a love affair with a wealthy man—very similar to the motives of the lonely and impoverished yet extremely motivated Carlotta in the nineteenth century. A product of a broken home, one in which her father abandoned her mother, Judy is an extremely insecure personality and clings to strong-minded males, needing to be constantly reassured that they love her and highly fearful of being abandoned once again. Yet, ironically, she is repeatedly abandoned, first by Gavin Elster, who leaves her behind and flees to Europe after Judy's usefulness to him is over, and then by Scottie, who can accept her only to the extent that she is the lost, apparently brought back to life, Madeleine, painstakingly resuscitated by Scottie as masterful conjurer, just like Consuelo. And Judy's life as Gavin Elster's new wife after the murder, even if the marriage had transpired, would seem to be as bleak and tormenting as is her ultimate relationship with Scottie. Indeed, the hapless Judy is loved by none of the males in her life—neither by father, Elster, nor Scottie.

In both *Vertigo* and *Aura,* the rapid absorption of the sensitive but highly frustrated male protagonists into a past which both initially idealize, romanticize, is keenly visualized. When Felipe Montero enters the old part of Mexico City, where the ancient Aztec Empire of México-Tenochtitlán—founded in 1136—had its center, and wanders down the Calle de Donceles, itself symbolic, as "doncel" signifies a young, virgin male, he gazes in fascination at the house of Consuelo, which Fuentes evokes as a

[16] Consult William Rothman, *The "I" of the Cinema: Essays in Film Criticism, History, and Aesthetics* (Cambridge University Press, 1988), p. 172.

house of Time, composed of a fusion of all of the epochs of Mexico, from the centuries of its ancient Aztec past, symbolized by the fact that it is made of *tezontle,* the ancient volcanic stone used by the Aztecs to construct their pyramids. Yet the style of Consuelo's house is baroque, alluding to the epoch of the Conquest and to the grandeur of colonial Mexico. Just as in the dazzling kaleidoscopic *La región más transparente*, Fuentes presents a multitemporal and multispatial Mexico, one in which all times and all historical and mythic personages are simultaneously present and alive—Quetzalcóatl and Huitzilopochtli, Moctezuma Xocoyotzin, and Hernán Cortés, Cuauhtémoc and Motolinía, Porfirio Díaz and Pancho Villa and Emiliano Zapata. Finally, the fact that there are two numbers on Consuelo's mysterious house, as if it were a palimpsest, alludes to the drastic changes that occurred as the result of the Mexican Revolution of 1910—changes which the dour, pretentiously aristocratic and monarchist Consuelo resolutely opposes. For Felipe, who previously has only studied history, history now becomes a *living* experience, and he remains fascinated by this confluence of times. The two stories of the dwelling also signify two vastly different dimensions. The lower, street level symbolizes the everyday reality—traffic congested, air polluted, contemporary Mexico, from which Felipe is eager to escape. The upper level, where Consuelo dwells, is characterized by an eery although inviting quietude.

It is significant that so powerful is the center city in both works that numerous tours have sprung up, taking myriad gawking tourists to the sights of *Vertigo*—from the dramatic Fort Point at the Golden Gate Bridge where Judy/Madeleine pretends to commit suicide, to the majestic Palace of the Legion of Honor, the exquisitely elegant museum where she gazes for hours seemingly stupefied before the portrait of Carlotta Valdés, to the exclusive restaurant *Ernie's* to the Portals of the Past, where Madeleine has, according to Gavin Elster, sat spellbound, to the Mission Dolores and Coit Tower, Nob Hill and Telegraph Hill, where Midge has her fashionable apartment, to the stately Brocklebank Building where Gavin Elster dwells with his mistress/accomplice Judy/Madeleine. Similarly, myriad students have been brought to central Mexico by Spanish professors giving them a tour of the heart of Mexico City and retracing the historic streets and colonial structures of *Aura*. In the case of both *Aura* and *Vertigo*, concrete geography is symbolic, spiritualized. In both works, physical geography over and over again is labyrinthine—the torturously winding streets of San Francisco through which Scottie relentlessly pursues Madeleine, the huge threatening trees that formidably, even menacingly, overshadow the highway down the Peninsula from San Francisco to San Juan Bautista and adumbrate the tragic ending of the spellbinding film, the immense and deserted and rapidly darkening hospital corridor down which Midge walks forlornly after realizing that there is no cure for Scottie's asphyxiating delusions and his impossible love for Madeleine—and that she has lost him forever. Midge's sad trudging down the suddenly darkened hospital corridor in a tragic sense constitutes a parallel scene to the suddenly congealing darkness in the *Argosy Book Shop*, as the gloomy hospital scene marks her permanent exit from Scottie's life. Yet, in this perfectly balanced film, as a critic has pointed out, Midge's disappearance down the suddenly darkened hospital corridor is countered by Judy/Madeleine's slow walk down the illuminated corridor of the Empire Hotel after she is almost completely transformed herself into a seductive Madeleine, into her hotel room where she will consummate her affair with Scottie.

In both *Vertigo* and *Aura*, space is incessantly labyrinthine, to underscore yet another classical Greek and Roman archetype—the myth of Theseus and the monstrous Minotaur with its head of a bull and body of a human—the product of the fornication of Pasiphaë and a bull. However, unlke the victorious hero Theseus, who slays the Minotaur and emerges victorious from the labyrinth, neither Scottie Ferguson nor Felipe Montero will ever emerge from the twisted, constrictive labyrinth that, at the end, permanently imprisons them. Indeed, just as existence for the increasingly tormented Scottie is reduced to a series of darkened labyrinths, from the *chiaroscuro* labyrinth that leads him to Madeleine at the elegant florist boutique to the ornate stairway leading to Madeleine Elster's unoccupied room in the eery McKittrick Hotel, to the darkened labyrinth that is the rickety stairwell to the tower top at San Juan Bautista Mission. Thus although a skillful Judy/Madeleine pretending to be frightened, speaks hauntingly, poetically of a darkened labyrinth at the end of which are mirrors and death—a twisting labyrinth that ironically becomes, at the end, a horrifying reality for the tortured Judy as she is dragged up the tower steps by a weirdly energized Scottie, all traces of his nonchalance and lassitude now dissipated. Scottie too, adumbrating Felipe in *Aura* plunges into these insidious labyrinths—and may as well find death at the end of the labyrinth.

This spatialization of time, in which the doomed, elevated then discarded the second story of a dwelling uncannily represents another world, a past world suspended in the present, is also found in *Vertigo.* Twice Judy/Madeleine appears fleetingly, more apparition than physical presence—indicating one more point of inspiration for *Aura*—at a second story window, once in the looming Hotel McKittrick, the second time at the Empire Hotel in downtown San Francisco. Similar to the dwelling of Consuelo, the Hotel McKittrick is a house of Time. Although now converted into apartments, in one of which Judy/Madeleine is apparently residing, in the nineteenth century it was the Great House, the towering and majestic mansion in which Carlotta dwelled—and indeed historically was the graceful Portman Mansion, now, unfortunately demolished and a nondescript, low-level building erected in its place. Just as Consuelo's house is linked with mystery, with strange appearances and disappearances, so too is the lofty Hotel McKittrick with its Victorian charm, captivating ornateness and luxuriousness. Although Scottie apparently has seen Judy/Madeleine at an early point inside the hotel, and viewed her at an upstairs window, when he climbs the stairs to investigate, he finds no one there. Similarly, from the start of *Aura,* which, like *Vertigo*, is composed of a series of No Trespassing Zones that are eagerly crossed by the male protagonist, the dwelling of Consuelo is symbolic of the hidden, of the mask, of the dual identity that is so characteristic of almost every aspect of this bizarre and convoluted narrative—temporal, spatial, historical, archaeological, psychological. Similar to *Vertigo* in the highly elusive, incessantly shifting world of Aura, everything—buildings, mansions, streets, art objects, personages—is something else:

> It's surprising to know that anyone lives on Donceles Street. You always thought that nobody lived in the old center of the city. You walk slowly, trying to pick out the

> number 815 in that conglomeration of old colonial mansions, all of them converted into repair shops, jewelry shops, shoe stores, drugstores. . . . on the greenish curtains that darken the long windows; on that window from which someone draws back when you look at it. You gaze at the fanciful vines carved over the doorway, then lower your eyes to the peeling wall and discover 815, formerly 69. (A, 11)

In both *Vertigo* and *Aura,* there is a constant process of both mythification and demythification. Consuelo's mansion symbolizes Porfirian Mexico City, whose center contained lavish Europeanized mansions of the powerful elite who disdained speaking Spanish and spoke in cultivated French tones, with mansard roofs emulating those of the European Continent to which many aristocrats fled after the violent upheaval in 1910, emulating the exile of their leader, Porfirio Díaz who once fought against the French and yet died and is buried in Paris, near the Arc de Triomphe. But with the cataclysmic Revolution came drastic change and demythification of the city still evoked as a cultural epicenter by upper class Latin Americans, including Vargas Llosa and of course, Carlos Fuentes himself—huge colonial mansions now compartmentalized, converted into apartment units and trade shops, epitomized in *La región más transparente* by the once elaborate mansion of the haughty relic Porfirista Doña Lorenza de Ovando, now subdivided and with an incongruous neon sign on its ornate rooftop. Fuentes's love of Mexico's extensive and breathtakingly beautiful architectural past is evident in the home where he once dwelled, in the historic *zona* of San Angel Inn near the Periférico.

In *Vertigo* as well, Scottie's rapid absorption into the past is expertly visualized as Scottie, after his sudden attack of *Vertigo*, his abrupt and permanent resignation from the police force, and his only tentative recuperation, receives an invitation to visit his old college friend Gavin Elster in the latter's plush office on the Embarcadero. Elster owns a shipbuilding company, and the walls of his office are ostentatiously lined with prints and paintings, all portraying San Francisco's seafaring past in a highly romantic way. In the sterile and purposeless lives of both Scottie and Felipe, the past seems to offer a richness, a fulfillment that the vapid present fails to contain. Indeed Gavin Elster himself, insidiously toying with Scottie, in a low keyed manner attempting to fire the detective's imagination and arouse his desire to plunge into the past, wistfully evokes a past that he holds up as heroic, one in which men had "freedom and power." Yet the highly cynical Elster has no love for San Francisco, as is evidenced by his rapid departure for Switzerland—to a Europe which for Elster signifies not only safety and anonymity but culture and refinement—the same lure that Europe has had for Latin Americans across the centuries. In the present, wearing a humiliating corset and forced to use a cane as the result of his accident, without a job and with no definite professional or personal goals, unemotionally related to Midge whom he responds to not as an impassioned lover but as a mother surrogate, Scottie has little freedom and no power. Indeed, he has been reduced from a person whose life had great purpose and ambition, to a dazed wanderer in search of identity. As such Scottie is very similar to Felipe, who is aimless, who is stalled in his doctoral dissertation and who is bored with his occupation as a secondary school teacher. Scottie has nurtured ambitions of leading the entire police force; after his accident renders these ambitions impossible, his pride prevents him from accepting what he views as a sterile, emasculating, confining desk job, and he resigns from the police force all together. Similarly, Felipe, although he has accomplished little on his dissertation, dreams of being a "conquistador intelectual," as he ambitiously envisions himself writing an all-encompassing thesis that will fuse all of the many diverse accounts of the Spanish Conquest of the New World significantly, an ambitious project that Carlos Fuentes himself has aspired to, and that this prolific Mexican author has actualized in his monumental, epic work of the Discovery and Conquest of the New World, the nine-hundred page Gargantuan novel *Terra nostra* (1978).

Upon entering the domain of Consuelo and seeing the beguiling Aura, the hitherto rootless existence of Felipe is suddenly imbued with purpose, and he immediately fashions himself as the prince who will rescue his trapped and exploited princess, Aura, from the despotic control of her harridan aunt. Both Scottie and Felipe are drifters, both are ripe for a takeover by an alternate identity which promises excitement, adventure, and most of all, instant self-actualization. Although Scottie is not responsible for the accidental death of the policeman, he continually blames himself for his failure to rescue him—adumbrating his self-flagellation after the sudden death of his adored "Madelene." Scottie's relationship with Madeleine parallels that between Felipe and Aura; in both cases weak and self-doubting males are seemingly given the opportunity to display their machismo, to become heroic protectors and rescuers of the suddenly appearing other worldly enigmatic and spellbinding female presences that deceive and destroy them.

In both *Vertigo* and *Aura,* buildings, rooms, and gardens are evoked both as realistic structures and as manifestations of the supernatural. Crossing the threshold into these buildings or rooms thus is not merely stepping into the remote past, it is passing into another plane of existence. For Felipe, entering the darkened chambers of Consuelo is entering a living tomb. Indeed, the weird door knocker, in the shape of a canine foetus, seems to grin demonically at him—an allusion to the three-headed dog Cerberus who guarded the entranceway to Hades/hell in classical Greek and Roman mythology. And Felipe has the sensation of departing forever from the world of modern Mexico, a world that, significantly, he is eager to abandon. Once he enters the domain of Consuelo, he will never emerge again. This is similar to Scottie, who once he becomes enamoured of the alluring Madeleine, will never be able to break away from her spell, despite the repeated attempts of the person who really cares for him, his ex-sweetheart Midge, to bring him back to reality. As Felipe is poised to enter the underworld, his attitude is both fearful yet welcoming:

> You rap vainly with the knocker, that copper head of a dog, so worn and smooth that it resembles the head of a canine foetus in a museum of natural science. It seems as if the dog is grinning at you and you let go of the cold metal. The door opens at the first light push of your fingers, but before going in you give a last look over your shoulder, frowning at the long line of stalled cars that growl, honk, and belch out the unhealthy fumes of their impatience. You try to

> retain some single image of that indifferent outside world. (A, 11)

Time and again in *Vertigo,* Scottie is depicted crossing the threshold of a building into the past, in a ritualized movement that parallels and most likely has influenced the way in which space and time function in *Aura.* Gavin Elster states to Scottie that his increasingly agitated wife, under the influence of the renascent spirit of Carlotta, sits by the San Francisco Bay at a place called, significantly and poetically, "The Portals of the Past." Yet it is not Gavin Elster's wife but the hapless Scottie who will constantly traverse those portals, first as he follows Judy/Madeleine to the beautiful and haunting Mission Dolores, one of the oldest intact buildings in San Francisco, its formidable construction with its enormously thick adobe walls leading to its surviving even the devastating San Francisco earthquake in the early twentieth century. The mission was constructed in 1776 and represents beautiful and haunting suspended Time in the commercial and technological world of modern San Francisco—just like the eery mansion of Carlotta in *Aura*—a mission built in the eighteenth century by the Spanish priests. The magical, dreamlike way in which Hitchcock films the entering of Scottie into the beautiful Mission Dolores—a profoundly sacred space—makes it seem as if he were entering a different world, one inhabited only by himself and the wraithlike Madeleine. Hitchcock has commented to Truffaut how he employed a special fog filter in this key cemetary scene—a filter that imbues Madeleine with a ghostly radiance—exactly as the ethereal Aura is evoked in Fuentes's masterpiece. Scottie then follows Madeleine to the Palace of the Legion of Honor, the famous San Francisco Museum of Art, and passes through more august portals to gaze again on the past. He avidly watches Madeleine as she in turn gazes spellbound on the portrait of Carlotta in the museum. The camera emphasizes the confluence between pictoral art and a fragile human reality that reflects the portrait, between past and present, between Judy/Madeleine and Carlotta, by focusing first on the whorls in the hairdo of Judy/Madeleine then match cutting to focus on a similar hair style of Carlotta—a scene, in this exactingly structured film, which anticipates the match-cutting at the end, when a startled Scottie gazes first at the incriminating necklace of Carlotta now donned by an unsuspecting Judy then flashes back to the necklace in the museum painting—and finally realizes how he has been duped by Judy/Madeleine. Once again the images are of enchantment, entrapment and possession. Yet ironically, it is not the seemingly victimized Madeleine but the increasingly hypnotized Scottie who is being entrapped—and increasingly enchanted, just as is Felipe in the lugubrious abode of the ever-devious Consuelo.

In the Museum of Art scene, Hitchcock gives us a striking visual equivalent of vertigo in the blonde whorls of the hairdos of both Carlotta and Judy/Madeleine—alluding constantly to an illness that is both physical and emotional, a fear of heights producing the physical sensation of vertigo along with a pleasurable sensation of letting the self go, of pleasure in falling—exactly paralleling Scottie's response to the person whom he mistakenly believes is someone else's wife, whom he is at first tricked into believing is Madeleine Elster yet even after constantly realizing that his beloved fantasy woman is an elaborate fraud, fanatically clings to his ineradicable misconception, insisting on calling Judy "Madeleine" even at the very end.

In both Fuentes's *novella* and Hitchcock's film, the labyrinth and the mirror are symbols that are repeated incessantly. The labyrinth indicates existence as conundrum; it is a graphic exteriorization of the situation of Scottie Ferguson, as he attempts to explicate the puzzling phenomenon of Judy/Madeleine, and in the case of Felipe Montero, the mystery that surrounds Consuelo, seemingly a *beata* but in fact a sorceress, seemingly in prayer to the saints but in fact in league with the devil, seemingly a benevolent employer but in fact the person who never pays Felipe any salary, who beguiles and entraps him and ultimately claims his body and his soul. The darkened labyrinth of Consuelo's house through which Felipe wanders has a mythic resonance—it alludes to the wanderings of the ancient Greek hero Theseus through the labyrinth on Crete constructed by the artesan Daedalus in quest of the ferocious Minotaur to which human victims of sacrifice were constantly rendered. But unlike the classic Greek and Roman myth, in which the bold and heroic Theseus slays the monstrous Minotaur and emerges triumphant from the labyrinth prison, the creature with the head of a bull and the body of a man, in *Aura* the

Figure 29. Right before Madeleine's fake suicide plunge and Scottie's vain heroics. Another striking example of the beauty of *Vertigo*.

Figure 30. Tumultuous cloud-covered sky and roiling waters of San Francisco Bay frame Pieta composition of fated lovers.

hapless Felipe/Theseus will be devoured by the monstrous equivalent of the dread minotaur—Consuelo. Corresponding to the dreamlike cemetary outside the Mission Dolores is the secret garden of Consuelo:

> You close the door behind you and peer into the darkness of a roofed alleyway. It must be a patio of some sort, because you can smell the mold, the dampness of the plants, the rotting roots, the thick drowsy aroma. There isn't any light to guide you, and you're searching in your coat pocket for the box of matches when a sharp, thin voice tells you, from a distance: "No, it isn't necessary. Please. Walk thirteen steps forward and you'll come to a stairway at your right. Come up, please. There are twenty-two steps. Count them. (A, 13)

Ironically, Aura at first seems to be Felipe's savior on the model of the Greek heroine Ariadne, who provides the lengthy cord to aid her lover Theseus in re-emerging from the sinuous and deadly labyrinth. Aura appears with a lamp, ostensibly to guide the feverishly questing Felipe through the labyrinth, just as the classical Ariadne, the lover of Theseus, holds the thread that will enable Theseus to retrace his steps through the foreboding labyrinth that is the dwelling place of the Minotaur. Yet Aura is but the mask of Consuelo. The purpose of the young girl is to entice Felipe, to keep him in the darkened quarters until he is totally possessed by the witchcraft of Consuelo. This is exactly the function that the dazzlingly beautiful Judy/Madeleine fulfills in *Vertigo*—to entice the love-starved and highly impressionable Scottie, to lure him down to San Juan Bautista, to set him up as the witness to what Scottie believes is a suicide that he could have prevented but which in fact is a murder that has already occurred. Then Gavin Elster, perhaps in league with the coroner at Madeleine's inquest just as he controls the sinuous hotel manager at the Hotel McKittrick, can emerge blameless from the brutal murder and claim his wife's entire fortune.

In *Vertigo,* the torturously winding streets of San Francisco are photographed by Hitchcock as an immense labyrinth, through which Scottie doggedly pursues Judy/Madeleine. The futility of his pursuit at the outset of *Vertigo* constitutes an adumbration of the fateful ending of *Vertigo*, in which Scottie is left with outstretched, empty arms. The crippling operation of cyclic time in *Vertigo* is indicated in that after he has one day followed the ever-elusive Judy/Madeleine as she makes innumerable turns through the streets, he finds that she has led him back to his own apartment, to which she is delivering a letter of thanks to Scottie for rescuing her! Indeed, this cyclical trajectory is a visualization of the essential hopelessness of Scottie's always tenuous relationship with Judy/Madeleine. Although Scottie is given several indications, on both the conscious and subconscious levels, that something is amiss, that he is being played for the fool, he continually—and blindly—seeks to further his relationship with Madeleine. Thus, for example, Midge attempts to warn him of the ridiculousness of his pursuit, by painting a portrait of Carlotta in her artist studio apartment in which she inserts her own features, including her definitely unromantic glasses, instead of the replicating of the nineteenth century woman by whom Scottie is becoming so entranced. Scottie, who previously has seemed to be nonchalant, almost indifferent, now reveals how fanatic—and irrational—he truly is, by summarily ending his relationship with Midge. She has dared to desecrate the portrait that for Scottie now looms as an icon, a portrait that he repeatedly in his imagination fuses with the image of the beleaguered Judy/Madeleine—indicating his rapid acceptance of Gavin Elster's highly improbable tale. And there is every indication that the dutiful Scottie is taking seriously the charge given to him by Gavin Elster not merely to keep watch on his wandering and highly unstable wife, but also *watch over* her—with the goal of facilitating Elster's interning his wife in a mental institution—ostensibly to save her life. Similarly, although Felipe on the conscious level is disconcerted by the darkness of Consuelo's domain, yet instead of imposing his own personality upon the house in which he is required to stay to work on the tedious task of editing Llorente's convoluted memoirs, Felipe meekly conforms to the darkness. Even more, the extremely pliable Felipe casts that darkness around himself, thus demonstrating how suitable he is for the role of victim:

> You could take the lamp down with you. You don't do it. This house will always be in darkness, and you've got to learn it and relearn it by touch. You grope your way like a blind man, with your arms stretched out wide, feeling your way along the wall . . . (A, 35)

Felipe is unable to discern that Aura is not enslaved but in fact is complicit with her aunt, sustained by the powerful and indefatigable will of Consuelo. Similarly, Scottie fails to understand until almost the very end of *Vertigo*, that Judy/Madeleine is not a helpless victim but in fact a hardened co-conspirator along with Gavin Elster. Far from being a weak and helpless victim of either supernatural fantasies or psychological visions, Judy Barton is in fact a cold-blooded accomplice to murder, and indirectly the destroyer of Scottie's identity. Ironically, too Scottie until the very end does not realize that the Judy Barton whom he is laboriously transforming into Madeleine was in fact Madeleine all along, that he is not painstakingly recreating a beloved but merely duplicating—and not nearly as well—what Gavin Elster has already done—punctiliously to train Judy to be Madeleine Elster. Yet both Scottie and Felipe have visions of the truth—yet, ironically, visions that both male protagonists repeatedly suppress. As he passionately embraces and kisses the Judy Barton in Judy's nondescript room in the Empire Hotel, finally transformed totally into Madeleine, Scottie experiences not emotional fulfillment but agitation, suspicion, even dread—he seems on some level to understand that Judy Barton is not just a remake that he has fanatically fashioned but the same Madeleine that he had passionately kissed before, in the livery stable at San Juan Bautista—another locale that is a fusion of reality and dream, and of historical time and prevarication—Judy trained by Gavin Elster to be possessed by the vengeful spirit of the mad Carlotta. Similarly, Felipe experiences a traumatic nightmare in which he gazes in horror on the features of the hag Consuelo superimposed over the beauteous countenance of his beloved Aura. Here again Fuentes demonstrates his mastery of cinematic techniques, as he effectively utilizes superimposition—adumbrating the final, devastating *superimposition* of the features of Llorente over those of the hapless Felipe Montero. Yet both

Felipe and Scottie up until the very end prefer to suppress the truth—that they have been lured, manipulated, betrayed and destroyed by these phantom women.

Both *Vertigo* and *Aura* trace the pathetic willingness on the part of the male protagonists to be deceived, indeed even to *collaborate* with the very persons who are brutally deceiving them. And when Aura at the end seeks to prod Felipe to actualize his goal of rescuing her, to flee with her while Consuelo has temporarily departed, Felipe now demurs, again manifesting not rebellion but submission to the inexorable will of Consuelo. Behind the veiled being who is seemingly Aura is the wizened Consuelo, and by the feebleness of Felipe's response, Consuelo finally is made certain that she now has him totally under her control, that there now is no possibility of his escaping. Aura, compliant with Consuelo, tempts Felipe by pretending that she is willing to flee with him. But Felipe demurs:

> [Aura] Yes, sometimes she does. She makes a great effort and goes out. She's going out today. For all day. You and I could . . ."
> "Go away?"
> "If you want to."
> "Well . . . perhaps not yet. I'm under contract. But as soon as I can finish the work, then . . ." (A, 123-125)

In *Vertigo,* the evidence of Judy's complicity with Gavin Elster finally becomes overwhelming. Whether out of carelessness or out of a desire to add something new to a relationship that is mired in sterile repetitiveness, echoing the comfortable but sterile relationship at the outset between Scottie and Midge, who is thus reduced to but one more dangling figure in the film, Judy/Madeleine finally dons the incriminating necklace of Carlotta that had been given to her by Gavin Elster as a payoff for Judy's successful participation in the crime. Upon seeing the necklace, Scottie immediately remembers the portrait of Carlotta and finally understands the connection between Judy and Gavin Elster. The belated realization impels him to take vengeance on Judy by compelling her to return to San Juan Bautista and to re-enact the circumstances of the crime. In the case of Felipe, the realization that he has been deceived, that he has been hired not merely to revise the memoirs of Llorente but to become him, comes too late, as at the end Felipe feels his own features being mercilessly torn away by a searing, supernatural force. The stricken Felipe now makes a vain attempt to hold on to his original identity as he frantically goes through his meager possessions, his final link with his original self that will be swept away forever. It is significant that just as Scottie arrives at the stunning realization of the truth through the evocation of a portrait, so also does Felipe, as he gazes upon an old photograph of Consuelo and Llorente and finds instead the images of Aura and of himself. As the frantic repetition "you, you, you" strikingly underscores in *Vertigo*, in which both Judy/Madeleine and Scottie and even the seemingly rational, pragmatic Midge are all captivated by the portrait of Carlotta, so too is Felipe enmeshed in the antique photographs of Consuelo and Llorente, suddenly transmorphed into Aura and Felipe:

> In the third photograph you see both Aura and the old gentleman, but this time they're dressed in outdoor clothes, sitting on a bench in a garden. The photograph has become a little blurred: Aura doesn't look as young as she did in the other picture, but it's she, it's he, it's . . . it's you. You stare and stare at the photographs, then hold them up to the skylight. You cover General Llorente's beard with your finger, and imagine him with black hair, and you only discover yourself: blurred, lost, forgotten, but you, you, you. (A, 137)

In *Vertigo*, Scottie is both Self and Other, and as he continues to exploit Judy Barton, he becomes cast in the mold of two alternate and extremely negative identities—both Gavin Elster and the nameless nineteenth century plutocrat who cruelly exploited Carlotta and drove his wife and the mother of his child to commit suicide. So also is the true identity of the fragile Felipe found in the past. Even moreso than the divided Scottie, Felipe is not integral self but Other; the circumstance that his narrative is always in the second-person singular form indicates his fundamental lack of an "I"—of a single, coherent, assertive identity:

> you fall exhausted on the bed, touching your cheeks, your eyes, your nose, as if you were afraid that some invisible hand had ripped off the mask that you've been wearing for twenty-seven years, the cardboard features that hid your true face, your real appearance, the appearance you once had but then forgot. You bury your face in the pillow, trying to keep the wind of the past from tearing away your own features, because you don't want to lose them. (A, 137-139)

In both *Vertigo* and *Aura,* the mirror is a key symbol, a paradoxical symbol of both doubleness—of the expansion of the self, of the self's capacity to extend itself, to re-create itself—and of duplicity. The fact that Felipe is from the start, perhaps even before entering Consuelo's domain, the Other, is indicated visually, through his narcissistic absorption with his mirror reflection. Felipe's identity seems to be as fragile as the mist that covers the mirror—that appears, disappears, and reappears again, that symbolizes the ghostly identities of both Llorente and of Aura:

> You look at yourself in the large oval mirror on the door of the wardrobe—it's also walnut—in the bathroom hallway. You move your heavy eyebrows and wide thick lips, and your breath fogs the mirror. You close your black eyes, and when you open them again the mirror has cleared. You stop holding your breath and run your hand through your dark, limp hair; you touch your fine profile, your lean cheeks; and when your breath hides your face again you're repeating her name: "Aura." (A, 33)

The essential unreality of Madeleine Elster is expertly symbolized by her constant appearance as but a reflection in a mirror—symbolizing too how much Madeleine from the very start—not merely when Scottie encounters her as Judy Barton—is an intricate creation of Scottie's febrile imagination. It is significant that the first time Judy/Madeleine is encountered by Scottie, in the elegant restaurant *Ernie's,* she is reflected in one of the huge gold-framed mirrors. And, after Scottie has pursued her to a florist shop, which Judy/Madeleine enters mysteriously, through the back way, via an alley entrance, Scottie opens the door to the shop and sees only the image of Madeleine—her glamorous reflection in a mirror. Even when Scottie forces his way into Judy's upstairs apartment at the Empire Hotel, the apparently coarse, street-wise Judy is repeatedly evoked in front of a mirror, to symbolize her doubleness and her continued duplicity. Thus does Hitchcock expertly symbolize Madeleine as but a mere illusion, as a projection, an emanation of Scottie's desperate consciousness, which is seeking a "damsel in distress" to rescue, just as is the inchoate Felipe in *Aura.* Through the reiterated emphasis on mirrors, the unreality of Madeleine is underscored, and also her deceptiveness—the fact that she is really not Madeleine Elster at all. In fact, Scottie only glimpses the real Madeleine Elster after she is dead, as he sees her body falling from the tower.

Curiously, instead of rushing to the body of his beloved to ascertain whether she is still alive, Scottie is so mortified at his failure to rescue Madeleine that he silently sneaks away—leaving the body to the attention of the nuns and not wishing to be seen by anyone. Indeed his cowardice and shame make him culpable of the one crime for which he never is formally charged—leaving the scene of a crime, whether that crime be suicide or murder. Similarly, when a terrified Judy at the end falls from the tower, instead of rushing to her side in an attempt to ascertain whether she may still be alive, Scottie for some reason never made clear and constituting one more of the mysteries of *Vertigo* assumes that she is dead and is horror-stricken and again incapable of heroic action or of any action at all—similar to the benumbed Felipe in *Aura.* In both *Vertigo* and *Rear Window*, Hitchcock, just as Fuentes so often will do, creates essentially weak male characters who constantly desire to be virile and heroic yet who result to be helpless and hopeless over and over again. Paralleling the continually stricken Scottie is the wheel-chair bound invalid L.B. Jefferies in the provocative *Rear Window*, another hero *manqué*. And the initially super confident and authoritative, even insolent San Francisco criminal lawyer Mitch in Hitchcock's thriller *The Birds* is subsequently rebuked as a weakling by his own mother and ultimately functions in a passive, totally defensive manner, never shooting at or even attempting to scare off the always menacing, biting birds, and at the end literally tiptoeing around them as he attempts to escape from treacherous, thoroughly occupied Bodega Bay. So too in Fuentes there are a plethora of male protagonists with heroic intentions—Artemio Cruz, Rodrigo Pola in *Where the Air is Clear*, Felipe Montero in *Aura*, Félix Maldonado in *Hydra Head*, all of whom are finally revealed as cowardly, ineffectual and even, like the initially adventurous Félix Maldonado, defeated and driven insane.

Cyclic time characterizes both *Vertigo* and *Aura*. Scottie at the end, as at the beginning, is suspended in time and space; it is likely that at the end, instead of returning to the sanctuary that is Midge's apartment—an ending initially filmed by Hitchcock but discarded as perhaps too conventional, too pat—Scottie will continue to wander endlessly in search of but another Judy Barton, whom he will obsessively remake into Madeleine, whose very name is suffused with an immateriality so different from Midge, whose name, rhyming with the nouns of stolidity, *fridge* and *bridge*, symbolizes her staidness and her concreteness—and her mundanity. In direct contrast, the alluring Madeleine constitutes an allusion to the marvelous Proustian novel *Le recherche de temps perdu*—the quest for the lost past—tantalizingly evoked through the tea and Madeleine pastries, in Marcel Proust's greatest work (1913-1927).

The theme of *Vertigo* is constantly visualized throughout the film, so that the spectator not only comprehends intellectually the plight of Scottie but is made to empathize with his illness through experiencing the vexing dizziness along with him. The theme of *Vertigo* is evident from the very start of the film, in the credits, in the multicolored spirals that emanate bewitchingly from the eyes of Judy/Madeleine and signify both her entrancing effect on Scottie and the circumstance that although he seeks in her relief from his debilitating illness, she will not cure him but only aggravate that unremitting and thoroughly unconquerable illness. The spellbinding credits, a slow, mesmerizing exercise in fantasy, as opposed to the very realistic backdrop to the credits initially envisioned by Hitchcock, were designed by Saul Bass, and stand as one of the most startlingly original credit designs in the whole history of Hollywood film—for which they won an Academy

Award. In effect the film begins not with Scottie pursuing the criminal across the San Francisco rooftops but with a concentration on the eyes—both fascinating and terrified— of Judy/Madeleine. Similarly, in *Aura,* there is an intense focus, a close-up on the mesmeric green eyes of Aura, that from the start bewitch the extremely pliable Felipe. Although he has balked at the curt directive of Consuelo that he remain with her in order to work on the memoirs, all resistance vanishes once he beholds the fluid green eyes of Aura. Corresponding to the stunning credits of Saul Bass in *Vertigo*, the multicolored vertiginous spirals that weave first a benumbed Scottie Ferguson then the viewer himself/herself into the film and hold that viewer spellbound from the very start, is the incantatory style of Fuentes, with its fluid movement and its use of the second-person singular—the same voice used by a hypnotist to entrance his subject: "You are getting drowsy, you are falling asleep . . . ":

> Finally you can see that those eyes are sea green and that they surge, break to foam, grow calm again, then surge again like a wave. You look into them and tell yourself it isn't true, because they're beautiful green eyes just like all the beautiful green eyes you've ever known. But you can't deceive yourself: those eyes do surge, do change, as if offering you a landscape that only you can see and desire.
> "Yes. I'm going to live with you." (A, 27)

The link of Aura's eyes with the foaming sea adumbrates her association with the Lorelei, the fantastic sirens along the Rhine who lured sailors to their deaths. In addition, the reference, a Germanic one, also constitutes an allusion to the ill-fated Hapsburg royal family of Maximilian, the same family that ruled Spain centuries earlier in the person of the Emperor Carlos V—whose first language was not Spanish, but German—at the time of the Conquest of Mexico City by Hernán Cortés in 1521.

In *Vertigo,* the way in which the opening close-up is presented, without a full-length view of Judy/Madeleine, without any establishing shot, makes the presence of Judy/Madeleine a disembodied one from the very start, and underscores the mood of uncanniness which will permeate the entire film, as it does *Aura.* This opening sequence has been perceptively analyzed by Wood:

> We see a woman's face; the camera moves in first to lips, then to eyes. The face is blank, mask-like, representing the inscrutability of appearances; the impossibility of knowing what goes on behind the mask . . . But the eyes dart nervously from side to side: beneath the mask are imprisoned unknown emotions, fears, desperation.[17]

The effect which Judy/Madeleine exerts is on the unstable Scottie alone. The savvy Midge rapidly understands what is really motivating her former beau, as she banters with him: "Was it fun? Is she pretty?," even though the solemn and extremely hypocritical Scottie, who tells Midge nothing of his risqué encounter with Madeleine, continues to believe that he is the noble protector and Judy/Madeleine, whom Scottie distortedly perceives as, exactly as the adventurous knight *en fleur* Felipe Montero perceives Aura, the victimized and helpless damsel in distress.

In *Aura,* from the very start Consuelo makes a shrewd plea to Felipe's narcissism, as the advertisement he reads seems to be directed to him alone, thus infusing him with a privileged status. This same exclusivity seems to be promised by Aura's gaze and even by Consuelo's tantalizing advertisement:

> You're reading the advertisement: an offer like this isn't made every day. You read it and reread it. It seems to be addressed to you and nobody else. (A, 3)

Unlike the straightforward, unpretentious but essentially unexciting Midge, Judy/Madeleine exercises an erotic attraction over Scottie from the very start. The contrast in the effect exerted on Scottie by Midge and Judy/Madeleine is underscored in the very way that both women are photographed. The candor of Midge, and her willingness to discuss any subject with Scottie, including the details of the new brassiere that she is sketching,

---

[17] See Robin Wood, *Hitchcock's Films* (London: A. Zwemmer, 1965), p. 74. Subsequent references are included in the text, preceded by HF.

Figure 31. Constant red and green contrasts imbue Vertigo with unmitigated tension. Judy cleverly projects vulnerability and wide-eyed innocence.

Figure 32. Judy/Madeleine as death-haunted. Striking black and white ensemble signifies Madeleine as beautiful, deadly paradox, irresistible for Scottie.

invented by the engineer who designed it on the model of the cantilever bridge—Midge's matter-of-fact approach to sexual allure contrasts so markedly with Madeleine's smoldering sensuality, not bold but softly insistent—are emphasized in the way that the witty and sensitive but unenticing Midge is photographed, directly, and with the use of a midshot and normative lighting. In contrast with this conventional presentation, the first time Judy/Madeleine is evoked, it is in a distant shot, and from the back—as Hitchcock cautiously focuses in an entrancingly slow traveling shot on her naked back. Instead of a direct focus on this unknown woman, the camera first concentrates on a rapt Scottie, then languorously pans left across the elegance of *Ernie's.* And the blood-red, ornately designed wallpaper of the luxurious dining room heightens the sensuality of the silent, mysterious Madeleine. In addition, the musical theme that begins when Madeleine is introduced, is a slow and haunting one, a theme that will accompany her throughout the film and that underscores her enigmatic nature. Wood (HF, 78) has remarked that Judy/Madeleine does not walk but seems to glide across the floor. Here again her ephemeral nature, the circumstance that she is not a human being, as is Midge, but an ideal, a ghost, is underscored. As she leaves *Ernie's*, Judy/Madeleine pauses, and her face is tilted upward. The lighting here is essential; she is backlit and her face surrounded by a brilliant glow. This stunning, unforgettable cameo shot underscores Judy/Madeleine as a twentieth century Venus, the goddess of love. In this shot Madeleine appears calm, even hopeful and very self-possessed, with no hint of the agitation she will later make manifest to an avuncular Scottie. Scottie essentially is a helpless child as he is initially evoked in Midge's apartment, yet one who is compelled to play the role of bold and commanding hero not merely to impress Madeleine but to restore his shattered male ego. The mesmeric effect that the unearthly, sphynxlike Madeleine is exerting on Scottie, who falls in love with her at first sight, is thus underscored. Similarly, in *Aura,* the hapless Felipe is infatuated by the alluring girl and from the start surrenders his identity to her—just as the weak Llorente more than a half century earlier had been totally subservient to his beloved Consuelo, becoming not merely her husband but her fanatic worshipper.

In *Vertigo,* the imprisonment of the characters in the past is given a stunning visualization by Hitchcock, through an expert combination of camera movement and back projection. For example, a culminating moment in *Vertigo* is when Scottie's meticulous transformation of a resisting and at best reluctant Judy into Madeleine is complete, and he is at last able to embrace her and make love to her. Yet instead of experiencing joy, Scottie is extremely troubled. Perhaps it is because upon kissing the transformed Judy, he realizes that this is the very same Madeleine whom he had kissed before, whom he had thought to be dead—and not merely his elaborate re-creation of Madeleine. Rather than salvation, Scottie's fanatic recreation of Judy/Madeleine signifies the destruction of Scottie. Here in Hitchcock is developed the Pygmalion theme in reverse—it is the contemporary equivalent to the ancient male sculptor himself who is turned into stone after breathing life into his marble goddess. The camera now begins a slow, sinuous vertiginous movement as it encircles the lovers—once again in Hitchcock as in Fuentes, technique masterfully conveys theme— and in the background, as a cinematic dramatization of Scottie's mental imagery, is reprised the scene where Scottie embraced and kissed a paradoxically willing and determinedly evasive Judy/Madeleine at the San Juan Bautista Mission in the livery stable just prior to her rush to the top of the tower and presumably, from the point of view of Scottie, to her death. Here the camera of Hitchcock in its serpentine movements that signify incarceration and asphyxiation for both doomed lovers is the twentieth century equivalent to Greek mythology, the enormous serpents sent by the Greek god Poseidon and Roman deity Neptune, god of the sea, to wrap themselves slowly and lethally around the anguished Laocöon and his sons and strangle them to death.

The revolving back projection in the room of Judy at the highly symbolic Empire Hotel emphasizes that Scottie is unable to experience a present, that all moments of his relationship with Judy are but *simulacra*, pale reflections of his original relationship with his beloved Madeleine. Rather than bliss or even contentment, expressions that one might expect now that Scottie's long desired goal has at last been reached, his expression is one of consternation and even of dread. Yet at this point Scottie rather than making any connection between the Judy Barton whom he has now totally transformed into Madeleine, and the Madeleine whom Gavin Elster has transformed into his wife, remains oblivious to the circumstance that he is once more being toyed with by Judy/Madeleine, and instead, very similar to the way in which the puppet Felipe will do, plunges unthinkingly into a devastating maelstrom.

Similarly, in *Aura,* behavior in the present is but a simulacrum of the past. When Felipe dines with Consuelo and Aura, four places are set at the table; once more Felipe's presence is necessary in order to conjure up Llorente. Felipe's victimized state is visualized by Fuentes in the grotesque, poorly sewn doll that the hapless protagonist encounters near his plate, with its stuffing coming out. The doll symbolizes the doll-like Felipe himself, his listlessness and his pliability. It is also a voodoo doll—the emergence of the stuffing symbolizes the imminence of the destruction of Felipe. Yet instead of destroying the doll, Felipe alternately rejects and then caresses it—an indication of his marked ambivalence toward Consuelo, his attempts to flee her realm and his desire to negate the Self, not to think, to let himself sink into oblivion—paralleling what Scottie in his relationship with the newly created Judy/Madeleine does:

> Beside your plate, under your napkin, there's an object you start caressing with your fingers: a clumsy little rag doll, filled with a powder that trickles from its badly sewn shoulder; its face is drawn with India ink, and its body is naked, sketched with a few brush strokes. You eat the cold supper—liver, tomatoes, wine—with your right hand while holding the doll in your left. (A, 97-99)

Like every aspect of the world of *Aura,* the nakedness of the doll has a dual significance: like the meal of kidneys and wine that act as aphrodisiacs, the doll symbolizes Felipe's function as an object of erotic desire for Aura, as well as Felipe's eagerness to consummate their relationship. Yet it also signifies his extreme vulnerability, and its shoddy construction symbolizes the basic contempt with which Consuelo holds Felipe as well as the fact that Felipe himself is on the verge of being destroyed.

When Aura embraces Felipe and begins to waltz with him, her behavior once again is to conjure up the past—the waltzes that the young and ravishingly beautiful Consuelo danced with Llorente in the extravagant court of Maximilian at the royal palace of Chapultepec that the Austrian Archduke and his captivating young Belgian princess had constructed in their exotic new kingdom. Consuelo at the same time is dancing with the empty tunic of Llorente. Paralleling the sensually whirling movement of the camera around the two fated lovers in *Vertigo* is the masterful style of Fuentes, one that with its breathless pyramiding of images conveys the giddiness of Felipe, as he allows himself to be seduced by Aura and to be caught up in her bizarre spell. The male protagonists of both *Aura* and *Vertigo* are evoked as willess, fated beings. The exquisite style of Fuentes itself is exceedingly cinematic, with its emphasis on incessant motion, as the movement of the waltz is paralleled by the erotic movements of the hands of Aura. Here Fuentes utilizes a series of action verbs that form a crescendo of motion and signify how rapidly and thoroughly Felipe is entrapped.

It is significant that although Scottie in *Vertigo* has been engaged to the pert at times even flippant, but thoroughly common–sensical Midge, it is she herself who breaks off their relationship, sensing perhaps that Scottie is not—nor ever will be—in love with her. And when Scottie asks her out, Midge demurs—Midge does not want to renew their romantic relationship, afraid of being hurt again by the seemingly sensitive but in fact perversely self-absorbed, extremely narcissistic Scottie. At the precise moment when a seemingly willing Scottie makes the invitation, Midge is suddenly seen in a dramatic and painful close-up, to underscore how much she longs to accept the continuation of the relationship but how futile she views it. Here Hitchcock affectively contrasts the nonchalance bordering on indifference of Scottie with the poignant, deep emotional commitment of Midge—a commitment that foreshadows the devotion of Judy Barton to Scottie at the end of the film and which parallels the abiding commitment of the captivatingly beautiful Lisa Fremont to L.B. Jefferies in Hitchcock's famed *Rear Window*. And indeed, Scottie constantly looks to the comforting, consoling Midge not for erotic love but for maternal support, as when he suffers an attack of vertigo in her apartment. Here Scottie quickly becomes reduced to a child first learning how to walk and anxiously seeking the praise of his mother, as he tentatively climbs up her three-stepped kitchen stool, then faints as the result of a sudden attack of vertigo as he gazes out the window and falls like a rag doll into her arms.

When Scottie jumps into the San Francisco Bay to rescue Judy/Madeleine, whom he believes has attempted to commit suicide, his male vanity is suddenly restored. It is significant that even though he believes that Madeleine is someone else's wife, after rescuing her, he takes her back to his apartment and strips off her wet clothing to leave her naked in his bed, all under the guise of being her avuncular guardian. It is evident that he desires to make love to her. Yet after he receives an opportunely planned telephone call from Gavin Elster, who feigns great concern for the welfare of his "wife," Scottie finds that the Madeleine who has always proved elusive to him—the Madeleine with whom he has fallen in love—has once again quietly and rapidly disappeared along with her underwear—an action that only increases his desire.

The effect is to augment the confusion surrounding Judy/Madeleine, to again underscore her essence for the dazed Scottie—that of a phantom being. Similarly, Aura, who one moment is in front of Felipe, suddenly disappears, only to reappear at night, as a succubus. Sensing that Felipe's unconsciousness is attempting to warn him of the doom that will befall him in her realm, the shrewd Consuelo materializes Aura and has her appear naked before him, so that the increasingly bewildered Felipe—paralleling the increasingly confused and now aroused Scottie—awakens from his nightmare not to reality but to another form of fantasy, to being caressed by the seductive Aura, who has rapidly escalated their relationship:

> When you're bored with them you undress slowly, get into bed, and fall asleep at once, and for the first time in years you dream, dream of only one thing, of a fleshless hand that comes toward you with a bell, screaming that you should go away; and when that face with its empty eye-sockets comes close to yours, you wake up with a muffled cry, sweating, and feel those lips murmuring in a low voice, consoling and asking you for affection. You reach out your

> hands to find that other body, that naked body with a key dangling from its neck, and when you recognize the key you recognize the woman who is lying over you, kissing you, kissing your whole body. (A, 75-77)

To make his behavior with the wife of Gavin Elster—supposedly a long lost college friend—morally acceptable to his conscience, Scottie quotes to Judy an "ancient Chinese proverb" according to which a person who saves the life of another is responsible for that *individual for the rest of her life*. Thus Scottie rationalizes his falling in love with a married woman. Similarly, Felipe is constrained to provide a moral purpose for his involvement with Aura; he does so by fashioning himself the valiant hero who will rescue the girl—whom he chooses to view as a tyrannized victim—from the clutches of her aunt.

The theme of impossible love, love rendered impossible either because of egomania, as in the case of both Gavin Elster and Consuelo, or because of death, as in the case of Scottie with Madeleine and Consuelo with Llorente, is underscored in both Hitchcock's hallucinatory film and Fuentes's supernatural novella. The love of the self-effacing Llorente for his dazzlingly beautiful bride is an all-consuming and self-abasing love that is never reciprocated by the supercilious and egomaniacal Consuelo. Instead, she reduces Llorente, as she will Felipe sixty years later, to a mere pawn or instrument of her fanatic desire to perpetuate herself. Similarly, both Gavin Elster and Scottie reduce Judy Barton to a mere pawn, even though she is sincerely—at times even desperately—in love with both of them. And the cruel behavior of these two males in the twentieth century is but the repetition of the monstrousness of the husband, never named, the controller of Carlotta in the nineteenth century, who re-created her to suit his whims and once she had been established in her role, shattered that role to exert his despotic power—just as Gavin Elster does in the case of Judy Barton, and just as Scottie will do after he discovers that Judy had deceived him. The intense fatalism of *Vertigo* is emphasized by Spoto, who insightfully analyzes the irony of Scottie's final transformation of the earthy and even coarse Judy Barton into the refined and ethereal Madeleine—a transfiguration that brings Scottie only renewed misery:

Figure 33. Agitated waters of Pacific Ocean symbolize turbulent union of benighted detective and Elster's puppet.

Figure 34. Midge desperately attempts to enter Scottie's secret world—and is permanently expelled, just as Carlotta was. Note how sky has blackened in contrast with Carlotta original.

> The moment has been recaptured. The woman of his dreams has been reborn. The romantic fantasy has been realized. All that can follow is tragedy. Herrmann's sensuous score is now an appropriate variation on the "Liebestod" or "Love-Death" from "Tristan and Isolde," which suggests death as love's ultimate, desired communion. [18]

Aura is one of the most perfect of the creations of Fuentes. It is so intricate a work, a *novella* so imbued with multiple meanings, that it can be analyzed line by line, as if it were an extensive poem. Every image, scene, character and event relates to every other one, like the strands in a spider's web. Similarly *Vertigo*, initally greeted with skepticism, but now considered by many critics to be Alfred Hitchcock's masterpiece, is a work in which Hitchcock's painstaking artistic perfectionism is demonstrated in scene after scene. In both *Vertigo* and *Aura,* the lighting is extremely important. Light is not only a physical force, it is metaphysical in nature, as it symbolizes the quests of the protagonists for mental and spiritual illumination, for the key to understanding the perplexing circumstances in which they find themselves. And, in the deepest sense, the constant interplay between darkness and light signifies the contrast between damnation and salvation. The extreme care that Hitchcock takes with the lighting is emphasized by Spoto:

> And at the California Palace of the Legion of Honor a guard remembers that Hitchcock took a week to shoot the brief, wordless scene there; that Hitchcock consulted the museum curator, and that the crew waited for the proper light, entering the translucent ceiling, to combine with the electric light within to get exactly the right effect. (AH, 297)

---

[18] Consult Donald Spoto, *The Art of Alfred Hitchcock* (New York: Doubleday, 1976), p. 330. Subsequent references are included in the text, preceded by AH.

Both Judy/Madeleine and Aura are constantly linked with the light, that seems to underscore their angelic nature, and for both Scottie and Felipe, new life. This is seen from the very start in *Vertigo,* in the brilliant light that envelops and deifies Madeleine transforming, even transfiguring her into a Greek goddess as she departs majestically from *Ernie's.* Even Madeleine's hairstyle is fashioned after that of a Greek deity like Aphrodite, or Venus, the ancient Roman goddess of love. And the very name of Aura, with its allusion to the poetic Aurora, the goddess of the dawn, seems to indicate her association with rebirth, not only for Consuelo but for the stunted Felipe.

Here is indicated that Felipe, like the dangling Scottie, has previously been frustrated in love. The radiant Aura stands in contrast to the palpable gloom in the house of Consuelo. And yet just as the light that so transfigures Judy/Madeleine is a false light, because the treacherous Judy will lead both Scottie and ultimately herself not to self-transcendence but into an inextricable trap, so too does the light which Aura bears not truly illuminating but deceptive for Felipe. Aura leads him but further into the labyrinthine world of Consuelo. Unlike the solicitous Ariadne, who provides the thread that enables Theseus to find his way out of the labyrinth after he has slain the Minotaur, the maleficent Aura with her lamp leads Felipe straight to the "Minotaur," to the ominous table at which Felipe will be drugged with the wine that he so eagerly imbibes.

Like Aura, Judy/Madeleine is continually linked with light, a light that at times seems supernatural in effect. Unlike Aura, who is submissive to Consuelo and ambivalent toward Felipe, Judy is more and more self-abasing to a petulant and ever more demanding Scottie. When the transformed Judy finally emerges into her bedroom at the Empire Hotel, complying even with Scottie's request that she change her last shred of being as Judy Barton—her hair style—into the tightly bound, whorlish bun of Madeleine, and after initially demurring Judy again concedes, she is enveloped in an eery greenish light. Although Hitchcock's vision is not supernatural, and the light has a rational explanation, for Judy/Madeleine is caught in the reflected glow of the huge green neon sign outside the window of her hotel room, it nonetheless seems as if she were a supernatural being—as if the dead Madeleine truly were brought back to life.

The nightmare that the apparently highly agitated Madeleine/Judy repeatedly experiences is one of a labyrinth that is lined with mirrors, and at the end of the labyrinth there is only darkness, the darkness of death—an indication of the deep *thanatos* impulse that is seemingly afflicting the tormented Madeleine. Significantly, what begins as a fanciful concoction of Gavin Elster painstakingly conveyed to be recited by his apt pupil Judy/Madeleine—the labyrinth lined with mirrors at the end of which is death, turns into macabre reality—the sinuous death-saturated labyrinth at the end characterizes the steep, twisting steps leading up to the tower at the San Juan Bautista Mission—steps that are treacherous and dimly lit. Here we encounter human mirrors—the black-robed nun suddenly emerging from the darkness is perceived by a dazed and hysteric Judy as an emanation of the real Madeleine Elster come back to life to kill her. When Judy/Madeleine lures Scottie to the forest of gigantic sequoias, there is once more an interplay between light, here frail and blotted out by the immense trees, and the threatening darkness.

Similarly, in *Aura,* light from beginning to end is imbued with a deep spiritual significance. In contrast with the darkness of the rest of her house, Consuelo is surrounded by the blazing lights of the votive lamps, light that is sufficient to blind Felipe, and which signifies how much he is deceived by the person who pretends to be a model of piety. It is significant that at the very end of *Aura*, all of the votive lamps have been extinguished—to indicate the triumph of the demonic. This is a victory that has been adumbrated from the very start of the shadow suffused narrative.

At the very end, only the light of the moon illuminates the setting. But once again this light is deceptive; it underscores the benumbed state of the hypnotized Felipe, who has now been transformed totally into the Other, who without realizing it is making love not to his cherished Aura but to the toothless hag Consuelo. Light in *Aura* as in *Vertigo* cannot truly illuminate, for although it reveals to him the features of Consuelo, not those of Aura, Felipe continues to embrace the disintegrating old woman, for he is now Llorente come back from the tomb to continue his adoration of his beloved Consuelo:

> . . . you're touching her withered breasts when a ray of moonlight shines in and surprises you, shines in through a chink in the wall that the rats have chewed open, an eye that lets in a beam of silvery moonlight. It falls on Aura's eroded face, as brittle and yellowed as the memoirs, as creased with wrinkles as the photographs. (A, 145)

Here light becomes dynamic, assertive—yet, ironically, illuminating nothing for the permanently entrapped Felipe. A Gothic touch, reminiscent of the scurrying rats in Murnau's shocking masterpiece *Nosferatu* that has so strongly impacted Fuentes, is seen in the fusion of beauty and vileness—the chink in the wall allowing the mesmerizing moonlight to prevail—the hole gnawed by the ubiquitous rats that proliferate in Consuelo's mansion just as they do around the coffins in which the zombielike Nosferatu travels. Lighting, and, in particular, the use of *chiaroscuro*, the paradoxical blending of darkness and light, are extremely important in the two major types of film that have significantly influenced both Hitchcock and Fuentes—the German Expressionist film of the silent era, of the twenties, and the American *film noir* of the forties. Films such as Robert Wiene's mystifying, highly artistic *Das Kabinett des Dr. Caligari* (1919), in which lights and shadows were painted right onto the sets, and Friedrich Wilhelm Murnau's chilling evocation of the Dracula theme entitled *Nosferatu* (1921), in which the horrifying shadow of the bloodsucking monster, eerily played by Max Shreck, seems to acquire a demonic life of its own, as the shadow falls across the breast of the willing victim of sacrifice, Nina, have had a great impact on novels of Fuentes such as *Cambio de piel* (1968).[19] Hitchcock made films such as the Expressionist thriller *The Lodger* (1926) in the silent era. In the Hollywood *film noir* of the forties and early fifties, in films such as *The Dark Corner* (1946), directed by Henry Hathaway, and *Night and the City* (1950), directed by

---

[19] For an extensive analysis of the impact of *Das Kabinett des Doktor Caligari* on the characterization and structure of *Cambio de piel*, consult my study, "The Artist Manqué in Fuentes's *Cambio de piel*," *Symposium*, XXXI, 2 (Summer, 1977), 126-150.

Jules Dassin, the stark contrast between the ever-menacing darkness and the stabbing light does much to underscore the atmosphere of betrayal, violence, and murder, and has influenced films of mystery and terror of Hitchcock such as *Psycho* (1960), as well as several novels of Fuentes.

In *Aura,* the feeble light that enters the dwelling of Consuelo indicates the impossibility of true salvation, both for Felipe and for Consuelo herself:

> You close the door and look up at the skylight that serves as a roof. You smile when you find that the evening light is blinding compared with the darkness in the rest of the house . . . (A, 31)

Similarly, in *Vertigo,* darkness constantly envelops the light. It is from the darkness at the top of the tower that emerges the ghostly form that Judy Barton in her terror and guilt believes is the resurrected Madeleine, and which so startles her that she plunges from the open window of the tower to her death.

In both *Vertigo* and *Aura,* it is exceedingly ironic that the male protagonists are investigators, because both prefer to remain in blissful ignorance rather than to ferret out the truth concerning the real, malicious nature of the persons with whom they have fallen in love.

Just as the eery Madeleine is continually suffused with an unearthly radiance, so also is the enigmatic Aura:

> Sitting on the bed, you try to make out the source of that diffuse, opaline light that hardly lets you distinguish the objects in the room, and the presence of Aura, from the golden atmosphere that surrounds them. She sees you looking up, trying to find where it comes from. You can tell from her voice that she's kneeling down in front of you.
> "The sky is neither high nor low. It's over us and under us at the same time." (A, 105)

The mysterious opaline light, which as light always functions in Aura, confuses rather than illuminates, is the perfect backdrop for the ambiguous words of Aura concerning the location of the "cielo," which itself is a word with a dual meaning, literally "sky" and figuratively, "heaven." If heaven is below them, then they are in a type of paradise; if it is above, then they may exist in a hellworld.

Testimony to the significant way in which *Vertigo* has influenced Fuentes is that even the patterning of light in both works is very similar. In both film and *novella* there appears a circle of light that itself is surrounded by darkness, to indicate the fatalistic nature of the works, that the male protagonists are being deceived, and also the inevitability that the light—signifying new hope, new life, redemption—will ultimately be consumed by the darkness. The expert use of lighting by Hitchcock is analyzed by Wood, who comments on a scene in which Judy writes a letter of confession to Scottie, a missive that the endlessly vacillating Judy will never send:

> As she writes her letter the camera half circles her, and the shade on her table lamp fills a large area of the screen, at one point obliterating her. The image recalls the scene where Madeleine came to Scottie at dawn to tell him her dream. She sat at his writing table, leaning forward in the light from his table-lamp as she described her terror of darkness. The effect was of the pitiful inadequacy of human illumination to combat the enveloping metaphysical darkness . . . by linking the two scenes through this image (the lamp and shade get great visual emphasis in both) Hitchcock links Judy's present situation and her inability to cope with it with Madeleine's darkness. (HF, 95)

When Judy/Madeleine is in Scottie's apartment, she is often left half in light and half in darkness. This *chiaoscuro* effect again symbolizes her dual nature, and her duplicity. Similarly, in *Aura,* whenever there is light, it seems only to intensify the darkness that it can never dispel:

> You make an effort to control yourself, diverting your attention away from her by listening to the imperceptible movement of a door behind you—it must lead to the kitchen—or by separating the two different elements that

> make up the room: the compact circle of light around the candelabra, illuminating the table and one carved wall, and the larger circle of darkness surrounding it. (A, 43)

This same fatalistic patterning of a small circle of light surrounded by darkness is repeated when Felipe encounters a lubricious Aura and is led to participate in a Black Mass, the result of which is the voluntary surrendering by Felipe of his identity, of his soul, to Aura/Consuelo:

> You push it open without knocking and go into that bare room, where a circle of light reveals the bed, the huge Mexican crucifix, and the woman who comes toward you when the door is closed. (A, 103)

A fascinating use of the contrast between light and darkness to signify both a psychological state and a metaphysical one is found in the brief encounter between Scottie, similar to Felipe an professional investigator of the past, and the person, Pop Liebl, the owner of the *Argosy Book Shop* to whom Scottie has gone for information on the legend of Carlotta. The very name of the book shop testifies to the meticulosness of the construction of *Vertigo*. The name *Argosy* alludes to the Greek hero Jason, the commander of a group of adventurers, the Argonauts, who in ancient Greek mythology set out to obtain the magical golden fleece—which in *Vertigo* becomes transmuted into the gleaming, golden-haired Madeleine. The disastrous outcome of Jason's quest, as he is compelled again and again to halt his journey to pick up the pieces of his children that his vengeful wife Medea has scattered over the sea in monstrous retribution for her husband's infidelity, foreshadows the doom that surrounds the desperate searches of both Scottie Ferguson and Felipe Montero in the contemporary world. Scottie seeks not scholarly or documented information but rather for oral, highly romanticized history, or as Midge states, "who shot who on the Embarcadero." These words of Midge, initially uttered lightheartedly, achieve sinister significance when we realize that the office of the velvet-voiced murderer Gavin Elster is on the infamous Embarcadero.

When the garrulous Pop Liebl begins his fatalistic narrative, evoking the tragic destiny of Carlotta, it is broad daylight, yet when he finishes his account, night has suddenly, and extremely fatalistically, descended. It is almost as if the very words of Pop Liebl had the power to conjure up the darkness. Similarly, at the very end of *Aura,* the darkness is doubled. Here again, as in *Vertigo,* the palpable gloom symbolizes both the ignorance of the male protagonist, his desire not to know, not to understand, and the ultimate triumph of the demonic Consuelo: "When you look up from the pillow, you find you're in darkness. Night has fallen" (A, 139). At the end of *Aura* as at the beginning, Felipe still naively believes that his employer is a devoted *beata* and that she has been absent the whole day.

Vertigo presents a similar, intricate patterning of both deceit and self-deception on the part of Scottie Ferguson. In the first half of the film, the naive and desperate Scottie wants to believe that Judy/Madeleine is falling in love with him. Still later, even though he strongly suspects that the Judy Barton whom he has transformed into Madeleine is the real Madeleine, he again suppresses his misgivings, so frantically does he yearn for the return of Madeleine from beyond the grave, a return that once again diminishes his overwhelming and indeed inexpungible feelings of inadequacy and guilt. Both Judy Barton and Scottie Ferguson, like Felipe Montero and Aura, are tools, the latter pair reduced to but instruments of Consuelo, the former debased into mere puppets of the always behind-the-scenes Gavin Elster. This is why Scottie turns so savagely on Judy at the very end, after he realizes that she was first and foremost the creation, the "Madeleine," of another, superior—and, ultimately and pervertedly successful creator—Gavin Elster, the most forbidding presence in Hitchcock's film, and the one who wears the most intricate mask—of urbaneness, concern, and even compassion, similar to the masks worn by several of Hitchcock's smooth villains and, of course paralleled by the myriad masks of the redoubtable Consuelo in *Aura*.

The way in which Madeleine moves through space, with a gliding movement that underscores her etherealness, also characterizes the ghostly Aura. It is significant that just as Scottie has been unable to establish a meaningful relationship with any human being, Felipe too has no attachments in the real world. For both of these pathetic males, the illusory woman is much more important than the terrestrial one. The sudden appearance of a distraught Madeleine to Scottie Ferguson in the middle of the night is paralled by the sudden, ghostly appearance of Aura who almost fuse herself to an accommodating Felipe:

> You look around and a girl is standing there, a girl whose whole body you can't see because she's standing so close to you and her arrival was so unexpected, without the slightest sound—not even those sounds that can't be heard but are real anyway because they're remembered immediately afterwards, because in spite of everything they're louder than the silence that accompanies them. (A, 25)

Similarly, in Hitchcock's *Vertigo*, when Judy/Madeleine unexpectedly appears at the apartment door of Scottie, it is still night. When Scottie opens the door, Madeleine's face is still bathed in shadow, but then it is suddenly illuminated. In a sense, this is the opposite of what has occurred in the *Argosy Book Shop*—Judy/Madeleine seems to have the power to dispel the darkness, the power of salvation—similar to the magical powers that the radiant Aura seems to possess. Yet, as we have seen, both of these light bearers provide only false illumination.

Few authors have as much sensitivity to the poetic, dramatic, and cinematic power of lighting as does Fuentes. In novels as diverse in scope and intent as *Terra nostra* and *La cabeza de la hidra, Cambio de piel* and *Gringo viejo,* the interplay of light and darkness serves to create mood and markedly to increase the suspense—and the mystery—or to establish an atmosphere of the transcendental or the otherworldly. Light in the ineluctable *Terra nostra,* which delves extensively into the myths of the ancient Aztec gods and goddesses, at times becomes vivified, personified, imbued with an almost tangible radiance. Light at times even becomes a central personage in a particular scene, such as this evocation of the dread god Tezcatlipoca in his animal form:

> And in my dream, Sire, I saw the Lady of the Butterflies. She was accompanied by a monstrous animal black as night, for there was nothing about it that reflected any light; it was like a shadow on four paws, huge and hairy. In vain I looked for its eyes. . . The woman with whom I had made love beside the ruined temple was bathed in an aureole of hazy light; the animal that was her companion began to dig on the earth, and as it dug, it growled terribly. When it had completed its task, the diffuse light of my dream became an oblique golden column emanating from the very center of the heavens; it fell into the hole excavated by the beast. That intense golden light was like a flowing river and as it poured into the depths of the cavity, the animal covered it up, throwing dirt upon it with its twisted feet, and the more dirt it scratched into the hole, the more the light faded. The Lady of the Butterflies wept.[20]

Here as in *Aura,* Fuentes dramatizes an incessant struggle between the powers of darkness, in the form of the god of night, Tezcatlipoca, and the powers of light, here personified by a female goddess who is linked with the consort of Quetzalcóatl—the love goddess Quetzalpilli. Although at this point the evil forces linked with the night gain the upper hand, *Terra nostra* as a whole is one of the most positive of Fuentes's works. At the very end there is a transcendental reunion between the youth Polo Febo, symbolizing the redemptive god Quetzalcóatl, and Quetzalpilli, at the symbolic time of dawn, to signify a new millennium. Fuentes thus poeticizes one of the most fundamental of the Aztec myths, that of the incessant struggle against the forces of the night, which terrified the Aztecs, because the sun, which they considered their redeemer, had disappeared, had "died" and the only way that the sun could be brought back to life was through human blood sacrifice. Since the sun rose and set daily, incessant sacrifice to propitiate the dread sun god Huitzilopochtli was thus required.

---

[20] Consult Carlos Fuentes, *Terra nostra* (Mexico: Joaquín Mortiz, 1975), p. 417. The superb translation, by Margaret Sayers Peden, is from *Terra nostra* (New York: Farrar, Straus, and Giroux, 1976), pp. 410-411.

Figure 35. Carriage house at San Juan Bautista Mission. First evoked as reality and then as ghost-ridden flashback in Scottie's increasingly unhinged mind.

Figure 36. Shadows symbolize marked ambiguities: is Madeleine complicit in a murder or is she attempting to halt the crime?

In *Vertigo,* the *chiaoscuro* effect, the blending of light and darkness, carries throughout the film, in both interior and exterior lighting. For example, as Scottie pursues Judy/Madeleine through the alley to the flower shop, one half of the alley is in shadow, the other half in light. Scottie is photographed not directly but only as a shadow, as the camera focuses on the opaque glass of the window in the door through which he enters the shop, evoked as another zone of quietness, great beauty, and unfathomable mystery. Similarly, the immense colonnades at the Mission of San Juan Bautista are photographed at a time of day in which they are half in light and half in shadow. This *chiaoscuro* effect, which adds immeasurably to both the beauty and the mystery of *Vertigo,* is reflected even in the way that Judy/Madeleine dresses, with a white overcoat and black gloves. Here again the exacting nature of the art of Hitchcock is evident, as he waits for just the right moment of the day to photograph San Francisco alleyways and the San Juan Bautista columns and to evoke the immense forest of sequoias at a time when there is a precise contrast between darkness and sunlight. These incessant light and dark contrasts underscore the complexity of the two central characters, Scottie and Judy/Madeleine, as well as the moral ambiguity of both of them. In addition, the *chiaoscuro* contrasts accentuate the intense mood of poetic revery and rapidly deepening mystery of this film that in its fusion of beauty and horror, Gothic terror and languorous sensuality, reflects the influence of another master of mystery and suspense, and of love that conquers the boundaries even of death, Edgar Allan Poe, in works like "Ligeia" and "The Fall of the House of Usher"—stories of the fantastic and the supernatural that have exerted so great an influence on Hispanic American writers like Carlos Fuentes and Julio Cortázar, the latter who translated into Spanish the complete works of the spellbinding master of suspense, horror, the macabre and the supernatural, Edgar Allan Poe.

The ambiguity that has characterized Judy/Madeleine from the start is present even in the final scene of *Vertigo.* Manifesting a cold rage, Scottie literally drags a protesting Judy—who perhaps feels that Scottie will hurl her off the tower just as Gavin Elster has done with his wife— by the throat, up the last steps to the very top of the bell tower. Although Judy now seems frantically to desire to emerge forever from behind the mask of Madeleine and makes a sincere and seemingly heartfelt plea to Scottie to begin their relationship anew, as themselves—as they really are, and not as man and ghost, we never know whether Judy in reality is declaring her steadfast love for him or merely buying time. Terrified that Scottie may kill her in vengeance for having tricked him, driven him to insanity and destroyed his precious dream of Madeleine, the wily Judy may only be humoring a murderous madman in order to save her life.

It is extremely ironic that the obsessive nightmare which Judy/Madeleine in the sequoia forest has so poignantly confessed to Scottie—a nightmare that has presumably been a key part of Gavin Elster's intricate deceit—is at the very end converted into a monstrous reality for the victimized Judy Barton. As Judy/Madeleine from out of her somnambulistic state utters to an increasingly agitated Scottie in the hauntingly poignant forest scene:

> Searching for something . . . Then I started to walk to the church . . .
> Then the darkness closed in and I was alone in the dark . . . being pulled into the darkness, not to wake up . . .

Being devoured by the darkness is for her the equivalent of death. Perhaps following the directions of Gavin Elster, perhaps artfully improvising her role, Judy/Madeleine cleverly dramatizes her nightmare to make it even more convincing to Scottie, as she first breaks away from him to plunge into the darkened forest, then begs to be taken by him back into the light. With horrible irony, at the end of *Vertigo* Scottie himself will drag Judy/Madeleine into the darkness at the top of the tower that is a prelude to her violent death. The nightmare of Carlotta that Judy/Madeleine has appropriated as her own is finally and horrifyingly actualized.

At the very end of *Aura,* light again becomes a significant presence. Once again Felipe, in a characteristic gesture, turns away from the light—indicating his desire not to know or to be forced to confront harsh and onerous reality. Instead, Felipe plunges into the comforting and obliterating darkness, which signifies self-negation and oblivion. Just as Scottie in his dazed state even at the very end, when he knows consciously that Judy has been all along only pretending to be Madeleine, continues to address her as "Madeleine," so too does Felipe, who cannot perceive that he is kissing the withered Consuelo, refer to her as his beloved Aura. At the end of both works, it is the fantasy identity—the identity from beyond the tomb—Felipe become Llorente and Scottie still questing for the dead Madeleine, that predominates.

Light that is linked not with clarity, not with revealing the truth of a situation or character, but rather with deepening a mystery, is also found in Fuentes's novel *Gringo viejo,* which traces the development of the young, headstrong school teacher Harriet Winslow, who grows up in a home in Washington, D.C. that has been abandoned by her father, who has been sent to Cuba to fight in the Spanish-American War and who remains there for the rest of his life with his Afro-Cuban mistress, finding the erotic love and the happiness that his marriage to his dour, sexually repressed wife in the United States could not provide him—signifying Fuentes's dramatic contrast between the sexually repressive North American society and the tropical sensuality and exuberance and *joie de vivre* of the Latin American, in this case the Caribbean experience. Light becomes a childhood companion for the lonely Harriet; it seems in a way to substitute for her absent father and to symbolize his secret life, which Harriet in her febrile imagination re-creates. It is an intriguing and spectral light, one that draws Harriet away from the tedious and sterile existence with her severely alienated mother and even adumbrates Harriet's subsequent rebellion and departure from Washington D.C., to plunge into the violent, sensuous world of revolutionary Mexico and the *villista* rebels. In Fuentes's world as in that of Alfred Hitchcock, light is much more than a mere accessory, it achieves a motion and purpose all its own, and becomes a significant character in both worlds. As throughout Hitchcock's films, from *Vertigo* and *Rear Window* to *The Birds* and *Marnie*, the physical is symbolic of the metaphysical; the decaying mansion inhabited by Harriet and a young girl is symbolic of the rotting relationship between her severely alienated parents:

> She had spent her childhood haunted by the brilliant yellow light she watched moving slowly from floor to floor in a

> recently constructed but already decaying mansion on Sixteenth Street. Hidden behind stubborn summer shrubs on a hill that plunged abruptly from an abandoned tennis court to a lawn covered with dead magnolias, she stared at the light as slowly it came and went, melting what must have been the soft interior, the buttery recesses behind the facade of carved stone, cut and assembled to resemble a fantasy of a Second Empire mansion, pompous and dank. [21]

Once more in Fuentes, the concrete symbolizes the abstract—the newly constructed but already disintegrating mansion symbolizes, along with the desolate tennis court and the dead magnolias, the sterile lifelessness of Harriet's mother, which the headstrong girl, thoroughly identifying with her absent father, does not wish to repeat, but which she at the end is compelled to re-enact.

Light in *Gringo viejo* operates as a fantastic, poetic, and , above all, as a redemptive phenomenon. The idealistic Harriet desperately seeks to transform her isolated and alienated mother, to resurrect her emotionally and spiritually, by means of a transference of light. The intense will of Harriet on the level of the main narrative operates to resuscitate the ghosts of her former lover, Tomás Arroyo and of her father surrogate, Ambrose Bierce. Just as Harriet will create for herself a new father to compensate for the one who never returns, she also attempts to give birth to a new mother:

> She didn't realize it, but the daughter's promise of happiness and youth was evident only on the mother's face. The light worked this transference, this gift from the daughter. A light. Perhaps the same light she had followed like a ghost through the decaying mansion; that same light had come here, to this tiny apartment, to fulfill Miss Winslow's desire: that her mother reflect the brilliant light

---

[21] Carlos Fuentes, *Gringo viejo* (Mexico: Fondo de Cultura Económica, 1985), p. 53. Subsequent references are to the English version, *The Old Gringo* (New York: Farrar, Straus, and Giroux), 1985, translated by Carlos Fuentes and Margaret Sayers Peden and are included in the text, preceded by OG.

> of her childhood; that the daughter no longer reflect the sorrowful shadow of the mother. (OG, 50)

The dramatically personified light that Harriet envisions is similar, in its sensuality, to the light that surrounds and transfigures Aura. It is a light that illuminates a secret and forbidden world—that of her father's adultery:

> She dreamed: the light stopped at the foot of the service stairway beside the cellar that was the last and darkest labyrinth in the unserviceable shell of the intimidating and ephemeral facade of Washingtonian luxury and duty, the stark whiteness of the pantheon of the city, its black wells, and the smell became stronger . . . as her father possessed the solitary Negress who lived there, perhaps in the service of absent masters, perhaps she herself the repudiated lady of the house. (OG, 50)

Harriet's subsequent experiences in Mexico, her romantic interlude with the arrogant *macho* Tomás Arroyo, who in contrast to her prissy North American beau Delaney fulfills her sexually, seems to be the acting out of this oneiric vision. Unable to be reunited with the principal object of her love—her father—Harriet emulates his life by taking a Mexican lover. Unlike her father, a character never evoked in his own right but who apparently is the only person in the narrative to find happiness and self-fulfillment—significantly, not in the United States but in far-off Cuba—Harriet abruptly rejects Arroyo and departs from Mexico forever, to return to an existence that in its solitude and alienation parallels that of her stultified mother. In childhood, adulthood and old age, Harriet's febrile imagination creates dreamworlds that, as in the life of Consuelo, must compensate for an irrevocable absence. In the case of Consuelo, it is the loss of Llorente, in that of Harriet it is the inconsolable loss of the father. So great is the devotion of Harriet to her forever lost father, Captain Winslow, that when Arroyo kills her surrogate father, Bierce, Harriet acts to precipitate her lover's death as an act of vengeance. Arroyo is executed by the very Revolutionary leader to whom he dies pledging his fierce loyalty—Pancho Villa.

What adds immeasurably to the immediacy and the power of both Fuentes's *Aura* and Hitchcock's *Vertigo* is the way in which the reader/spectator is rapidly drawn into the vortex of these artistic creations. In *Vertigo,* this breaking down of the barriers between film and reality, between the actors on the screen and the audience in the theatre, is accomplished through several means. First and foremost, through his masterful direction and expert utilization of the camera, Hitchcock not only tells of the crippling *Vertigo* that Scottie suffers, but makes the spectator repeatedly experience that sensation—once when Scottie is on the rooftop chasing the criminal, a second time when he merely attempts to climb to the top step of a three-rung kitchen stepladder in the apartment of Midge, and a third time as he attempts to prevent the suicide of Madeleine by rushing to the top of the bell tower. Hitchcock uses the technique of a forward zoom then a track out expertly to produce the sensation of dizziness. According to an interview that Hitchcock conducted with Truffaut, to obtain this sensation within the bell tower at San Juan Bautista, Hitchcock constructed a mock tower, placed it on its side, and filmed its interior from the perspective of the stricken Scottie. Over and over again in the thriller films of Hitchcock, *Vertigo* and *Psycho* (1960) and *The Birds* (1963), the spectator is hurled into the middle of the on-screen action, so close does the camera bring us into contact with the characters. In his book-length interview with Truffaut, Hitchcock explains how this sensation of immediacy is obtained:

> Planting the countryside to shoot a passing train would merely give us the viewpoint of a cow watching a train go by. I tried to keep the public inside the train, *with* the train. Whenever it went into a curve, we took a longshot from one of the train windows. The way we did that was to put three cameras on the rear platform of the *Twentieth Century Limited,* and we went over the exact journey of the film at the same time of the day. One of our cameras was used for the long shots of the train in the curves, while the two others were used for background footage.

Figure 37. Masterful chiaroscuro as Hitchcock stresses fusion of sacred and demonic, Love and Death.

Figure 38. Why doesn't a stricken Scottie rush to the aid of his apparently dying beloved?

> F.T. In your technique everything is subordinated to the dramatic impact; the camera, in fact, accompanies the characters almost like an escort.[22]

Fuentes masterfully accomplishes the same goal as Hitchcock, so that reader/spectator is rapidly drawn into the artistic creation, as Fuentes makes the reader not a passive observer but part of the action, experiencing the perplexity and the bewilderment as well as the astonishment of the hapless Felipe. Fuentes accomplishes this through his expert utilization of the second-person narrative, one seldom encountered in fiction, that draws the reader into the ambience of the work and into the action in several ways. First, the second-person narrative refers not only to the Other within Felipe, the Llorente identity that finally and excruciatingly emerges, but also to the very reader of *Aura*, thus effectively abolishing the distance between reader and protagonist. And the hypnotic mood that the reiteration of the "you" establishes also serves to sweep the reader into the story.

Samuel Taylor, who collaborated with Hitchcock on the script of *Vertigo*, has stated that Hitchcock is a master short story writer. Here is another bridge between director and writer, between Hitchcock and Fuentes. Indeed, Hitchcock's preoccupation with the details of cinematic imagery parallels the preoccupation of Fuentes with verbal imagery. And Hitchcock's great awareness of the cinematic medium as a means not merely of recording external reality but of creating a unique, imaginative vision of its own, corresponds to Fuentes's aesthetic mode, in which apparently real locations—Mexico City, Paris, the border between the United States and Mexico—are all symbolic of inner states of mind and of often frustrated ontological quests by the characters.

As Hitchcock states, commenting on the intense discipline of his craft:

[22] See François Truffaut, *Hitchcock*, revised edition (New York: Simon and Schuster, 1985), p. 265. This volume was first published in France as *Hitchcock/Truffaut* by Editions Ramsay in 1983. Subsequent references are included in the text, preceded by HT.

> The placing of the images on the screen . . . should never be dealt with in a factual manner. Never! You can get anything you want through the proper use of cinematic techniques, which enable you to work out any image. There is no justification for a short cut and no reason to settle for a compromise between the image you wanted and the image you get. One of the reasons most films aren't sufficiently rigorous is that so few people in the industry know anything about imagery. (HT, 265)

Thus, in the key scene when Scottie first views Madeleine at *Ernie's*, focus on the back of Madeleine is paralleled by reiterated emphasis on the back of Scottie's head—to underscore how inpenetrable mystery characterizes not only mercurial, illusory Madeleine but complex, opaque Scottie Ferguson as well. And the secrecy characteristic of Judy/Madeleine is further underscored visually by Hitchcock as he focusses intensely on the back of Judy/s neck when she is about to reveal to the audience a confession of complicity and guilt with the crime of murder that she never reveals to Scottie.

It is significant that Hitchcock, unlike most directors, repeatedly focuses on the backs of the heads of his central characters, in this case Scottie and Judy/Madeleine. Indeed, back photography is a significant artistic phenomenon in Great Britain. Because of the unusualness of the camera angle, because the spectator is impatient that he or she cannot see the way in which the character is responding to a certain situation, because in effect the back of the head constitutes another mask over the identity, the effect is both intriguing—increasing the mystery of the character—and highly unsettling.

Repeatedly in *Vertigo*, Hitchcock uses pan shots, which move very slowly over a setting, such as the sweeping vista of San Francisco, or the interior of *Ernie's*, thereby tantalizing the viewer. Similarly, in his intensely visual style, Fuentes in *Aura* as in other works such as *La región más transparente* (1958) and *La cabeza de la hidra* (1978), uses a *camera stylo*, such as this slow pan shot over the antique furnishings in Consuelo's domain:

> Then you glance around the room: a red wool rug, olive and gold wallpaper, an easy chair covered in red velvet, an old walnut desk with a green leather top, an old Argand lamp with its soft glow for your nights of research, and a bookshelf over the desk in reach of your hand. (A, 33)

It is ironic that the light which the lamp gives off is a "luz opaca," thus constituting an illusion to the fact that it will provide, like all the light in the realm of Consuelo, not illumination but ambiguity and obfuscation. And the red and green combination that appears again and again in *Vertigo* even in the shifting red to green of the traffic lights in the city, is also characteristic of *Aura*.

Although film critics have commented on the difficulty that the cinema has in conveying the inner, psychological states and moods of the characters, their private thoughts and reactions, Hitchcock in *Vertigo* demonstrates how in the work of a master director, the consciousness of the protagonist can be effectively penetrated and exteriorized. As a solemn, intense Scottie pursues Madeleine's car through the sinuous streets of San Francisco, the camera focuses relentlessly on only his face, thereby pursuing *him*, like a scalpel delving into the way that his doubts, hesitations, and anxieties are registered, capturing both his puzzlement at Madeleine's bizarre behavior and his determination to complete his mission, which like that of Felipe is one linked with personal salvation. Hitchcock in this undeviating camera shot radically departs from the way in which a chase scene is typically filmed in a Hollywood movie. Whether it be a madcap pursuit by the Keystone Cops or a chase by the determined posse of an outlaw band in a Western movie or a pursuit by the police of fleeing gangsters, a chase scene is usually filmed with a shot/reverse shot technique. First those being pursued and their desperation are evoked, then the camera changes point of view to train itself on the grim and relentless pursuers, then switches again back to the fugitives then again back to the obsessed avengers. The effect of Hitchcock's focusing solely on Scottie is to underscore from the very beginning of the film how much Scottie's tracking of Madeleine is really an inner pursuit, the pursuit of a dream and not of a real person. Similarly, Felipe in the mystifying realm of Aura/Consuelo undertakes both an external investigation, into the life of Llorente, and an inner one, into the nature of his own incipient and divided self. It is very significant that the memoirs of Llorente are incomplete. Thus it is indicated that his identity is an open one; both the memoirs and the life of Llorente are ironically and tragically completed in Felipe.

In his public lecture at a Hitchcock Symposium in New York City in June of 1986, Taylor has stated that *Vertigo*, despite the appearances of Midge, a character he himself created, is really the story of only two persons, Scottie and Madeleine: Midge is but a bystander. Yet we may also contend that *Vertigo* is a story of but a single obsessed and tormented consciousness, that of Scottie Ferguson, which perhaps in some sense reflects the obsessions with creation and re-creation of Hitchcock himself. Indeed, the way in which both Gavin Elster and Scottie Ferguson remold the pliant Judy Barton to conform to their desires repeats the way in which Alfred Hitchcock, who reputedly disdained actors and actresses and who contemptuously referred to them as cattle, exactingly molded a reluctant but highly professional Kim Novak to conform to the role that he thoroughly controlled. It has been stated that Miss Novak had declared that she would never act in a gray suit and black shoes, and yet the role of Madeleine called for precisely this attire, the grayness of the clothing symbolic of the existential nebulousness of Judy/Madeleine—as if she had just emerged from the San Francisco fog, here symbolic of dream and nonbeing and mystery. Yet despite Novak's objections, Hitchcock apparently convinced the statuesque actress to don this attire—just as Scottie convinces Judy Barton to don the stylish gray clothing originally worn by Madeleine and indeed, even after the crime, a possessive Judy keeps Madeleine's elegant gray suit in her closet—as an indication of how much the shop girl was entranced by her aristocratic role—or perhaps a subconscious desire of Judy to play the enticing, elegant role of the exquisitely dressed and elegantly crafted Madeleine again.

Indeed, the puppetlike status of Judy/Madeleine signifies concentric circles of identity manipulation of the female by powerful males. Beyond the molding of the pliable, awed Novak by the ever authoritative Hitchcock is the way in which Harry Cohn, the then autocratic head of Columbia pictures, crafted the star that Kim Novak became, in films like *Jeanne Eagels* (1957),

Pal Joey (1957) and *The Eddy Duchin Story* (1956), taking the gorgeous beauty who started her career in advertising as "Miss Deep Freeze" touring the United States demonstrating refrigerators, and converting her into a sultry sex symbol to rival Marilyn Monroe and to replace Columbia's fading superstar, Rita Hayworth. Indeed, Kim Novak, was designated by critics as a "manufactured star," an epithet that she very much resented, as in reality she was both highly talented and a perfectionist in her art.

Aura perhaps more than any other work reflects the obsessions with Self and Other, psychological and mythic and historical, time, love and death, life, death and immortality, of Fuentes, who has stated that he was born in 1927—the very year in which the Empress Carlotta died, as if to imply some connection between death and new life, perhaps even alluding to a transmigration of souls, with Carlotta, who appears in several of Fuentes's works, including *Terra nostra* and in his second drama, *El tuerto es rey*, becoming some type of alter ego of Fuentes himself. In a letter, Fuentes has stated that the inspiration for the character pairing of Consuelo and Aura came to him after he had seen two dramatically contrasting images of Carlotta—the first, a painting in the Castle of Chapultepec in Mexico City of Carlotta as a young and beautiful girl, as a cosseted Belgian princess, and the second, a photograph from the Casasola Archive, of the aged Carlotta in her coffin, the Empress having been reduced to a madwoman recluse, who died at the age of eighty-six in her native Belgium, in her castle at Bouchot which was spared from destruction when Germany invaded Belgium during World War I and the marauding German conquerors left the castle intact after reading the sign in front: *Kaiserin von Mexiko*. Fuentes brilliantly fuses these two images in *Aura*, immortalizing Consuelo/Carlotta, just as Scottie Ferguson constantly fuses the images of Carlotta Valdés and Madeleine, bringing back to life not only the stylish Madeleine but the deranged Carlotta as well.

Wood penetratingly analyzes the way in which *Vertigo* begins, as we see a bar that will be grasped first by the fleeing criminal and then by the extremely determined but vainly pursuing Scottie:

> The first image is of a horizontal bar standing out against a blurred background: a single solid object against an undefined mass. The shot is held for a moment, then two hands grab the bar, the camera moves back, the focus deepens, to reveal a city spread out beneath the night: suggestions of clinging and falling set against a great wilderness of roof-tops. (HF, 74)

The viewer is jolted by the initial image. The beginning of *Vertigo*—fatalistically—is its ending. It is not the criminal, the pursued but the pursuer, in this case Scottie, who is in mortal danger, and the policeman attempting valiantly to rescue Scottie falls to his death; the criminal, however, escapes. This situation adumbrates the ending of the work, in which the murderer of Madeleine, Gavin Elster, flees safely to Switzerland and apparently remains there, living in quiet luxury. Ironically, Gavin Elster is the only figure in *Vertigo* who emerges victorious.

It is highly significant that an ending in which Scottie, a stiff drink in his hand, now safely in the comforting confines of Midge's apartment, hears on the radio the news of Elster's capture in Switzerland—a moralistic, justice triumphant ending to please the censors, constitutes a finale that Hitchcock initially filmed but subsequently deleted. Instead, the final, horrifying and mystifying shot is of Scottie framed in the window ledge of the monastery, transfixed by the gruesome sight of the body of his beloved on the pavement below, perhaps tempted to hurl himself from the tower. The ending of *Vertigo,* like that of *Aura,* is ambiguous and intensely cyclical. Consuelo, in order to bring back Aura once more, after she has used up Felipe, will undoubtedly place another advertisement in the newspaper for a young historian, for a victim-lover—a new impersonator of Llorente, just as it is very probable that a dazed and delirium-enshrouded Scottie will begin but another pursuit of a ghostly Madeleine. Both Hitchcock and Fuentes shun realism for the maelstrom of fantasy and delusion.

Similar to *Vertigo*, in *Aura* the very beginning is also its ending. The crumbs on the bed of Consuelo which Felipe sees at the beginning of the narrative are the remnants of previous Black Masses in which Consuelo/Aura lubriciously places the communal wafer between her thighs. These crumbs indicate that there have been a fatalistic series of sacrificial victims. Similarly, *Vertigo* is bound by a fatalistic, cyclical time. At the beginning as at the end of the film, Scottie is seen at the top of a tall building. And, each time he ascends to the top, there occurs a violent death.

The ending of both the *novella* of the Mexican author and of the magisterial director the film is highly ambiguous. Is Felipe finally redeemed or destroyed as the result of his liaison with Consuelo/Aura? Is he granted a new identity or is he bound inextricably to a past identity? Similarly, the ending of *Vertigo* is ambiguous. Hitchcock had initially filmed a typical Hollywood "happily-ever-after ending," but he discarded it. The ending as actually filmed shows Scottie alone, suspended in space, at the top of the tower. In one sense, this outcome is positive, because Scottie has accomplished what he had set out to do, *i.e.*, to conquer his vertigo, successfully to climb to the top of the tower. Yet his posture, arms outstretched as if he were a stricken Christ figure, seems to indicate that it is not self-transcendence but renewed agony that Scottie is experiencing. Now his guilt is tripled, as he feels responsible for the deaths of the self-sacrificing policeman, the real Madeleine Elster, and finally the phony Madeleine, Judy Barton. It is conceivable that Scottie will again begin the search for a new "Madeleine," after he is once again hospitalized for his recurrent insanity. Or it is possible that he will hurl himself from the tower, joining Judy/Madeleine in death. This suicidal ending has been adumbrated in Scottie's terrifying nightmare in which, apparently to alleviate his intense feelings of guilt, he imagines himself falling from the tower into Madeleine's open grave.

In addition to cinematic techniques, another aspect of *Vertigo* that increases audience identification is the shrewd casting by Alfred Hitchcock of James Stewart as Scottie Ferguson. The screen *persona* of James Stewart prior to his role as Scottie has been carefully crafted since the 1930's as the "All American Hero" and "Mr. Nice Guy." Indeed, one of the biographies of Stewart is entitled *Everybody's Man*. In films of idealism such as Frank Capra's *It's a Wonderful Life* (1946) and *Mr. Smith Goes to Washington* (1939), as well as biographical films concentrating on American national heroes, such as *The Spirit of St. Louis* (1957), directed by the inimitable Billy Wilder, the story of the daring aviator Charles Lindbergh, who accomplished the first trans-

Atlantic flight, alone in the cockpit, and *The Glen Miller Story* (1954), evoking the career of one of the greatest Big Band leaders of the 1940s, an Air Force Officer whose plane was lost during World War II and Miller's body never found, another national icon, his biography directed by the masterful Anthony Mann. Stewart, who plays the starring role in most of his films, is always the embattled hero, struggling against great odds for high moral principles. Stewart, the consummate Hollywood actor, shrewdly underplays his roles, combining a boyish naivete with a halting, at times even stammering delivery that facilitates audience identification with him as the "common man," the good-hearted, sincere and idealistic person, combining casualness with devotion to duty. Yet in *Vertigo*, Hitchcock casts James Stewart against the types he had for decades played so successfully—Scottie Ferguson slowly emerges as a monster of sadistic fury. And Hitchcock, in but another twist, masterfully plays against the screen *persona* of Stewart as awkward but likeable good guy evident in the first part of *Vertigo*. The tendency of the audience is to identify with the seemingly casual, unassuming, victimized, Scottie Ferguson as a firm continuation of the gentle and gentlemanly and bastion of idealism screen *persona* that Stewart had continually built up over decades. Only in the second half of the film, where the ruthlessness of Scottie becomes more and more exposed, is the shock apparent—instead of the even-tempered and noble hero, Scottie has turned vicious, toying with and finally capable of destroying the life of Judy Barton, emulating both the cruelty of Gavin Elster and the exploitativeness of the anonymous nineteenth century entrepreneur who transformed, elevated, then cast aside a helpless, devastated Carlotta.

This Dr. Jekyll-Mr. Hyde transformation in Stewart is all the more powerful because it is so unexpected. Gradually, without really being conscious that we have realized it, as we would have had the role of Scottie been played by a "heavy" or "killer actor" such as Charles Bronson in *Death Wish (I, II* and *III*, all directed by Michael Winner; 1974, 1982, 1985) or the late Lee Marvin or James Cagney in thrillers like *White Heat (*directed by the great Raoul Walsh, 1945) and *Public Enemy (*directed by William Wellman 1931) , we witness not only the transformation of Judy into Madeleine but the deliberately slow transformation of Scottie

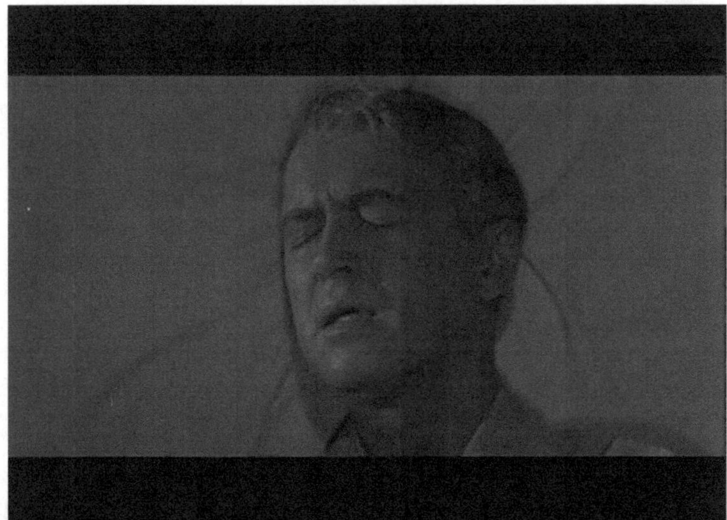

Figure 39. Scottie feverishly tormented by nightmare of double suicide and unexpurgated guilt.

Figure 40. Weird orange filter: Carlotta alive, embracing, and conspiring with Elster. Scottie's subconsciousness attempts to warn him.

into the murderous Gavin Elster—a murderous Dr. Jekyll/Mr. Hyde transmogrification. At the end of *Vertigo*, as a merciless Scottie drags Judy/Madeleine by the throat to the top of the tower, his monstrousness underneath his façade of nonchalance and affability and boyish charm which are initially so captivating, is stunningly revealed.

Adding to the fatalism of *Vertigo* is the way in which key phrases are repeated throughout the film. It is Gavin Elster who with his restrained eloquence first conjures up the image of men in the nineteenth century as having "power and freedom." His exact words are echoed by Pop Liebl, this time not in a romantic but rather a sinister light, as Liebl alludes to the terrible control and the freedom from punishment that men like Carlotta's husband in the nineteenth century—the very epoch so romanticized by the vicious Gavin Elster, whose idealistic vision is rapidly absorbed, then even eagerly shared by an initially doubting and extremely reluctant Scottie. Pop Liebl alludes to a lethal power exerted both to amass huge fortunes and to control and destroy women. This is the same type of power that will be cruelly exercised over Judy Barton, first by Gavin Elster and then by Scottie. And here lies one of the main differences between Hitchcock's vision and that of Fuentes. Hitchcock adopts a feminist perspective—women are throughout the centuries manipulated and eventually destroyed by the powerful and ruthless male, and even those like Midge who attempt to control the male are doomed to isolation, rejection, and total abandonment. Fuentes's vision is just the opposite—women are all-powerful—behind the fierce and fanatic Consuelo is the ambitious and ruthless Carlotta, Empress of Mexico and behind Carlotta is the monstrous and terrifying, both life-sustaining and life-devouring ancient Aztec goddess of Life and Death, Coatlicue. The immense stone statue of Coatlicue, whose name signifies "Goddess with the Skirt of Serpents" which now stands in the Museo de Antropología in central Mexico City, depicts a goddess who instead of a head has two immense serpents, signifying flowing blood—the blood necessary to sustain the universe, the serpant theme repeated in the immense skirt of serpants that the goddess wears. Victims of sacrifice to Coatlicue were beheaded to celebrate her self-immolation. She is the paradoxical goddess of both Creation and Destruction, both life and death—death symbolized by the necklace that she wears, of human hearts and the centerpiece a human skull. She is a venerable Earth Goddess, the earth both as generating womb and as fateful tomb: Ashes to Ashes and Dust to Dust.

Finally, at the very end of *Vertigo*, a stricken Scottie, extremely jealous of Gavin Elster because Elster had been much more dedicated and successful in his transformation of Judy, and, indirectly, because Elster had been the lover of Judy/Madeleine before Scottie got to her, refers to him—with intense jealousy—as possessing "all that freedom and all that power." Surface reality in both *Vertigo* and *Aura* is porous and constantly shifting. No perception is reliable, and characters like Midge who represent a potential center of integrity and cool-headedness, are permanently cast aside.

In *Aura*, the proliferation of rats in the musty and tomblike house of Consuelo indicates that there have been no cats present for many years. Yet Felipe is tormented by a hellish vision of writhing and screeching cats. Once again it is not the present but the inexplicable past which holds all significance. These are the spirits of the cats that had been tortured more than a half century earlier by the demented Consuelo in her desperate attempt to restore the fertility of Llorente. In both *Aura* and *Vertigo*, only on the level of the subconscious mind or the level of the unconsciousness, is the negative truth about their situation revealed to the two often dazed male protagonists. Ironically, even though they receive many admonitory visions that could have resulted in their escaping their predators, both Scottie and Felipe disregard them in their obsessive quest for their dream women. In one of his many nightmares, Felipe's unconsciousness reveals to him the truth about Consuelo's destructive nature, her terrifying reality as a *mater terribilis*, not a harmless old woman, fanatically consecrated to her husband's memory:

> *moving her fleshless hand, coming toward you until her face touches yours and you see the old lady's bloody gums, her toothless gums, and you scream and she goes away again, moving her hand, sowing the abyss with the yellow teeth she carries in her blood stained apron.* (A, 95)

The phantasmagorical level of *Aura* is accentuated through Fuentes's extensive use of disconcerting italics. Once again the deep mythic level of *Aura* is apparent, Fuentes's allusion is to the sowing of dragon's teeth by the ill-fated Greek hero Jason, teeth once sown producing warriors in mortal combat. Felipe, paralleling the stricken, nightmare prone Scottie Ferguson, also is given a vision of the truth concerning the nature of Consuelo and Aura. On the conscious level, he has perceived Aura, who eats mechanically, whose every movement seems to follow that of her aunt, as the entrapped and exploited victim of Consuelo, but his nightmare indicates that both woman are the same—a rapidly ensnaring and devouring force:

> *your scream is an echo of Aura's, she's standing in front of you in your dream, and she's screaming because someone's hands have ripped her green taffeta skirt in two, and then she turns her head toward you with the torn folds of the skirt in her hands turns toward you and laughs silently, with the old lady's teeth superimposed on her own, while her legs, her naked legs, shatter into bits and fly toward the abyss . . .* (A, 95-97)

In the mind of the tormented Scottie Ferguson as well, the true nature of Judy/Madeleine as complicit with Gavin Elster is revealed and utilizing the exact same technique, that of a terrifying nightmare. One of the most original and spellbinding parts of *Vertigo* is the extended dramatization of Scottie's subsequent nightmare after the jaundiced coroner's inquest, when Scottie is cruelly and insistently rebuked by the coroner who, like the concierge at the Hotel McKittrick, seems to be in league with the *titiritero*, the glacially smooth Gavin Elster, for having allowed two persons—the policeman and now Madeleine, to die. Although Scottie officially is cleared of all blame, and Madeleine's death is technically ruled a suicide, Scottie is held morally responsible by the sadistic coroner, while not the slightest suspicion accrues to the ever self-possessed and chillingly articulate Gavin Elster, whose outstretched hand after the inquest is concluded Scottie now refuses to shake. In Scottie's nightmare, the colors that play across his face are the same as the multicolored spirals that emanated from the eyes of Judy/Madeleine at the very outset of the film. Here, on the unconscious level, is indicated that Judy/Madeleine is not really the cure for Scottie's intransigent *Vertigo* but the person who is exacerbating it. The images of disintegration that characterize Felipe's nightmare in *Aura* and that adumbrate not only the final disappearance of Aura, her merging back into the cadaverous Consuelo, but also the destruction of Felipe, are also found in Scottie's nightmare. A key symbol of Madeleine and Carlotta is the bouquet of flowers, held by Carlotta in the museum portrait, a similar bouquet purchased by "Madeleine," who believes she is Carlotta, a fatally symbolic bouquet torn apart immediately before Madeleine plunges into San Francisco Bay in a suicide attempt that supposedly emulates the tragic death of Carlotta. Yet the flowers in Scottie's nightmare are not realistic but rather gigantic, cartoonlike flowers—fake flowers, the huge bouquet rapidly torn apart to indicate to him that Judy/Madeleine, the holder of those flowers, is a fake, that her death is a phony. It is also highly significant that Carlotta is revivified in Scottie's nightmare and appears not as a tremulous victim and not as an icon to be worshipped—as Scottie previously had envisioned her—but as a co-conspirator, in the arms of Gavin Elster, and gazing balefully at Scottie. Previously, on the conscious level, Scottie's mind has fused the portrait of Carlotta with the image of Judy/Madeleine. The implication is clear; Carlotta/Madeleine, far from being a distraught victim, is in league with Gavin Elster against Scottie. For the extremely gullible Scottie, Carlotta becomes, on the subconscious level, a sinister figure, but Scottie, like Felipe after his recurrent nightmares, refuses to act or is utterly incapable of acting upon these oneiric revelations.

Russell comments perceptively on the increasing monstrousness of the initially fragile and almost pathetic Scottie Ferguson:

> . . . in *Vertigo*, the whole emotional situation is invested with a nightmarish intensity because its true nature is unacknowledged and its natural course diverted. The hero's passion for the girl in the second half of the film is perverse not because he continues hopelessly to love someone he believes dead—bereavement is not such an unnatural

> situation—but because he is incapable of reacting to a real, living woman until he has dominated her completely and transformed her completely against her will, into the image of his lost lover. In other words, he has chosen fantasy over reality, and found to transform reality into fantasy by the sheer force of his obsession. (243)

Throughout *Vertigo* there occurs a complex process of self-assertion of his identity by Scottie, undermined by an equally strong desire for self-negation and expertly captured by Hitchcock's ever prowling, ever intrusive camera movement through reiterated use of the forward zoom then back tracking shot, that mysteriously, poetically, captivatingly demonstrates vertigo, ambivalence, and attraction-repulsion. When he compels Judy/Madeleine to return with him to the Spanish colonial mission at San Juan Bautista, Scottie is determined to transcend the past by confronting it, by reliving it. Above all he wants to conquer his *Vertigo*. Yet the fatalistic words of Midge, stated matter of factly at the very start of the film, cast a pall over all of Scottie's efforts, when she states to him that the doctor has deemed his illness incurable, "There's no losing it, you know." Indeed, Midge seems quietly to delight in the news, because Scottie's incapacitated state makes him even more dependent on her, enabling her to play the role that she does best, that of mother-comforter-protector.

It is significant that both Scottie and Felipe experience nightmares of falling. In the life of Felipe Montero as in that of Scottie, the urge to assert the Self is countered and finally defeated by the down-dragging urge to negate the self, by the quest for oblivion. Although one moment Felipe, whose grasp on reality, like that of Scottie, is always tenuous, envisions himself as the gallant hero who will brave the monstrous forces that hold his beloved princess captive and free her, the next moment he succumbs to an incapacitating lassitude:

> ...enter your own room feeling the rough bristles on your chin, turn on the bath faucets and then slide into the warm water, letting yourself relax into forgetfulness. (A, 117)

Fuentes repeatedly in his work emphasizes the theme of the Fall in the same biblical terms as does Alfred Hitchcock. In both *La región más transparente* and *La muerte de Artemio Cruz*, for example, the male protagonists, titanic figures cast in terms both of New Men, of Adamlike creations thrust into power and wealth as the result of the cataclysmic Mexican Revolution, and isolated and defeated figures, like Adam cast forth from Paradise and both plutocrats eroded by guilt. And Fuentes, in one of his least appreciated but outstanding narratives, *Los años con Laura Díaz* (*The Years with Laura Díaz*; 1998) develops the countermyth—Adam and Eve not falling from Paradise but ascending to Heaven–as sinners transformed into sanctified figures. Similar to the beleagured Felipe, Scottie experiences, on the oneiric level, multiple deaths of the self. The first death he envisions is a literal one—his falling at breakneck speed from the top of the tower at San Juan Bautista into the open grave of his adored Madeleine. The second death is even more terrifying, as Scottie's head, within his nightmare, now expands to fill the entire screen, a decisive influence on Hitchcock of the German master director, Fritz Lang, who in his epic film *Dr. Mabuse* (1922) evokes the menacing image of the diabolical protagonist first as but a small disembodied head gleaming on a solid black background, a head that rapidly, terrifyingly grows monstrously to encompass the full screen—and the puppetlike Scottie plunges into a frighteningly limitless space. It is the maximum extreme of *vertigo*, as Scottie's head accelerates frenziedly toward a weblike backdrop, indicating how imprisoned the detective is not only in the elaborate schemes of Gavin Elster but also, and perhaps more significantly, within the shocked and stricken self. Soon after his nightmare, the disaffected Scottie is committed to the mental institution, with Midge experiencing a lengthy, futile visit with a zombielike Scottie, so benumbed that he never even recognizes her nor speaks a single word to her. Indeed, he exists in a catatonic state, listless, unable to respond at all to the patient, loving attempts of Midge to comfort him. This scene in the mental institution is a key one; it both terminates forever the problematic relationship between Midge and Scottie and adumbrates the repetitive, stagnant relationship between Judy/Madeleine and a seemingly contented but encrusted and zombielike Scottie.

Figure 41. Carlotta's ruby necklace: Judy's cherished souvenir of a crime.

Figure 42. Spiderweb that has entrapped Scottie from the beginning is now inextricable for hapless protagonist.

Even after his release, the fated nature of Scottie's life is symbolized visually, as the rootless and helpless detective stands in front of the luxury apartment building on Nob Hill where Madeleine formerly dwelled—the exclusive Brocklebank Apartments. The benumbed Scottie stands near a traffic sign saying "One Way." The camera lingers on this sign, to signify the fated nature of Scottie's existence. Twice he travels down the Peninsula to the Mission at San Juan Bautista, twice he enters the fated tower from which Carlotta had plunged to her death; twice he is the helpless witness to the death of a person whom he has obsessively but vainly loved.

Underscoring the fatalistic, weblike nature of reality in *Vertigo* is the way in which certain ominous images are reiterated throughout the film. At the very beginning, a handicapped and vexatious Scottie complains bitterly to Midge over the necessity of wearing a corset and using a cane, and in reference to the latter he states that he feels like throwing "the miserable thing" out the window—a veiled reference to what the sadistic Gavin Elster will do with his wife's body. This phenomenon of throwing away applies not only to objects but to people. Scottie will discard one of the most important, perhaps the most important person in his life, Midge, after she dares even to question his involvement with Madeleine. The theme of throwing away is echoed in the story told by Pop Liebl, in reference to the callous behavior of Carlotta's husband, that, as we have seen, establishes the mold for the duplicitous acts of both Gavin Elster and Scottie Ferguson in the twentieth century: "He kept the child and threw her away. You know men could do that in those days. They had the power and the freedom." With savage irony, Hitchcock demonstrates how men could act with total impunity not only in the tumultuous San Francisco of the lawless Barbary Coast days of the nineteenth century, but also in contemporary society, characterized, seemingly, by refinement and gentility.

And indeed, "throwing away" is exactly what Gavin Elster does with the body of his wife, whom he has murdered by breaking her neck, and then hurls the body the top of the tower. Elster will take no chances that his wife would survive the fall, and thus the real Madeleine Elster dies twice—symbolizing how the identity of the real Judy Barton is twice effaced. "Throwing away" is also what Scottie does—first with the steadfast devotion of Midge and then with the genuine love of Judy Barton, and Judy's sudden death by falling from the tower is a tragic culmination of this attitude of discarding of human beings once their usefulness to the powerful, corruptible but unpunishable males has terminated.

Another example of the negative operation of cyclical time in *Vertigo* is that at the exact moment when Scottie reads the name of Carlotta Valdés on the tombstone in the small graveyard outside of the Mission Dolores, a mission bell rings out fatalistically. This moment adumbrates the very ending of the film, in which Carlotta's restless spirit seems to have emerged to act in precisely the way in which Gavin Elster said it would—to mesmerize and control and destroy her descendants. The figure emerging from the gloom at the top of the tower, the figure who so terrifies Judy, whose words, "I heard voices" could very well have been uttered by the distressed and insane Madeleine Elster, proves to be one of the black-robed nuns at the Mission, whose first act after the death of Judy Barton is to ring the bells of the tower—like the scene in the spectral garden of the Mission Dolores, a peal of doom reminiscent of the funeral bells in the anguished, doom-laden poems of Edgar Allan Poe.

Both *Vertigo* and *Aura* evoke spectral, narcotized presences—Judy/Madeleine and Aura—who are markedly ambivalent. Although Judy has been meticulously trained by Elster to deceive Scottie, after she apparently falls in love with him she makes several attempts to discourage him, even to attempt to break off their relationship—as a means of protecting him. Thus, even though Judy/Madeleine leads Scottie to the forest of sequoias, playing to the hilt the role assigned to her by Gavin Elster as the distressed and demented Madeleine, her plea to Scottie, "Please don't ask me, please don't ask me" indicates her heartfelt desire not to draw Scottie further into the elaborate trap set for him by Elster. Even when they have arrived at the Mission at San Juan Bautista, and Scottie embraces her, a highly—and unusually—emotional Madeleine/Judy begs him not to follow her to the tower—which may be construed again as Judy's resolve to end her complicity with Elster, and to protect Scottie. Yet Madeleine/Judy's words to Scottie not to pursue her may be an integral part of the role she is playing as the shill for Elster—

knowing that her imprecations will make the relentlessly pursuing Scottie all the more determined to follow her to the tower.

Similarly, the vaporous Aura too is ambivalent creation. Most of the time she acts as the minion of Consuelo, exactly paralleling the way Judy Barton acts, as the willing instrument of Gavin Elster. Yet at times Aura appears as an admonitory force, both within Felipe's nightmares and in the domain of Consuelo. Indeed, just as Judy/Madeleine is a highly paradoxical phenomenon throughout *Vertigo*, both alluring and destructive, both a redeeming force in Scottie's vapid life and a seemingly successful criminal accomplice, so too does the beguiling Aura both save and destroy Felipe Montero.

Both Felipe and Scottie are presented as dangling men. At the outset of *Vertigo*, Scottie is literally a dangling man, as he hangs from the damaged gutter of the roof after slipping and almost falling to his death. After presenting the traumatic scene of the death of the policeman, Hitchcock cuts directly to the quiet apartment of Midge—a seemingly ideal setting for Scottie's recuperation—and concentrates on a time several days after the death. Hitchcock thus leaves a marked ambiguity in the film, as Wood points out:

> We do not see, and are never told, how he got down from the gutter; there seems no possible way he could have got down. The effect is of leaving him, throughout the film, metaphorically suspended over a great abyss. (HF, 75)

Scottie's physical suspension adumbrates his whole subsequent social, psychological, and metaphysical suspension. When asked by Judy/Madeleine what his profession is, Scottie states casually—and evasively, for he is as elusive as Madeleine—that he is a wanderer. Yet, in fact, the meticulous and extremely uptight Scottie is just the opposite—a control freak, one who hates wandering; he despises the limbo state in which he must exist after his traumatic attack of v*ertigo*, and the purposelessness of his life in retirement and longs to assert the shattered self—even to command and compel—which he does at the end with the increasingly terrified Judy Barton.

Indeed, despite his air of nonchalance, Scottie is a deadly serious person who by temperament is not a drifter but a hunter, a tracker, a relentless pursuer of a dream. Similarly, Felipe Montero in *Aura* is too is a pursuer, a hunter—an occupation symbolized by his last name, Montero. Just as his pursuit of Madeleine gives Scottie newfound energy and purpose, so also does Felipe's fated encounter with Aura imbue him with renewed energy, and he begins work on the thesis that he had long neglected. The colorless, nebulous lives of both Felipe and Scottie are ironically fulfilled, even transcended, through their relationships not with real women—indeed, neither is capable of understanding or relating to a flesh and blood woman, as Scottie demonstrates in his inability to relate to the Midge who adores him, and Felipe in his mentioning of no friends or family or even acquaintances in the external world.

Aura's name too underscores her wraithlike nature, her evanescent quality. As *Vertigo* progresses, Scottie dwells more and more in his private fantasy world, severing all of his ties with reality, first cutting off Midge when he becomes irked that she is attempting to bring him back to secure but prosaic and mundane reality, and then shutting out Judy Barton as well. Just as Scottie's honor and dignity and virility all are restored after he believes that he has singlehandedly rescued Madeleine from her suicidal plunge, so too does Felipe experience the birth of a new and heroic *machista* identity, yet one that is immediately undercut by his inherent timidity and passivity, as instead of rescuing the princess whom he has deemed is being held against her will, he waits for Aura to come to him:

> And the more you think about her, the more you make her yours, not only because of her beauty and your desire, but also because you want to set her free: you've found a moral basis for your desire, and you feel innocent and self-satisfied. When you hear the bell again you don't go down to supper because you can't bear another scene like the one at the middle of the day. Perhaps Aura will realize it, and come up to look for you after supper. (A, 75)

Significantly, the obstinate but essentially passive and nebulous Scottie finds it impossible to correspond to the love now genuinely offered to him by the real Judy Barton, but instead can love only the phantom Madeleine that his desire and his imagination as well as his severe frustration and guilt and sense of inadequacy have created—the cold, aristocratic Madeleine who is fragile and vulnerable and totally dependent on him. So too can Felipe, like Scottie a highly unstable and introverted personality, one who also is given to incessant fantasizing, love only the Aura whom he has created in his imagination.

The themes of death and resurrection are fundamental to both *Vertigo* and *Aura* and perhaps serve to explain why Fuentes, who throughout his work is preoccupied with the theme of immortality, should be so attracted to and so decisively influenced by Hitchcock's vision. In his perceptive analysis of *Vertigo*, Spoto quotes from T.S. Eliot's "Four Quartets," in which life and death are evoked not as opposites but as inseparable and even interacting phenomena:

> We die with the dying: See, they depart, and we go with them. We are born with the dead: See, they return, and bring us with them. (AH, 290)

These haunting verses resonate throughout both *Vertigo* and *Aura*; indeed they provide a poetic summation of the warped and tragic existences of both Scottie and Consuelo—Scottie in his desperate and poignant longing to bring back the dead Madeleine, and Consuelo in her fierce and unrelenting desire to bring back her long lost husband from the dead. At the very end, the determined Consuelo again fulfills her name as she attempts to console Felipe with her vow to bring back Aura:

> You plunge your face, your open eyes, into Consuelo's silver-white hair, and you'll embrace her again when the clouds cover the moon, when you're both hidden again, when the memory of youth, of youth re-embodied, rules the darkness.
>
> "She'll come back, Felipe. We'll bring her back together. Let me recover my strength and I'll bring her back . . . " (A, 145)

Both the desiccated Scottie and the vapid Felipe are in a sense reborn with the dead, with the renascence of both Madeleine and Llorente. An echo to the poem of T.S. Eliot comes in the epigraph to *Aura*, which also stresses the theme of birth and death, a quotation by Fuentes from Jules Michelet's *Le sorcière*. Here the dread Consuelo looms as a modern emanation of the ancient Aztec goddess Coatlicue, the Earth Goddess, dread goddess of womb and tomb, of life and death, goddess with a skirt of serpents signifying new life and a necklace of severed human hands and a human skull, that signify her deadly nature:

> Man hunts and struggles. Woman intrigues and dreams; she is the mother of fantasy, the mother of the gods. She has second sight, the wings that enable her to fly to the infinite of desire and the imagination . . . The gods are like men: they are born and they die on a woman's breast . . .

Ironically, Felipe is reborn with Consuelo, and at the end dies into her, just as Aura is continually born from Consuelo's witchcraft and irremediably dies into the crone. As we have seen, much of the pervasive mystery of *Aura* and *Vertigo* is the result of the profound spiritual resonance in both of them. It is no accident that both works are the creations of authors who have been profoundly influenced by Catholic theology, Hitchcock as the result of his strict, even punitive schooling in a Jesuit seminary at Saint Ignatius in Great Britain, and Fuentes the product of a Catholic Latin American culture and traumatic childhood experiences under the control of strict Mexican priests, painfully recounted in *La región más transparente* through the character of Rodrigo Pola, initially a budding poet and a stand-in for the young, idealistic, extremely talented Carlos Fuentes himself. Ironically even in a post-Revolutionary Mexico that separated Church and State, prohibited priests from wearing their frocks in public, converted monasteries into public schools and basketball courts, Catholic doctrine still reigned, particularly in the exclusive schools in Mexico which Fuentes attended. In the post-Revolutionary Mexico of the 1930s and 1940s, priests vociferously condemned sex before marriage and held over the miscreant the spectre of damnation to Hell for transgression. Thus even though both artistic creators may reject specific dogma, or burlesque that religion, as Fuentes does in his depiction of necromancy and the Black Mass in which Aura glances nervously at a crucifix that symbolizes the fate of Felipe, the concentration on life, death, and resurrection in both works testifies to the lasting, indeed indelible influence of Catholic theology on both the famed British-American director and the distinguished Mexican author.

Hitchcock's *Vertigo* is replete with terrifying images of the Fall of Man; the themes of profound, even inexpiable guilt and retribution permeate the work. Both Scottie and Judy Barton suffer intense feelings of inadequacy and guilt, unlike the glib but lizard-like Elster. *Vertigo* twice alludes to one of the most famous statues of Michelangelo, the exquisite, white marble *Pietá*, depicting a mournful Virgin Mary cradling the head of her martyred Son—alluded to in the way that a stricken Scottie falls from the step-stool, fainting into Midge's arms, tears welling in her eyes as she cradles him devotedly, tenderly clutching his unconscious head. Later on, when Scottie carries the limp, seemingly unconscious body of Madeleine from the turbulent waters of San Francisco Bay, the image of the Pietá again dominates the screen, only this time it is an ironic image, since Judy/Madeleine merely pretends to commit suicide and expertly fakes a near drowning. Crucifixion imagery is found even in the evocation of the psychologically tormented, maniacal serial killer Norman Bates in *Psycho*. Christian iconography also pervades *Aura*, and the emphasis on the demonic, as Aura is seen skinning a goat, her hair and clothing splattered with blood, the goat both an allusion to Satan, with his cloven-hoofs and spiking tail and the skinless goat, grisly symbol of the ultimate fate of Felipe, as he feels his features being stripped from him, demonstrates the power of the vision of purgatory and hell, of salvation and damnation, that are all part of the intricate Catholic faith that Fuentes both rejects and satirizes and yet whose impact on him from the epoch of his early childhood down to the twenty-first century has been profound and to which he dedicates a portion of his autobiographical dictionary, *This I Believe* (2005).

When Aura states cryptically to Felipe that one must die in order to be reborn, she alludes on one level to the martyrdom of Christ. Felipe has urged her to free herself from the clutches of Consuelo, to be reborn, just as he feels himself reborn with her:

> "She's trying to bury you alive. You've got to be reborn, Aura."
> "You have to die to be reborn . . . No, you don't understand. Forget about it, Felipe. Just have faith in me." (A, 123)

It is not only Aura but Felipe too who will be reborn. Indeed, as the result of the weird Black Mass, it is Felipe not Aura who feels pregnant—the prelude to his being reborn as Llorente. But to be reborn he must die, as the identity as Felipe Montero is suddenly and permanently swept away:

> When you wake up, you look for another presence in the room, and realize it's not Aura who disturbs you but rather the double presence of something that was engendered during the night. You put your hands on your forehead, trying to calm your disordered senses: that dull melancholy is hinting to you in a low voice, the voice of memory and premonition, that you're seeking your other half, that the sterile conception last night engendered your own double. (A, 117)

The epigraph to *Aura* acquires new meaning as, toward the end, Felipe makes a vow of eternal love to the dual feminine presence, a vow that seems to renew the vow made by Llorente to Consuelo:

> Then you fall on Aura's naked body, you fall on her naked arms, which are stretched out from one side of the bed to the other like the arms of the crucifix hanging on the wall, the black Christ with that scarlet silk wrapped around his thighs, his spread knees, his wounded side, his crown of thorns set on a tangled black wig with silver spangles. Aura opens up like an altar. (A, 109)

Once again, Fuentes masterfully utilizes cinematic techniques—here a series of bizarre superimpositions that reveal the influence of the scathing anti-Catholic vision of Luis Buñuel.

The naked, lubricious body of Aura is metamorphasized first into an immense crucifix, and the naked body of Felipe implicitly is transformed into an ironic Christ-on-the-Cross figure, as prelude to yet another superimposition that combines eroticism with ironic sanctification, as the writhing, receptive body of Aura is further transformed into an alter. And Felipe is mocked and degraded by the evocation of himself fused with the caricature of Christ "his crown of thorns set on a tangled black wig with silver spangles."

In this extraordinarily complex, labyrinthine work, it is first the tormented Felipe who is identified with the crucified Christ. Yet now, ironically, Aura herself is identified with the Cross of Crucifixion, and the key phrase "Aura opens up like an altar" blasphemous and probably the factor leading to the censure of the novel and its being deleted from the reading list at a Catholic girls school in Mexico, precipitating a scandal that resulted, as Fuentes himself gleefully stated, not in successful censorship but only in increased sales of *Aura*. The case against *Aura* was leveled by a minister of the PAN, the conservative Partido de Acción Nacional, and apparently after much hullabalu in the 1990s, more than a generation and a half after the publication of *Aura*, was dropped.

Although the Christ figure has initially been linked with Felipe, as a symbol of martyrdom, it is now transferred to Aura/Consuelo, as a figure of resurrection. Aura is the human, spectral cross on which Felipe is both crucified and, ironically, resurrected.

It is significant that Aura can remain with Consuelo for only three days at a time. Her disappearance, perhaps "resurrection" from the realm of Consuelo, seems to constitute an ironic allusion to the Resurrection from the dead of Christ on the third day. Yet salvation is denied to Felipe, just as it it is denied to both Judy Barton and Scottie in *Vertigo*.

Ironically too, Judy is called once more by Scottie at the very end, at the top of the fatalistic tower, by the name of *Madeleine*. Instead of instinctively seeking the protection of Scottie's embrace to hold off what appears to her as the spectre of Madeleine/Carlotta, the anguished Judy abruptly moves away from her lover, thereby indicating the depth of the terror that she is experiencing—and testifying once again to the tentativeness of her relationship with Scottie.

If we interpret *Aura* from a theological standpoint, Felipe is destroyed because he has passively allowed himself to participate in the Black Mass with Aura, who washes the feet of Felipe, then gives him half of the Divine Host, which he reluctantly consumes:

> You feel the warm water that bathes the soles of your feet, while she washes them with a heavy cloth, now and then casting furtive glances at that Christ carved from black wood. . . . she offers you half of the wafer and you take it, place it in your mouth at the same time she does, and swallow it with difficulty. (A, 107-109)

Similarly, in the world of transgression and punishment depicted by the ever-crafty moralist Hitchcock, the punishment for Judy's complicity in the murder of Madeleine is death, and the castigation of Scottie for his inhumane treatment of Judy is permanent madness. Yet it is also significant that the truly guilty, in the final version of the film, goes unpunished; Gavin Elster enjoys his lavish inheritance in Switzerland, safe from the authorities, with only the extremely unreliable Scottie left to corroborate any accusation against him. And indeed, with the one key person whose testimony could indict him—Judy—now deceased, Gavin Elster is safer than ever. And in the enigmatic *Aura*, while the complaisant Felipe is destroyed, the true culprit, the demonic Consuelo, at the end seems about to renew her powers, on the model of the dread Coatlicue. Although this ancient mother goddess, is depicted with flaccid breasts, because she has been exhausted by her tremendous effort of living life, of daily giving birth to the sun, her titanic, seemingly invincible force will be endlessly replenished, like that of her descendant and contemporary *máscara* Consuelo, by massive and reiterated human sacrifice.

In both *Aura* and *Vertigo*, the themes of time, death, and immortality are poetically visualized. A key scene in *Vertigo*, which represents a masterful evocation of the consciousness of mortality on the part of Judy/Madeleine and her anxious and eloquent desire to transcend the apparently battered Self, is found in the interlude between Scottie and Judy, both of whom are falling in love with one another, in the forest of giant sequoias, the

Figure 43. Existence as recurrent nightmare: Scottie plunges from tower to join Madeleine in death.

Figure 44. For Scottie, Madeleine is both redemptive new life and an open grave. Note harsh, stony backdrop.

enchanting Muir Woods in Northern California. Both Hitchcock and Fuentes are masters of creating and sustaining mood, and the atmosphere created by filming in the eery forest, containing the oldest living things on earth, is one of mystery and reverence. Time in both *Aura* and *Vertigo* is dramatically spatialized. Corresponding to Felipe's perception of the house of Consuelo as a series of temporal layers, is the gazing by Judy/Madeleine on the concentric rings of one of the giant sequoias, whose life span has encompassed events as remote as the Battle of Hastings in 1066, and that was finally cut down in the 1930s. Seemingly out of the haze of her Carlotta identity, Judy/Madeleine touches the rings and speaks hauntingly, "Somewhere in here I was born, and there I died. It was only a moment for you, you took no notice." The words are ostensibly those of the ghost of the embittered Carlotta, which has invaded and possessed Madeleine, acrimonious words hurled by a stricken Carlotta against her authoritative and finally heinously cruel husband, and against the society that had passively condoned her degraded status, as she wandered through the streets, wailing "Where is my child? Where is my child?" But on another level, the plaintive words are prophetic of Judy Barton's own fate, as neither her life nor her death essentially mean anything either to Gavin Elster or to an increasingly vexed Scottie Ferguson.

The concentric rings of the giant sequoia also symbolize Time not as a linear but as a recurrent, cyclical force, in which old identities resurge to dominate the new. The immense trees are photographed as ominous, as blocking out the light, as symbols of a past time that is so powerful that it crushes the present and denies the future. Throughout the film, the phenomenon of characters entering a dark labyrinth, symbolic of their entrapment and in the case of Scottie, self-entrapment, is reiterated. For example the forest of gigantic sequoias looms as an immense labyrinth, in which Judy/Madeleine loses herself. Entering a hallway photographed by Hitchcock as a tunnel-like enclosure and being consumed by the darkness is also seen in the way that Midge, in utter defeat, walks forlornly out of the corridor of the mental institution after realizing the hopelessness of Scottie's condition. Yet *Vertigo,* like *Aura,* is a work in which the forces of darkness and death are constantly balanced by those of light and life. The opposite of the corridor entry as disappearance and death, that of emerging from a darkened corridor into a new light and life, is perceptively analyzed by Wood:

> To anticipate, it is the significance that has accrued to the corridor image that gives the scene of Madeleine's re-creation—Judy's return from the beauty salon with face and hair transformed—such emotional intensity; she appears at the end of the hotel corridor in the light, walking towards Scottie (us), precisely reversing the previous corridor images and thereby intensifying the effect of resurrection that is the more poignant in that we know it, (as Scottie doesn't) to be in a normal sense, illusory. (HF, 84-85)

Corridors, passageways, labyrinths and chasms proliferate in both *Vertigo* and *Aura*, to emphasize existence as both a struggle and an enigma, and finally, for Judy and Scottie, and for Felipe, as well, as an inextricable trap.

The past which is brought back to impose itself upon the present and future in both of these spellbinding works is neither romantic nor liberating but fiendish. To resuscitate Llorente, Felipe's independent identity must be destroyed, and his soul must be captured and delivered to Satan. To convoke the spirit of the mad Carlotta, as Judy Barton does by assuming the role of a person who is transfixed by her, is to suffer the same horrible fate as the doomed Carlotta suffered. Even before the devastating climax of *Vertigo*, Scottie is essentially entrapped at the end in a sterile relationship with the transformed Judy. All that both can think of is to endlessly return to the same haunts where a glamorous and eloquent and silent Madeleine had so bewitched Scottie. Nothing new must ever break the spell cast permanently over Scottie by the lost Madeleine. So it is once more off to *Ernie's*—and beyond that, presumably, once again to the Palace of the Legion of Honor and to the Mission Dolores. Judy Barton allows herself to be dehumanized, roboticized and even when Scottie mysteriously, threateningly takes her one hundred miles down the peninsula to San Juan Bautista, gloomily and with increasing anxiety nevertheless obeys his wishes without even a whimper.

In a key scene after the laborious transformation of a vulgar Judy into a sophisticated and aristocratic Madeleine is complete, now all of Judy's hesitancies and anguish over the transformation have vanished; she actually seems to enjoy playing the role of Madeleine. Previously doubting and apprehensive, it is now a newly assertive "Madeleine" who takes the initiative by suggesting that they again go to luxurious and elegant *Ernie's* to dine. And Judy/Madeleine has donned the same black dress that she wore on the first night that Scottie saw her at the plush restaurant. Indeed, a frightening sign of the essential meaningless of the relationship between Madeleine and Scottie is that no element that was not part of the original and short-lived relation between Scottie and Madeleine is allowable in the painstakingly re-created relationship with Judy. Thus this final and seemingly contented association essentially goes nowhere. It is significant that Scottie, although seemingly happy, is now as narcotized as he was in the insane asylum. And he has not brought Judy/Madeleine back to his handsomely furnished apartment, rather they remain in her plain, sparse accommodations at the Empire Hotel. It is almost as if Scottie were unwilling to allow what he still believes is but a cheap, imperfect imitation of his radiant and seductive Madeleine into his own apartment. There are no acquaintances, of either the reborn Judy or the tranquilized Scottie, and no outsiders can be allowed into their "perfect" fantasy world, since none were part of the original relationship. Indeed, Judy/Madeleine and Scottie both dwell in a hermetically sealed world, just as do Consuelo and Felipe. In *Aura*, the sterility, literal in the case of Llorente, symbolic in the case of Consuelo, who consecrates her entire existence to a mere phantom, finally enmeshes Felipe as well, since his identity remains forever circumscribed by a phantom. Perhaps Judy's sudden and extremely careless and infortuitous donning of the incriminating necklace is the result of a strong subconscious urge to break out of her stultifying role, toward which she all along has been markedly ambivalent—or the desire to add something new to the relationship—the New ingredient that, ironically can only be the Old, and, in this case, the powerfully incriminating ruby necklace.

The clever and tenacious Scottie has used a combination of wheedling, implorations, and threats to withdraw his affection in order to compel the reluctant and complaining and resisting Judy to undergo the many changes that will convert her back into Madeleine. It is significant that shortly after she encounters Scottie on the street, Judy selects for herself a flower from a street stand. This is the last act of free will that will be allowed her by the increasingly dictatorial Scottie. This is similar to the mere token resistance that Felipe puts up to Consuelo. When Felipe states that he must leave temporarily to bring his personal effects, Consuelo informs him that a servant will go for his things. This is but another lie, for no servant is ever seen. As we have seen, the power of fate rules in both *Vertigo* and *Aura*.

In Fuentes, this deterministic vision is underscored by the very style of the work, the narrative voice in the future, corresponding to the second-person voice of Cruz's subconsciousness and oneiric unconsciousness in *La muerte de Artemio Cruz*. In *Aura*, as in *La muerte*, the future tense is not an open one but rather an imperative future. This future voice signifies what other young males who have preceded Felipe as victims of Consuelo have done and what he too must now do. Correspondingly, the extremely fatalistic vision of Hitchcock is commented upon by Hirsch, who sees Hitchcock as a master of the powerfully deterministic film noir:

> Like the traditional noir director, Hitchcock maintains a decided distance from his characters, looking down on them as they become entangled in the nets he carefully spreads. His typical posture is one of amusement—what fools these mortals be—as he masterminds the often catastrophic fates that confound his protagonists. Awful things happen to them—the Hitchcockian world is a series of traps for unsuspecting victims. Like Lang and his compatriots, Hitchcock watches dispassionately . . . a terrible pre-ordained destiny overtakes his characters.[23]

[23] See Foster Hirsch, *The Dark Side of the Screen: Film Noir* (San Diego: A.S. Barnes, 1981), p. 139. Subsequent references are included in the text, preceded by DS.

This is similar to the deeply ominous and bewildering world in which the hapless Felipe plunges in *Aura*, a world where even the votive lamps, normally symbols of hope, of the resurrection of the soul, are depicted in sinister terms, as "the spider's web of those devotional lamps" (A, 53). Even the glance of Consuelo is duplicitous. It is animalized in terms of a wild animal that suddenly scurries to take refuge in its darkened cave.

Just as Hitchcock presents a complex interplay between chronological time and immortality, so masterfully and symbolically captured in the forest of gigantic redwoods—towering symbols of eternity—so also does Fuentes. In both works, human life is reduced to but an insignificant span, as it becomes subject to a fiendish and eternally recurring past:

> You don't look at your watch again, that useless object tediously measuring time in accordance with human vanity, those little hands marking out the long hours that were invented to disguise the real passage of time, which races with a mortal and insolent swiftness no clock could ever measure. A life, a century, fifty years: you can't imagine those lying measurements any longer, you can't hold that bodiless dust within your hands. (A, 139)

Hirsch's analysis of the way in which a perilous world entraps the protagonists in Hitchcock's films can also be applied to the phantasmagorical and very ensnaring world of Fuentes's *Aura.* Indeed, both creators stress the dangers of giving oneself over, as do both Scottie and Felipe, Consuelo and Judy Barton, to a fantasy existence:

> In his films, the normal waking world is covered with quicksand. It is always dangerous for Hitchcock's characters to step beyond normal boundaries . . . In Hitchcock, to borrow Robin Wood's useful formulation, the night world often invades and gradually overtakes the day world; dark forces penetrate the most seemingly ordinary characters and settings. (DS, 140)

In fatalistic *Aura* as in night-enshrouded *Vertigo*, the night world ultimately dominates the fragile, evanescent day world. Although it has been stated that Hitchcock was displeased with the reserved acting style of Kim Novak, and indeed declared that she began to act convincingly only in the second half of *Vertigo*, when Novak played Judy Barton, and that he initially wanted Vera Miles, who had starred in *The Wrong Man* (1957), and who was under personal contract to Hitchcock, to play the role of Madeleine Elster, it can be seen that the great reserve which Novak projects as an actress, her air of restraint and remoteness—the perfect icy blonde goddess—is a decided asset in playing the role of the enigmatic, zombielike Madeleine. In the world of *Vertigo*, it is the dead, not the living, who are of major concern to the male protagonist, and Novak has the demanding task—at which she is very successful— of playing a role that has both a human side, in the person of the frank and earthy, even blunt Judy Barton, and an otherworldly, illusory, phantasmal side, in that of the spectral Madeleine. Indeed, the calm and even expressionless face of Kim Novak, her face that is many times frozen into a mask of voluptuous beauty, her distinctly nonemotional style of acting, with never a smile nor a frown nor a laugh nor a grimace such as characterize the histrionic acting style of Bette Davis or Joan Crawford, is perfect for the part of Madeleine. And, Kim Novak's highly restrained facial and full body gestures that freeze her into a Greek Aphrodite and Roman Venus, a twentieth-century love goddess, make her the perfect actress for the part of the ethereal, zombielike Madeleine. Another actress with stronger emotional responses, with facial contortions and gestures, would break the spell of the phantomlike being that Novak so perfectly plays. It is no accident that one of the very few biographies of the ever-elusive Novak, who now for decades has dwelt in seclusion, never returning to Hollywood, should be entitled *The Reluctant Goddess.*

And just as Judy/Madeleine is the *golem* created by the suave, sophisticated and seemingly concerned and compassionate but inwardly ruthless Gavin Elster, so too is Aura the creation of the outwardly frail and pious but essentially plotting and fierce and diabolic Consuelo.

Both *Vertigo* and *Aura* are characterized by a reductive, restrictive and ultimately tomblike space. At the outset of *Aura*,

Consuelo complains bitterly over the imitations society has placed on her dwelling, hemmed in on all sides by the modern buildings:

> They've walled us in, Señor Montero. They've built up all around us and blocked off the light. They've tried to force me to sell, but I'll die first. (A, 51)

As Scottie enters the Mission Dolores in pursuit of the always elusive Madeleine, his entering the old mission, a pocket of congealed time just as is the house of Consuelo, is viewed by Spoto as the equivalent to his entering a tomb:

> Scottie follows her to the Mission Dolores, where he enters a dark side door entrance to the old chapel which in turn leads to the cemetery garden. It is as if Scottie were stepping right into a large, dark tombstone. (AH, 309)

Although confining, space in both *Vertigo* and *Aura* is not sheltering but frightening—and brutally demonized. The second time that Scottie and Judy/Madeleine travel down the Peninsula to the Mission at San Juan Bautista, the immense trees lining the highway, which cover the automobile like a tremulous yet sinister canopy, are photographed hurtling by, and provide a graphic exteriorization of the atmosphere of increased menace with which *Vertigo* terminates. The towering trees symbolize the closing in of Fate on both occupants of the car, and undermine the expressed goal of Scottie, which is to directly and obstinately confront and repeat the past in order to free himself from it.

Similar to Scottie's entering the Mission Dolores is Felipe's entering the gloomy house of Consuelo, which, ironically, he seems initially to envision as a sanctuary from the outside world, but which ultimately becomes a hellworld for him. The theme of the *facile descensus averno*, from Virgil's *Aeneid, Book VI*, the ease with which one descends to hell—is summoned up by Fuentes, who like Hitchcock is a master of mythology. The door to the house of Consuelo, which like all the other doors is easy to open, having no lock, shuts quickly and permanently behind the still unsuspecting Felipe, signifying his irrevocable entrapment. In *Aura*, Felipe, once he has entered the domain of Consuelo, never re-emerges. Although the locales in *Vertigo* are much more variegated, most of them reflect a cramped, enclosed, and finally suffocating space, from the overcrowded apartment of Midge to the claustrophobic tower at San Juan Bautista, specially constructed by Hitchcock for the film, and from the menacing forest of sequoias to the way in which Judy/Madeleine's apartment is finally evoked, as a confined and stultifying space—an existential vacuum. External space is but the equivalent of Scottie's severe and irremediable self-incarceration.

It is ironic that both Scottie and Felipe Montero are connoisseurs of the past, because for both of them the past will change from romantic to terrifying. That Scottie is a collector of antiques adumbrates the way he perceives Judy Barton, as one more precious, fanatically desired object to be valued exclusively for its relationship with the past, as he accepts Judy both as a person and as a sexual object only for the spirit of Madeleine that seems to be present within her. Similarly and ironically, when Felipe appears in response to her advertisement, the first aspect of his credentials that Consuelo checks is his profile—-and she is satisfied because it matches that of Llorente. This scene parallels one of the key scenes of *Vertigo*. Although Judy Barton is a very attractive and personable individual in her own right, when Scottie first invites her to dinner, he is attentive only to the women who in some aspect are similar to his beloved Madeleine, elegantly dressed, aristocratic looking women whom he in his delirium wishes desperately to believe are the lost Madeleine come back to life. Although Judy is humiliated at Scottie's finding her repulsive and unwilling to touch her, she lacks sufficient self-integrity and assertiveness to sever the increasingly warped relationship. It is only after they have returned to Judy's apartment at the Empire Hotel and Scottie sees her in profile, in a darkened room, illuminated only by the eery green light of the neon sign outside her window, that Scottie can begin to love her. Seen in silhouette, her profile of course is a perfect match with that of the lost Madeleine, and Scottie at last begins to respond amorously to her, a girl who up to that point had been as cast-off and barely tolerated—as was the ever-willing and continually rejected Midge. And the greenish glow that encircles the beauteous but pedestrian

Judy transforms her into the phantasmagorical being that Scottie so persistently pursues.

It is ironic too that Scottie, whom the imperiously English Gavin Elster condescendingly refers to as the "hard headed Scott," insistently seeks at the beginning to convince Madeleine that she is not possessed by a demonic spirit, that her recurrent visions and nightmares are the result of a psychological disturbance that can be readily cured. Perhaps this is a type of wish fulfillment—Scottie's desperate longing to find a cure for his own essentially psychological disturbance which as his destructive *Vertigo* develops, explodes into full blown but, after Scottie is released from the sanitarium, carefully controlled dementia which is unleashed again only at the very end of *Vertigo*.

One of the crucial ironies of *Vertigo* is that Scottie, who will be forever plunged into the maelstrom of the irrational and the phantasmagorical is at the outset, the epitome of rationalism and pragmatism. Hitchcock, like the Fuentes who remains so much under his shadow, reveals the depths of passion and jealousy and vindictiveness and indeed even lust for vengeance underneath the façade of rationalism. Thus when Madeleine comes to Scottie's apartment at night with the account of her distressing nightmare of a tower and a livery stable, an apparently highly rational and pragmatic Scottie urges her to return with him to San Juan Bautista, following the theory that when she confronts the reality of the location, she will realize that her mind is playing tricks on her and her illness will suddenly dissipate. This is the same cure that Scottie at the end seeks to apply to himself—plunging into the conflictive past, repeating the traumatic events at San Juan Bautista that led up to the murder of Madeleine, will somehow cure him permanently of his crippling and highly debasing vertigo. Scottie, like Felipe, is extremely naive in both his theorizing and his lack of suspicion concerning the person with whom he is falling in love. The singlemindedness of Scottie, who discards everything and everyone, including the person who has been closest to him, the ever loyal Midge, in his obsession with Madeleine, is paralleled by that of Felipe, who ultimately is indifferent to the account by Llorente of his own experiences, attentive only to his evocation of Aura, as Felipe laboriously evokes the diary of the militaristic, staunchly monarchistic Llorente:

> . . . pays his respects to Napoleon the Little, summons up his most martial rhetoric to proclaim the Franco-Prussian War, fills whole pages with his sorrow at the defeat, harangues all men of honor about the Republican monster, sees a ray of hope in General Boulanger, sighs for Mexico, believes that in the Dreyfus affairs, the honor—always that word "honor"—of the army has asserted itself again.
>
> The brittle pages crumble at your touch: you don't respect them now, you're only looking for a reappearance of the woman with green eyes. (A, 131)

Just as Scottie remains so bedazzled by Madeleine that he time and again misses cues, disregards warnings and intuitions concerning her destructiveness, so too is Felipe so entranced by his beloved Aura, that he remains from start to finish oblivious to the signs, which multiply as the work continues, of her destructive and even deadly nature. Thus, toward the end, Felipe discovers an old photograph of Consuelo/Aura and again remains spellbound. Yet just as at the beginning, when he has failed to notice that Consuelo is not praying to God and the saints but to the Devil, so now does he fail to heed the final warning—Consuelo/Aura is posed against a painting of Lorelei—an allusion to the sirens along the Rhine whose beguiling chant caused the shipwreck and death of sailors:

> Then the photograph of Aura, of Aura with her green eyes, her black hair gathered in ringlets, leaning against a Doric column with a painted landscape in the background: the landscape of a Lorelei in the Rhine. Her dress is buttoned up to the collar, there's a handkerchief in her hand, she's wearing a bustle (A, 135)

Why are Scottie and Judy Barton, Felipe Montero and Consuelo, so easily absorbed by the Other, so that all of these characters basically dedicate their existences to the cultivation of mere fantasy beings? Perhaps it is because there is a horrible vacuum at the center of the existences of all four of these insecure

Figure 45. First Madeleine now Judy Barton repeatedly transformed into mirror image, both to underscore duplicity and evanescence.

Figure 46. Anguished close-up of Judy Barton as prelude to key flashback to traumatic tower scene of murder.

and increasingly desperate individuals, all of whom prefer to dwell in a limbo state.

Both *Vertigo* and *Aura*, masterpieces of their respective genres, are stories of thwarted love, of impossible love, and of the desperate and obsessive attempts of the living to bring back the beloved from beyond the tomb. This is the paradox of Consuelo—on the one hand an egomaniac whose cult of the past and of death requires the spiritual sacrifice of the living, on the other hand a person steadfastly devoted to the memory of Llorente and even when she herself is close to death fiercely seeking erotic love. The devastatingly beautiful Consuelo was the *raison d'etre* of her publicly vainglorious but privately self-abasing husband. Indeed, after his demise, Consuelo finds it impossible to live without Llorente and thus begins her bizarre death cult.

Similar to Consuelo, Scottie's love for the lost Madeleine is so great that it leads him, again and again, to quest for the fulfillment of that lost love in the Other. In a sense, the stunned reaction of Scottie once he learns that Judy has tricked him, is understandable, but not forgiveable, because he has surrendered so much of his own identity to guard and protect her. At the end, Scottie is particularly distressed at realizing that his major heroic achievement, that of plunging into the roiled waters of San Francisco Bay to rescue Judy/Madeleine, is a false attempt, a phony victory, that Judy in reality is an excellent swimmer, and he now derides Judy mercilessly for her deceit that so incisively undercuts what he believed to be his new found virility.

The oversensitive Scottie feels himself debased, once again, just as in his failure to rescue the policeman who falls from the roof to his death. Once more, Scottie's attempts to prove himself, to assert himself, to reclaim his lost masculinity, are all futile. Scottie's reaction to Judy/Madeleine rapidly evolves from voyeuristic attraction to deep emotional commitment to paternal protection and finally to a dangerous consecration of his entire existence to her—in a sense paralleling the consecration by the weak-willed, increasingly despondent Llorente of his whole identity to Consuelo, especially after the bitter loss of his especially exalted position in the imperial court of Maxmilian, a loss from which Llorente never really recovers. Both Llorente and Scottie never recover from the shock of their professional upheaval—Scottie from the permanent loss of his ambitions to head the San Francisco Police Force, Llorente by the collapse of his ambitions—his quest of power and glory through being a member of the splendid but extremely vainglorious and ephemeral court of Maximilian and Carlotta, ambitions permanently shattered after the capture of the Emperor by the forces of Benito Juárez and the subsequent trial and summary execution of Maximilian—despite pleas to an obdurate Benito Juárez from leaders throughout the world—at Querétaro at the Cerro de las Campanas, the ill-fated Hill of the Bells. Both Scottie and Llorente turn from the outside world of status and power-striving to the personal world, only to be shocked again, Llorente by the realization that he is losing to permanent insanity the last person on earth who means anything to him; Scottie by the sudden loss of his beloved Madeleine. Both males remain essentially unconsolable. As the anguished and helpless Llorente states, as pitifully unable to help his beloved Consuelo as is Scottie to rescue Madeleine:

> And finally: "Early this morning I found her walking barefooted through the hallways. I wanted to stop her. She went by without looking at me, but her words were directed to me. 'Don't stop me,' she said. 'I'm going toward my youth, and my youth is coming toward me. It's coming in, it's in the garden, it's come back . . .' Consuelo, my poor Consuelo! Even the devil was an angel once." (A, 133-135)

The anguished and lyrically eloquent and moving words of Llorente constitute an echo of the poignant, highly poetic words that Gavin Elster uses to evoke a similar alienation, a similar madness in his wife. The glacial eloquence of Elster contrasts with the halting, at times even stammering speech of the distressed Scottie. Both Elster and Llorente are power figures; both are exceedingly ambitious.

The difference, of course, is that while Gavin Elster is the shrewd dissimulator, paralleling Consuelo with Felipe, Llorente, like Scottie, is genuinely heart-broken. Llorente succumbs to death because of this extreme despair—a quiet desperation that also characterizes the extremely egotistical but at the same time incessantly self-doubting and extremely malleable Scottie

Ferguson. Llorente cannot exist without his Consuelo, without the love of the woman who deceives him as much as Judy/Madeleine deceives Scottie, for Consuelo is devoted only to Self, to the demonic perpetuation of her beauty. Thus, ironically, at the end, all three of the central characters—Felipe, Felipe/Llorente, and Consuelo, remain dedicated to and consumed by, a mere phantom—the ever young and ever tantalizing Aura. And here is the final parallel with *Vertigo*—at the very end, as he is suspended once more in time and in space, the anguished Scottie seems to reach out in his agony for the spirit of the seemingly lost yet eternally returning Madeleine.

Yet even though the stubborn Scottie and the indomitable Consuelo obsessively attempt to revive the dead, they succeed but temporarily. Consuelo through an intense effort of will and imagination revives both Aura and Llorente, only to lose them again and again. And, again similar to the classical hero Orpheus, Scottie painstakingly brings back his precious "Madeleine" to life only to see her once again torn away from him—and, like the classical Eurydice, twice lost to death.

Of all the cities in the United States, San Francisco is the one closest to dream. It is not only the all-enveloping fog that wraps the fabled city in an otherworldly mist, but the combination of swirling fog penetrated by brilliant sunlight and the effect of ocean water combined with steep hills laden with sinuous streets. San Francisco is a city easily romanticized, as the love song, inimitably recorded by Tony Bennett, "I Left My Heart in San Francisco" attests. And cinema, of all the arts, is the one closest to dream, so that in *Vertigo* we have the remarkable phenomenon of multiple layers of fantasy and dream. The eminent film critic Parker Tyler has affirmed that all good films have the quality of dream. And the acting of Kim Novak that is characterized by a lack of emotion; the face that most often is expressionless, just the opposite of a melodramatic actress like Joan Crawford or Bette Davis, complete with facial grimaces and contortions, adds to the aura of the impenetrable—and alluring—mystery so characteristic of *Vertigo* from start to finish. Ironically, Novak is not the slender, wraithlike actress who ostensibly would be far better suited to play a ghost. She is a large woman, finely proportioned, but almost heavy-set—and fully voluptuous, sensuality that is heightened by her form-clinging costume, as the provocative, superficially sassy but essentially pliant and ready-for-love subordinate—one catering insistently to male fantasies. Yet her carnality is not the exposed, taunting, almost lascivious fleshiness of another superstar of the 1950s, Marilyn Monroe, who was most often provocatively photographed with mouth open, lips pouting and ringed with fiery red lipstick and in extremely tight-fitting, revealing clothing often with full cleavage. In contrast, Kim Novak, who was propelled to worldwide fame by the studio director Harry Cohn to be both a rival to Marilyn Monroe and a replacement for Columbia Studio's scintillating but in the 1950s now aging screen goddess, Rita Hayworth, is extraordinarily restrained—a cold fire—her surface iciness contrasting with her desperately muted but seething sexuality, first projected in the film *Picnic* (1955, directed by the masterful Joshua Logan) and then in the film *Pal Joey*, in which she wins out over the extremely wealthy and sophisticated Rita Hayworth for the love of the errant, rakish playboy, Joey/Frank Sinatra.

It is extremely ironic that the equally restrained, soft-spoken Gavin Elster, in conveying to Scottie the increasing insanity of his wife, states emphatically but cryptically: "And she wanders, my God how she wanders." But Judy/Madeleine in her travels around San Francisco does everything but wander—her visits to the Mission Dolores, to the exclusive florist of Podesta Baldocchi, to the elegant all but deserted Palace of the Legion of Honor, are all highly deliberate, all planned to bait an elaborate trap for the naïve, unsuspecting Scottie. And the former detective too is everything but the wanderer that he self-deprecatingly describes himself as—indeed, his actions are all painstakingly deliberate, from his relentless even obsessive tracking of Madeleine to his obsessive quest for any sign of a resurrected Madeleine after he believes she has committed suicide—the seemingly pleasant, seemingly nonchalant Scottie again mistakenly believing, desperately wanting to believe—that she has appeared alive. And as the film comes to an inexorable climax, Scottie is more and more intense, fanatically badgering a resisting Judy to modify her appearance—by first donning an exact version of the clothing worn by Madeline, then insisting that Judy dye her auburn hair blonde, relentlessly hectoring a highly intimidated

Judy/Madeleine, who is willing to obey all of Scottie's demands if only he will love her—ultimately surrendering to an extremely adamant Scottie, the very last shred of her independent identity. In both *Vertigo* and *Aura*, the self is but a simulacrum; the reality of Judy Barton, despite her beauty and her affability and her willingness to love Scottie, are all irrelevant to him; indeed, he can hold her, touch her, kiss her, make love to Judy only to the extent that she is the Other, that she is the reincarnation of the ghost of Madeleine. Perhaps it is by re-creating the lost Madeleine that Scottie can finally assuage his powerful feelings of guilt in failing to rescue her. Similarly Consuelo in *Aura* has little but contempt for Felipe; it is Felipe transmogrified into Llorente that she fanatically seeks.

The color green is used extensively in both Hitchcock's mesmerizing film and Fuentes's fascinating and riveting short story—one of his finest works. In *Vertigo*, green is the color of Madeleine's car, her ever-elusive Jaguar, signifying new hope and new life for a shell-shocked Scottie, who has seen his career ambitions vanish after the sudden and permanent onset of his emotionally crippling illness. With aspirations of becoming police chief, Scottie refuses the boring nature and tediousness of a desk job at the San Francisco police department. Scottie exists in a state of suspended animation, from the devastatingly traumatic outset to the excruciating end of *Vertigo*. As Judy Barton, Kim Novak dresses in green, and it is an oneiric green light—literally the immense neon light of the street sign of the Empire Hotel where Judy has been residing, that mysteriously, even magically envelops and transforms her. Green also dominates *Aura*: the eyes that mesmerize Felipe are green, and Consuelo at one point wears a green dress. In both Hitchcock's masterpiece and Fuentes's *novella*, green is highly ambivalent; it signifies both renewal and destruction; it acquires in both works an unearthly, spectral glow, to signify uncanniness.

Indeed, the color green dominates both *Vertigo* and *Aura*. Even the headboard of the bed in Judy's hotel room at the Empire Hotel is green, as is Judy's skirt, as is the eery greenish light that falls over her as she emerges from the bathroom with her hair tightly coiled—the last element necessary to transform Judy Barton totally into Madeleine, thus fulfilling Scottie's obsessions. In *Aura*, the eyes of the bewitching phantom are a mesmerizing green, as is Aura's dress. Green represents a magic color that has a dual, ambivalent significance—both the color of hope, of renewal, of resurrection, and the color of the robes worn in medieval times by witches. Julio Cortázar's cynical remark about hope, in his superb novel *Rayuela* "esa puta vestida de verde" "That whore dressed in green," also applies to the entrancingly green-eyed Aura who has enjoyed multiple young lovers, who gives Felipe only false, unredeemed hope of transcendence and self-fulfillment. Thus green is symbolic both of new life and of death, both of the spiritual-hope, new life—and of the demonic.

Both Scottie Ferguson and Felipe Montero are essentially drifters; both are apt victims to be absorbed and destroyed in fantasy worlds. Scottie prior to his obsession with Madeline is a middle-aged drifter, with no strong attachments either to a romantic interest or to friends or family, none of which he ever mentions. And this is exactly the case with the inchoate dreamer and daydreamer and archetypal loner, Felipe Montero.

The invasion of Madeleine's fragile identity by a demonic figure from the past is but an elaborate hoax perpetuated by the eloquent and cunning Gavin Elster. But fantasies in both *Vertigo* and *Aura* become real for the highly gullible male protagonists, both of whom willingly embrace the dead that they bring to life. Scottie is transfixed not by Judy Barton but as Judy converted into a dead woman—as Judy becoming a resuscitated Madeleine—thus not only also allaying his deep, corrosive feelings of guilt played on viciously by Gavin Elster, who at the farcical inquest sadistically informs Scottie "We know who killed Madeleine," seemingly alluding to the invasive force of Carlotta that possessed Madeleine and drove her to suicide, yet so ambiguous that it also implies that Scottie killed Madeleine, that Scottie's vertigo impeded him from rescuing his beloved, whom Scottie knew was in mortal danger because of her rapidly escalating insanity, killed by the delusion that had possessed her. Both Scottie and Felipe are easily mesmerized by alluring, spectral women, who continually play upon their extreme vulnerabilities.

Hitchcock astutely plays with time in *Vertigo*, again and again returning to San Francisco's oldest architectural monuments, such as the haunting Mission Dolores, or the old Spanish colonial mission at San Juan Bautista. Indeed, cyclic time characterizes both *Vertigo* and *Aura*. Scottie at the end as at the outset of *Vertigo* is a suspended being—at the beginning grasping the collapsing gutter for dear life, at the end dazed and stricken and spellbound by the dead body of Madeleine. Cyclic time prevails in both *Vertigo* and *Aura*. In an ending never filmed but implied by Hitchcock, Scottie will once more embark on an endless wandering to search for yet another Madeleine to bring back to life. And, after Felipe has, like all of Consuelo's young lovers, become aged and spent, she will immediately discard him for a new young lover—one more reincarnation of Llorente.

Both *Vertigo* and *Aura* are works in which incessant masks predominate. *Vertigo* presents a congeries of masked characters. Behind his façade of suavity, sophistication and ever feigned gentleness, Gavin Elster is a ruthless killer, and the real Madeleine Elster never appears alive—only as a lady impeccably dressed in a gray suit whose neck has been broken by Gavin Elster, and the bruised body dragged to the top of the tower—ironically foreshadowing what a vindictive and enraged and savage Scottie will do at the end with the living body of a frantically struggling Judy.

But the impersonator of the real Madeleine Elster, her mask, Judy/Madeleine is a highly contradictory character—perhaps the most complex woman character ever created by Alfred Hitchcock—the seemingly confused, highly distraught, drop-dead gorgeous Judy/Madeleine. Edith Head remarked that Hitchcock wanted Madeleine to look as if she had just stepped out of the ubiquitous San Francisco fog—hence the imperative of Madeleine's gray suit—a garment that, ironically, Kim Novak considered confining to act in. Indeed, the color gray washes out silver blonde hair, striking blonde hair that is most thoroughly highlighted by a solid red or blue—as it is in the key scene after the attempted suicide, when Madeleine dons Scottie's bed robe and emerges seductivwely from his bedroom to act demurely but patiently, reclining at his feet, in front of a romantic fire.. But Hitchcock insisted on both the gray suit and the black pumps that Novak declared she never wore, because they accentuated the fleshiness of her calves. Beneath the mask—the apparent aloofness and at times even frostiness of Madeleine/Novak—is a voluptuous eroticism and a scarcely restrained sexuality, evident in the key scene in Scottie's apartment where the quirky protagonist suddenly turned hero and rescuer—at least in his imagination—quickly undresses a soaked Madeleine after her apparent suicide attempt when after contemplating the bouquet of flowers she has purchased, suddenly and, for Scottie, unexpectedly jumps into San Francisco Bay. Ironically, just as Judy, once an insistent Scottie encounters her at the Empire Hotel, totally becomes what she has vowed never to become—the reincarnated Madeleine—to delight the increasingly demanding and even maniacally possessive Scottie—just as Judy herself proposes dining at *Ernie's*—to which Scottie happily acquiesces—Judy's seemingly secure world suddenly and permanently disintegrates, like the huge cartoon-like flower petals in Scottie's nightmare.

Indeed, in one of the key, final scenes of *Vertigo*, a relaxed, joyous Judy/Madeleine's words to Scottie are laced with irony "*Now* I have you," she coos, just at the moment when she is losing him forever, as Scottie spies Carlotta's necklace that Judy has donned—perhaps in a semiconscious attempt to make her Madeleine transformation complete—to satisfy Scottie utterly, just as she has dutifully satisfied her first puppetmaster, Gavin Elster.

Both Scottie and Judy are sexually repressed, both find erotic fulfillment in one another, but only briefly. It is unclear whether Judy's final, desperate pleas of love to Scottie at the top of the tower at the end are sincere or perhaps instead constitute a desperate means of prolonging her life, as she confronts an increasingly vengeful and even vicious Scottie. Judy's relationship with Gavin Elster, the first re-creator of Judy as Madeleine and ironically, even more exacting than Scottie, cares nothing for her. Immediately after the murder, Elster drops Judy permanently and flees to Europe. Indeed the only person in *Vertigo* who does not wear a mask is the open, insightful, highly irreverent Midge Wood, expertly played by Barbara Bel Geddes. Yet underneath her insouciant manner, Midge too is impassioned, and rapidly becomes extremely jealous of Madeleine. Despite Scottie's reticence to reveal anything about his relationship, the fiercely intelligent Midge quickly infers what Scottie is after—sexual fulfillment with a dazzling blonde, with whom Midge tries desperately—and futilely—to compete. Although Midge is attractive and vibrant—

and blonde—she cannot compete with the smoldering, animal-like sexuality combined with the aloof, other worldliness of Judy/Madeleine.

Like Judy/Madeleine, like Gavin Elster—and paralleled by Felipe Montero in *Aura*—Scottie from start to finish is a series of masks. He doggedly pretends to be the reliable friend and faithful companion of Midge, even though he has no real interest in her, and, after his internment in a sanitarium as the inevitable result of mental collapse under the intolerable burden of guilt, exacerbated by the criminal Gavin Elster, Scottie is unable to respond to Midge, who attempts to play the role of a surrogate nurse, at all. Just as Judy Barton pretends to be an increasingly suicidal Madeleine—effectively to prepare an unsuspecting Scottie for the traumatic and murderous tower sequence—Scottie pretends to Midge that he has merely an avuncular interest in Madeleine. And an extremely savvy Madeleine, who understands that the best way to incite Scottie's love is to play hard to get—what the extremely honest Midge never is capable of doing—as in a low, sensuous voice Judy/Madeleine warns after being brought to Scottie's apartment and undressed by him, seems to warm the now testosterone enhcaned Scottie, stating directly, "I'm *married*, you know," even while entrancing him with her carefully controlled sensuality. This is similar to the way Aura, who repeatedly seems to warn Felipe away by ringing a death-tolling bell that is compared to one rung by lepers—and yet suddenly appears naked and seductive before him. Scottie from the very first moment he gazes on Madeleine at *Ernie's*, falls in love with her, and rapidly becomes obsessed by her. Even though Scottie casually refers to his incessant following of her as his "wandering," it is not only to fulfill his promise to Gavin Elster—the trailing of what apparently is an irrational wife possessed by the revenant spirit of her great grandmother who had committed suicide at exactly the same age that Madeleine is now—twenty six. It is apparently to impede this suicide and to gain the information necessary to hospitalize Madeleine that the Machiavellian Elster retains the services of Scottie.

The solemn coroner at the inquest of the real Madeleine Elster is merciless toward a still dazed and utterly passive Scottie, who is not even permitted to testify on his own behalf. The inquest into Madeleine's death is for Scottie an extremely traumatic experience indeed which exacerbates his already severely traumatized condition, at which Scottie is condemned at length and even sadistically for his extreme negligence in allowing two people to die quickly, a superficially objective inquest at which the corner quickly assumes the role of prosecuting judge at what is supposed to be merely a hearing, yet which rapidly assumes the status of a jury trial of Scottie. Indeed, a vexed Scottie appears to be but not what he is in reality—a material witness—but a guilty person under arraignment for murder. Although a mere witness to the death of Madeleine Elster, the hapless Scottie—a still benumbed victim—is irremediably condemned by the coroner—superbly played by Raymond Bailey, in one of his best, albeit briefest roles.

Thus Scottie's guilt is repeatedly exacerbated, as even the police chief, Scottie's former boss, seems unwittingly to be against him, as the chief bluntly testifies to the first time that Scottie had apparently caused the death of a fellow officer, as Scottie's vertigo prevented him from lifting himself off the gutter and grasping the hand outstretched to save him. Similarly in this film of dread and fatalistic cyclic time—so much like *Aura*—at the end it is a stricken Judy Barton—paralleling the self-sacrificing policeman on the rooftop at the outset of *Vertigo*—who professes love and concern for Scottie and who offers him the promise of salvation—and who again passionately kisses a distraught Scottie—in a repetition of the livery stable scene in which the deep and prolonged and seemingly redemptive kiss of Madeleine and Scottie is suddenly broken off by a startled and even terrified Judy, who states enigmatically "There's something I must do." Those words will be fatalistically echoed by Scottie at the very end, as he morosely drives a mute and increasingly disconcerted Judy/Madeleine down the Peninsula, down to the crime scene and to her death. At the end, Scottie is alone, shocked and, heedless of his vertigo, gazing on the body of Judy/Madeleine, perhaps wanting to follow her in death—reality coinciding with his traumatic nightmare in which he envisioned himself hurtling down at terrifying speed into Madeleine's open grave.

Figure 47. How many Madeleine's are found in Vertigo? Two or four—or six?

Figure 48. Judy's excruciating ambivalence: a new love life or unmasking and sentencing as a criminal accomplice?

At the end, both Scottie in *Vertigo* and Felipe in *Aura* are unredeemed, dangling figures, both shocked and bewitched by ghosts that they themselves have perpetuated. Indeed, *Vertigo* has been alternately titled "To lay a ghost" and this title applies equally as well to *Aura*, as it is the revenant spirit of the lost Llorente that Consuelo insists on bringing back to life in order to perpetuate their timeless love—a love that can be sustained only by the repeated physical and spiritual sacrifice of a series of young and malleable lovers who must become instantaneously Llorente. Indeed, just as the theme of the makeover—the itinerant Judy Barton from Salina, Kansas, a highly insecure, lower middle class working girl made over painstakingly by Gavin Elster as a refined blonde aristocrat, just as Judy will again be made over by a fanatic Scottie Ferguson—just as the highly talented yet malleable Hollywood superstar Kim Novak is made over by the excruciatingly exacting director Alfred Hitchcock, who throughout his directoral career in both Great Britain and the United States was entranced by a series of young, sensual blonde actresses whom he starred in his films: Madeleine Carroll in *The Thirty-Nine Steps* (1935) and *The Secret Agent* (1936), Grace Kelly in *To Catch a Thief* (1955), *Dial M for Murder* (1954) and *Rear Window* (1954), Vera Miles in *The Wrong Man* (1957), Eva Marie Saint in *North by Northwest* (1959), Janet Leigh in *Psycho* (1960) and Tippi Hedren in *The Birds* (1963) and *Marnie* (1964). In *Aura*, it is the hapless and in many senses unctuous Felipe who is made over by the demonic artesan, the fanatic Consuelo.

Everything in *Vertigo* has multiple meanings. Do the words "There's something I must do," allude to Judy's need to go through with the elaborate and deadly charade and run up the tower to implicate the innocent Scottie in the murder of the real Madeleine Elster, or is Judy implying that now that she has fallen in love with Scottie, she needs to prevent the crime from taking place, to protect her newfound lover? Similarly, the scream of Judy as Madeleine Elster's body falls from the tower is ambiguous. Is Judy pretending to be a stricken Madeleine who, supposedly, like her great-grandmother Carlotta takes her own life, as the pliable Judy conscientiously aids her master, Gavin Elster in his murder of his wife, or is Judy screaming at Gavin Elster in an attempt to stop him from committing a crime or is she doing just the opposite, complying with Elster's scheme to implicate an innocent Scottie, now the man whom she apparently loves? And even beyond this, is Judy/Madeleine's professed love for Scottie real or just one more aspect of her elaborate stratagem? It is ironic that the person at the end who is indeed very available is not Scottie but Judy/Madeleine. Scottie at the end asks Judy plaintively, and never gets an answer from an extremely reticent Judy—"Why did you scream, Judy?" The implication, however, is that Judy screamed to carry out her role as an accomplice to murder.

The ending of *Vertigo* anticipates the end of *Aura*, that is also suffused with ambiguity. Is the final embrace and kiss of Judy/Madeleine and Scottie a signal of Scottie's newly emerged forgiveness of Judy, of his being convinced that Judy's newfound love for him at least resulted in her desire to stop the equally fanatic Gavin Elster? Ironically, just as what seems to be the prelude to a typical Happily-ever-after Hollywood ending, there is a brutal and shocking *cambio de piel* in *Vertigo* that Fuentes most assuredly would appreciate, as the black-robed nun suddenly emerges from the darkness and is perceived by the anguished and unstable Judy as the dread spirit of Carlotta Valdés returning from the dead to destroy Judy Barton for being an accomplice in the murder of her great-granddaughter, or as the revenant Spirit of Madeleine Elster arisen from the tomb, to demand vengeance on The Other Woman. Thus, at the end, it is not only Scottie but Judy who is highly susceptible to delusions and who shares Scottie's mental and emotional instability—an unbalance that led Judy in the first place into collusion with Gavin Elster—for only a brief interval a temporarily contented Judy Barton, as she is comfortably ensconced in her relationship with an all-approving Scottie at the Empire Hotel and even takes the initiative in their love-making "muss me a little."

"I just put on my face," remarks Judy/Madeleine ironically, to warn Scottie not to muss her up before their departure, yet again, for *Ernie's* and yet Judy/Madeleine ambivalent and contradictory once again, as she immediately relents with the seductive "Well maybe just a little"—until Scottie abruptly changes his mind and takes her again to the fated monastery of San Juan Bautista. Ironic too is Scottie's exclamation to an increasingly terrified Judy/Madeleine—a terror evinced from the very start of *Vertigo*, as

Judy's eyes, nervously flitting from side to side, suddenly open wide in terror. Says Scottie enigmatically: "We have to go up to the top of the tower again, and then we'll both be free." His words prove to be ironic—the climbing again to the top of the tower results not in freedom for either of the doomed lovers but in death for Judy and recurrent madness for Scottie. Ironically, the only person in *Vertigo* who is at the end truly free is the criminal, Gavin Elster. Scottie's climb to the very top of the tower at the climax of *Vertigo* constitutes his desperate attempt to break the fatalistic curse of that psychosomatic illness. Yet as Midge has expressed matter-of-factly, at the very beginning, referring to the inexorability of Scottie's affliction: "There's no getting rid of it." Undoubtedly Scottie's guilt and his vertigo are both increased exponentially at the end, as he will suffer increased anguish and guilt for having compelled Judy/Madeleine to climb the tower from which she falls accidentally to her death, at the very moment when it seems that they both might have the chance to permanently exorcise the ghosts of the past. Perhaps it is this unresolved ending of *Vertigo*—just the opposite of a user-friendly, optimistic Hollywood ending that resulted, at least initially in the fifties, in *Vertigo*'s not achieving box office success but that now, in the twenty-first century, that has transformed it into an enduring masterpiece.

Geography in both *Vertigo* and *Aura* is both precise and symbolic. Gavin Elster weaves to a highly skeptical Scottie the alluring vision of a mysterious Madeleine, one who sits for hours at a point named the *Portals of the Past.* Thus from the very start the power of the past as a controlling force over the characters is underscored in a highly poetic manner. Elster, who in direct contrast to the always open, direct, sincere Midge is eloquent, commanding, and highly elusive and deceptive, with the huge window of his office overlooking his immense shipbuilding empire, and confirming his wealth and power, nonetheless complains about contemporary, twentieth century San Francisco and how much it has changed. Perhaps in a bold attempt to lure Scottie out of his sudden retirement, Elster creates an elaborate vision of a romantic San Francisco of the nineteenth century when men had unbridled freedom and power. He alludes to the callous husband of Carlotta, who after building her a lavish mansion and after she had borne him a child, abruptly threw her away. Here is an adumbration of the fate of both the real Madeleine Elster and the fake one—the Judy Barton who after the murder is successfully perpetrated is quickly and permanently abandoned by Elster. It is Scottie in the twentieth century who along with Elster represents freedom and power—the power to reshape a socioeconomically inferior and initially protesting Judy into the restrained and elegant Madeleine when he believes he has failed to rescue his beloved Madeleine Elster from an early, tragic death.

Vertigo, initially underappreciated, is now regarded as Hitchcock's greatest film. And *Aura*, the *novella* that the eminent Argentine short story writer Julio Cortázar has stated that he wished that he had written, stands as one of Carlos Fuentes's greatest works, from his early period that produced his masterworks: *La región más transparente*, *La muerte de Artemio Cruz*, and *Cambio de piel* and that, along with the spectral *Aura*, constitute the cuadrivium in which is contained the essence of Fuentes's artistic achievement.

Madeleine, unlike the constantly hovering and fitfully intervening Midge, continually eludes Scottie—and thus increases his desire for her. A key episode is the witnessing by Scottie of Madeleine stopping at the once elegant Hotel McKittrick and going up to the second story, where she is glimpsed by Scottie at a window. But the mystery is increased when the duplicitous hotel clerk—in league with Gavin Elster—denies that Madeleine ever entered the hotel, and maintains staunchly that the room which Madeleine has briefly occupied is vacant—Madeleine's key to her room still at the front desk. The mystified Scottie—and the spectator of *Vertigo* as well—now begins to doubt his own perceptions. Is Madeleine real or a ghost? Is the sarcastic hotel clerk in on the deception of Scottie, is she another loyal collaborator of the *titiritero* Gavin Elster, who silkily plays the Machiavellian role that is also so often portrayed by males in Fuentes's works, from the demiurge arch-plotter Ixca Cienfuegos in *Where the Air is Clear* and the shyster and manipulator Artemio Cruz in *The Death of Artemio Cruz* to the chameleonlike and sinister forces in *La cabeza de la hidra*, incarnated in the maleficent figures of the shadowy Director General of Pemex, Petróleos Mexicanos, whom Fuentes stunningly evokes in terms of

Mexico's arch traitor Victoriano Huerta, and the seemingly noble and heroic but in actuality scheming and ruthless narrator—another of Fuentes's many killer narrators—the diabolic Timón, whose true name is never revealed, as he hides behind a munificent role from Shakespeare's drama, *Timon of Athens.*

An extreme fatalism characterizes both *Vertigo* and *Aura*. From the very start, Felipe Montero like Scottie Ferguson, is doomed. Both continually thwarted males have great, never-to-be fulfilled ambitions. Scottie disdains the possibility of a desk job on the force after his crippling disability makes the police chief position impossible. Yet Scottie clings fiercely to the vision of himself as Superhero—an allusion that is, temporarily at least, fulfilled by the inveigling Madeleine, who pretends to be confused, hysteric and extremely vulnerable—just the opposite of the redoubtable Midge. Indeed, Barbara Bel Geddes as the determined Marjorie Wood, truly exemplifies the "hard-headed Scot" as Scottie is derisively called by Gavin Elster, whereas a hitherto restrained Scottie is drawn toward a torrid love affair made even more enticing because it is with someone else's wife—the highly unstable, haunted wife of a Gavin Elster of whom the rootless Scottie—as alienated as is Judy Barton—cautious and of whose exalted status Scottie is secretly envious—not Judy, who is always extremely pliable. Love signifies entirely different things for Scottie and Judy; the highly insecure Judy who comes from a family where the father abandoned her mother, and fervently desires above all security and protection from males, views love as necessary for what she most desperately desires, protection and devotion and comfort, whereas Scottie perceives love as the fulfillment of romantic illusion, sexual desire, and male prowess.

Thus the initially enigmatic words that the apparently hallucinatory Madeleine states to Scottie, "One shouldn't live alone" apply not to Madeleine Elster's sheltered but unsuspecting wife, but to the alone—and lonely—Judy Barton herself. In a film, like *Aura*, based on continual ellipses, we never really know what the real Madeleine Elster is like—a pampered socialite or a battered recluse, since she is evoked while alive only from the jaundiced, hypocritical and utterly calculating perspective of Gavin Elster. Judy wants above all to be loved for herself alone, which for Scottie is impossible. Even at the very end, right before Judy's accidental fall from the tower, Scottie cries out in desperation and genuine anguish, "Oh Madeleine, I loved you so," underscoring the extreme difficulty of his ever being able to love Judy Barton for herself, which for the disdainful hero, who becomes closer and closer as a soulmate to Gavin Elster in his elitism and his cruelty.

Paralleling the over vacillating Judy/Madeleine, in *Aura* is the fragile self evoked constantly in terms of the insubstantial Other—Felipe. Even structurally, he never is an "I," only a "you"—the "you" signifying but another ghost, this time that of Llorente. The words of Elster that Scottie initially scoffs at prove grimly prophetic:

> "I believe that some harm may come to her."
> "From whom?"
> "Someone dead."

The dry, clipped, unemotional delivery of these threatening lines by a poised Elster—one of the finest roles of the English actor Tom Helmore—makes them all the more ominous. The poetry of San Francisco is remarkably captured by Hitchcock in a series of *chiaroscuro* shots. Thus the alleyway that leads to the back entrance to the exclusive Podesta Baldocchi Floral Shop is photographed in darkness and light, to signify entrancing mystery. The wordlessness of this key episode compels the spectator to concentrate on the at once beautiful and mystifying images. As he silently spies on her, Scottie himself is derealized by being photographed through the opaque glass door—as a shadow, not as a human being. A similar shot is utilized when Scottie enters the lugubrious monument to the past, the eery McKittrick Hotel, deliberately set up by Gavin Elster as a residence of ghosts. There seem to be no other inhabitants of the huge mansion—once Carlotta's mansion, the nineteenth century paradise from which she was permanently expelled—except the duplicitous concierge and Judy/Madeleine, and even Madeleine quickly and mysteriously disappears after a bewildered Scottie initially catches sight of her at an upstairs window. But when Scottie prods a sinuous, initially forceful and mocking landlady, expertly played by the petite but recalcitrant character actress Ellen Corby—to show him the room, Madeleine has vanished and Scottie—and even the viewer of

Vertigo—begin to doubt her reality. Indeed, we begin to suspect that Scottie is delusional. Significantly, for all the traffic and people in downtown San Francisco—in reality a populous, major U.S. metropolis—the City in *Vertigo* emerges as an extremely lonely place, dominated by the insistent pursuit by Scottie of an apparent victim—Madeleine—who is really the predator, and the hapless Scottie, who rapidly and hopelessly falls in love with her—the highly gullible prey. Although Gavin Elster disappears from the film after the tortured inquest scene, he continues to be the manipulator—a behind-the-scenes but powerful force on both Judy Barton and Scottie Ferguson.

Although Scottie, toying with Midge, casually defines himself as "available Ferguson," he is never available for Midge—and indeed it is Judy who is, toward the end available for Scottie—but only because, like Carlotta before her, Judy has been abruptly and permanently ditched by Gavin Elster, the wealthy and powerful male who finds her, elevates her to high society, coldly and remorselessly exploits her—perhaps with the enticing promise that she will be the next Madeleine Elster—then quickly and permanently abandons her after paying her off. Indeed, adding greatly to the enchantment of *Vertigo* is that throughout the film Hitchcock focuses not on the pedestrian, as he deliberately eschews ordinary people and unimpressive shops and diners, aspects of San Francisco that appear in many Hollywood films like the menacing *Dark Passage* (1947, directed by Delmar Daves and starring Humphrey Bogart and Lauren Bacall) but almost always on the most exquisite and impressive settings—from the lavishness of *Ernie's* and the luxuriousness of the office of Gavin Elster on the Embarcadero with its imposing, expensive, mahogany-paneled walls and immense picture window through which is seen the gigantic and the immense ship building crane in ac tion, symbolizing Elster's power and authority, to which Scottie initally is deferent, to the fashionable and highly exclusive Men's Club where Gavin Elster meets Scottie to receive the detective's report on the strange activities of Elster's supposedly deranged wife, to the grandiose ballroom of one of San Francisco's most luxurious hotels, The Fairmont on Nob Hill, where Scottie dances listlessly with an apprehensive, disconsolate Judy Barton.

When Scottie glimpses Madeleine purchasing a small bouquet of flowers at the chic Podesta Baldocchi it is, once more, first from the back, again to underscore both Madeleine's elusiveness and her mystery—and Scottie's rapid entrancement. Alfred Hitchcock began his film career as a titler in the Silent Film in Great Britain, and much of the first part of *Vertigo* occurs in silence—character and plot conveyed through the images that are reinforced by the mysterious, haunting music of Bernard Herrmann, who also did the superb music for Orson Welles's *Citizen Kane* (1941) and the piercing, violin studded score for *Psycho*. And in the haunting world of *Vertigo*, the mood of the otherworldly is enhanced by the slow, sinuous movement of the film as well as by the haunting, violin suffused music of the great Bernard Herrmann. The sense of unreality deepens as Scottie stealthily enters another symbolic door—that of the Mission Dolores—to view Madeleine before the gravestone of Carlotta Valdés. Hitchcock uses a special filter expertly to create a fog-like atmosphere in this intensely poetic scene, as if it were an impressionist painting of a garden brought to eery life—photographed in sunlight that nonetheless acquires an transcendental, mistlike glow, as if the sequence were a waking dream. Once again Madeleine in the ghostly cemetery is first photographed in a distant shot, to underscore her mystery, her elusiveness and her unattainability. Similarly, in *Aura* the mood masterfully created by Fuentes is one of otherworldliness, even though, as in *Vertigo*, there is a detailed, even exacting concentration on physical reality.

The dialogue in both *Vertigo* and *Aura* is incessantly opaque. Madeleine continually plays a cat and mouse game with Scottie, appearing and disappearing, leading him on a futile chase through the labyrinthine streets of San Francisco back to his own apartment near Coit Tower. Similarly, Aura suddenly appears to Felipe and then vanishes; she is the beauteous and alluring bait to hold Felipe entranced until the sorceress Consuelo can claim his soul. When she is with Scottie in the cavernous Muir Woods, the seemingly unstable Madeleine repeatedly breaks away from him, first to plunge into the dark woods that seem menacing and later to rush toward the roiled ocean at Cypress Point—giving Scottie the impression that she is once more about to commit suicide—and thereby increasing both Scottie's protectiveness and his physical desire for the alluring girl. Judy/Madeleine, smooth and exceedingly accomplished in her Madeleine role, carefully and repeatedly plays on Scottie's thwarted *macho* instinct—to re-create him as her hero. The elaborate process of re-creation, first practiced astutely by the master Gavin Elster on an eager Judy Barton, is continued by his apt pupil, Judy, who re-creates a befuddled and aimless and depressed Scottie as a bold, adventurous hero, singlehandedly rescuing his damsel in distress—exactly the role that Felipe in *Aura* seeks to play, as he fashions himself the noble knight who will rescue his beloved, highly distressed Aura from the clutches of the dragoness Consuelo. But both male protagonists are easily duped—the difference is that Scottie is extremely resentful of being toyed with—as at the end, he remarks bitterly that Judy must be an excellent swimmer—since the rescue at Fort Point that he has found so gratifying to his *macho* ego is but a sham—and he is but the pathetic dupe of the woman whom he loved. Similarly, the spectral and provocative Aura, who appears naked before Felipe and rapidly seduces him, is not imprisoned by her harridan aunt as Felipe mistakenly believes, but instead is sustained, vivified, empowered by Consuelo, the most powerful force in the narrative.

Judy/Madeleine declares that it's wrong to live alone and reaches out to Scottie. Here again the dialogue is suffused with mystery and with irony and Scottie's fateful words adumbrate the tragic ending of his amatory relationships, first with Midge, then with Judy Barton:

> Madeleine: "Only one is a wanderer. Two are always going somewhere."
> Scottie: "No, I don't think that is necessarily so."

Is Madeleine uttering the words that Gavin Elster has taught her in what must have been many rehearsals, or is she improvising? The poetic quality of her utterances leads us to believe that these are words that Gavin Elster placed in her mouth—corresponding to the filmscript architected by Hitchcock, Samuel Taylor and others that is delivered to Kim Novak. And there is even a link—a mysterious one, like everything else in this haunting film—of Gavin Elster with the shadowy Alfred Hitchcock—who is, played on the directorial level, the master manipulator, the role so brutally yet successfully played by Gavin Elster. It is Hitchcock, who like Gavin Elster takes beautiful blonde actresses like Kim Novak and, ultimately Tippi Hedren, molds them to conform to his elaborate, erotic fantasies, then, as occurred with the mesmerizingly beautiful Tippi Hedren, abandon them when they fail to fulfill his desires. It is Scottie who unwittingly predicts the tragic outcome of the relationship which goes nowhere, which after the fanatic transformation of Judy into the reborn Madeleine, lapses into a sterile patterning with repeated dining at *Ernie's*—becomes closed and even suffocating. It is highly significant that Scottie, once his Pygmalion-in-reverse transformation of Judy into Madeleine is complete, does not take Judy/Madeleine back to his apartment; she is holed up by him in a weird colloidal suspension at the seedy Empire Hotel. Indeed, the relationship is less of love—either emotional or physical—than it is of perversity and perversion.

The key scene in Muir Woods, with the towering sequoia trees, the oldest living things, becomes but one more twisted stage for the artful Madeleine. The outspokenly effervescent Midge is always dressed smartly but casually; her attitude ranges from flippant to mocking: "Was she a ghost?" "Was it fun?" In contrast, Madeleine is regally coiffed and elegantly dressed—she wears a white coat with a black blouse and a matching black bag—a living, stylish *chiaroscuro*, as she lures Scottie out into the cavernous Muir Woods and then to the Oceanside. Ironically, the ancient trees for a complaisant Judy playing Madeleine, signify not strength but death. As Judy/Madeleine states emotionally, seeking to lure an ever-willing Scottie into her trap by playing the *thanatos*-haunted victim: "I don't like it . . . knowing that I have to die." She attempts to give Scottie the impression that just as the stricken Carlotta took her life at age twenty-six, so too is she possessed by Carlotta's tormented spirit, about to die—and thoroughly awakens Scottie's heroic instincts—the same ones that led him to fanatically seek the position of Police Chief. In direct contrast to the coy, seductive Madeleine, Midge's mistake again and again is coming on too strong, too self-possessed, leaving no

Figure 49. Greenish mist envelops living ghost into which Judy has been fanatically transformed by compulsive Scottie.

Figure 50. False embrace as prelude to frantic and enraged dragging of Judy to top of tower and to her death.

room for Scottie to play the *macho*—it is not only that the highly sensual Madeleine is so great a sexual turn on that Midge cannot compete with her. And Judy/Madeleine, who in reality is a far tougher person than Midge, is also far more experienced is projecting vulnerability:

> "Oh Scottie. . . I don't want to die"
> "I'm here. I've got you now."

Scottie's comforting words will later be repeated by Judy/Madeleine right before she dons Carlotta's incriminating necklace: "I've got you now, haven't I," ironically at just the precise moment when she is about to lose a now suddenly enlightened Scottie forever.

It is significant that, before *Vertigo* even begins, the credits first focus on the enticing red lips of Kim Novak, or an actress playing Novak—highlighting her sensuality—and only then on her eyes. It is also significant that the vertigo symbols—the elaborate whorls that enticingly emerge from her eyes, spirals colored red and gold and blue and purple and signifying dizziness—and entrapment—also retreat back into her eyes. Madeleine will become the hypnotic focus of Scottie from the very first moment he catches sight of her at *Ernie's*, to the last time that he embraces and kisses her at the top of the bell tower of San Juan Bautista. *Vertigo* is a story of male obsession and male control and of female complaisance—Judy desires above all to please. The readily moldable Judy Barton is presumably much more than Gavin Elster's accomplice, she is his lover, and she willingly becomes his accomplice because she, like the gullible Carlotta, wife of the nameless power baron in the nineteenth century, the Carlotta who initially was an impoverished dance hall girl whom he initially cherished and then destroyed, is drifting through life and like Carlotta's husband and Scottie, has haunting but highly corrosive ambitions. Indeed Judy Barton is both delighted and intrigued by the suave, debonaire, and extremely wealthy Gavin Elster, and above all willing to be manipulated by Elster. And Judy Barton becomes as cold-blooded as Gavin Elster—it is not only the money that impels her to become the alluring pawn that bewitches Scottie, but also the promise of becoming the new Madeleine Elster. Thus the shock that Scottie experiences after the merciless attack by the sadistic coroner at the inquest of Madeleine Elster is paralleled by the devastating shock that Judy no doubt experiences after she successfully aids Gavin Elster, because instead of entering the wealth and power world of the man whom she fashions as a husband-to-be—as his permanent mistress or even his new wife—she is suddenly and permanently abandoned by the wily, cynical, and brutally opportunistic Elster and she is thrown back into a life of drudgery and of only marginal economic stability—until once more initially and very temporarily rescued by Scottie.

Thus, when Scottie, after his release, still uncured, from the insane asylum, encounters Judy on the San Francisco street, they both once more have been reduced to wanderers—and they both begin *again* to wander together—and they both, as Scottie has unwittingly stated previously, go nowhere. Extremely attractive and personable, Judy is highly insecure, particularly after having been jilted by Gavin Elster, who knows that Judy can do nothing to incriminate him. The question is why the initially frightened and suspicious and crafty Judy dons the necklace of Carlotta, knowing that Scottie has seen the necklace several times, as he not only followed but remained himself hypnotized by Judy/Madeleine. Does Judy subconsciously desire to be revealed for what she is—an accomplice to a murder that resulted in psychic damage to an innocent man who fell in love with her—or does Judy wish to communicate to Scottie—without revealing it in words—that she is guilty, so that she may obtain what she really desires—that Scottie love her for herself and not as a mere *simulacrum*. Does Judy seek even before Scottie desires to do it, to free herself from the ghosts of the past? This is one of the many unsolved mysteries of the extremely complex *Vertigo*. Judy does not don the necklace out of stupidity or indifference—perhaps she seeks to gratify Scottie even more by being as "Madeleine" as she could be.

The deliberate expressionlessness of Kim Novak as Madeleine/Judy is key to understanding *Vertigo*. First and foremost, Kim Novak has the most challenging role in the film, as she must play Madeleine/Judy, the extremely artful creation of Gavin Elster, then a meretricious Judy Barton, and then finally a Judy turned into Madeleine by Scottie, who deeply resents that he was not the consummate artesan that Gavin Elster was. Indeed, just as cyclic time, the re-appearance in contemporary Mexico of the hidden Aztec gods and goddesses, so expansively evoked by Carlos Fuentes in *La región más transparente*, just as the ghosts of Hernán Cortés, Bernal Díaz, Moctezuma II, Cuauhtémoc and Pedro Alvarado all inhabit Fuentes's epic and magical Mexico City, so does Hitchcock create a magical San Francisco, mythifying the haunting city in scene after scene. The nineteenth century gold rush days of San Francisco are once again, as in so many Hollywood films like *Hello Frisco Hello* (1943, directed by Bruce Humberstone and starring another blonde Hollywood goddess, Alice Faye) now converted into exuberant myth and permeate *Vertigo*. Indeed, the figure of the domineering *macho*, revelling in his "freedom and power" characterizes least three of the males in *Vertigo*: Gavin Elster, villainous, grave, highly manipulative, a perfect façade of gentility; Scottie, who is rapidly jealous of Gavin Elster's social position and affluence and above all his role as exacting Pygmalion, and the thirdly, nameless plutocrat, the husband of Carlotta Valdés, who encountered her as a dance hall girl, elevated her to social prominence, even building a mansion for her, then suddenly and permanently abandoning her—just as Gavin Elster does with his mistress Judy Barton as soon as her usefulness to him is over—an abandonment that Scottie up until the very end of *Vertigo* intends to do again, as he lashes out against Judy and only in the final moments before her suicide seems willing to forgive her—and to grant at least partial credence that Judy screamed at the top of the tower to attempt to prevent Elster from killing his wife. Yet this story seems to be but another lie, since Judy in her flashback to the murder scene envisions the lifeless body of Madeleine—killed in essence *twice*—the wife whose neck an extremely cautious Elster, taking no chances that his wife might survive the fall, breaks prior to hurling the body off the tower. The scream of Judy that Scottie is so obsessed with thus is of key importance. It is to convince Scottie that Madeleine, is terrified at hurling herself from the tower—to make it seem as if Madeleine Elster—the real one—was still alive when in fact her already dead body was thrown from the tower. And the probable, highly fatalistic conclusion to *Vertigo* is Scottie's hurling himself from the tower to join Judy in death—monstrously foreshadowed in his nightmare of falling himself onto the roof of the mission at San Juan Bautista to join his beloved Madeleine in death. Why does Judy at the end of *Vertigo*, terrified by what looms as the return from the dead of Carlotta, move out of Scottie's protective embrace and suddenly falls accidentally from the window? This is but one more center of ambiguity in Hitchcock's now classic film.

This is the dark, fatalistic world that is meticulously constructed by Hitchcock. The key scene in Scottie's apartment of the self-possessed Madeleine right after her suicide attempt by leaping off the Golden Gate Bridge and the discussion about falls—whether Scottie has ever fallen into the San Francisco Bay—constitutes an opening for Scottie to reveal his great weakness to Madeleine as he has obsessively done so to a maternally understanding and forgiving Midge—that he almost fell to his death from a high building. Instead, Scottie tells Madeleine nothing about the incident or about his devastating vertigo, preferring to keep in her mind the romantic image of Scottie as bold and valiant hero, which he will subsequently play to the hilt, masking his increasing sexual desire for Madeleine behind a façade of sheltering paternalism toward her. Indeed it is impossible to imagine that Scottie would expose his vulnerability —his corset and his cane, his fear of heights that are only as high as a stepladder—to Madeleine. Now that he has saved her life, he is responsible for her. Like Gavin Elster although not to the extent of committing murder—which nonetheless it becomes finally apparent to a terrified Judy Barton that the deranged Scottie is capable of when he drags her by the throat to the top of the tower at San Juan Bautista—Scottie is devious, callous, and cruel. He is totally exploitative of Midge, but when she attempts to find out about her glamorous competition, Scottie tells her nothing. Here, Hitchcock carefully exploits the diffident "Aw, shucks" boyishness of Jimmy Stewart, seen in a countless number of Stewart's films like *Mr. Smith Goes to Washington* (1935, directed by W.S. Van Dyke) and *It's a Wonderful Life* (1947, directed by Frank Capra) to create the façade of casualness, even innocence that is but an elaborate mask for Scottie's fanaticism and his aggressive and dominating and thoroughly demeaning treatment of Judy Barton. It is significant that even after Judy has surrendered the last shreds of her identity—her hair style, which as a down-to-earth Judy she has worn casually draped over the neck—to force her to fasten her hair into a tight whorl—Scottie does not take her to his apartment to live but is content to keep her in the Empire Hotel, in amorous suspension, perhaps even granting her a probation—to see how much she will continue to fulfill his expectations/demands in the Madeleine role that so excites him and indeed is essential for him in order to make love to her. Perhaps this is the reason—to be totally accepted by Scottie, to become his wife—that Judy deliberately dons the necklace right in front of him, to excite him and to prove that she can play the Madeleine role to the hilt—just as the ambitious, perfectionist Kim Novak initially reluctant and objecting, finally strove to please her demanding master, Hitchcock, needing to prove her abilities in a way that Jimmy Stewart, already legendary, never had to prove. Indeed, although Htichcock fanatically chose the elaborate costumes for his blonde divinitries—Grace Kelly and Kim Novak and especially Tippi Hedren, to whom he presented as a gift the sable mink coat she wore as the elitist melanie Daniels and spent more on her wardrobe than he did on her initial salary. And Cary Grant has stated that in a lavishly and elegantly costumed film like *To Catch a Thief*, he himself was given the freedom to choose his own expensively tailored wardrobe[24]. Both *Vertigo* and *Aura* are ridden not only with ghosts but with characters—both male protagonists and female ones—who rapidly become versed in deception. Just as Scottie Ferguson plays double and a triple role with Madeleine Elster, so too does a crafty Felipe play a double role with Consuelo, pretending to work assiduously on the memoirs of Llorente that Felipe finds overwritten, pretentious, and boring, but in reality cheating on his employer to return to long-postponed work on his doctoral dissertation. Thus not only Gavin Elster but Scottie as well becomes a master of evasion and deception—paralleling the seemingly noble-hearted Felipe Montero.

Not only in *Aura* but in many of his works, from *La región más transparente* and *La muerte de Artemio Cruz* to *Cristóbal nonato* and *Los años con Laura Díaz*, Fuentes demonstrates both

---

[24] See *Writing with Hitchcock: The Collaboration of Alfred Hitchcock and John Michael Hayes*, by Steven DeRosa (New York and London: Faber and Faber, 2001) p. 113.

his obsession with and his great ambivalence toward Mexico City. Indeed, no other Mexican city or for that matter other world city—with the exception of London in *Cumpleaños*, is developed in so much detail, with so great an evocation of the streets and buildings and monuments, cathedrals and palaces, fashionable districts, from the elegant Las Lomas to Coyoacán and the Zona Rosa to Polanco as Fuentes does in his many novels and short stories, particularly those of *Agua quemada* (*Burnt Water*; 1981), right up to his monumental narrative *El destino y la fortuna* (*Destiny and Desire*; 2010).

Similarly, Kraft and Leventhal, in their fascinating, picture-filled work *Footsteps in the Fog: Alfred Hitchcock's San Francisco* (Santa Monica: Santa Monica Press, 2002), comment on Hitchcock's love for San Francisco and its wonders and its mysteriousness and how the master director skillfully incorporated San Francisco and its environs into *Vertigo* as well as many other of his films:

> Hitchcock captured the romance, mystery and elegance of the City in one of cinema's classics, *Vertigo* . . . San Francisco's tall buildings, steep and twisting streets, and dramatic bridges make it an ideal setting for *Vertigo*. San Francisco's steep hills create winding streets, gorgeous vistas, and a jagged skyline. The coastline too is rugged, with dangerous cliffs and steep curves which only add to the suspense. The blend of the city's unique character with Hitchcock's keen ability to weave a sinister fate creates a brilliant psychological suspense film.
>
> . . . *Vertigo* seems like a travelogue of San Francisco and the surrounding area's famous historical sites, monuments, architecture, and luxurious businesses from the 1950s. Hitchcock had a remarkable ability to capture the subtleties of time, place, and spirit in his films. Even in cases where the actor's filming occurred in a studio set [Hollywood] far away from the original location, Hitchcock captured the essence of a setting by the meticulous use of authentic details. While *Vertigo* is a notable suspense masterpiece, it is also a remarkable testament to Hitchcock's passion for the San Francisco Bay Area. (74)

Both *Vertigo* and *Aura* are filled with incongruities and ironies. Nothing is ever stable or finished, and nothing—neither character nor setting nor motive—is ever definite. The San Francisco fog stunningly symbolizes the precariousness the evanescence of all—of relationships, of love, of life itself. Madeleine's seemingly positive remark to a doubtful Scottie: "Ah, but only one is a wanderer. Two are always going somewhere," is initially hopeful but finally ironic in several senses, as we have discussed—Madeleine leads him literally into the darkness of Muir Woods and toward deception and destruction.

Hitchcock has stated in an interview "The thing that interests me most of all is a change of perspective within a shot."[25] Here is emphasized the incessant change that so characterizes *Vertigo* and which also suffuses *Aura*.

Vertigo is one of the most haunting and beautiful films ever made. It masterfully combines the quiet, reserved, but tense and voluptuous beauty of Kim Novak, with the extraordinary beauty of San Francisco—not only its landmarks like the awe-inspiring Golden Gate Bridge, so powerfully photographed in *Vertigo* that it looms as a surrealistic structure, the imposing, classically structured with lawns and arches Palace of the Legion of Honor, the venerable Mission Dolores, but the stunning architecture found in the cathedrals and the ornate lavish, monumental hotels like the *Fairmont*, where a nervous, apprehensive Judy, now wearing on two occasions the same purple dress—perhaps in an attempt to erase from Scottie's mind the elegant gray dress of Madeleine that he has consecrated—dances uncomfortably with Scottie, because Judy is not yet Madeleine Reborn, but also the stunning nature of the Northern California coast—the rugged mountains and jagged cliffs, the turbulent Pacific Ocean at Cypress Point, caught in back projection as well as the imposing Muir Woods with its gigantic and, for Hitchcock, imposingly symbolic trees.

Vertigo is a testimony both to the ineradicable power of the past and, paradoxically, to its relentless disappearance. In the reality of the twenty-first century, the lavish *Ernie's* is gone, the

---

[25] Consult Murray Pomerance, *An Eye for Hitchcock* (New Brunswick, New Jersey: Rutgers University Press, 2004) p. 217.

stately McKittrick Hotel, originally the elaborate Portman Mansion, was demolished a year after *Vertigo* was completed, and a nondescript building erected in its place. Hitchcock passed away in 1980; James Stewart died in 1997 and Kim Novak, now in her late seventies, lives reclusively in the California hills and is seldom or never photographed—unlike Bette Davis and even Joan Crawford, who exposed the inevitable cracks and wrinkles of age in their late seventies, in a more realistic era before the discovery of Botox. Yet through the magic and grace of the film art, both places and human beings are preserved forever, granted cinematic resurrection and immortality. Similarly, Fuentes has declared that he seeks to conserve the past, in a modern age that he states is founded on amnesia. Like the fierce and indomitable Consuelo of *Aura*, Fuentes is a staunch holdout, adamantly refusing to let go of the past, relentlessly exploring that past—both recent and ancient, both Mexico and Aztec-Mayan, fatalistic pasts that in Fuentes's often deterministic universe forcibly and indelibly impose themselves on the present. The haunting beauty and ineluctable mystery of *Vertigo* are thoroughly reflected in *Aura*, one of Fuentes's most beautiful and mystifying works, to which a mountain of criticism has been dedicated, and which in the twenty-first century, almost fifty years after its publication in 1962, continues to be a best-seller.

For all her braininess Midge, unlike both Judy Barton and Gavin Elster, is not savvy; over and over again she is clueless regarding the sudden emergence of vertigo that so afflicts the man she loves. "There's no getting rid of it" is what Midge almost satisfactorily pronounces as she repents what the physician has told her, because she seems at least subconsciously to desire that inevitability—so that she can forever play what she does best—the role of a protective, nurturing, surrogate mother. Indeed, Midge is clueless to the way to ingratiate herself with Scottie and how she can gain his approval and even his love. Directly contrasting with the sensuousness of Judy/Madeleine, evinced even in her low, soft, seductive voice, the matter of a fact Midge in the very first scene in which she appears, launches into the description of the new brassiere that she is sketching—at once coyly but definitely unseductively telling Scottie that it was designed by an engineer and is based on the principle of the cantilever bridge! Rather than enticing and alluring, the sexual theme here is made technical and, at best, bantering—testimony to the impossibility of the amorous relationship with Scottie that Midge so desperately desires as she continues to state bluntly to him: "You know there's only one person for me, Johnny-O." For example, Scottie at the outset tells Midge explicitly that he hates classical music as he petulantly asks for the Bach music which Midge is playing to be turned off, yet this is the type of music—this time, Mozart—that a stubborn and seemingly uncomprehending Midge plays for a totally unresponsive Scottie when he is interned in the mental institution. She seems to be clueless regarding the probability that playing music that Scottie hates only drives him further away from her. The on situation which she clearly intuits is that Scottie was in love with the dead Madeleine Lester—and still is. Ironically, the absolute silence and unresponsiveness of a thoroughly devastated Scottie to a maternal, protective Midge is but an extension of his absolute silence at the judicial inquiry into the bizarre circumstances of Madeleine's death—the latest of which Scottie for the whole time is speechless, and, significnatly is not once called upon by the coroner to give testimony as to what transpired in the tower.

And, instead of intuitively recognizing its significance, Midge mocks Scottie's obsession with Madeleine/Carlotta by painting herself in an unflattering manner, glasses and all, into her re-creation in caricature of the cherished, stark unglamorous portrait of Carlotta that Scottie is beginning to view as a sacred icon—primarily because he is falling in love with Madeleine and more and more is embracing Gavin Elster's interpretation that Madeleine is being driven to take her own life by the demonic invasion of the spirit of revenant Carlotta. Here is the implicit warning to Midge—not to meddle with Scottie's obsessions, or at least not to mock them. After the key incident of her caricature of Carlotta/Madeleine, a painting that Midge in her extreme anger and frustration at her own stupidity violently defaces—and in an ironic way, foreshadows what Scottie himself will savagely attempt to do at the very end with the criminal accomplice Judy Barton—there is no relationship whatever between Midge and Scottie. Indeed a psychotic Scottie is incapable of even speaking to an ever-devoted Midge. In contrast, to the increasingly frustrated and finally powerless Midge, on her own, without needing and coaching from Gavin Elster, the astute and highly intuitive Judy/Madeleine senses how to manipulate Scottie, by constantly confirming him in the role he most desperately wants to succeed in, a role of hero/protector/savior—thus rapidly reducing his overwhelming guilt over the accidental death of the policeman, who had vainly attempted to rescue him and ameliorating the devastating blow to his ego that Scottie's precipitous retirement from the police force has occasioned. Even details, like Madeleine's affirmation that John is a strong name, require significance in Judy/Madeleine's patient strengthening of Scottie's damaged ego. And even the last words of Judy to Scottie before her untimely death are to keep her safe—what Scottie had repeatedly vowed to do with the unbalanced Madeleine but which he once more—as he had with the real Madeleine Elster—fails to do. Ironic too, in this film, so much like *Aura*, of endless mirror images, of constant duplications, toward the very end, when Scottie hurls a resisting Judy against the wall of the tower, Judy remains in the same position that the dead Madeleine Elster had occupied before her body was thrown from the tower.

Critics have commented on the keen use by Hitchcock of ellipses—we never know how Scottie got down from the collapsed gutter, at the outset, for example. There is a similar use of ellision in *Aura*, one of Fuentes's most compact, densest works. There is no lead in to the dramatic mutations of Aura, from young and virginal and even timid to bold and provocative, from evanescent and ethereal to witchly and brutal in her skinning of a goat for blood sacrifice. Her transformation, even transmogrification in the time of three days from *doncella* to courtesan to old hag is mystifying, and can be explained only by the need of the domineering yet increasingly desperate Consuelo to act rapidly, because her powers as sorceress are very limited, and she can keep the ghostly Aura with her for only three days at a time.

Auiler gives one of the most penetrating interpretations of the significance of *Vertigo*, a summation that also can be applied to Fuentes's elusive and fascinating *Aura*. Auiler's commentary underscores the universality of *Vertigo*:

Figure 51. Judy's desperate plea for forgiveness:"I was safe when you found me." Note how she appears to be behind prison-appearing bars.

> *Vertigo* is an expression of longing for what we can never have again, whether it be embodied in a person, a location,or an emotion. Those of us who are "healthy" do not wander the old places, looking for ghosts. But the film expresses a truth that may be dark but is unavoidable: Health falters, time destroys as well as heals and one day we find the living crowded by the dead. In that sense, we all stand with Scottie in the tower.[26]

Similarly, we all stand with the fierce and indomitable Consuelo in Fuentes's enigmatic work, an impassioned woman who refuses to submit to time and encroaching death, who struggles mightily and unswervingly to re-create herself as the young and beautiful and enticing *Aura*. We seem to identify much moreso with the seemingly invincible Consuelo than to the doomed adventures of the conceited and timorous Felipe, who falls

---

[26] See Dan Auiler, *Vertigo: The Making of a Hitchcock Classic* (New York: Saint Martin's Press, 1998), p. 208.

so rapidly and thoroughly under Consuelo's dark and pernicious spell. *Aura*, like the narrative written at the same time, *The Death of Artemio Cruz*, bears testimony to the desperate need for erotic love—not only in youth, when the flow of sexual hormones is the most intense, but through middle age, old age, to the very borders between life and death.

The smooth sensuality of Kim Novak, evident from the very first moment she is sighted by a nervous, highly insecure and quickly enraptured Scottie in *Ernie's*—is paralleled by the figure of the spectral but, paradoxically, extremely carnal Aura, the living ghost in Fuentes's brief but spellbinding work. Despite Hitchcock's apparent fury at losing the talented and attractive Vera Miles—whom he starred in the 1957 film *The Wrong Man*—as Madeleine, after Miles announced her pregnancy, Miles's far more reserved, beautiful but less sensual blonde personality could not compete with that of Kim Novak. It is erotic love—difficult if not impossible for Scottie with the willing but domineering Midge—that is a central theme of *Vertigo*. And in both *Vertigo* and *Aura*, love is deadly. Gavin Elster is not interested in love, only in power and his wife's money; Scottie can love only a dead woman brought back to life; Judy loses the love of both Gavin Elster—a love she never really had, as Elster, the master *titiritero*, duped not only his wife, but also Judy, Scottie and the coroner, who even goes so far as to face Elster from all blame for his wife's tragic death, and yet emerged scot free—and loses as well the death-haunted love of Scottie. And even Consuelo, whose Nemesis is not Felipe but Time, continually loses both her husband and worshipper, Llorente, and all successive lovers and finally is evoked not as triumphant but expectant of Aura's longed-for return, which can occur only as the result of the physical and spiritual destruction of but another Felipe Montero—on the model of the Aztec blood sacrifices that were carried out in almost every month of the Aztec calendar year.

It is ironic that of all the central characters in *Vertigo*, all of whom desire to escape the past, only one—the murderer Gavin Elster, can successfully do so. At the end, the now openly obsessed Scottie compels Judy/Madeleine to return again to San Juan Bautista and to climb with him to the very top of the tower to free himself of the past—to conquer his vertigo—to expunge the dead and fatalistic past by directly confronting it. Judy's secret wish after she encounters Scottie on the San Francisco Avenue is also to escape the past, as she hopes that Scottie will begin to love her as Judy Barton, "I want you so to love me as I am, for myself, and so forget the Other and forget the past," she declares beautifully, lyrically, in her poignant soliloquy in her hotel room at the Empire Hotel as she abruptly changes her blunt, even coarse diction which seems to be but another part of her dexterous acting before Scottie, this time deliberately accentuating her vulgarity in an initial, frustrated attempt to warn Scottie off. Yet despite her frequent protestations about being made over for the second time as Madeleine, Judy is not strong enough to break away from Scottie and affirm an independent identity. Thus in both *Vertigo* and *Aura*, the destinies of the principal characters are all fated, all determined by the past—Judy Barton is forever Madeleine; Scottie Ferguson is forever denied freedom from his affliction, and ironically, although his intention at the very end is to free himself once and for all from the crippling past, from his destructive vertigo, at the end he is more anguished than ever, and the guilt that has tormented him is now increased again—as he feels responsible now for three deaths—that of the policeman, Madeleine Elster, and now Judy Barton. And Midge, despite her insistent attempts to bring Scottie back to her, loses him forever.

Dialogue in both *Vertigo* and *Aura* is double-edged. When Scottie, finally turned on by Judy/Madeleine, is eager to caress her to continue his role as Judy/Madeleine's keeper, she initially demurs, stating ironically "Too late. I've got my face on." Kim Novak is very adroitly playing the role of Judy Barton, who knows what Scottie at this point still does not realize, that Judy really was Scottie's Madeleine from the very start—a still deceived, still earnest and devoted Scottie. A bemused and amused Scottie at this point is responding to the beautiful mask, that he egotistically and self-satisfiedly believes that he alone has created. Gavin Elster molds Judy Barton painstakingly to achieve his purpose—to become the sole heir of Madeleine Elster's vast fortune. But Scottie is extremely proud of his role as Pygmalion for sociopsychological not economic reasons, because it grants him the power and the outlet for his intense frustration—over the collapse of his ambitions—a professional status-driving—that his crippling illness has all but destroyed.

Judy is so overconfident, naively believing that she has thoroughly duped Scottie, that she literally puts the noose around her own neck as she not only dons Carlotta's necklace, but even asks Scottie to help her fasten the clasp, and when Scottie has difficulty, states with another *double entendre* "Don't you see?"—ironically commenting as well on Scottie's final ability to see through the elaborate fraud that has so thoroughly engulfed him. And the irony rapidly escalates in this crucial scene. Just when an extremely contented Judy declares to Scottie, "I *do* have you now, don't I," it is the very moment that she will lose him forever.

The two engage in a dialogue of the deaf. Just as Judy pleads with Scottie at the very end at the perilous top of the tower in San Juan Bautista—the confined, murderous space—to reassume the hero's role "keep me safe," Scottie in a trancelike state disavows Judy, concentrating totally on Madeleine—the Madeleine that he has conceitedly believed he has brought back to life—and once more expressing either his inability or his perverse unwillingness to love anyone but Madeleine:

> "I loved you so, Madeleine"
>
> . . . .
>
> "It's too late, there's no bringing her back."

From a common sense point of view, we wonder why Scottie, after seeing the first Madeleine fall from the tower, did not rush to the body to determine whether his beloved were still alive and, if so, in desperate need of emergency assistance. Scottie fails to take action at a crucial moment because he is totally absorbed not in Madeleine but in Self—he is so consumed by guilt that he can only slink away—behavior that the pitiless coroner repeatedly faults him for. Scottie's heightened sense of self-loathing, of self-diminishment, is expertly caught by Hitchcock after the fall of the first Madeleine Elster from the tower—in a high angle shot with a tiny, evasive Scottie at the very edge of the frame—almost imperceptible as if he were suddenly reduced to the status of a little black scurrying insect. And despite this sadistic berating of the pitiless coroner as cruel as Scottie himself will finally become,

Scottie at the very end, instead of what would be the normal reaction of now rushing to the *bottom* of the tower to ascertain if Judy were still alive and in any case to summon rescuers, Scottie, at the end as at the outset of the film is paralyzed, incapable of even descending the tower—his vertigo not cured but savagely exacerbated. As in the insane asylum, Scottie is mute and catatonic. At the end of *Vertigo* as at the beginning he is left dangling, suspended between life and death—exactly as is the nebulous, anguished Felipe Montero in *Aura*. Similarly, when Felipe is granted the opportunity actually to fulfill his heroic ambitions and carry off his beloved Aura to freedom, he suddenly demures—behavior consistent with his puppetlike behavior in the realm of Consuelo from the very start:

> "She's going out? But she never…"
> "Yes, sometimes she does. She makes a great effort and goes out. She's going out today. For all day. You and I could. . ."
> "Go away?"
> "If you want to."
> "Well . . . perhaps not yet. I'm under contract. But as soon as I can finish the work, then . . ." (A, 123-125)

The fated Felipe will never finish his work. As we have seen, Felipe is in reality bored with the revision work for which he has been hired and readily abandons it; thus his protestations about dedication to duty ring hollow—in reality Felipe is a coward, completely incapable of heroic action and characterized much more by compliance and even submissiveness to Consuelo.

Madeleine's essence has been incisively captured by Wood, in terms that can also be applied to the phantomlike Aura:

> Madeleine is so much more than erotic because of this combination of grace, mysteriousness, and vulnerability. She is from the start the representative of another world of experience beyond the grasp of the cards-on-the-table reality of Midge. A higher reality, or an allusion? Or, to shift to the Keatsian terminology, "vision," or "waking dream"? It seems more reasonable to add… "Lamian" or

> the "Nightingale Ode" in this connection than to make the classification of *Vertigo* as a "mystery thriller." (HR, 114)

In both *Vertigo* and *Aura*, the male protagonist finally makes desperate attempts to assert the self, to extricate himself from his fantasy world. Upon suddenly realizing how much he has been duped by Judy/Madeleine, Scottie resolves to confront his vertigo head-on by compelling the woman whom he finally sees not as a beautiful ghost but as an alluring accomplice to murder and to his excruciating frame up, to climb again to the top of the fatalistic tower at San Juan Bautistia. He wants vengeance on Judy/Madeleine and more—he wants his integrity, his self-esteem back, and he wants permanently to be cured of his crippling vertigo. The way in which a finally clued-in Scottie suddenly rejects Judy/Madeleine is conveyed cinematically by Hitchcock is expertly explained by Wood:

> From the close-up of the necklace around Carlotta's neck the camera tracks back to take in Madeleine staring in the art gallery. . . the backward tracking shot contrasts with the frequent forward tracking shots that characterized the earlier part of the film, to suggest recoil, Scottie extricating himself from the quicksands of illusion. (HR, 126)

Yet, as we have seen, Scottie never can successfully emerge from his entangling delusions. Similarly, when it is too late, Felipe also recoils from the nightmare, and frantically begins to count the objects in his travel case—symbolizing his desperate attempts to cling to the last shreds of his identity as Felipe Montero just as a desperate Judy Barton insistently struggles to retain the last bit of Judy Barton—her casual hair style, worn down around the neck—before once again surrendering to the demands of her longed-for lover and putting her hair up into the tightly-coiled, vertiginous whorl. Yet like Scottie, Felipe's attempts are futile; like Scottie in the quicksand film that is *Vertigo,* Felipe too is psychologically, spiritually destroyed:

> . . . you count the objects in your traveling case, the bottles and tubes which the servant you've never seen brought

> over from your boarding house: you murmur the names of those objects, touch them, read the contents and instructions, pronounce the names of the manufacturers, keeping to these objects in order to forget that other one, the one without a name, without a label, without any rational consistency. (A, 119)

The Pygmalion theme is an intricate part of the works of both Alfred Hitchcock and Carlos Fuentes. In *Vertigo*, Scottie is the eager but frustrated Pygmalion—he desperately desires to mold the supple clay that he perceives Judy Barton as, into an exact replica of his beloved Madeleine. Yet when his obsessive, querulous attempts prove at least temporarily successful, Scottie rather than being ecstatic, is shaken and suspicious. And even after becoming the perfect copy of Madeleine that he so desires, Judy at the very end makes a seemingly heartfelt plea to be recognized—and loved—for herself alone Scottie draws back into his shell, even addressing a stricken and terrified Judy at the top of the tower as Madeleine—"Oh Madeleine, I loved you so." The Pygmalion theme thus emerges as an extremely ironic one—Scottie has his goddess incarnate at last, but Judy, perhaps in order to perfect the Madeleine that Scottie so adores, makes the fatal mistake of donning the incriminating necklace.

In Fuentes's masterpiece, *The Death of Artemio Cruz* (1962), the highly complex, paradoxical Cruz, both tragic victim and ruthless exploiter, Cruz too is ironically and sadistically successful in his Pygmalion role. He takes the young, idealistic, and extremely impressionable son—his only son—Lorenzo—and patiently shapes him into the fighting hero that Cruz himself was too cowardly to fulfill. Cruz, like Scottie Ferguson, is wracked by guilt—in the case of the Mexican revolutionary fighter for betraying his comrades in the Mexican Revolution as the military officer Cruz abandons them to die on the battlefield, and, like Scottie, is compelled to expiate his corrosive guilt. Cruz does this by bringing his son to Cocuya—to Veracruz, and the sea, where Cruz instills in Lorenzo a quest for adventure and a heroic idealism. Cruz is successful in his constant attempts to play Pygmalion. The idealistic Lorenzo, who deludedly believes that his father had acted as a bold, valiant, Revolutionary hero that he seeks to emulate, Lorenzo crosses the sea to fight on the side of the liberal Republic against the fascists in the Spanish Civil War of 1939, in a major sense to gratify his father's expectations of him—and dies tragically—thereby at the same time both expiating Cruz's cowardice and betrayal of his comrades in the Revolution of 1910 and yet, compounding Cruz's guilt at sacrificing his beloved son, whose face—symbolic of the courageous martyr Lorenzo that Cruz himself has created—Cruz cannot summon to memory on his deathbed, although, ironically, at the very moment of his death Cruz can remember with extraordinary detail his vast material possessions.

The Death of Artemio Cruz has been extensively influenced by one of Fuentes's most lauded film directors, the great Orson Welles. And *Citizen Kane,* Welles's finest film, is an epic both celebrating the United States and capitalism and sharply critical of its excesses, just as is *The Death of Artemio Cruz* both a celebration and an acidulous critique of twentieth century, post-revolutionary Mexico and a detailed evocation of both the promise and the failure of what official government ideology exalts as the glorious, national redeeming Revolution of 1910.

Like Scottie Ferguson, like the domineering Artemio Cruz, the highly manipulative and egomaniacal Charles Foster Kane also seeks to emulate the Greek sculptor Pygmalion by molding a young, beautiful but very pliant person into an ideal, in this case into a world-famous operatic star. To justify himself after his bitter defeat at the polls after his scandalous affair with his blonde lover Susan Alexander is revealed by a rival newspaper, Kane takes his mistress, who has a sweet but frail voice, and obsessively attempts to transform her into an opera star, even building the Chicago Opera House for her. At first Susan Alexander allows herself to be molded uncomplainingly but is terrified on her debut in *Salaambo*, and when Kane even after Susan's disastrous debut insists that she continue her career, Susan attempts suicide. Like Scottie Ferguson, Charles Foster Kane is reduced to a frustrated Pygmalion, despite his enormous financial and emotional investment in Susan's transformation. Kane wants to be loved by the voters, the American public, by his mistress and above all by his mother, the very mother who for Kane's own good—to get him away from his drunken, abusive father, abandons him, signing him over to the care of the mercenary Thatcher. Another Pygmalion in reverse, Kane selects his first wife, the niece of the President of the United States—Emily Monroe Norton— and turns her into a collectible. As his fawning associate Bernstein remarks, "He ain't only collecting diamonds, he's collecting someone who collects diamonds." In Fuentes's labyrinthine narrative *A Change of Skin*, Fuentes develops the Pygmalion theme in reverse just as Alfred Hitchcock does in *Vertigo*—the sadistic protagonist Javier Ortega takes his strong and beautiful and extremely sensual wife Elizabeth and obsessively attempts to reduce her from an assertive, impassioned being whom he finds threatening to his fragile masculinity into an artistic image—a painting by Modigliani, or a Greek *stele*—into a fixed image that Javier— paranoid and highly insecure yet relentlessly manipulative—just like Scottie Ferguson—can summon up or dismiss at will.

Welles's Susan Alexander alludes to the talented Hollywood actress Marion Davies, whom the newspaper magnate and politician who ran unsuccessfully for governor of New York and who had presidential aspirations—William Randolph Hearst—attempted to mold into a Hollywood superstar—and yet, despite his immense wealth and extensive control of the media, was unsuccessful in so doing. Hearst himself can be seen as an ironic Pygmalion, as is the brash, enigmatic, highly energized figure so much based on both his tumultuous career and the turbulent, scandal-ridden career of Orson Welles himself—the dark, impetuous, ultimately demonized Citizen Kane. Indeed, Hearst first encountered Marion Davies when she appeared in the Ziegfield Follies. One of Marion Davies's most successful films, the silent screen classic *Show People* (1928, directed by the eminent King Vidor) provides an ironic mirror of the beautiful blonde starlet, herself, as Davies plays the role of Peggy Pepper, who comes to Hollywood with aspirations of becoming a dramatic actress—just as Hearst sought to transform his mistress into a serious actress of costume dramas—when the only work that Peggy Pepper can obtain is as a comedienne—in the pie-throwing comedies of Billy Boone. Despite Hearst's constant attempts to transform his beautiful and talented lover into a dramatic star, Marion Davies achieved but limited acclaim—and as a sparkling comedienne.

The emphasis by Hitchcock on fatalism, particularly surrounding the harassed Scottie Ferguson, is perceptively analyzed by Sterritt:

> A number of terms might serve as metaphors for Scottie's problem, from "fatal flaw" to "Achilles heel," and many of them relate in some way to the concept of original sin. Scottie's condition is indeed *original*, a part of his being and his nature, rather than an illness or eccentricity imposed on him by the random circumstances of an active life. It has been observed of Hitchcock's films . . . that things happen to his characters—that they are more acted on than acting . . . In Scottie's case . . . he is specifically not acted on by his rooftop trauma. If he has been acted on at all, it is by fate, shaping the deepest characteristics of his personality before adulthood and perhaps before birth itself.[27]

Both Scottie and Madeleine are among the most complex and ambivalent of Hitchcock's characters, just as are Consuelo/Aura and Felipe in Fuentes's brilliant *novella.* Felipe is both a fierce opponent of devastating, twentieth century change and a historian *en fleur*, ardently consecrated to the past. Similarly, the reclusive Consuelo is fiercely devoted to a lost love and to her once shimmering beauty that Consuelo succeeds in resuscitating over and over again, yet is continually and vexatiously evanescent. The great complexity of Scottie and Judy/Madeleine has been commented on by Sterritt (p. 90):

> The performances here are impressive on the movie-acting level as well as on the narrative level. Stewart expertly conveys Scottie's mixture of compassion for Madeleine, bewitchment with the mystery surrounding her and absorption in his own growing infatuation. Novak is also in top form, especially given the complexity . . . of her character.

---

[27] Consult David Sterritt, *The Films of Alfred Hitchcock* (Cambridge and New York: Cambridge University Press, 1993), p. 87.

The way in which Hitchcock at times captures, at times entices the viewer into the maelstrom of *Vertigo* is amply paralleled by the way in which Fuentes rapidly submerges the reader in *Aura*. The opening sequence of *Vertigo*—the action-packed chase of the criminal across the San Francisco rooftop at night and the subsequent traumatic spell first of acrophobia then of vertigo masterfully captured by Hitchcock by a simultaneous track-out/zoom is shot to make the spectator experience the dizziness of Scottie, is commented on incisively by Wood:

> The sequence represents the most extreme and abrupt instance of enforced audience identification in all of Hitchcock—an effect to which the technical means front of view, alternating, vertigo shot, even the jarring rhythmic lurch at the policeman's fall, all contribute. Usually, however, he is far more circumspect, building identification gradually through a complicated proces of curiosity, sympathy, emotional involvement....[28]

Fuentes surely has been influenced by the incessantly dreamlike state in which Scottie Ferguson finds himself. Paralleling the bruising nightmare of Socttie in which he envisions his own destruction and death—seemingly revelatory of his intensified *Thanatos* impulse or his deep desire to consumate his love with Madeleine through joining her in death—when Scottie wakes up it is not to relief or self-possession but to continued affliction. As Keane comments incisively:

> When Stewart/Scottie sits bolt upright in bed and lunges toward the camera at the end of his dream, his eyes are fixed open and his face is filled with terror. He projects himself directly toward the camera, but his eyes, immersed in his dream, do not take in the camera....Figured in his dream, this man's dream is that he is nothingness, that he

---

[28]Consult Robin Wood, "Male Desire, Male Anxiety: The Essential Hitchcock, in *A Hitchcock Reader*, Edited by Marshall Deutelbaum and Leland Poague (Malden, Massachusetts: Blackwell Publishing, 1986) p. 224.

> can be penetrated completely. We might characterize this as his fear that he too is a ghost [29]

Keane disagrees with critics who see Scottie as an essentially negative figure, and analyzes the detective as a constantly suffering hero:

> Mulvey describes the Stewart figure as possessing, brandishing and relishing a position of active power in relation to the woman, but the truth is that he suffers throughout *Vertigo*. He suffers from the moment he painfully covers his acrophobia on the rooftop, though his involvement with Madeleine, under the condescending and barbed censure of the court officer at the hearing, and up to his dream, the final nightmare of his life until the end of the film. [30]

Keane sees the protagonist of *Vertigo* not as Scottie Ferguson—despite the fact that James Stewart appears in almost eleven scenes—but surprisingly, Madeleine and Judy, and goes on to interpret Hitchcock as identifying with the victimized and finally destroyed Judy Barton, whom Keane views not as accidentally falling through an open tower in her terror but as deliberately leaping from that tower—thereby equating her desire with that of Carlotta Valdés, whom Keane sees as an object too of Scottie's attraction and love. That *Vertigo* has found so many, often times conflicting interpretations—as has *Aura*—is a remarkable testimony to its open, conundrum nature, one which, anticipating *Aura*, will never be fully disambiguated by the spectator/reader or the critic. Both *Vertigo* and *Aura* thus become the most re-creatable, most universal of the many works of their respective creators.

It is significant that as artists and creators, both Hitchcock and Fuentes view women in the same iconic, mystifying way. According to West:

---

[29]See Marion E. Keane, "A Closer Look at Scopophilia: Mulvey, Hitchcock, and *Vertigo*, included in *A Hitchcock Reader, op. cit.*, pp. 240-241.
[30]Consult Keane.*op. cit.*, p. 236

> Hitchcock seemed especially conscious of the magical qualities of women. He often characterizes women's powers as verging on the supernatural[31]

Similarly, throughout Fuentes's works, from the intensely baroque, epic *La región más transparente* in the figure of the venerable Teódula Moctezuma, a twentieth century Coatlicue, to the domineering superstar Claudia Nervo in *Zona sagrada* a protagonist again developed in terms of an ancient Aztec goddess, this time Tlazoltéotl, to the wily, supernatural Inez in *Instinto de Inés* to the sorceress Consuelo in *Aura* and the demonic Carlotta in "Tlactocatzine del jardín de Flandes," women in Fuentes are imbued with mystery, magic, and infused with a supernatural aura. Apparently the Catholic organization, the Legion of Decency objected to the underwear that Scottie had stripped from Madeleine after rescuing her from the turbulent waters of Fort Point, and therefore to comply with their dictum that any sort of sexual relationship between the two of them not be made evident, for one reason because Judy/Madeleine was ostensibly a married woman, the ever artful Hitchcock deliberately blurred the undergarments, with the result that the audience only imagine that it is viewing the undergarments—in reality images of non-descript clothing. In the 1940s and 1950s a sexual relationship could only be hinted at—thus the emphasis on prolonged, passionate kisses filmed in dramatic close-up, such as the kiss between Scottie and Madeleine in the livery stable of San Juan Bautista—because this ecstatic kiss was as far as Hitchcock could go at the time. Ironically, although not censored in the sixties when it was first published, *Aura* came under scrutiny a generation later: in the 1980s, in Mexico City, when a member of the Partido de Acción Nacional, the PAN, sought to ban it in an all-girls secondary school because of its blasphemous content—the Black Mass in which Aura and Felipe make love. And even in 2010, in Puerto Rico the outstanding *novella* was banned for secondary school reading because of its

---

[31] Consult Ann West. "The Concept of the Fantastic in *Vertigo*," in *Hitchcock's Rereleased Films: From Rope to Vertigo*, Edited by Walter Raubicheck and Walter Srebnick (Detroit: Wayne State University Press, 1991), p. 163

supposedly salacious language. Ironically, eroticism of an intense nature, including fellatio, found in *Gringo viejo* caused no outcry—perhaps because unlike *Aura*, the eroticism is of a secular nature. As we have seen, both Fuentes and Hitchcock are products of a very strict Catholic, Jesuit upbringing—against which, paradoxically, both of these creators rebel and yet at the same time are deeply influenced by throughout their lives and creative works.

Just as Consuelo/Aura constitutes the most complex, ever-changing center of *Aura*, so also does the enigmatic, ever paradoxical Judy Barton/Madeleine Elster constitute the center of paradox and ambiguity in *Vertigo*. On the one hand a *femme fatale*—blonde, alluring, deceptive, and ultimately destructive, an accomplice to murder; on the other hand Judy/Madeleine is a highly insecure, very vulnerable and exceedingly malleable victim. Kim Novak in this extremely demanding role exudes both sensuality and extreme vulnerability—thus quite different from the tough, wise-cracking, street-wise *femme fatale* of *film noir* like the roles played by Gloria Grahame, in films like *The Big Heat* (1953). Novak expresses pliability, confusion, vulnerability, dependency, not ruthlessness or toughness or cynicism. In addition, it is remarkable how addicted to solitude Judy Barton is—despite her gorgeousness, she is not surrounded by a bevy of eager males when Scottie by chance encounters her on the San Francisco Streets after he is released—far too soon, because he is not cured—from the Sanitarium. It is clear that Judy Barton is attracted to older males who are wealthy or at least, like Scottie, well off, and there is a notable class difference not only between the waitress Judy and the millionaire Gavin Elster but between the comfortably financial Scottie and the coarse Judy—a coarseness that Judy intentionally exaggerates at first in an attempt to dissuade an eager Scottie from pursuing her.

In both *Aura* and *Vertigo*, there predominates a constant symmetry that reinforces the fatalistic ambience of both works. When Scottie drags a protesting Judy to the very top of the tower, he hurls her against the wall in the exact same spot where Judy had witnesses Gavin Elster with the body of the real Madeleine Elster—thus constituting a visual signal by Hitchcock that the fate of Judy and Madeleine will be the same. The fact that Judy finally confesses to Scottie that Madeleine was already dead before her body was thrown from the tower leads to a further ambiguity. When Judy screams, it may be as fulfilling Elster's directions—as a means of drawing Scottie's attention to the falling body—or it may be Judy's cry to halt Elster in his actions in order to save Scottie from being implicated in the murder.

CHAPTER III: VOYEURISM AND DEATH: HITCHCOCK'S *REAR WINDOW* AND FUENTES'S "EL AMANTE DEL TEATRO"

As opposed to the breathtaking *Vertigo*, which again and again delves into expansive space—including the masterful, spectacular panoramic shot of the skyline of San Francisco seen through Scottie's still dazed perspective after he is prematurely released from the sanitarium, as well as Hitchcock's extended focus on the forest of immense, seemingly immortal gigantic redwoods—awe-inspiring symbols of Timelessness, and yet, in Hitchcock's highly paradoxical vision, fragile entities. As Judy/Madeleine pauses to contemplate the rings of one of the fallen redwoods, Judy magnificently plays to her increasingly appreciative audience of Scottie, her role as death-haunted victim —as transhabited by the spirit of the doomed Carlotta, despised by her powerful husband: "Here I was born and here I died and you took no notice of me." Ironically, it will be Scottie, not Madeleine, who will be consumed by a *Thanatos* impulse that is fatalistically added to his vertigo affliction. What Judy really is pondering is her future life as the socially prominent wife of Gavin Elster, as a reward for her successful duping of Scottie.

Scottie is surrounded by deceit, epitomized by both the suave Gavin Elster and the artful Judy Barton, and yet, ironically, when offered genuineness and sincerity and unconditional love by a devoted Midge, Scottie, similar to the misanthropic L.B. Jefferies in *Rear Window*, thoroughly rejects that unadulterated love, so willingly consumed is he by the romantic world craftily and persistently built up around him, first by Gavin Elster and then by his star pupil Judy Barton. Timing is everything in this film, as it is in *Rear Window* and as it is in *Aura* as well, in which the pressured Consuelo has only three days to capture Felipe's soul before her magic powers wane and disappear, along with the lubricious Aura

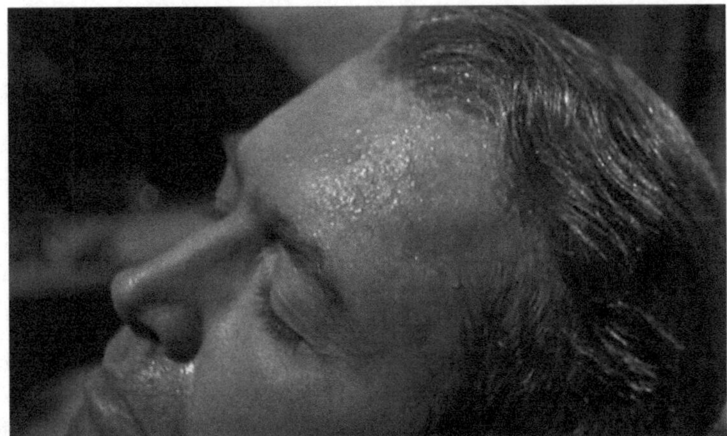

Figure 52. Jefferies suffering excessive physical heat but very low libido.

Figure 53. Miss Torso: vicarious erotic fulfillment for Jefferies and viewer. Refrigerator competes with wide-open windows.

—the equivalent of Elster's prized pawn—the alluring Madeleine Elster copy.

The freedom and power which existed for males in the ninteenth century which the shrewd, even Machiavellian Gavin Elster seems to long for, as he projects to Scottie a distinct disenchantment with contemporary San Francisco, in reality a crafty catering to the romantic longings of the seemingly pragmatic and realistic, even hard-headed but inwardly shaken and highly susceptible—and passionately romantic—Scottie Ferguson. As opposed to Scottie, whose façade of indifference and boyish charm rapidly dissipates, who becomes more and more entrapped—as is L.B. Jefferies—in his middle age insecurity and apprehension—Gavin Elster is essentially rootless, as he abruptly departs forever from the San Francisco that he has so painstakingly romanticized to Scottie. Indeed, Gavin Elster in the twentieth century is as calculating and cruel as is the nameless plutocrat who elevated Carlotta from her impoverished status as a dance hall girl, placed her at the pinnacle of upper class San Francisco society, then suddenly and brutally abandonded her, driving her into lunacy and then into suicide. Gavin Elster will also repeat the success of the nameless nineteenth century power baron—both men with triumph with impunity—Hitchcock´s trenchant commentary on unbridled male power.

There is a cluelessness that characterizes Midge and Judy and Scottie, just as it is so characteristic of the ever naïve, ever guillible, bumbling and increasingly deceived and self-deluded Felipe Montero in *Aura*. Despite her apparent brightness and witty remarks—which contrast so markedly with Madeleine's soft, purring, understated sexual innuendoes—Midge is essentially clueless about Scottie's tastes. Knowing what the doctors at the Sanitarium do not know—that Scottie hates classical music and when she plays Bach on the phonograph, an irritated Scottie asks her to turn the music off, she nonetheless continues on her classical music binge, playing Mozart to a wheelchair bound, shocked, catatonic, stupefied Scottie Ferguson. Judy too is, at crucial moments, clueless; indeed Judy seems most happy, most fulfilled, playing the Other and not being herself, whom she seems to despise just as Scottie is scarred by a loathing of his psychologically crippled self. Indeed, so insecure is Judy and so

Figure 54. Frustrated composer of "Lisa" feverishly at work. Stagelike curtain is always up.

Figure 55. Thorwald digging in flower garden: body parts of wife buried here.

willing is she to please Scottie's every whim that she goes overboard when she not only dons the highly incriminating necklace of Carlotta but even asks Scottie to fasten it around her neck—in a scene that subtly enchoes the breaking of the neck of the real Madeleine Elster by her murderous husband.

In contrast to the bold, incessant expansion—at least on one level of the ever restless *Vertigo*—through the winding streets of modern San Francisco, to the pocket of congealed time that is the Mission Dolores, to the majestic Palace of the Legion of Honor, to the regal Fairmont Hotel, in the magnificent ballroom in which the alienated couple of Judy and Scottie dance dispiritedly, Hitchcock's *Rear Window* is a tightly composed, inwardly turning film. *Rear Window* is a claustrophobic film, never leaving the point of view of the jaundiced L.B. Jefferies, who since he is bound to his wheelchair and in his but very limited mobility, has been reduced to merely fantasizing about his past life of adventure and peril—what he vainly hopes will be his action-filled future. For the extremely privileged Jefferies, fantasies—the eager, extraordinarily beautiful, intelligent Lisa Fremont who caters to his every whim and despite his frequent rejections and insults promises to fulfill his sexual fantasies unreservedly—are made real, yet he retreats from the insistent advances of Lisa. Indeed L.B. Jefferies's characteristic avoidance of a marital relationship with the stunning Lisa is paralleled by the refusal of the willful male protagonist of Carlos Fuentes's short story, "El amante del teatro," Larry O'Shea, to make the slightest attempt to get to know the mysterious, sensual, and enticing blonde woman across the way, who is obviously attracted to him and is attempting to reach out to him as more than a mere avid spectator of her reherasals for her dramatic role as Ophelia in Shakespeare's blood-drenched drama, *Hamlet*, which in Fuentes's narrative seems to become shockingly real.

Vertigo is very similar in major aspects to *Rear Window*—just as Scottie, throughly obsessed with his lost Madeleine, keeps rejecting Judy's pleas almost to the moment of her accidental death, keeps spurning the most attractive Judy who like Lisa Fremont, repeatedly throws herself at him, so too does the circumspect L.B. Jefferies, expertly portrayed by one of Hitchcock's favorite male leads, Jimmie Stewart, a veteran

Figure 56. Handicapped Jefferies leads an unreal existence: this time it's the mere shadow of Lisa.

Figure 57. Dream princess—beautiful, seductive, but disdained by intransigent Jefferies.

Hollywood professional whose brilliant career began in the thirities when he was starred with Joan Crawford and Carole Lombard—attempt to keep an aroused glamor girl at bay—until Lisa at the end proves to be the true adventurer, the true risk-taker, boldly and surreptitiously entering the apartment of Thorwald, accomplishing what Detective Doyle could have easily done by legal means but is too reticent to do so. It is Lisa who runs the risk not only of assault but of death—and a self-vaunting L.B. Jefferies who in a moment of extreme danger to Lisa is suddenly ineffectual, even powerless, and reduced to a squirming, frantic, impotent onlooker—an ironic commentary by Hitchcock on the easy entrapment that is voyeurism

Lisa Fremont, vivacious, wealthy and head-over-heels in love with the far more modestly living Jefferies—who perhaps is intimidated by a future in which there is a distinct probablity that he will be reduced to a Mr. Fremont—to an adjunct of the relentlessly active, overwhelmingly successful fashion model. In contrast to Lisa and her lavish tastes and free-spending ways, L.B. Jefferies lives from paycheck to paycheck and he perceives the highly accessible Lisa as, ironically, too perfect for him.

Vertigo, which constantly alternates between psychological space—the initally quizzical but rapidly fanatical and ultimately dislocated and agonized consciousness of the male protagonist, Scottie Ferguson and then a sudden delving into expansive space—the skyline of San Francisco, seen through Scottie's dazed perspective as he continues his fanatic wanderings through the romantic settings of the past which he has forever consecrated in his still delirious imagination, as well as the extensive evocation of the forest of gigantic redwoods initially emerging as all powerful, timeless symbols and yet ultimately viewed as highly vulnerable, fallen gods. The ever-artful Judy Barton, playing to the hilt a double role, both the stricken Madeleine Elster and the transhabited descendant of the vengeful Carlotta, reprimands Carlotta's exploitative husband—and indirectly Scottie himself—for his callousness. Both *Vertigo* and *Rear Window*, like so many of Hitchcock's films are suffused with morbidity. In *Rear Window* it is the obsession that Lars Thorwald's suspected dismemberment of the body of his anonymous wife—whom he has apparently murdered—has for all three of the occupants of L. B. Jefferies's

Figure 58. Lisa continually takes initiative; Jefferies prefers unattainable Miss Torso.

Figure 59. $1000 designer dress: for jaundiced Jefferies it's frivolity and decadence.

apartment—Thelma Ritter, masterfully playing the role of Stella, the sarcastic insurance nurse who rapidly becomes absorbed with the killing, Lisa Fremont, ever beguiling, ever affable to a constantly repelling L.B. Jefferies, who deems her too perfect for him and dreads the prospect of marriage to a fashion model and business woman whom he finds suffocating, and finally, the increasingly mesmerized and ghoulish Jefferies himself, who becomes increasingly convinced despite the frequent objections of his good friend and detective, Doyle, that Lars Thorwald is a cold-blooded murderer.

In *Vertigo*, there is a constant contrast between the fake *thanatos* impulse by which Madeleine Elster/Judy Barton is presumably consumed, and the real impulse toward suicide of Scottie Ferguson, who longs to join his beloved Madeleine in death and has horrifying visions of falling into Madeleine's open grave —a suicide impulse still present at the very end of *Vertigo*, which may very well terminate in his hurling himself from the tower. Thus despite the appearance of the end that the tremulous Scottie has at last conquered his crippling vertigo, as he stands at the very top of the tower, he is still irremediably and irredeemably afflicted. Indeed, Scottie at the end rather than experiencing catharsis, is left increasingly shocked and tormented. Ironically, although Judy Barton suffers an accidental death, at the very end she has emerged as a life force, as again and again she begs Scottie to begin their relationship anew and to love her as a human being, as Judy Barton, not as a ghost—a love that for Scottie is just as impossible as it is for Consuelo in *Aura* to love anyone but a zombie of Llorente.

Vertigo, like Fuentes's *Aura* and *Cambio de piel*, and *Una familia lejana* is a film of transformations; *Rear Window* is a film of incarcerations in social and psychological roles. At the end, although a seemingly relaxed Lisa Fremont keeping watch over a blissfully sleeping, incapacitated Jefferies who now suffers from two broken legs, ostensibly is reading a book about adventures in the Himalayas—on the surface a seeming indication that the hyperactive fashion princess will fervently become the adventuress and explorer—the male L. B. Jefferies —that Jefferies wants her to be as he, like Scottie Ferguson, like Consuelo in *Aura*, determinedly plays the role of a twentieth century Pygmalion.

Figure 60. Miss Lonelyhearts meticulously prepares dinner for two: herself and phantom lover.

Figure 61. Reflection of Lisa's elaborate supper for Jefferies: Dinner for None.

Jefferies does not reject Lisa, he is really not even rejecting marriage—he is disdainful of and dismissive of a life-long marital relationship with someone who is not a soulmate—a mirror reflection of his own love of hardship and danger and suffering and exploration in distant lands. That the subtle and shrewd Lisa Fremont has no intention of becoming Jefferies's double is indicated in that at the very end she quickly discards the Himalayas tome to pick up *Harper's Bazaar*—a prominent fashion magazins-—as soon as she is certain that Jefferies is fast asleep. And the Pygmalion theme is also a present in Fuentes's captivating short story, "El amante del teatro" ("The Theatre Lover") which has been decidedly influenced by Hitchcock's *Rear Window* ethics, in the form of the tyrannical director of Shakespeare's *Hamlet*, Peter Massey, who seems to have been inspired by the great British director Peter Brooks, one of whose most famous works is the highly original *The Persecution and Assassination of Jean-Paul Maurat as Performed by the Inmates of the Asylum of Charenton under the Direction of the Marquis De Sade*. The apparently cruel and demeaning Peter Massey—like most all of the characters of *Rear Window* evoked only from the point of view of the mesmerized and highly vulnerable male protagonist—turns his strikingly bold and innovative theatrical production into a horror show, as he apparently murders in reality the actress playing the sister of Hamlet, Ophelia.

In the breathlessly expansive vision that is exemplified by *Vertigo*, Hitchcock's camera ranges extensively and relentlessly over both San Francisco and the Peninsula. In contrast, *Rear Window* is much more exclusive and confined, as the spectators see only what the handicapped and the almost ever vigilant Jefferies is capable of seeing from his apartment window. Both *Vertigo* and *Rear Window*, like "El amante del teatro" are intense depictions of voyeurism. Like the Peeping Tom that is the handicapped and temporarily imprisoned L.B. Jefferies, the protagonist of Fuentes's short story spends hours contemplating the window across the way with the shade drawn up. Paralleling the amusement and the vicarious sexual pleasure that Jefferies gains from watching the well endowed Miss Torso, whose face we seldom see because it is her body that is the sole object of Jefferies's fascination, is the rapt attention on a gorgeous blonde

Figure 62. Marital discord: Thorwald on phone to lover. Both windows of severely estranged couple wide open.

Figure 63. Anna Thorwald intently listens in on Thorwald's conversation with lover.

female seen in a window across the way that quickly changes into obsession of the solitary male protagonist Larry O'Shea of Fuentes's stunning work.

Complementing *Rear Window*, a film that in many senses is like a stage play brought to the screen, "El amante del teatro" is a story whose basis is both cinematic—the protagonist works as a film technician and processor, and dramatic, as he escapes into the theatre, initially to find pleasure but ultimately, like Jefferies, to encounter horror and murder. Both male protagonists are self-incarcerated beings whose fantasy lives grow with great rapidity—to compensate for a prior identity as world adventurer that he wants to regain, in the case of Jefferies, or for a drab, circumspect, alienating existence that he flees from, in the case of Fuentes's equally estranged protagonist, who like Jefferies enjoys escaping into fantasies.

Like *Vertigo*, in which Kim Novak expertly playing Judy Barton playing both the revenant spirit of the mad Carlotta and the glacially smooth Madeleine Elster, constantly puts herself on display for Scottie, who from the very first moment that he sees her in *Ernie's*—an initial appearance of the enticing Madeleine made even more tantalizing by the way in which Hitchcock deliberately prolongs the scene, slowly unveiling Madeleine with his camera shots—is spellbound by her beauty and poise, grace, and sophistication, *Rear Window* parallels *Vertigo* in that it evokes an even more aggressive, stunningly beautiful, even angelic woman who this time sincerely and relentlessly throws herself at a decidedly recalcitrant Jefferies. It is important to realize that Jefferies does not vigorously object either to Lisa's advances or her splendidly royal treatment, including the elaborate, catered dinner from the exclusive Club 21 and her seductively unpacking her suitcase out of which spills her enticing negligee as she blatantly informs him that she is spending the night with him. What Jefferies is not keen to is marriage itself—which is paramount for Lisa—but perceived by Jefferies as a straitjacket perhaps even a hellworld of confinement and stagnation. Indeed Jefferies finds impossible a marriage to someone as energetic and exacting and needing to be constantly dressed exquisitely and wined and dined sumptuously as is the tantalizing but for Jefferies, deadly Lisa Fremont. Indeed, Jefferies makes it perfectly clear that

Figure 64. First it's binoculars, but Jefferies's voyeurism insatiable.

Figure 65. Thorwald's suitcase filled with costume jewelry and later with human body parts.

he does not want to lose Lisa—that he wants the relationship to continue exactly as it is—with sexual fulfillment but without the increasingly constrictive demands that he knows she will place on *him* if she becomes his wife. Indeed, Jefferies fully realizes that the lovely and alluring and relentlessly active Lisa, whose days are brimming with appointments, fashion shows, modeling assignments and press conferences, will never leave New York City and will never, ever abandon her modelling profession—and that it would be hell on earth for her to accompany him on overseas assignments in which extreme privation, wild animals, jungle habitats, miserable food, inelegant clothing, are all the rule.

There are two sets of characters in Hitchcock's major film *Rear Window*—first of all the protagonist, the adventurous photographer L.B. Jefferies and his girlfriend Lisa Carol Fremont, who constantly pressures him to get married and thereby indicates that she is capable of nagging him relentlessly, just as does Thorwald's wife and even the initally demure but sexually unsatisfied new bride across the way. Corresponding to the human characters are the inanimate ones—the many, variously styled windows of the huge apartment complex in Greenwich Village that constitutes Hitchcock's imposing set for *Rear Window*, indeed one of the largest sets ever designed and built for a Hollywood film, rivaling the huge sets of Cecil B. DeMille. The major importance of these windows is stressed from the outset of Hitchcock's masterful film, in that one after another, the rolling blinds in the three windows in Jefferies's cramped, two-room apartment are very slowly, very enticingly rolled up—as if the windows themselves were magically performing a striptease—in anticipation of the behavior of Miss Torso and her frustrated rival, Lisa Fremont. And, to provide exquisite aesthetic balance to the film, at the end one by one the blinds roll down.

Like Carlos Fuentes, who always has his readers in mind, enticing them, baffling them, overwhelming them with his Niagara Falls of cascading prose, so too Hitchcock is also ever mindful of his audience—and the viewing of semiclad enticing beauties like Miss Torso endlessly rehearsing her ballet exercises in her bra and panties, is designed to titillate the staid but thrill-seeking audiences of the 1950s—a vicarious excitement and fulfillment which film, like literature, has always afforded. L.B. Jefferies returns again

Figure 66. Gigantic telephoto lens acts as ironic phallic symbol to underscore Jefferies's voyeuristic obsessions that may mask impotence.

Figure 67. Romantic tryst meaningless for illusion-engulfed protagonist.

and again to to focus on the antics—a private performance— of Miss Torso, until finally an increasingly exasperated Lisa abruptly draws the blinds as preparation for her own erotic performance—designed to rival that of the sensuous Miss Torso, just as does the bra-clad Janet Leigh/Marion Crane in bed with her lover played by John Gavin at the beginning of *Psycho*, entice the spectator at the very outset of Hitchcock's most commercially successful film in which Hitchcock's restless camera hovers over Phoenix Arizona then relentlessly and voyeuristically moves in to an open window of a downtown hotel in which the two lovers are still engaged in "afterglow." Similarly, the alienated protagonist of Fuentes's masterful short story occupies a small apartment, this time in London, and the first section of Fuentes's narrative is captioned "La ventana," with its promise of vicarious thrills at viewing the forbidden.

Rear Window, with its theme of double and triple voyeurism —the seated audience in the darkened movie theatre watching a mesmerized L.B. Jefferies in his darkened apartment watching a host of characters in turn watching one another, or like the pathetically lonely and desperate Miss Lonelyhearts at the outset, entertaining an invisible lover and toasting him with her wine glass—a scene of silent desperation that so amuses a highly cynical L.B. Jefferies that he raises his own wine glass in a silent corresponding and mocking toast of her. Jefferies regards Miss Lonelyhearts just as he does Lisa. For the aloof Jefferies, the alluringly beauteous Lisa is but an object of diversion, of romantic attraction but one whom he desires to turn off and on just as she regally turns on the lamps of his apartment to underscore her breathtaking entrance—which a doubtful Jefferies greets with a combination of bemusement and disdain. *Rear Window* is one of Hitchcock's most complex films, along with *Vertigo*, and it is readily apparent why *Rear Window* has so fascinated Carlos Fuentes. The number of windows, each of which acts as a huge television screen, is mirrored in the very busy alleyway adjacent to the monstrous set, as the viewer is led out of the complex multi-story into the street, which leads to the restaurant where Mis Lonelyhearts picks up her young, oversexed lover—the very opposite of the sedentary, middle-aged, undersexed L.B. Jefferies. Ironically, although at the very end, the forlorn Miss Lonelyhearts,

Figure 68. Lisa attempts vainly to assert herself by condemning Jefferies's sick obsession.

Figure 69. Lisa more hypnotized than her fixated partner on murder-mystery across the way.

who at one point is on the verge of suicide, seems to grow younger and more glamorous and finally finds companionship and possibly even a romantic relationship with the music composer who finally finishes his entrancing song, significantly entitled "Lisa," the consolidation—matrimony—of the lead couple, Jefferies and a bouyant yet stubborn Lisa, is far more problematic. Indeed, the open-endedness of *Rear Window*, paralleled by the *apertura* of *Vertigo* and *The Birds*, is mirrored in the ambivalent, ambiguous endings of so many of Fuentes's works, from his initial epic novel *La región más transparente*, to his supernatural Neo Gothic work *Una familia lejana*, to his scathing critique of pollution infected, violence ridden contemporary Mexico, *Cristóbal nonato*, to the murky "The Theatre Lover."

One of the most crucial aspects of the contrast between L.B. Jefferies and Lisa is the difference between the physical incapacity of Jefferies—at the beginning, one leg in a cast, and at the end, both legs in casts, and the emotional vulnerability of the physically powerful Lisa, who over and over again is put down, sometimes suddenly, sometimes coarsely by L.B. Jefferies, a highly sensitive Lisa who again and again registers pain and disappointment with Jefferies's continued opposition and depreciation of her. Indeed the disputatious relationship between Lars Thorwald and his invalid, shrewish wife, who nonetheless appears as sensual creature in her slip in bed demanding, nagging, at times even infuriating with her stocky and always morose husband, who when he is doing his best to be attentive to her, dutifully serving her meals in bed—an attentiveness to his wife which L.B. Jefferies throughout the film lacks, feeling slighted and expressing dismay only once, when it seems as if Lisa were going to walk out on him for good, until she returns to form, telling him that she is leaving him, but only until tomorrow night. Indeed, there is a reason why Jefferies, very comfortable in his relationship with Lisa, should be so adverse to making it permanent—and the disintegrating marital relationships all around him—Lars Thorwald and Anna, as well as the petulant, oversexed bride who summons her exhausted man back to the bridal bed, confirm Jefferies in his conviction that bachelorhood has all the advantages of marriage and none of its confining argumentative negativities. Similarly, Fuentes's bachelor protagonist has no desire for a real-life,

Figure 70. Lisa as perfect Love Goddess—too real for dessicated Jefferies.

Figure 71. Lisa changes from skeptical to highly absorbed in solving murder as way of getting her man.

demanding relationship in which he would inevitably have to sacrifice—or at least compromise—his highly treasured privacy and individualism.

The characteristically aloof and a times even cruel Jefferies readily demonstrates keen interest in Lisa only when she becomes a duplicate of himself—or rather—the Indiana Jones that he once was—a man of action, who to get a dramatic shot of a race car careening out of control stands right in the path of that race car—and suffers both irreparably damaged camera equipment and a very slowly mending broken leg. Jefferies wants Lisa as a wife but only his terms—one who will be an adventuress, who will suffer extremes of heat and cold and malnutrion, in far off, underdeveloped lands, one who will gladly sacrifice her glamorous, princesslike elegant life of meals at 21 and thousand dollar dresses and high life of upper class New York. Yet as this provocative film proceeds, it is evident that energy and daring action and even defiance of death are all exemplified by the overly refined Lisa, not the former adventurer and now ardent window shopper L.B. Jefferies. Lisa is extremely active in her successful modelling career and successful too in her unmasking of the murky Lars Thorwald as a murderer. Yet, ironically this antiheroic status of Jefferies is one of the ways in which the highly intricate portrait of L.B. Jefferies has influenced Fuentes. When it comes time for Jefferies, who watches as Lisa is thrown to the ground and attacked by Thorwald who is capable of killing her as quickly as he dispatched his wife, L.B. Jefferies will not even cry out to startle the attacker as a desperate response to Lisa's frantic calling out for help, as she repeatedly yells out his name. Yet when Jefferies himself is attacked and comes close to being killed by Thorwald, he screams out the names of Doyle and Lisa, who immediately come running to his assistance. When Jefferies himself—a self-proclaimed man of action—is faced by extreme danger, a frustrated and anguished Jefferies can respond only with a strange passivity. When Jefferies is put under extreme duress—ironically, he who is so fond of living vicariously, watching the erotic displays of Miss Torso and the pathetic life of Miss Lonelyhearts like an entomologist, closely observing a group of active, aggressive bugs, when he sees Lisa on the verge of being killed, he turns away in despair, displaying an avoidance that parallels the

Figure 72. Acid-tongued Stella initially rebukes Jefferies then enthusiastically joins him.

Figure 73. Unrelenting, even fierce intensity of *Rear Window* ethics.

passivity and retreat into self of Scottie Ferguson in *Vertigo* who, we recall, also had illusions of a virile, heroic, even commanding role in life—yet who, with supreme irony winds up at the excruciatingly painful and tragic end of *Vertigo*, alone and devastated. Indeed, there is much of the vertigo-stricken, forever out of action Scottie Ferguson in L.B. Jefferies.

Time and again, as every attempt by Lisa—provocative, sensual, loving, endearing, dutifully serving him a lavish meal from the exclusive 21—is slighted and even rebuffed, she frequently registers the pain of disappointment and rejection. It is for this reason that Lisa so thoroughly identifies with the lonely and frustrated and even despairing middle-aged, unglamorous Miss Lonelyhearts on the first floor of the apartment building across the way as well as with the athletic, strong and sophisticated and nubile and erotic Miss Torso on the second floor, surrounded by a horde of eager admirers whom she is successful in fending off. The ending of *Rear Window*—the sudden return from the Army of the boy, Stanly, whom Miss Torso really loves, a lover who appears in uniform, shorter than she is and a stocky boy who immediately runs to the refrigerator, is a let down—and perhaps foreshadows the inevitable decline of relationship between L.B. Jefferies and Lisa, and an unhappy ending to the film that ends, as do most all of Fuentes's challenging works, ambiguously, allowing great space for the reader/viewer to complete the mystery—to resolve the many ambiguities—in his or her imagination. This heightened space of ambiguity characterizes another one of Hitchcock's terrifying films which has decisively impacted the narrative art of Fuentes—*The Birds* (1963) with its open, unsettling, but indeterminate ending, similar to the shocking but highly ambiguous ending of one of Fuentes's finest short stories, "Vlad" which evokes the demonic vampire Dracula in but another reincarnation—a Mexican Dracula with a sinister Minea, his daughter who becomes more powerful than ever he is.

So ambiguous is *Rear Window* that again and again the spectator doubts that Thorwald has really murdered his wife. The detective Doyle, an Air Force buddy of Jefferies's, now a Police Lieutenant, projects a quiet authority when he states confidently that Thorwald is no more a murderer than he is—and with an impressive certainty. Lisa, who at first scoffs at Jefferies's

Figure 74. Twins: Lisa's chic light green ensemble refracted in Miss Lonelyhearts's drab green dress.

Figure 75. Two hands: Telephoto lens too heavy for obsessive gazing but Jefferies undeterred.

absorption with Thorwald and views it as a threat to her own conquest of Jefferies , suddenly turns into her would-be husband's greatest ally, and even becomes his arms and his legs—doing what apparently a reinvigorated Jefferies would have done—entering boldy and surreptitiously the supposed crime scene, the menace-filled apartment of Thorwald. Just before the climatic scene when a suddenly athletic and aggressive Lisa singlehandedly scales the fire escape and enters the rear window to Thorwald's apartment alone and unprotected, it first seems as if cirumstances were corroborating the polished and self-assured Doyle's continued skepticism—when Stella digs in the flower bed, in the court yard of the apartment complex, instead of what she is expecting to find––dismembered parts of Anna Thorwald's body, her digging turns up nothing—Thorwald has removed what he initally buried there after "the dog who knew too much" smells the cadaver pieces.

The controlled structure of *Rear Window* matches that of "El amante del teatro," the lead story of one of Fuentes's stellar short story collections, *Inquieta compañía* ("Disquieting Company"; 2004). The story is dedicated to Harold Pinter, the great English dramatist and Antonia Fraser, and combines theatre and film—paralleling *Rear Window*—a film that could well have been a theatrical production since it, significantly, never leaves the elaborate set of the Greenwich Village apartment buildings, to concentrate almost *in toto* on L.B. Jefferies who has been rendered immobile but who, although initially protesting against his enforced inactivity, seems more and more to find satisfaction in his state—paralleling the sedentary yet highly enjoyable passivity of the afflicted protagonist of "El amante del teatro." Not only Jefferies, but first Stella, who repeatedly chastises Jefferies and stresses the criminal penalty—the years of imprisonment that he will be sentenced to for being a convicted Peeping Tom, yet readily becomes absorbed herself into *Rear Window* antics, enthusiastically spying on Thorwald to corroborate her suspicions––—maybe even her morbid desire—to find Thorwald guilty of murdering his wife then cutting her body into pieces more easily to dispose of it. Similarly, Lisa initially rebuking Jefferies and finding his voyeuristic activities sick, suddenly joins him and most enthusiastically in his spying—and like him is deeply disappointed when at first it seems as if Anna Thorwald is still alive.

Figure 76. Lisa continually brings light but not illumination to benighted Jefferies.

Figure 77. Jefferies is right: sophisticated Lisa could not permanently exist in this humdrum environment.

Action, however, proceeds simultaneously on many planes in *Rear Window* as in "The Theatre Lover." In contrast to the sleeping Jefferies is the on-the-move, ambitious Lisa Carol Fremont—fashion shows, appointments, placing newspaper stories to give immediate publicity to Jefferies, all in a single day—full of activities which do not fatigue her as she at the end of a grueling day is primed for an erotic night with the obstinate and jejune L.B. Jefferies. Indeed, in the fashion industry Lisa relishes the equivalent to the fast-paced life of the death-defying L.B. Jefferies. But unlike Jefferies , who wants her in his life only to the extent that she *refashions* herself in his daring and rough-hewn image, Lisa is willing to compromise—at least at the beginning, as she wistfully asks to be a part of his life in contrast to an adamant Jefferies , who wants no part of her life, which he implies for a daring Spartan hero is sissified, pretentious, wasteful, sterile, and even decadent. Thus the significant incompatibility of Jefferies and Lisa—mirrored in the antagonism between the sensuous but highly querulous Anna Thorwald and her brutish husband—is forcefully stressed by Hitchcock. With the object of his obsession with whom Fuentes's protagonist believes that he is in love but will never approach—the woman who entrances him—because he fears rejection—or perhaps because, like L.B. Jefferies, Larry O'Shea is most content, most satisfied with a purely vicarious relationship. Just as in his daring professional career, where he positioned himself in the path of a speeding race car, Jefferies "asks for it" by deliberately provoking the raging bull—the killer animal—that is the morose, heavy-set Thorwald, masterfully played by Raymond Burr, who is most famous for his role on the other side of the Law—as the redoubtable defense attorney Perry Mason.

Both Hitchcock's L.B. Jefferies and Fuentes's Larry O'Shea are evoked as clinging to their dependent state, to their comfortable passivity. Even when the strangely alluring girl across the way begins to moan, the protagonist Larry O'Shea is not alarmed enough to come to her aid, again paralleling the distance between L.B. Jefferies and the ready for love Grace Kelly who throws herself at him and repeatedly attempts to seduce him but to no avail. For a while, the aggressive Lisa wants to remold Jefferies into the extension of her lavish world upper East Side Manhattan

Figure 78. Everything in film is something else. Lisa's handbag is overnight case for love.

Figure 79. The lovebirds: temporarily blissful, paralleling newlyweds across the way.

existence, to obtain for him dozens of photographic assignments for fashion shows—to transmute him into a fashion photographer, into an extension of *her own* professional world. Neither wants to to give an inch to overcome their professional incompatibility. Significantly there are no children in the tenement area—only the sounds of children playing in the background. Thus a major element of 1950s domesticity—the station wagon mom and the house full of kids—is deliberately absent from *Rear Window*. The energy expended by several of the tenants contrasts with the lethargy of L.B. Jefferies. The frustrated music composer is always in action, writing, playing the piano, throwing endless parties, hosting even a brief, comic appearance of Alfred Hitchcock himself in his spacious apartment. The vibrant Miss Torso, who is always exercising, most always alone, but at one time even with a willing partner—contrasts with the highly uncomfortable immobility of Jefferies. When Lisa first enters Jefferies's cramped and very hot apartment, she has a flair and a charm and a preciousness that are all lost on Jefferies —who is for the most part of the film far more turned on by the amply endowed, scantily clad Miss Torso, displaying to him repeatedly both above the waistline and below it, as she always prances about in the briefest of costumes, most often in her bra and panties. At one point, in order to highlight her own striptease—complete with lavish white negligee, Lisa peremptorily draws down the blinds and exclaims that if she had to rent a nearby apartment to do the Dance of the Seven Veils for Jefferies on the hour, she would do it. It seems that Lisa's very obsession with capturing Jefferies makes him extremely anxious and highly defensive and even leads to his repeatedly insulting her—just as Anna Thorwald throws away the flower on her tray that has been dutifully placed there by her obsequious but errant husband. Lisa brooks no competition from the ravishing Miss Torso, who provides the only sexuality Jefferies is capable of maintaining—vicarious fulfillment, again very similar to the extremely passive Larry O'Shea in Fuentes's captivating short story. At one point, Lisa attempts through uninterrupted kissing in which she promptly takes the initative, to arouse a hopelessly passive Jefferies—just as Janet Leigh, the Hollywood actress who compellingly played the challenging role of the thieving then suddenly repentant Marion Crane was prompted by

Figure 80. Lisa in close-up not as satisfying as prancing Miss Torso in distant shot.

Figure 81. The silken armaments of love dramatically emerge from suitcase, where love is also buried.

Alfred Hitchcock to excite a wooden John Gavin at the provocative beginning of *Psycho*, again a film in which the spectator is from the start thrown into the role of voyeur, as the camera teasingly approaches then penetrates the hotel room window where Marion and her reluctant lover are finishing up their tryst, and are still on the love bed. But Jefferies is much more interested in proving to an initally uninterested Lisa that Thorwald is a murderer, and relishes not the prospect of a romantic evening with his ardent lover but is very preoccupied in how difficult it would be to cut up the body of Miss Torso, who suddenly becomes not only the object of Jefferies's sexual fantasizing but also of his ghoulishness! This ghoulishness not only penetrates *Rear Window* but is markedly heightened in *Psycho*, where a demented Norman Bates carries around the stuffed corpose of the very mother whom he has murdered, along with the lover at whom Norman is outraged but is found in many other of the fifty-four films of Hitchcock, like *Frenzy*. Indeed a terror film by Hitchcock like *The Birds* is definitely a foreshadowing of the ghoulish activities of the zombies feeding on human cadavers that relentlessly attack the house of terrified humans in George A. Romero's thriller, *Night of the Living Dead*. Finally, disappointed that she cannot excite him, Lisa seems suddenly electrified in the realization that by joining his detective activities she can prove herself and immediately become his mate.

Corresponding to the gory, murder and suicide-filled, thriller drama of *Hamlet* that O'Shea in Fuentes's short story returns to again and again, in *Rear Window* Jefferies occupies a prime seat—and finally is mesmerized by the action as he is seated in the front row, in front of his window—overlooking the courtyard and the mini-dramas that continually unfold day and night before him, rendering him almost oblivious to the glamorous Lisa Show going on right before his eyes in his own neglected apartment. What Jefferies wants—similar to Fuentes's frustrated and forever lonely, forever longing and misanthropic protagonist—are a series vicarious relationships in which he can overcome his feelings of dejection, frustration, confinement, boredom, and can repeatedly affirm, even in his crippled state, his superiority to his often quarrelsome, nagging, depressed, oversexed neighbors—as is the initially demure, newly wed wife who at first even declines to

Figure 82. Detective Doyle: the eternal, overconfident skeptic.

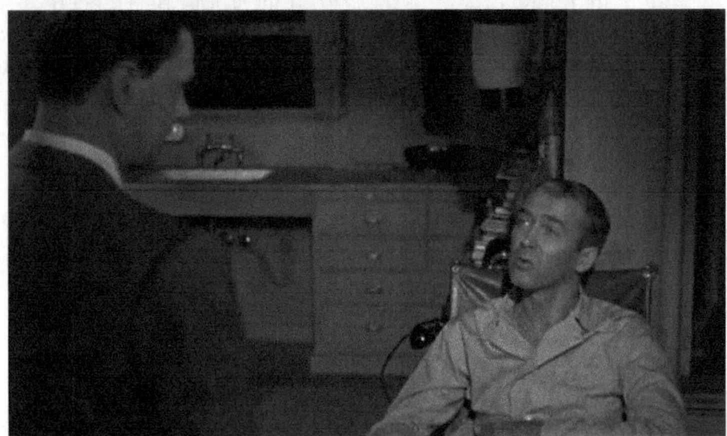

Figure 83. Jefferies considered delusional by all around him but stubbornly persists.

kiss her new husband in front of the landlord who gives them the keys to their new apartment, but who soon becomes possessively amorous, as she repeatedly calls her new and exhausted husband back to the love bed, from which he cannot escape—again an external confirmation of a future, highly exhausting and contentious marriage with the hyperactive Lisa Fremont which Jefferies fears will reduce him to a permanent invalid—which he at the end, nevertheless seems on the verge of becoming.

Hitchcock at times adds comic touches to *Rear Window*, such the female artist with her rather trite depiction of hunger—as a metallic statue that is headless and armless, with a prominent hole where the stomach would be, and whose misshapen design ironically foreshadows the dismembered corpse of Anna Thorwald, the cut-up body that we never see—just as we never see the way in which Peter Massey murders the actress playing Ophelia—presumably, by poisoning her—just as a poisoned cup is used by both Claudius and later, successfully, by a vengeful Hamlet in Shakespeare's convoluted drama. Even the often sarcastic insurance nurse Stella in the visually fascinating *Rear Window*, after being apprised that part of Anna Thorwald is in the East River and part in a hatbox in Thorwald's apartment states, "I want no *part* of it"—and immediately does a double take on her own remark.

Indeed, the incompatibility of Lisa and Jefferies, despite her Girl Friday exploits, her extreme loyalty, her protectiveness, and her very enticing seductiveness, is at the end alluded to by the fact that the newlyweds have finally emerged from their love cocoon and are now heatedly arguing—the groom has lost his job and his hitherto all too willing bride now turns against him—adumbrating what an impatient and highstrung Lisa is capable of doing if dropped in the middle of the High Himalayas with a demanding even exacting, and endlessly judgmental and condemnatory Jefferies. Indeed, it seems as if their extremely fragile relationship can only exist in Jefferies's apartment—not Lisa's lavish, spacious, 63rd Street, Upper East Side apartment to which Hitchcock deliberately never brings us, just as he never shifts to the railroad station to follow the strapped trunk of Thorwald's—apparently filled with Anna Thorwald's clothing but in fact containing parts of her cadaver—and Hitchcock never

Figure 84. Dejected Jefferies when Doyle deflates his ardent investigation.

Figure 85. Lisa has now joined the battle and stands by her man.

entering one of the glamorous fashion studios in which the extremely persistent—indeed as obsessed in obtaining what she desires as is Jefferies in his resistance of her—wants him to obtain a position as well-paid fashion photographer, and certainly not in the wilds of Borneo which Jefferies vociferously yet rather unconvincingly slavers after.

Like *Rear Window*, which has so much inspired it, "El amante del teatro" is filled with ambiguity. Who is the tantalizing, solitary girl across the way, seen only from the torso above by the voyeuristic protagonist? Is she finally murdered, as the febrile mind of the highly unstable protagonist comes to believe—or is she but playing to the extreme, the famous Shakespearean role of the fated, demented Ophelia, the sister of Laertes who commits suicide, in the masterpiece Elizabethan play? In any case both Fuentes's gripping short story and Hitchcock's suspenseful thriller are suffused with intense ambiguity and heightened suspense and sudden, chilling violence. At one point in the ever-shifting world of *Rear Window*, corresponding to the psychedelic universe of "The Theatre Lover," the morbid Stella with hidden relish contemplates the fact that the murder of Anna Thorwald must have occurred in the bathroom, so that the murderer could more easily clean up the splattered blood—which at one point Thorwald as glimpsed through Jefferies's high-powered, telephoto lense, is seen apparently doing.

The Man Who Knew Too Much, Dial M for Murder, Psycho, Vertigo, *The Birds*, and *Marnie*, the films of the master which have received the most critical attention, are all spellbinding works of Hitchcock, all of which combine beautiful sexually charged, icy blonde stars—Grace Kelly, Vera Miles, Kim Novak, Janet Leigh, Tippi Hedren in thriller stories of attack, mystery, and murder, which elevates Hitchcock to one of the finest of Hollywood directors just as Carlos Fuentes has emerged as one of —perhaps now even *the* leading Latin American and world author, one whose consummate fusion of language, innovative and intricate and theme, matches the masterful fusion of cinematic technique and psychological, sociological and metaphysical content by the redoubtable and inimitable Alfred Hitchcock.

It is unclear whether L.B. Jefferies at the end of his misadventures will continue his voyeurism, but there is a strong

Figure 86. Normally passive Jefferies most animated when propagating his murder hypothesis.

Figure 87. Jefferies tormented; Doyle projecting false superiority. Is the detective far more attracted to Lisa than is Jefferies?

probability that because of his severe incapacity, he will, inspiring again Fuentes's protagonist who at the end is mired in contemplation of an empty window across the way, as if desirous that someone else will take the place of the doomed Ophelia. The stationary L.B. Jefferies is evoked at the end of the film as at the beginning, fitfully but apparently contentedly asleep, but this time with both legs in casts. There seems little doubt that Jefferies will continue his life of voyeurism just as at the end of *Vertigo* in the case of the highly disturbed and self-destructive and excruciatingly ambivalent protagonist, the Thanatos-driven Scottie Ferguson—just as the self-destructive Scottie even if he encounters a third Madeleine Elster, is doomed but once more to lose her. Similarly, the ending of "El amante del teatro" exemplifies cyclic time—the protagonist is once more at his window, once more gazing, this time repeatedly, obsessively, his gaze transfixed by a marvellous blue flower—as if hoping his beloved Ophelia would some day return.

L.B. Jefferies occupies a two room walk-up in a downscale Greenwich Village, and Hitchcock contrasts his close, cramped quarters with the spacious up-town apartment of the wealthy Lisa Carol Fremont, which we never see, as Hitchcock, much moreso than in the vertiginous and space-expansive *Vertigo* in which the canny director takes us repeatedly across San Francisco, north to Muir Woods, south, as the camera swoops twice down to the Peninsula to the fateful Jesuit mission of San Juan Bautista. Fuentes's frustrated male protagonist dwells, similar to L.B. Jefferies, alone and stultified in a small, rented apartment in Wardour Street in central London. L.B. Jefferies is ambivalent toward his handicapped status—he both chafes against it, as he longs to return to the action of journalistic photography, particularly in far off exotic lands, and yet strangely enjoys, even clings to the voyeuristic existence that his helpless state gives him.

In both Hitchcock and Fuentes, fantasies are piled up on mere fantasies. Significantly, Miss Lonelyhearts who at first is portrayed as a despondent, suicidal spinster, seems to grow younger—and more beautiful, as the film progresses. It is she who finds and takes pity on the dead dog killed by Thorwald, a dog to which Lisa refers, alluding to a Hitchcock film, *The Man Who Knew Too Much* as "the dog who knew too much." At the end,

Figure 88. Lisa and Jefferies, never united as lovers but determined partners in detection. Grace Kelly stunning in role.

Figure 89. The Lisa Show: enticing, but cannot compete with acrobatic, scantily clad Miss Torso.

Miss Lonelyhearts, instead of committing suicide as the wisecracking insurance woman Stella—as confident in her misapprehensions as is Detective Doyle—thinks she is about to do, is seen in the company of the triumphant composer of the song that Lisa finds so enchanting, and Miss Lonelyhearts seems on the verge of a fulfilling relationship. Ironically, to Miss Lonelyhearts, not to Lisa Fremont, belongs the captivating song "Lisa," finally completed by the frequently tempermental and highly despondent, and deliberately nameless, composer. Indeed, the initially forlorn and abused Miss Lonelyhearts is perhaps the only character in *Rear Window* to succeed in love.

The fantasy that is the fashion industry is fully displayed by the flowing, $1000 dress spectacularly worn by Grace Kelly in her entrance costume, again underscoring the highly dramatic qualities of *Rear Window*. Indeed, it is L.B. Jefferies who at first emerges as a stubborn, petulant fool, both from the jaundiced perspective of Stella, and that of the audience who find unbelievable his being willing to throw away the person, slim, elegant, intelligent, wealthy, charming—who is so in love with him—again just as the highly dependent Scottie Ferguson throws away the engaging, intelligent, attractive, over solicitous Midge who is so unerringly devoted to him, even without the marital vow of "in sickness and in health." Jimmy Stewart, in his key roles in both of these thrillers of Hitchcock, is masterful at playing in a subdued fashion extremely complex roles of both intense suffering and insistent cruelty—yet unfailingly gaining the audience identification with his plight. Indeed, it is Jefferies not Lisa, who with his victimization and his increasingly desperate plight controls the development of *Rear Window* and to whose perspective—at first curious, bemused, then riveted, especially by Thorwald's activities in the dead of night, and finally degraded into the lone, helpless, crippled victim of a looming maniac—just as the stricken protagonist of "El amante del teatro" depicts himself as the helpless, defenseless victim of an outraged and murderous and suddenly attacking Peter Massey.

There is parallel costuming in *Rear Window* to underscore similar predicaments: the conservative, even out of style, prim dark green dress worn by Miss Lonelyhearts to pick up a male and bring him back to her apartment is echoed and enhanced in the highly

Figure 90. Seduction suddenly erased by murder.

Figure 91. Everyone in apartment complex rushes to window to view dead dog except the strangler, Thorwald.

fashionable, light green and white ensemble worn by the Lisa, who so identifies with the loneliness and dejection of Miss Lonelyhearts—just the opposite of the unemotional reaction toward the forlorn spinster of the callous Jefferies. Lisa is over and over seen only in relationship first to Jefferies, and then, antagonistically to Thorwald. When she is caught by Thorwald in his apartment, Lisa puts on and triumphantly flashes to an amazed Jefferies the diamond wedding ring of Anna Thorwald which, in essence, the extremely brazen Lisa has stolen from Lars Thorwald. The meaning is double—this is the wedding ring that not only incriminates the sinister Thorwald but is a victory ring for Lisa, who now feels she is in a good position to get a wedding diamond for herself as Jefferies's new bride. Throughout the multifaceted *Rear Window*, Hitchcock expertly contrasts the utter devotion to marriage of the highly desirable Lisa with the obstinate and intransigent attitude of Jefferies, whom Stella brands as foolish and deluded. Similarly, Fuentes contrasts the desperate attempts of Ophelia to reach out in the only way she can to Larry O'Shea, with the male protagonist's profound ambivalence toward the beautiful, mysterious girl, paralleling the dreamlike Lisa, whose own identity is mirrored fragmentarily—in the rejection by males of Miss Lonelyhearts and the seemingly successful male manipulator yet ever loyal, the ever-energetic Miss Torso.

The cold fascination that Jefferies has for the warped lives of his neighbors is paralleled by the obsession of Fuentes's alienated and friendless protagonist—a Mexican rootless in London without being accepted either by his elitist British film associates or by his Latin American companions, doubly alienated in that his heritage is Irish—O'Shea. Fuentes's Cortázar-like character, inspired in part by one of the Argentine master's greatest short stories of the theatrical experience that turns a theatrical murder of the female lead to an actual murder of the fated actress, "Instrucciones para John Howell" which also takes place on the London stage and also like "El amante del teatro" contains a play within a play—the threat to the female lead by her fellow actors who are also her captors in reality, and who incite John Howell—initially only a spectator of the play—to murder her.

In *Rear Window*, James Stewart from his wheelchair assumes the role both of spectator—in which he is joined by an

Figure 92. Anguished owner of the "Dog who knew too much."

Figure 93. Jefferies as remarkably energized; Lisa as rapt, willing accomplice.

increasingly enthusiastic Stella and a zestful Lisa—a team operation that in this meticulously constructed work is adumbrated from the start—as Stewart's vain attempt to gaze on two girls who take off their clothes to sunbathe on the roof immediately draws a helicopter to the scene to enjoy the view that Stewart is attempting to see but is frustratingly deprived of. Both *Rear Window* and "El amante del teatro" are stories of overly zealous male fantasies—first of female beauty and desirability and provocativeness and then of apparent murder, a crime that in *Rear Window* is finally confirmed, and in "The Theatre Lover" remains definitely problematic.

Fantasies pile up upon fantasies in the vertiginous works of both Fuentes and Hitchcock. At the end of the convoluted *Rear Window*, Lisa is seen seemingly absorbed in an adventure book *Beyond the High Himalayas* that would presumably mark her increasing, sustained absorption into Jefferies's heroic world—yet as soon as the wily Lisa determines that Jefferies is fast asleep, she quickly abandons the adventure book to turn to her true obsession––the glamorous fashion world that Jefferies loathes. The extremely narcissistic L.B. Jefferies seems to view his photographic exploits as a combination of the prize-winning Margaret Bourke White, her masterful photographs gracing many issues of *Life Magazine* to which L.B. Jefferies has also contributed prized photos, and the daredevil stuntman Evil Kenevil, in combination with the daring, and reckless and death-defying the Flying Wallendas, who perform their high wire acrobatics without a safety net resulting in the tragic deaths of several of their family members. Yet Jefferies is not really a hero—he was extremely reckless in standing right in front of a speeding race car which crashed and hit him, and now he is faced both with increasing age and enforced sedentariness, all of which render his return to a daredevil existence as rather improbable. In this film the person who risks being assaulted and even murdered by Thorwald first is Lisa, whom Jefferies now from his sheltered apartment only silently addresses, quietly imploring her to get out of the dangerous cage that is of Thorwald's apartment. Throughout *Rear Window*, Hitchcock constantly and subtly moves between the satiric and comic and the foreboding and tragic. Romantic interludes are permanently cut off

Figure 94. Spellbound: a trio of unrepentant voyeurs in concentrated action.

Figure 95. Stella joins Jefferies in morbidity, concocting lurid details of Anna's murder.

by acts of murder—just as they are in Fuentes's captivating narrative, "The Theatre Lover."

The two sudden screams that are heard in the night, in the relentlessly paced *Rear Window*, first that of Anna Thorwald, presumably as she is being murdered by strangulation, and later the piercing scream of the dog owner that has just discovered that her beloved dog has been killed—the cry that cuts short Lisa's coyly announced seduction performance of Jefferies, exemplify the exacting parallelism that characterizes so many of Hitchcock's works, like *Vertigo*, *Psycho*, *Marnie*, *The Birds*, in the last film in which even the elaborate French-inspired hairdo of Melanie Daniels, the outside presence in claustrophobic Bodega Bay and a formidable threat to the highly possessive and extremely insecure mother of Mitch, Lydia Brenner, is reflected in the fashionable hairdo of the hateful Lydia—two very determined, initially antagonistic women, two rivals for the affection of Mitch Brenner, who is pursued not only by fierce, biting birds but by relentlessly aggressive women. Indeed, the attacking birds are paralleled by far more subtle but equally fierce rivalries among the three women in *The Birds* as Hitchcock's films, like Fuentes's works, continually move between the physical and the psychological, and geography as well as architecture—streets, alleyways, palaces, mansions is symbolic of emotional states and metaphysical concerns like time, memory, immortality, and oblivion.

What exactly happened to Ophelia in "El amante del teatro"? Her fate is left ambiguous—the only certainty is that when the play closes, she no longer appears in the window across the way. She could have been fired from the theatrical company by the dictatorial, temperamental Peter Massey for breaking the code of the drama and interacting with the spectators. Massey is a demonic perfectionist. Or she could have been eliminated by a vindictive Massey—paralleling the outwardly obsequious but in reality diabolical Thorwald—who is ready to kill again—first the dog, then threatening both Lisa and finally Jefferies, before he is successfully apprehended by the police—something that never occurs with Peter Massey in Fuentes´s chilling story—Massey whose fate parallels that of the invulnerable manipulator Gavin Elster in *Vertigo*.

Figure 96. High angle shot: provocation of brutish Thorwald.

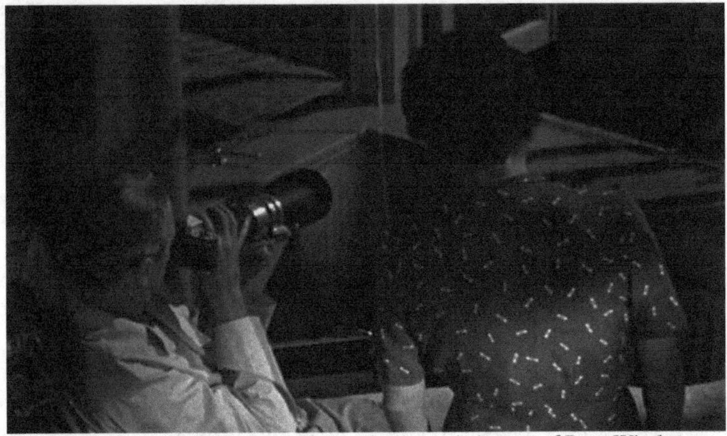

Figure 97. Vicarious thrills for Jefferies, Stella, and viewers of Rear Window.

Indeed, Larry O'Shea seems to be a Mexican expatriate version of Hitchcock himself, as he depicts his film and television profession in exacting terms "my work consists in following the intentions of a director to make certain but a single thing: the narrative fluidity and the technical perfection of the film."[32] As he meticulously defines the nature of the word *film*, the narrator is also defining the contours of his bizarre story of spying, on a beautiful, erotic woman, and finally on a brutal murder that remains highly ambiguous, as well as his thwarted attempts to halt the crime and rescue his beloved—whom he has previously, zealously, kept at a comfortable distance.

> "The English word *film* perhaps is better because it is more technical or abstract than the Spanish term [*película*]. *Film* indicates a membrane, a fragile skin, fog, veil, opacity. I have looked up the word in the dictionary to avoid verbal fantasies and to concentrate on what film is in my work: a flexible roll of celluloid and emulsion." (AT, 10)

Ironically, the painstakingly precise O'Shea, who asserts his desire to avoid "verbal fantasies" may in his lurid account of the torture then murder of his beloved Ophelia be doing just that—elaborately concocting his own, personal drama, one which reflects his own increasingly alienated, tormented existence.

Just as in *Rear Window*, where all three of the amateur detectives in Jefferies's apartment —Stella, Lisa, and Jefferies himself—at times concentrate with morbid fascination on what at first is the purely speculative, dismembered corpse of Anna Thorwald—the parts of his wife that Thorwald is apparently disposing of by surreptitiously, he thinks, carrying them off to various parts of the city in his metallic sample case at night, to the extent that the exceedingly refined Lisa refers to herself and Jefferies as "ghouls," so too is the violence and the horror about to

---

[32] Consult Carlos Fuentes, "El amante del teatro," in Fuentes's short story collection *Inquieta compañía* (México: Alfaguara, 2004) p. 9. Subsequent references are indicated parenthetically in the text. The translations are all by L.G.

Figure 98. Life reduced to hours-filled, nights-filled armchair detection.

Figure 99. Lisa takes action and startlingly delivers denunciation of the suspected murderer.

come indicated at the start of "El amante del teatro" by the circumstance that the deliberately unbalanced narrator moves from an emphasis on *film* to a focus on *skin*, as the extensive film that covers up body parts the meticulous and somewhat morbid—again paralleling the ghoulish L.B. Jefferies—as a professional film developer exposes:

> ...but I nonetheless cannot (or will not) separate myself from the vision of the fragile human skin, superficial, the thin costume of appearance. The skin with which we present ourselves to the gaze of others, since without the skin which covers us from feet to hand, we would be only a butcher store of short-lived visceral organs, without any ultimate armament than the skeleton —the cranium. *Alas, poor Yorick*! (AT, 10)

Indeed, the repeated, gleeful morbidity of the characters in *Rear Window* is reflected in the exultant ghoulishness of the narrator of "The Theatre Lover" as he exultantly echoes the cry of Hamlet as he gazes upon the skull of the lost Yorick in Shakespeare's drama of passion and murder.

Just as Jefferies is misanthropic, as he basically enjoys being a daring-do and an inveterate loner, so also is Fuentes's narrator, who seems also to cling to—or to relish—his friendless state, rationalizing it by claiming that the English "are not particularly open to the foreigner" and citing a series of racial epithets commonly employed in England to insult and isolate the foreigner. But there is a sense that just as Jefferies enjoys being a loner and repeatedly links marriage—even to someone as perfect as Lisa Fremont—with castration and mummification and the deadly whir of kitchen appliances that he finds enslaving—even though the function of home appliances in the 1940s—and for many persons even today in the twenty-first century—is designed not to enslave but to liberate the houseperson from the drudgery of eighteenth and nineteenth century domestic chores—appliances almost universally regarded not as prison guards but as domestic servants. And, Larry O'Shea, paralleling the obtuse, self-absorbed L.B. Jefferies, clings to his uniqueness and his prized, well-

Figure 100. Lisa demonstrates lust for adventure by recklessly climbing into Thorwald's apartment.

Figure 101. Brooding, sinister Lars Thorwald: One of Raymond Burr's (Perry Mason) finest supporting roles.

guarded solitude, which makes him, like Jefferies, prone to excessive—and obstinate—fantasizing.

Like the highly ambitious L.B. Jefferies , who is very proud of being at the top of his profession, to the extent that his boss does not want to send him on dangerous assignments anymore, Jefferies who is talented enough to do covers for *Life Magazine*—for more than fifty years the leading photographic weekly news magazine in the world and devotedly read by the Master of the Visual, Alfred Hitchcock—Larry O'Shea is also highly ambitious but keenly frustrated in his aspirations, and because of his hermit-like nature unable successfully to make the contacts necessary for his professional advancement—or for the amelioration of his love life, of which he is even worse off than L.B. Jefferies—O'Shea literally has none:

> I didn't realize it until very late on my thirty-third birthday which is my age today, the implacable competition which reigns over the world of film and television. My disagreeable character, my foreign origin, perhaps a lassitude very disagreeable to admit, chained me to an editor's desk as well as to a solitary life because, for identical reasons, I did not wish to be a partygoer, to belong to the life of the pubs and sports and the fascination with the Royals and their comings and goings....I wanted to reserve for myself the free aloneness of the gaze after nine hours glued to AVID. (AT, 11)

O'Shea eloquently depicts himself as the "fourth wall" of the theatrical setting—that fourth wall that is also so important in *Rear Window*, as both L.B. Jefferies and the spectator of *Rear Window* throughout this highly theatrical film also occupy the position of the "Fourth Wall." Indeed, of all Hitchcock's many films, black and white and in color, from the silent era to the sound films, *Rear Window* is the most theatrical and consists, on one level, of a series of exclusive minidramas avidly watched by the imprisoned Jefferies , who for most of the film is, just like Larry O'Shea, a defenseless spectator. *Rear Window* consists of a dialogue among characters in a fixed space—everything is viewed either inside or from the apartment of Jefferies—and almost

Figure 102. Mystery after mystery: what does Anna Thorwald's alligator purse contain?

Figure 103. Jefferies alone and highly vulnerable: door invitingly unlocked.

exclusively limited to exactly what the highly immobilized protagonist can view through his window, during the day and throughout his mostly sleepless night. Similarly, in Fuentes's tightly woven short story, there is but a single author observer and nothing occurs outside of his visual perception and exuberant, even overly zealous mental fantasizing.

Indeed, O'Shea speaks with a gusto for the enterprise of *looking*, of deriving great pleasure from merely viewing, that corresponds to L.B. Jefferies's incessantly voyeuristic life even before his accident, as his very profession is one of again and again viewing other peoples' lives for pleasure and profit. As O'Shea states energetically:

> I've become insatiable. The theatrical scene provides me with *the living distance* that my spirit requires (that my eyes demand). I am *there* but illusion itself separates me from the scene. I constitute the "fourth wall" of the scene. The acting is love. (AT, 11)

Much of the fantasy that is *Rear Window* consists of the windows that are always conveniently shadeless or curtainless—those of Miss Lonelyhearts, with the sole exception of the time when she is entertaining—and even in the violent scene where the man whom she hopes would be a romantic lover and who turns out to be brutal, the would be lover whom she has picked up, we are still allowed to peep through the narrow slots of the Venetian blinds of her desolate apartment. Openness reigns in *Rear Window*; the immense artistic designer windows of the music composer which are never covered, just as are the always uncovered windows of the provocative Miss Torso and, surprisingly even those of the criminal Lars Thorwald, to the extent that Detective Doyle sees Thorwald's apparent openness as an indication of his definite innocence, because a truly guilty murderer would hide himself all the time. Thus we can conclude that if Jefferies is an inveterate Peeping Tom, most of his neighbors—with the sole exception of the newlywed couple in their conjugal bed—are exhibitionists. This is precisely the situation in "El amante del teatro"—it is clear that the sensual woman across the street wants to be incessantly looked at, and she constitutes the delectable

Figure 104. Unlike statuette, crippled Jefferies is unarmored.

Figure 105. Melding contradictions: sophisticated elegance and blunt plainness side by side in adventure and intrigue. Note exquisite but adumbratory pearl choker necklace.

exhibitionist who delightfully fulfills the passive existence of the extremely voyeuristic Larry O'Shea. Why she wants this attention seems to be because she is practicing her role as Ophelia, but beyond this there are other reasons—the beautiful blonde woman seems to be reaching out desperately, plaintively to O'Shea—paralleling the repeated actions of the gorgeous Lisa toward a resisting Jefferies—yet like Lisa, she is *not* responded to by the intransigent narrator, who, again like Jefferies, prefers to remain solely ensconced within his incorrigible voyeurism. Indeed, this reaching out of Ophelia achieves its maximum extreme when the stricken woman in her final performance as the doomed Ophelia and perhaps even the final moments of her life—tosses to O'Shea the magical blue flower, which at the end he cherishes as a symbol that is indeterminate—either of immortality or of everlasting love.

Indeed, the self-satisfied and self-exalting L.B. Jefferies is really turned on by Lisa only when he starts *viewing* her entering Thorwald's apartment, at the climactic moment when Lisa deliberately and enthusiastically converts herself into one more of Jefferies's prized "Rear Window" objects. Then he at once becomes ecstatic about her. At first Lisa is shocked, as Jefferies abruptly interrupts her passionate kisses with a morbid observation "Just how would you start to cut up a human body?"—which changes the emphasis from "Did Thorwald kill his wife?" to a rather ghoulish concentration on what the monstrous Thorwald did *after* he murdered her, in order to dispose of the corpse. Initially Lisa is startled "Jeff, I'll be honest with you, you begin to scare me!" Yet her highly negative attitude toward her extremely reluctant lover immediately changes, and for multiple reasons.

It is important to underscore the fact that silent dreams played out by nonspeaking personages form an important part of both *Rear Window* and "The Theatre Lover." Much of *Rear Window* is in silence. Indeed, the greater part of Thorwald's role is a silent one. Thorwald speaks only briefly, first on the telephone when Jefferies calls him, to rattle him, and finally when Thorwald in a cold rage easily—perhaps even too easily—invades Jefferies's apartment. In New York, a city of locked doors—with triple locks even in the relatively halcyon fifties and sixties, it is ironic that the door in Jefferies's apartment is always left open—on one level a cinematic concoction—paralleling the ease with which theatrical

Figure 106. Now Jefferies has yet another, this time personal, drama to watch fixedly.

Figure 107. Lisa's initial triumph: the mysterious alligator purse of Anna Thorwald.

actors and actresses move and out of stage center. Yet it is strange that even after Jefferies has deliberately provoked Thorwald by sending—delivered by the active, intrepid Lisa—the note "what have you done with your wife!," Jefferies fails to sensibly lock his door—almost as if he were welcoming an encounter with the highly menacing Thorwald—in order to demonstrate Jefferies's prized theory concerning Thorwald's guilt and need to be punished for his dastardly crime—as well as Jefferies's need to vindicate himself before his best friend Doyle, who regards Jefferies more and more as a deluded pervert—just as first Stella then Lisa have regarded him. Perhaps Jefferies deliberately leaves his door open because subconsciously he relishes a fierce encounter with his antagonist—as a means of self-vindication.

Indeed, the one noble aspect of Jefferies is his stubborn adherence to his conviction that Thorwald is a murderer—despite the initial skepticism of all of those around him—and despite the sustained opposition of Doyle, Jefferies's comrade and best friend, probably the only friend of the finicky and even at times curmudgeonly protagonist. In Fuentes's short story, the relationship between the solitude-seeking O'Shea and Ophelia is, most of all, a silent one—when she is in her apartment, he never speaks or calls out to her. And, more importantly, Peter Massey in his *Hamlet* of striking originality and tyrannical abuse of his actors, all of whom are treated with contempt—paralleling Alfred Hitchcock's famous remark that actors are like cattle——Massey commands Ophelia to play a silent role as a prelude to her theatrical suicide—which the extremely agitated and even anguished narrator deems a murder—thus constituting a morbid extension of the phenomenon of "living theatre" and a severe and grisly smashing of the barriers between stage acting and real life. Or is the supposed murder of Ophelia only in the mind of the avid, even rabid and increasingly unhinged Larry O'Shea? The reader, as is customary in the world of Carlos Fuentes and that of his fellow Boom Author Julio Cortázar, is compelled to play an active role in the story—either to agree with O'Shea that Peter Massey is not only a deranged tyrant but a cold-blooded murderer, a director wildly applauded by an audience ever-willing to be duped, fully believing that the demise of Ophelia, who seems to drown before their very eyes, is part of Massey's stunning originality, or to label

Figure 108. Time and again in roller coaster Rear Window, exhilaration turns into disconsolation.

Figure 109. Voyeurism becomes more intricate: simultaneous actions.

him a madman—a parallel to the monstrous way in which O'Shea depicts the despotic Peter Massey. Ironically the condemnation of Massey by O'Shea contrasts with the enthusiastic approbation of the theatre audience of the highly original version of Shakespeare's most famous tragedy.

The increasingly agitated narrator created by Fuentes even skips work, so fascinated has he become with the young, provocative, scantily clad blonde next door—undoubtedly inspired by Hitchcock's energetic ballet dancer Miss Torso, more appreciated by L.B. Jefferies for her unattainable provocativeness than he ever appreciates the real fashion model—the calculating Lisa Fremont——who insistently throws herself at him. And just as Lisa first appears as an unreal phenomenon, as a looming shadow over the face of the sleeping Jefferies, as a magical princess bestowing a kiss upon a chaste, sleeping lover, so too is the nameless blonde in "The Theatre Lover" loom as an unreality—as a marvellous erotic fantasy. As O'Shea declares excitedly, as aroused by the enigmatic blonde woman as is L.B. Jefferies by the teasing Miss Torso:

> She did not have eyebrows—that is to say, she had shaved them completely off. This gave her an unreal air, very strange, that's certain. But it was sufficient for me to lower my gaze towards her breasts, practically visible because of the provocative nature of her gown, to discover in them a *tenderness* that I didn't dare to evaluate. A marvellous tenderness—that of a lover, perhaps maternal, but above all desirable, a tenderness of desire, that was it. (AT, 15)

The narrator, like Jefferies, gazes on his fascinating subject with both his eyes and his imagination, attributing to her a tenderness that she may or may not possess, but clearly indicating how deeply O'Shea is immersed in her as a fulfilling erotic fantasy for an alienated, surly man. Indeed, O'Shea becomes just as fanatic a voyeur as is L.B. Jefferies , who even stops sleeping in his bed at night, so glued to his windows has he become, and who rapidly moves from viewing his neighbors with the naked eye, first to using binoculars, which he quickly discards as inadequate, and

Figure 110. Heightened suspense: Thorwald returns far too soon.

Figure 111. Will Thorwald murder again?

finally employing a huge telephoto lense which clearly picks up what Jefferies surmises are the murder weapons—a huge butcher knife and a gleaming saw both wielded by Thorwald, who apparently is packing them in his trunk. Here again why Thorwald would be so careless as to wrap these so menacing objects in newspaper without drawing the blinds remains a mystery, unless Thorwald subconsciously wants to be observed, wants to be caught. But the bullish Thorwald is much bolder than the basically cautious Jefferies —particularly after the racetrack acccident in which the defiant Jefferies could have been killed. Indeed Thorwald is surprisingly very incautious, even phoning his lover long distance from the living room of his apartment while his wife, whose rising antagonism towards her seemingly servile spouse may be due not so much to physical illness but to her increasing suspicions that her husband is conducting an affair right under her nose, are indicated in her surreptitiously approaching the living room entrance to listen in on Thorwald—becoming one more voyeur/evesdropper in this tightly constructed film, one of Hitchcock's most exacting and suspenseful works, similar to Fuentes's tightly composed narrative suffused with dramatic action that, again paralleling to the circuitous *Rear Window*, takes many twists and turns.

And Fuentes's entranced narrator is even more captivated with his voyeuristic object than is the obsessed Jefferies. Just as Jefferies will remain immobile for an extended period of time with little to do but to return to his vicarious existence as voyeur, so too does Fuentes's bizarre, lonely, mesmerized protagonist melt into a permanent Freeze Frame at the end:

> I would never again leave my place at the window. There probably would be interruptions. Accidents, perhaps. Yes, unforseeable acts of chance, but never stranger than the absolute, necessarily born instantaneously, like a companion of the great fortune of having discovered her (AT, 15)

So obsessed by his platonic lover—whom he clearly wants to *remain* platonic—despite his circumscribing himself in the category of Latin lover to his physician, from whom he wheedles

Figure 112. Jefferies in agony; not the adventurous daredevil hero he self-exaltedly proclaims.

Figure 113. Paralyzed Jefferies unable to intervene directly to save Lisa.

an excuse to stay home from work, does the beleagured protagonist become, that he even gives up his love for the nocturnal theatre to participate vicariously in this living theatrical performance across the way, which he desperately desires to continue as mere performance, not a consummated relationship, which would inexorably pull him out of his dreamworld to possibly discomfitting reality.

The behavior of O'Shea toward his appetizing, would-be mistress is as vacillating and eccentric as is that of L.B. Jefferies toward the paradoxically angelic and erotic Lisa. Instead of ringing the bell of her apartment and introducing himself, the vacillating protagonist O'Shea becomes the mirror image of the vicarious adventurer that the crippled L.B. Jefferies has now become reduced to:

> It was an infernal dizziness that overwhelmed my heart. I only wanted to see her from the window. I had fallen in love with the girl in the window. I did not wish to break the illusion of that untouchable beauty, silent, drawn away from my voice and my touch by a narrow alleyway in Soho, although very near to me thanks to the mystery of my own gaze, fixed on her. (AT, 19)

The scene reflects that of *Rear Window* in its claustrophobia. The same suffocating heat of summer plagues both L.B. Jefferies, for most of the time alone in his sweltering apartment, and the bizarre narrator of "The Theatre Lover" who now abandons his beloved theatre for a new, but totally vicarious love affair. The intrinsically passive Larry O'Shea is just like L.B. Jefferies, who when confronted by a real-life willing, gorgeous girl repeatedly turns her aside, essentially disdaining her, to welcome his midnight entertainment with Miss Torso. Indeed, O'Shea even lords over his voyeurism, not a prelude to sexual and emotional intimacy but superior to both forms of attachment of one human being to another:

> Could her skin, her touch, her uncertain kisses, satisfy me more than the distance that allowed me to look at her—to possess her—completely? (AT, 19)

Figure 114. Voyeurism doubled: Stella is activated and begins digging.

Figure 115. Exuberant donning of Anna's wedding ring: a marital future for Lisa?

Indeed, Larry O'Shea is very similar to the highly introverted protagonist of Fuentes's *A Change of Skin* (1968), Javier Ortega, who incessantly seeks to reduce his oversexed wife Elizabeth to an artistic object—to a woman painted by Modigliani or to a Greek *stele*, in order to control her, to summon her up or abolish her by an act of his will—and who also is entranced by a dark-haired "Woman in the Window" about whom he can freely fantasize without surrendering anything of his precious Self. Indeed, the introspective, voyeuristic Javier may also be inspired by the contemplative control freak L.B. Jefferies.

There is, in L.B. Jefferies's initial desire to break up with Lisa, a genuineness, which Lisa herself recognizes, not to lead her on, not to marry her and then place her in situations which she would find awkward, disgusting and even terrifying. And yet although it is clear that Lisa has many male alternatives to L.B. Jefferies —indeed, this is one of the reasons why Lisa speaks with so much authority when she states that Miss Torso, far from being, as Jefferies enviously sees her, the Queen Bee surrounded by a pack of well-dressed male drones devoted to her, is instead performing a woman's most difficult task—that of juggling wolves. Indeed, at the end, Lisa's contradictory interpretation that Miss Torso, far from being a temptress, loves none of her well-to-do admirers, is borne out when the boyfriend/lover of Miss Torso —short, with glasses, and immediately desirous of raiding the refrigerator rather than making love to Miss Torso, returns on leave from the Army—reminiscent of L.B. Jefferies who was an Air Force pilot and who seems perfectly content with an existence of eating, drinking wine, and obtaining his sexual thrills vicariously—just as does the narrator of Fuentes's short story, who much prefers, similar to L.B. Jefferies, to exist in suspended animation. And once again Hitchcock's wry humor is evident—there is a marked compatibility between Miss Torso and her boyfriend—both love food—Miss Torso throughout *Rear Window* constantly returning to her refrigerator and even to continue to dance while devouring her food—possessed of a ravenous appetite for food not sex that is paralleled by that of her hungry G.I.

Lisa Fremont looms as an eagerly willing love, suddenly emerging, seemly out of nowhere in the night to kiss L.B. Jefferies—a goddess of perfection, blonde, slender, warm,

Figure 116. Thorwald finally recognizes his pursuer; vengeance is imminent.

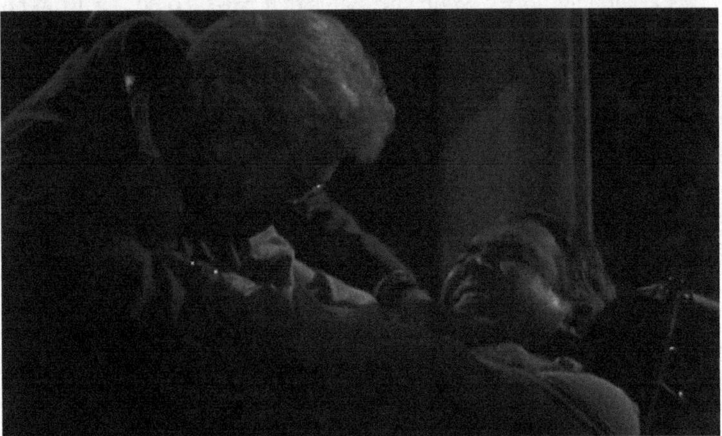

Figure 117. Suddenly pleasurable vicarious thrills become horrifying for incapacitated Jefferies.

embraceable and more importantly, steadfast—yet for Jefferies suffocatingly controlling. But just as Stella wryly remarks that Jefferies's frequent gazing on the semi-naked bathing beauties has not raised his temperature one bit, neither can an adoring, willing sexual goddess like Lisa, literally throwing herself at Jefferies , arouse his erotic passion. Similarly, Larry O'Shea is in the throws of ecstacy over his dream girl—that, like the ancient Greek master sculptor Pygmalion with his beauteous marble statue of Galatea, can fashion and refashion at his will, without the slightest risk of rejection:

> What didn't I see in my marvellous creature! Her long blonde hair, blown about in reality by the electric fan which purred by her shoulders, from my viewpoint, tossed by the flowing of a marvellous and inevitable river which bathed her hair in refulgent waves. And her eyes: because they were dark, were more liquid than the green of the sea or the blue of the sky. (AT, 18)

Significantly, O'Shea's mentioning of the flowing of an invisible river—an allusion to the river in which Shakespeare's forlorn Ophelia commits suicide—the astonishing, magically appearing river in Fuentes's story as it concentrates on the concluding, doubly fatalistic performance of *Hamlet* ominously adumbrates the horrifying ending of "The Theatre Lover"—the marvellous but treacherous river that in the concluding performance of *Hamlet*—a true showstopper—suddenly opens up in the theatre, to drag a doomed Ophelia down the orchestra pit and to stun, amaze, and delight the highly enthusiastic audience, which unlike the skeptical then condemnatory O'Shea, idolizes the highly iconoclastic Peter Massey.

Ironically, what a typical male admirer of the "woman in the window" would consider normal—the blonde's returning his gaze, perhaps amorously or invitingly, is received with dread by the suddenly strangely prudish narrator, who even deems such mutual recognition by the woman to be a perversion:

> A single time I realized that she was on the verge of averting her unmindful gaze to fix it on me. I felt terror.

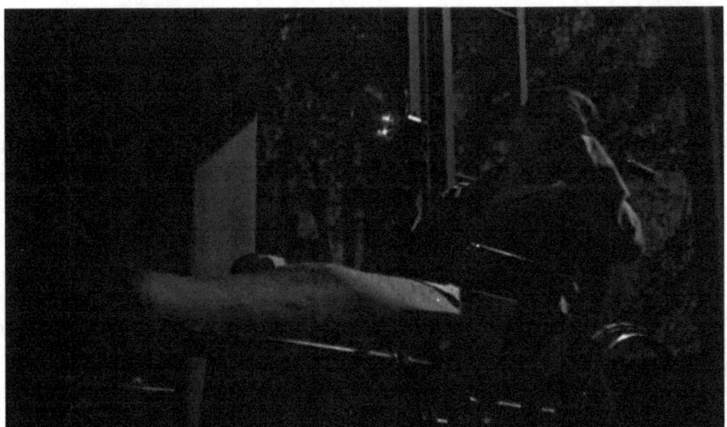

Figure 118. Jefferies only weapons to save his life, flashbulbs, prove ineffectual.

Figure 119. Will Thorwald murder again?

> With a brusque motion I withdrew from the window and I covered myself, cowardly, with the curtain. There, like an invisible spider, I wanted to contemplate with lucidity the dimensions of my strategy. Like a cockroach, I hid myself in the anonymous obscurity of the drapes, more fearful of what I desired than of what I feared. Fear over fear. (AT, 20.)

This apprehension finds its source in *Rear Window*, in which the fixated gaze of Jefferies on his multiple neighbors is returned only once—by a monstrous Thorwald after he confronts Lisa in his apartment and then looks out the window piercingly, ominously—foreshadowing his crossing over the courtyard easily to enter Jefferies's apartment with the intent to kill him, although a savvy Thorwald is soft-spoken, in measured tones—even seemingly rational—asking Jefferies what he wants of him and that he needs the wedding ring back. Jefferies is fully aware as he has been when Thorwald confronts Lisa in his apartment and throws her to the floor, that the menacing but calm, smooth-voiced Thorwald is ready instantly to kill him, which the savage attacker almost does.
Just as when a frightened Lisa, attacked by a bullish and powerful and enraged Thorwald, cries out desperately to Jeff for help, but Jefferies, despite his self-satisfied *machismo*, is incapable of yelling back or even approaching the window to scare off Thorwald—one of the key incidents in *Rear Window*, which parallels the anguished moment in *Vertigo*, in the tower of San Juan Bautista, when Scottie's vertigo impedes him from climbing to the very top of the tower to rescue his beloved and even idolized Madeleine. Indeed, the impotent Jefferies can only attempt to summon *others* to rescue Lisa, when he frantically calls the police to report the attack in progress—knowing that before the police even arrive, Lisa could be dead—just as Anna Thorwald is instantly killed. The same helplessness at moments of crisis afflicts both Scottie Ferguson and L.B. Jefferies as well as the terrified male protagonist of "El amante del teatro." Indeed, although Ferguson is middle-aged and has inescapable vertigo, apparently, a latent perhaps even genetic fallibility, it is only as the result of a crisis situation, as he is terrifyingly suspended at the outset over the street below on the verge of death, that his inexplicable vertigo

Figure 120. Soft-voiced, dark-suited, dark-shadowed menace. Note light on hands, ready to strangle again.

Figure 121. Happily ever after: Jefferies dreaming contentedly, but not of Lisa.

suddenly appears—and after that, in moments of crisis, never leaves him. In *Rear Window* Hitchcock develops the case of another stricken male protagonist who, again has victimized and increasingly anguished status. Indeed L.B. Jefferies becomes a portrait of writhing anguish as Hitchcock's camera turns from focus on the victimized Lisa to a Jefferies tormented, twisting feverishly in his wheelchair and even turning away from viewing what is happening to Lisa because he knows what Thorwald is capable of. And an impotent Jefferies even cries out to Stella "what are we going to do?" revealing that he is just the opposite of the reckless hero that he has smugly and vauntingly projected himself as—in the face of imminent danger.

If Jefferies suffers from a castration complex, Larry O'Shea does even moreso. As soon as he hears the first, bizarre moaning—mooing sounds issuing from the lips of the blonde Venus across the way, O'Leary is terrified. There is a direct parallel between the cries for help of the greatly endangered Lisa, facing her Minotaur —Thorwald—the heavy-set, always scowling, tramping, bullish foe—and the suddenly shocked O'Leary, who instead of rushing to the aid of his beloved, shuts his eyes in terror and when he opens them, the apartment across the way is deserted:

> An animal mooing, like that of a cow, but also demented like the powerful roaring of the wind and terrible like the enraged cry of a stricken love.
>
> She mooed.
>
> She mooed and she looked at me for the first time. (AT, 23)

His style highly cinematic, Fuentes in his series of short, choppy sentences gives us the equivalent of the quick, rapidly cut series of shots that Hitchcock accomplishes so masterfully such as that of the terrifying ending of *Rear Window*, when a brutal Thorwald, attempting to kill a helpless Jefferies, lunges toward him and hurls his body out the window.

> I thought that I as going to be turned into stone. But she was not the Medusa. (AT, 23)

Figure 122. Hanging on for dear life: from this peril, Jefferies is rescued.

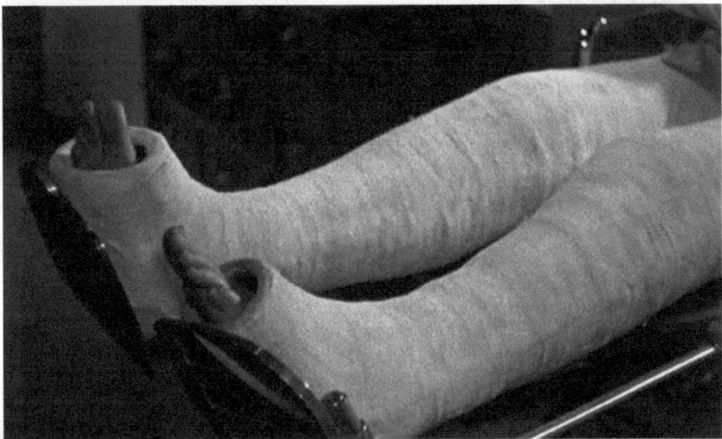

Figure 123. Doubly wounded: Jefferies with both legs in casts and under Lisa's control.

Yet despite the fact that the narrator understands that her cry is one of desperation, he is characteristically passive—similar to a panicked Jefferies, who seeing his Lisa brutally attacked can only grip the arms of his wheelchair more tightly then, in his intense frustration, bring his hands to his neck, never thinking of startling Thorwald by the flashbulbs of his camera—as Jefferies will do when he himself is ultimately confronted by the murderer or even of hurling something at Thorwald's window to disrupt his cold fury; or even crying out. Similarly, a panicked O'Shea—as Jefferies will do when he is subsequently attacked himself by Thorwald—who, characteristically, has an initial impulse when confronted by danger to flee, perceives the blonde's outcry as one of begging for help, yet refuses to respond. Why does Fuentes leave O'Shea's motivation deliberately ambiguous? It is for the active, engrossed reader who essentially is placed in the same role of bewildered spectator that Larry O'Shea occupies, to complete the story—to accept O'Shea's twisted testimony at face value, to regard O'Shea either as a lunatic or to elevate him as a stricken hero—a counterfigure to the demonic Peter Massey.

> Her size, accompanied by that fierce mooing and plaintive outcry at the same time, was one of abandonment, was a cry for help, was the cry of a madwoman. (AT, 23)

Just as both the sardonic and the dismayed Stella initally condemns Jefferies as a pervert who faces possible imprisonment for years if caught, or, as Lisa exclaims, as a sick person because of his fixation, spying on the private activities of on his neighbors, so too does Fuentes's highly agitated protagonist depict his behavior as a "sick obsession." Both Fuentes and Hitchcock are exacting creators.

O'Shea refers to the new production of Strindberg's *Danza de la muerte* (*The Dance of Death*), an allusion that foreshadows what is about to occur in the new, thrillingly, innovative Peter Massey production of the classic tragedy of *Hamlet*—just as the death of the lovable dog in *Rear Window*, his neck broken by the killer, echoes the brutal murder of the wife committed by Thorwald. And O'Shea's reference to the drama of Michael Sheen, *Caligula*, adumbrates in its allusion to the monstrous, sadistic,

Figure 124. Lisa as beautiful mask: vicarious adventuress, permanent fashion model.

degenerate behavior of the Roman Emperor, the seemingly perverted machinations of the dictatorial Peter Massey:

> —I shall return—states the monstrous Caesar when he has just died.
> —I am alive.
> They always return. Because they constitute a single being. Tyranny is an immense hydra. Cut off one of its heads and one hundred more are reborn, said Corneille in *Cinna.* (AT, 24)

The narrator, who has totally abandoned the very woman whom he had consecrated once she breaks the spell and cries out to him, suddenly finds her again, in a stellar production of *Hamlet*, playing the role of the stricken Ophelia, the demented sister of Laertes, the agitated Ophelia who will later commit suicide in Shakespeare's blood-soaked drama. The narrator is an extraordinarily emotional person, who when he encounters Ophelia believes that she is addressing her words exclusively to him—and becomes so agitated that he rushes out of the elegant Royal Haymarket Theatre, stricken with conflicting feelings, once more responding to the bizarre woman as a lover:

> I didn't hear the first words of the young actress. I knew them by heart, she directed them to me of course, I realized it without hearing her, because my hearing was blocked by my emotion.
> OPHELIA: You doubt it?
> To whom was she speaking? To Laertes? To me? To her brother? To her lover? (AT, 24)

Once more the heightened ambiguity of "El amante del teatro" paralleling Hitchcock's complex and fascinating *Rear Window*, is evident. The distraught narrator is compelled to return again and again to the performances of *Hamlet*, bewitched by the enticing Ophelia whom he does not even know, but about whom he concocts fantasies of illicit love and condemnation for this illicit love that have nothing to do with reality.

Throughout *Rear Window*, Hitchcock expertly uses many devices to dramatize—strikingly to visualize—ambiguity: rain, a gloomy night, filters that cover projections through various types of windows, from the majestic four-paned bay windows of the initially depressed, gregarious and ultimately successful composer, to the small, most always covered window of the newlyweds, so that the imaginations of both L.B. Jefferies and that of the viewer can play over the blank screen that is repeatedly, soundlessly evoked as well as a series of fadeouts at key points in the film that leave the viewer in suspense—just as are an increasingly baffled Jefferies , Lisa, and Stella.

Vividly to convey to the reader the increasing agitation of O'Shea, Fuentes utilizes a series of brief, staccato-like questions that intensify the dramatic situation:

> Hadn't my relation with the girl across the way been intense? Was it love that is never consummated precisely the most ardent of all, the most condemned type of love, as well, by the Church Fathers because it is inflamed passion that constitutes the boiling point of sin? (AT, 29-30)

The next time the volatile O'Shea attends a performance of

Hamlet at the Royal Haymarket Theatre, when his longed-for scene of Ophelia and Laertes appears, Ophelia has been suddenly transmuted into a silent actress, one who merely moves her lips. Why? The narrator responds personally to the abrupt changes in the spectacular production, villifying Massey for his egotistic desire to control all of the other actors, viciously to subordinate them so that his *Hamlet*—the title role that Massey himself forcefully, imperiously plays, will be the self-glorifing Peter Massey/Hamlet alone. Yet, significantly, Ophelia is the only one who is condemned to silence—Laertes continues vociferously vocalizing his role. Again the extremely agitated O'Shea rushes out of the theatre, perplexed and anguished. Once more the mental and emotional instability of the distraught O'Shea are underscored. And, just as Jefferies seeks, actively and unrelentingly in the case of his Air Force buddy Doyle, to engage others in entering and solving the case that Jefferies is building against Thorwald, so too does O'Shea take a lateral attack—to condemn Massey for oppressing his fellow actors in order to glorify himself. O'Shea, like Jefferies, excitedly seeks confirmation from others of Massey's deviant, murderous personality—a confirmation that O'Shea never encounters—possibly because the image of Peter Massey as a megalomaniacal murderer is one that exists only in the mind of severely dislocated O'Shea:

> Why hasn't anyone written that in this version Ophelia is silent? Is the actress a mute? Or is it a matter of an omnipotent caprice, a vanguardist extreme, or even a perversion, of the actor and director Massey? (AT,)

Does "The Theatre Lover" reflect the increasing madness not only of the stricken Ophelia on stage, whose father, Polonius, has been slain by Hamlet, but also the descent into madness of the increasingly hostile O'Shea? Just as the highly ambiguous from beginning to end *Rear Window* is one of the finest, most celebrated films of Hitchcock, "El amante del teatro," is one of the most daring and complex of Fuentes's short stories, from a superb collection that includes many narratives of surprise, shock, vampirism, and horror.

Both Jefferies and Lisa, as the result of Doyle's failure to encounter incriminating evidence, succumb to depression. The apparent picking up of a trunk full of her belongings by a live and happy Anna Thorwald who has seemingly gone on vacation, leaves both Jefferies and Lisa who now is so throughly engrossed in the murder case, perplexed and depressed, so that they change their minds about condemning Thorwald as a murderer. They are both dejected when confronted by the terse testimony of the overconfident Doyle that the mysterious trunk of Thorwald, fastened with a thick rope, which they believe contains the cut up body parts of Thorwald's wife, was received by Anna Thorwald who seemingly is on a pleasure trip. So too does the narrator of Fuentes's short story become increasingly dislocated as O'Shea first expresses a hatred and a condemnation of Massey because of his monstrous ego and his tyranizing over his fellow actors, but then suddenly, lavishly, even schizophrenically praises the Massey whom has just villified as a genius for providing a highly original Ophelia whose silence is for O'Shea not at all a manifestation of Massey's oppressiveness but an excitingly original way of conveying Ophelia's madness and despair. Indeed, the volatile O'Shea, apparently over-immersed in fantasizing—the same offense that Jefferies is repeatedly accused of—O'Shea suddenly becomes an eloquent *apologist* for Massey:

> No, she didn't pronounce a single word, but I didn't have any recourse but to recognize the genius of Peter Massey. The silence was, forever, the madness of Ophelia. Her *actions* ought to reveal her words, since those were nothing but verbalized thoughts and a thought doesn't need to verbalize itself in order to be understood. (AT, 36)

Here in Fuentes's convoluted work appears a bizarre Dr. Jekyll/Mr. Hyde doubling process that mirrors the refraction of the essentially misogynistic and marriage-despising L.B. Jefferies into the sadistic and brutal Lars Thorwald—whom some critics see as carrying out what L.B. Jefferies secretly wishes to do to a relentlessly nagging, stultifying future spouse. O'Shea even expands his role to move from ardent spectator to drama critic. The narrator reveals his increasing insanity as the delirious O'Shea now breaks the invisible barrier between passive spectators and actors on stage, and cries out, urging his beloved Ophelia to sing:

> I began to hear musical phrases, bells inside my head, and was certain that the same thing was being experienced by Ophelia. Ophelia was the ghost of Hamlet! His feminine Double! I stood up suddenly and shouted: "Sing, Ophelia!" (AT, 36)

But the tormented, insane Ophelia is not the double of Hamlet, as O'Shea maintains, but the weird, projected double of the dislocated O'Shea himself, who now peremptorily orders Ophelia to sing because he himself in his increasing delirium is hearing bells and musical phrases. And O'Shea finds another Double in the despotic Peter Massey, as both men become bizarre Directors of the stage action, both egotistical males attempting to control the victimized Ophelia. Just as an increasingly obsessed L.B. Jefferies uses more and more powerful instruments to penetrate into the mystery of the private lives of his neighbors, finally employing a huge telephoto lense that is so heavy that the debilitated Jefferies has difficulty holding it, and which constitutes an ironic phallic symbol because Jefferies is not only an inconstant lover but no lover at all—similar to the voyeuristic O'Shea, who is much more a theatre lover than a woman lover. Fuentes's finally emasculating hero Larry O'Shea may even constitute an ironic parallel to the *double entendre* uttered by Lisa who shows a hostile Jefferies her petite, svelte overnight case and says demurely "*yours* can't be this small," referring not only to Jefferies's suitcase but to his masculine appendage.

O'Shea, for the final performance of *Hamlet*, is seated in the front row, and now, for the first time Ophelia as actress looks directly at *him*. Yet is O'Shea describing what is actually occurring, that Ophelia is truly responding to him as a lover, or is O'Shea in his volatile, febrile imagination investing her with his sexual fantasies, symbolically controlling her, just as he has imagined the cruel and tormenting Massey watching her performance, castrating her, depriving her of the few lines that William Shakespeare has granted her?

It is exceedingly ironic that Jefferies, who fashions himself a bold, *macho* hero, when actually confronted by a perilous situation, cries out helplessly to Stella, "what are we going to do?" Here, ironically, the self-styled Man of Intrepid Action that Jefferies sees himself as, is nowhere to be seen, and Jefferies responds to the perilous situation just as he had supposed that an elegant, refined, afraid to soil her dress or mess her hair Lisa would respond in a danger-filled exploit in the far off Himalayas. That Thorwald is an overwhelmingly powerful force who can kill at one blow has been evidenced in that the episode of his murdering his wife is not a prolonged struggle but a single stifled scream—indicating that in the brief time taken by the policeman to reach and enter Thorwald's apartment, he would have slain Lisa. Lisa thus proves that she is—when she wants to be—the daring-do soulmate of Jefferies and, thus, most worthy of being his wife on Jefferies's own egotistical terms. Yet that this marriage will ever occur is ambiguous—Hitchcock provides no typically Hollywood "Happily-Ever-After" endings to his films, as we have seen in our discussion of the exceedingly enigmatic *Vertigo* and will surface in our examination of the highly ambiguous *The Birds*. "El amante del teatro" in many scenes becomes the mirror image of *Rear Window* with its emphasis on the totality of the Gaze:

> The night I was that privileged spectator. But at once I realized that the glance of Ophelia was not foreseen in the stage directions. Ophelia kept on looking at me with the same intensity that was communicated in the message of all my passion for her, all the melancholy of never having loved one another physically. (AT, 37)

Indeed, it seems as if the marked originality of Peter Massey as Director is paralled by Ophelia's need to break out of her customary interpretation of Ophelia as dazed and passive. Just as critics have interpreted Jefferies as desirous of eliminating Lisa from his life just as Thorwald has eliminated a vexatious wife, so too does the mentally disturbed O'Shea reveal a strange, sick parallel between what he in dreams does and what he attributes to Massey as in fact doing—becoming the attacker and murderer of Ophelia, in the case of Massey, apparently both to display his unbridled power over his drama and to dominate a rebellious actress who has dared to break his ironclad rules and break the line between on-stage actress and audience. Here again the figures of Larry O'Shea and Peter Massey seem to dissolve into one another perfectly reflecting the way that Hitchcock's character creations—Scottie Ferguson and Gavin Elster and the nameless nineteenth century plutocrat; Judy Barton and Midge; Judy Barton and Madeleine Elster; Carlotta and Madeleine; L.B. Jefferies and Miss Torso's Army swain; Melanie Daniels and Annie Hayworth and Lydia Brenner in the terrifying film *The Birds*; and, horrifically, Norman Bates and his mother *and* his mother's corpse, constantly blend into one another just as they do at the very end of *Psycho*, when the skull of Bates's mother is gruesomely superimposed over a grinning Norman wrapped in a blanket and held in isolation at the Police Station. Indeed, O'Shea's gruesome words constitute an echo of what the demented Norman Bates will do with the hapless Marion Crane in the infamous shower scene in *Psycho*:

> That night I dreamed that I violated a woman who could not scream. And if she could not scream, why not kill her instead of possessing her? (AT, 38)

This is exactly what a demented Norman Bates, dressed as his condemning mother, carries out, as Norman's own instincts to ravish the sensual Marion in the shower, reacting ecstatically to the falling water, are thwarted by a sanctimonious and punitive "Mother" internalized by a schizophrenic son. In Fuentes's chilling narrative, the macabre nature of O'Shea is manifested which seems also to be inspired by the delight in morbidity of L.B. Jefferies. The climax of "The Theatre Lover" is the bold desire of O'Shea to rescue his beloved as in yet another shocking change in the drama, in the final performance, there is apparently a torrent of water that opens up where the orchestra pit once was, and the dead body of Ophelia comes floating down toward the audience. The scene is astonishing but the exacerbated spectator O'Shea believes that Ophelia is not acting a suicidal role but, like the tormented invalid wife of Lars Thorwald, has been brutally murdered by a megalomaniac Massey. Paralleling the anguish of L.B. Jefferies as he watches the grim consequences of his voyeurism—the attack on Lisa and her brush with death, which a terrified Jefferies will soon experience himself—is the incapacity of O'Shea to act heroically to save Ophelia from her doom:

> It was a river inside the theatre and the cadaver of Ophelia passed floating by, accompanied by the flower of death—daisies and nettles, *aciazo* and fingers-of-death, long purple flowers; the wide skirts floating; Ophelia similar to a mermaid who drowns under the weight of the oozing mud. (AT, 39)

Now the unhinged mind of O'Shea even begins to supply dramatic dialogue to an imperious Massey, whom O'Shea regards as a homicidal maniac:

> "If God has died—the look of Massey was telling—there only remains in His place The Devil and The Angel. I am both. Who are you?" (AT, 40)

And the wild imagination of O'Shea who once again flees the theatre, even imposes a fitting ending for the dictatorial and homicidal Massey:

> I tried to imagine him old, solitary, maniacal, forgotten. (AT, 41)

Yet O'Shea in his judgment and condemnation of Massey further expands the marked ambiguity of Fuentes's narrative. If Massey is guilty of murder, why doesn't O'Shea demand his trial and the judgment of imprisonment or execution? Why be content with a punishment of abandonment and oblivion? And here an embittered O'Shea expands his role even further, as if he is yearning to compensate for his insignificance and his failure to gain the promotions he feels he deserves in his filmic profession; he now emerges as a dramatist *en fleur*:

> I felt the tempation of forcing my way through the dressing room. I stopped myself in time. The idea that Ophelia had really died overwhelmed me. Sacrificed to the Revolutionary Realism of Peter Massey. Would he himself, one day, die, run through by the poisoned dagger of the

> fierce sergeant, Death? In the meantime, would he murder his anonymous heroines, hidden for months in solitary rehearsals? (AT, 41)

There is a direct, poignant, even searing contrast between the apparent resolution of conflict in the concluding scenes of *Rear Window* and that of "El amante del teatro." In Hitchcock's film, loose ends—but not all of them—are tied up. The initially frustrated and highly depressed music composer triumphantly finishes his new composition, over which he has painfully labored throughout the film and by which Lisa Fremont is entranced, and is seen in the company of a new, revitalized, even glamorous Miss Lonelyhearts. Miss Torso's long absent lover returns on leave from the Army and heads straight for the refrigerator—another one of Hitchcock's whimsical touches, because the refrigerator and its contents have been the constant goal of the energetic and alluring Miss Torso, whose many—ardent and wealthy—male companions result to be irrelevant. The middle-aged, childless couple who nightly sleep on the balcony to avoid the oppressive heat, now have a new dog, and the walls of Thorwald's apartment are being repainted in anticipation of a new tenant, all symbolic of a restoration of peacefulness and order to a chaotic, irrational universe. But Fuentes's narrative, in contrast, ends on a sustained note of ambiguity, as O'Shea advises the reader not to believe the newspaper accounts that a deranged spectator has attempted vainly to kiss and breathe life into a dead Orphelia, and according to printed accounts repeatedly denied by the narrator—who perhaps now has become completely unbalanced—even states that Massey as Hamlet had unsheathed his dagger and attempted to kill the agitated spectator—O'Shea himself. But what the bizarre narrator affirms is that even after the attack of Massey on O'Shea, as the enraged director plunges a knife into his back—the show goes on: it is said that the work continued as if nothing at all had happened." (AT, 43)

Similar to *Rear Window*, in which the vicarious activities of Jefferies, carried on throughout much of the film, finally end in direct confrontation with a cold-blooded murderer whom Jefferies himself has unleashed by sending him the provocative note, being caught by a piercing look out the window by an enraged Thorwald and finally mistakenly spoken to again on the telephone, as a confused Jefferies initially believes that the party on the other end of the line is Jefferies's erstwhile ally Doyle, in "El amante del teatro" the obsessive voyeurism and coveted passivity of O'Shea, who like Jefferies, is very fond of making sarcastic, cutting remarks to his office companions that result in his further estrangement, finally is compelled—apparently—to leap into action, to heroically attempt to resuscitate a dying or already dead Ophelia, whether dead or alive. Yet the stricken Ophelia never returns to the apartment across the way. The narrator, like Jefferies, has broken through his passivity, apparently risking his own life to attempt to save the one he loves. Indeed, at the end, a dazed, rapt Larry O'Shea continues his obsessive gazing, his gaze fixated on the blue flower that the dying Ophelia has thrown to him—as opposed to the flowers of death surrounding Ophelia on stage, this is a flower of life, the flower which does not die, whose immortality signifies O'Shea's lasting love for Ophelia.

Throughout the artistic creations of both Hitchcock and Fuentes, style and form and content masterfully coalesce. Even the marked fragmentation of *Rear Window* at the very end, in the climactic struggle between Jefferies and Thorwald, the human form is edited by the masterful Hitchcock in sharp cut up focuses on arms, legs, eyes—that eerily symbolize the dismemberment of the body that cannot be shown—that of Anna Thorwald, whose parts are scattered across Manhattan, some even in a hatbox in Thorwald's apartment, that Lisa did not have time to discover in her bold invasion of Thorwald's apartment that the reluctant Doyle had the authority to search but refused to become involved.

Ironically, the enthusiastic line that Stella delivers, casting aside her customary sarcasm, as she attempts to play the role of matchmaker "Lisa's loaded to her fingertips with her love for you" could also be applied to Ophelia at the end of "The Theatre Lover," who singles out O'Shea, her obsessive admirer and would be lover. In Hitchcock's masterpiece *Rear Window*, what initially begins as a seeming fantasy murder concocted by the overwrought imagination of the laid-up Jefferies is slowly then with increasing avidity subscribed to both by Stella, who at the beginning has even warned Jefferies that the penalty for his exorbitant voyeurism used to be putting out the eyes of the Peeping Tom with a red hot poker, becomes herself engrossed in the apparent murder down to her continual speculating on its gory details. Stella sarcastically refers to Jefferies as a "window shopper," underscoring his atraction to Lisa but his refusal to commit himself to her. Similarly, over and over again O'Shea hesitates even at ringing the apartment bell of the woman whom he consecrates—only imaginatively—and at the end, perhaps intervenes to attempt to save her but perhaps merely concocts in his guilt-stricken conscience an ending to the suspenseful murder-mystery that will exonerate him for his failure to rescue his princesss, just as a pathetic L.B. Jefferies is both physically and psychologically incapable of rescuing Lisa. And even here, O'Shea's characteristic ambivalence is evident, as he denies the very newspaper stories that initially he is touting. Fuentes has often experimented with the unreliable narrator—Felipe Montero in *Aura*, the chameleonic Freddy Lambert in *Cambio de piel*, and Larry O'Shea is a continuation of this unreliable and vacillating and oftentimes confused and continually tormented narrator. Indeed, the initially rational appearing O'Shea finally emerges as a paranoid schizophrenic.

Similar to Scottie Ferguson, who feels emasculated by his cane and his binding corset and states in reference to his cane that he "wants to throw this miserable thing out the window," Jefferies at the outset of *Rear Window* exclaims in exasperation that, in reference to his large and cumbersome cast: "I want to get this thing off and get moving." Ironically, he never does; instead at the very end he will be confined for many more weeks, now with two casts, just as the handicapped Scottie can never divest himself of his vertigo and has delusions of the ghostly Madeleine.

Both "El amante del teatro" and *Rear Window* are suffused with irony. On the one hand, the male protagonist of Fuentes's story is exceedingly ambitious, yet he makes little attempt to smooth over the differences between himself and his competitive English co-workers and ironically, even alienates his fellow Latin American associate, the initially friendly Bolivian, whom the ever sarcastic O'Shea alienates by his adopting a smug superiority over a fellow Latin American with whom O'Shea could have created a personal—and professional—alliance but whom Larry permanently, even deliberately, alienates:

—It seems as if there is an agreement, an unspoken one, between the business people and the newspaper reporters
—An unsaid agreement? —I permitted myself the enrichment of the vocabulary of the denizen of High Peru with a certain Mexican arrogance, I readily admit it. (AT, 32)

In *Rear Window*, the desperate Miss Lonelyhearts at the ouset dines with an imaginary suitor as she listens to Bing Crosby crooning on the photograph: "To see you is to love you, and I see you all the time." The song constitutes a tragic commentary on Jefferies and Lisa as well, for although Lisa is constantly in his apartment, fussing over him, kissing him repeatedly—throwing herself at him—Jefferies too does not really see her. And the irony extends even to the constantly quarreling Lars and Anna Thorwald—for a reluctant Jefferies, constituting proof at hand of having to cope with a nagging wife—underscoring Jefferies's repeated apprehension of the monstrous creature the initially soft and seductive Lisa will inevitably become once she has successfully set her mantrap and snared her prize.

Both "El amante del teatro" and *Rear Window* are jagged/open-ended in that they explore a number of suppositions that turn out to be false or unjustified or improbable and thus prolong the suspense. For example, although Jefferies is certain that Thorwald has buried body parts of his wife in the flowerbed that Thorwald has carefully tended, Stella's digging in the bed uncovers nothing, and it once more appears as if Thorwald were innocent. Similarly, the narrator of Fuentes's work is so vacillating, so contradictory in his accounts at the astonishing end both of *Hamlet* and of "El amante del teatro" at the end even denying that the newspaper stories which he himself first cites, then rapidly denies are true, and at times damning Peter Massey and at other times praising him, so that the reader of "The Theatre Lover" is baffled as to what to believe regarding the apparently shocking ending to the final performance of *Hamlet*—which the theatre audience with the notable exception of O'Shea heartily applaud.

Incidents in *Rear Window* constantly reflect and refract one another. The anguished outcry in the night of the woman who owns the dead dog "Which one of you did it?" finally and with consummate irony breaking the barriers between all of the neighbors—and provides Lisa with another clue to the mystery, as she states that only Lars Thorwald did not come to his window to view what caused the commotion, yet he was in his apartment, his cigarette ominously burning in the darkness. The anguished words of the dog owner are echoed in Jefferies's message: "Lars Thorwald, what have you done with her?" Similarly, Fuentes's work consists of a series of doublings—Larry O'Shea is extremely jealous of the fame of Peter Massey, which contrasts with O'Shea's own feelings of inferiority and resentment that he has not achieved the success that he feels is due him in the cinema production world. O'Shea searches in vain for some newspaper columnist who could be as outraged as he is, that the supporting actors in *Hamlet* are being mistreated by Massey in several ways—no credit even given to them in the lavish advertising that glorifies, even deifies Peter Massey, no mentioning that would justify the cutting out of Ophelia's lines in the production and reducing her role to a silent part—as if she were being gagged by an all-controlling Massey.

What at first seems to be a suicide attempt by Miss Lonelyhearts detected—and misdetected—by Stella, who states that she is an expert on the type of pills that an unbalanced and depressed Miss Lonelyhearts is apparently overdosing with, turns out to be but another false alarm—and another indication that Stella's gruesome conclusion about Thorwald's actions in killing his wife and dismembering her corpse in the bathroom where the blood could more easily be washed off, may be but the concoction of Stella's overactive and increasingly morbid, hyperactive imagination, one also possessed by the unstable narrator of "The Theatre Lover."

And O'Shea's gruesome testimony of the death of Ophelia in reality is never corroborated—the only perspective on the apparent murder of Ophelia by a fiendish Peter Massey/Hamlet is provided by the convoluted account of the increasingly delusional O'Shea himself.

Both *Rear Window* and "The Theatre Lover" are suffused with ambiguity. The beautiful woman across the way that so fascinates the recalcitrant, loner narrator in Fuentes's work emerges as an ambiguous entity—O'Shea remains dumbfounded by her strange cry; he is perplexed that she is without eyebrows. It is only after seeing her play the part of the tragic Ophelia that O'Shea finally realizes that his alluring neighbor has been constantly rehearsing a theatrical performance. In *Rear Window*, the reality of what Jefferies sees markedly contradicts the verbal commentary he hears——in Hitchcock *seeing*, and indeed the visual—continually trumps the verbal, what is also starkly exemplified by Gavin Elster's sleek, poetic evocation of a distressed Madeleine and the reality of Judy/Madeleine as Kim Novak playing the role of Judy Barton in turn playing the role of Madeleine Elster—the real Madeleine Elster whom neither Scottie Ferguson nor the spectator of *Vertigo* ever see alive and who is known primarily only to Gavin Elster and only partially, by a perpetually conniving Judy Barton.

In *Rear Window*, Jefferies's boss, like Stella attempting to convince him of the wonders of marital bliss, encouragingly tells him that "Wives don't nag; they discuss." But here again words are deceptive; the true reality is the visual one, as simultaneously Jefferies witnesses the increasingly antagonistic relationship between a morose Lars Thorwald and his bed-ridden wife Anna Thorwald—one which confirms him in his conviction that marriage would be a stifling hellworld, particularly to the demanding perfectionist that is the ever restless and unsatisfied perfectionist that is Lisa Fremont. Lars Thorwald dutifully waits on his demanding wife, apparently caregiving that is in fact a coverup, because his real lover is brazenly telephoned by Thorwald from the very living room of his apartment. Thus while it appears at first as if a querulous Anna Thorwald cannot be pleased or pacified no matter what her obsequious husband does, it seems as if her temper tantrums and quarrelsome attitude have justified cause in Thorwald's infidelity. Indeed Lars Thorwald's dissatisfaction with his marriage reflects Jefferies's desire—expressed to an uncomprehending Stella—to terminate his relationship with Lisa Fremont on the grounds of incompatibility. For the hostile Jefferies, Lisa is perfect as a friend and erstwhile companion—continually loving him while he is an invalid but not the suitable female Indiana Jones for an adventerous superhero that he will again strive to be as soon as his vexatious cast comes off.

Ironically, at the end of *Rear Window*, Lisa appears, not submissive but even more in control of the relucant, even at times openly antagonistic Jefferies, who is now even more dependent on her and more distant than ever from his treasured photographic career in which he concludes that a refined and delicate and hypersensitive Lisa can play no part.

Ironically, Lisa is perfect for L.B. Jefferies *the invalid*, just as the untouchable—the girl whom O'Shea seeks to keep in the status of distant, remote, unattainable goddess—is perfect for a rabid theatregoer whose life is primarily a vicarious one and who like Jefferies, is extremely relucant to move from detached idealization of his beloved to the excruciating trauma of actually having to interact with her. The Peeping Tom role so adeptly played by Jefferies is reflected and refracted in the obsessive voyeurism of the misanthropic Larry O'Shea.

Both Hithcock's vision in *Rear Window* as in *Psycho*, and Fuentes's vision in "El amante del teatro," are lurid. The viewer of *Rear Window*, identifying with the now totally committed Stella, repeatedly contemplating the horror scene in Lars Thorwald's apartment, corresponds to the reader of Fuentes's compelling narrative, who identifies with the narrator's belief that Peter Massey has viciously murdered his actress to satisfy his egomania and to crush her for daring to break out of her role by desperately reaching out to the wildly emotional, stricken O'Shea in the Haymarket Theatre. And Stella's opening remarks to Jefferies: "We've become a race of Peeping Toms" echoes throughout the film—Lisa quickly joins the surveillance as do the millions of viewers of *Rear Window*—as do the myriad readers of Fuentes's thriller narrative.

Both Jefferies and O'Shea are presented as unreliable witnesses—Jefferies throughout most of *Rear Window* and O'Shea throughout most of his increasingly agitated first-person testimony. Jefferies's misinterpretation of reality is corrected by the intuition of Lisa—an adumbration of her understanding that Lars Thorwald could not have left his apartment with his wife because a woman would never leave her wedding ring behind—not even to go to the hospital! Lisa's conclusion is confirmed by Stella, who categorically asserts that she would have her finger cut off rather than having her wedding ring removed from it. Thus ironically, the woman whom Jefferies views as frivolous and spoiled and super-refined and unfit to be his jungle companion eating fish heads and suffering below zero temperatures is much more perceptive—and finally—much more adventurous and even daring, despite her elegance and her impeccable grooming and her expensive, stylish clothing, than he.

Indeed, the often obtuse Jefferies mistakenly perceives Miss Torso as a royal Queen Bee, surrounded by a pack of wealthy drones, but Lisa, correctly sees her as juggling wolves —her astute perception carried out by the constant sexual advancements toward Miss Torso by her male companions—and Miss Torso's continual, vigorous, and successful rejection of their advances. In her luring them and then rejecting them, the sensual Miss Torso reflects Jefferies's marked ambivalence to Lisa, whom at times he responds to lovingly and at other times abruptly and coarsely tells her to shut up—corresponding to the marked ambivalence of Larry O'Shea to the radiant blonde across the way, whom he initially idealizes, even depicts rapturously and yet suddenly abandons her as she attempts to establish communication with him—to break the spell of aloof, alluring, but inaccessible goddess. And Lisa's remark that the seemingly dominating Miss Torso loves none of her admirers proves correct when at the end Miss Torso's true lover appears—and is enthusiastically welcomed by Miss Torso—a suitor totally distinct from the wealthy, elegantly dressed and impeccably groomed flock of would-be lovers that result ultimately to be merely boy toys. Jefferies predicts a future for the ravishing, incessantly dancing Miss Torso, whose whirling reflects the dash through her daily modelling activities of the hyperactive Lisa Fremont, as ending up "Fat, alcoholic, and miserable"—a future Miss Torso, whose ultimate fate seems to be what gracious, wistful and enchanting Lisa will turn out to be after years of stultifying marriage with him which she will be able to escape only through the bottle. Similarly, Larry O'Shea is capable of responding to the beautiful blonde goddess across the way only as a picture, an image, a phantom much more the creation of his ceaselessly active, febrile imagination. Sudden, excruciating, highly dramatic reversal is a fundamental charactersitic of the art of both Fuentes and Hitchcock.

Rear Window, like "The Theatre Lover" demonstrates how

rapidly the viewer, primed in both cases for a voyeuristic experience, can be drawn into the action. At first a witheringly sarcastic Stella has repeatedly and sharply condemned Jefferies for voyeurism, as does a Lisa eager to convert him into her impassioned lover; as Lisa attempts to shift his gaze to fasten that gaze on her in a seductive negligee and not on the sexy *but* unattainable Miss Torso—whose name, bestowed upon her by an admiring Jefferies, ironically reflects what Anna Thorwald will be reduced to. Both women quickly become first his enthusiastic accomplices then finally his ardent leaders in unraveling the Thorwald case—unlike the detective Doyle, who is relucant to detect, to pry, to search Thorwald's apartment, and whose investigation of the Thorwald trunk of the train station we never see—so imprisoned does Hitchcock wish to keep the spectator that he never drastically changes locales, thus producing a type of claustrophobia that is similar to the closed-in world of Larry O'Shea in Fuentes's tautly delineated story. When Jefferies asks a skeptical Stella to take his binoculars out of their case, she first remarks negatively "Trouble, I can smell it" but then immediately plunges into the surreptitious viewing, and becomes, like Jefferies and like Hitchcock's spellbound viewer, rivetted on Thorwald's suspicious behavior.

Both *Vertigo* and *Rear Window* dramatically convey incessant restlessness, but in highly contrasting manners. The restlesness of *Rear Window* derives from its intense inwardness, from its insistent probing into the many lives of the afflicted characters inder scrutiny. The restlessness of *Vertigo* is the result of incessant motion—speeding cars, sweeping vistas, dramatic shift in locales. Indeed, *Vertigo* again and again delves into expansive space—a spectacular panoramic shot over the skyline of San Francisco seen through Scottie's dazed perspective after he is released from hospital confinement—a shot that ironically echoes the opening night panoramic shot across the San Francisco rooftops that signified Scottie's sudden and tragic plight. Now a bold daylight shot that seems to promise emancipation and victory for the harried protagonist, the extended focus on immense all powerful redwoods, symbols of timelessness, awe-inspiring symbols—beautiful and majestic and yet after they are evoked alive one of which is seen dead—as Hitchcock and

Judy/Madeleine focus on the huge severed trunk and its concentric rings, and both director and female star concentrate on the death of Madeleine—the fake obsession with death, since what Judy is really thinking of is new life as Mrs. Gavin Elster, eminent San Francisco socialite. The freedom and power which the shrewd Elster seems to long for as he unflappingly conveys a disenchantment with San Francisco, is really a crafty contemporary catering to the romantic illusions of the middle-aged, increasingly entrapped Scottie Ferguson. Indeed, Gavin Elster is essentially rootless, he abruptly departs forever from the San Francisco he has so romanticized to flee to the safety of Switzerland but because he is essentially as cold and restless as is the nameless nineteenth century plutocrat who cruelly abandoned Carlotta, the nameless plutocrat of whose success will be fatalistically duplicated in Gavin Elster's triumph in marrying the beautiful but reclusive socialite Madeleine Elster then literally throwing his wife away after he has broken her neck. There is a cluelessness that characterizes both Midge and Judy, Midge is clueless about Scottie's tastes—knowing what the director of the asylum doesn't know, that Scottie hates classical music, she continues her Mozart which she blithely goes on playing to a shocked, totally unresponsive Scottie. In contrast, the bold, dynamic Lisa Fremont is highly perceptive, successfully manipulative, and instead of ruefully withdrawing from the love frey after initially suffering defeat, as does a dejected Midge in *Vertigo*, triumphantly reinvents herself as a super-Jefferies.

The cynicism and the basic indifference and even coldness of Jefferies toward the plight of his neighbors all contrast with the poignant sensitivity of Lisa. When the frustrated composer arrives home drunk and tosses his pages in the air in his frustration, Jefferies is supremely and self-satisfiedly amused. His lack of genuine empathy is noticeable especially with Miss Lonelyhearts, who seems to exist primarily for his amusement; in contrast, Lisa identifies with her frustration, her loneliness, because the cossetted Lisa sees herself as essentially shut out from the life of the man whom she loves. Although Jefferies does not treat her aggressively, brutally to satisfy his sexual urges, as does the pickup who attempts to molest Miss Lonelyhearts, Lisa is frustrated because Jefferies is just the opposite—impossible to warm up, evasive, at times even argumentative toward her, and applying the same disdain for her career in the high fashion industry that he applies to the activities of his neighbors—all of whom he essentially looks down on—physically from the height of his window and psychologically from the vantage point of his ability not to become ensnared in relationships with the opposite sex that he sees as stifling and strangling.

Similarly, Larry O'Shea is clearly a misfit, but he too has a superiority complex that is evident in the condescending manner that he treats the only Latin American in his work place—the Bolivian with whom he could readily have formed an alliance. In a major sense, Fuentes's alienated protagonist is much more human than L.B. Jefferies, because he cares about the future of the beautiful blonde across the way and is preoccupied with the possibility that she is looking at him. This mutual gazing never seems to interest L.B. Jefferies because he essentially is detached from all of his neighbors whom he views with the gaze of an entomologist discovering curious, frenetic activities of his specimens under the lens. And Jefferies finds in the initially demure just married couple across the way another reflection of entrapment and marital misery. The young married couple with their sexual intensity demanded by the bride, whose initial reticence and shyness give way to lustful action—all hidden by the single shade over the bedroom that is only opened rarely, when the bridesgroom comes up for air and takes a break by the open window before he is summoned back to the conjugal bed constitute a fatalistic future that Jefferies stubbornly seeks to avoid. Just as in *Rear Window*, obsessive gazing, both real and imaged, is predominant in "The Theatre Lover":

> I would never fall asleep with the hope that she would then direct her gaze toward me. At first, I accommodated my sleeping hours to her … But one day I had a fatal suspicion. And if she was taking advantage of my being asleep to direct her gaze toward me and only encountered some blinds that were closed? She very well could, possibly, be so bashful that she only searched for my gaze when she knew that I could not return it. (AT, 21)

In *Rear Window*, when the middle-aged couple who own the dog and sleep on the fire escape scramble to avoid the rain by frantically taking in their mattress, Jefferies continues his supremely amused response. Indeed, the anguished outcry of the wife after finding her dog dead, as the wife shouts that the animal was the only one of the group who liked anyone, applies to Jefferies as well, who essentially neither likes nor identifies with any of his neighbors—precisely the attitude of the surly and curt and disdainful loner that is Larry O'Shea in Fuentes's narrative that has been so profoundly influenced by *Rear Window*.

What essentially unites Hitchcock's masterpiece and Fuentes's short story is a fascination with the art of viewing. The theatrical experience for the vexed narrator is horrifying—he again and again rushes out to the Royal Haymarket Theatre only to be compelled to attend more performances. Indeed, the most satisfying spectacle of his life is not any of the many dreams that he mentions but the daily routine of observing the rehearsing of Ophelia at her window. Similarly, in *Rear Window* at first Stella wants only to get out of the cramped apartment and to terminate her relationship with an obtuse client whom she sees as a pervert, but then is suddenly drawn in to the murder mystery—just as is Lisa, just as is Hitchcock's rapt audience looking along with Jefferies and Lisa through the rear windows, becoming enthusiastic fellow voyeurs. At first Lisa condemns Jefferies's incessant spying as diseased but suddenly she too undergoes a dramatic *volta faccia* and declares to a Jefferies who suddenly has a co-conspirator in his surveillance— and, ironically, one who will become much better at it than he is:

> Let's start from the beginning, again Jeff. Tell me everything you saw, and what you think it means.

So eager does a highly energized Lisa participate in Jefferies's obsessive sleuthing that after she has checked out the exact address in which Thorwald lives she asks breathlessly "What's my next assignment?," as if she were already Jefferies's new wife and companion in adventure—symbolized by her triumphant flashing to him of Thorwald's wedding ring that Lisa has immediately donned—not merely as a piece of evidence that incriminates

Thorwald, since she states that a woman would never leave behind her wedding ring, but in anticipation that now she has proved herself as an equal to Jefferies in enduring hardship and peril, she is fit to be his wife—she is not the delicate society girl afraid of getting her dress soiled or her expensive shoes wet but thrives on danger—exactly as Jefferies does.

In contrast with the bold expansion of *Vertigo* to San Francisco, to the Mission Dolores of San Francisco to the Mission Dolores, then to the Palace of The Legion of Honor, to the regal, Fairmount Hotel, *Rear Window* concentrates on a tight, enclosed space. Yet, paradoxically, *Vertigo* is very similar in major aspects to *Rear Window.* Just as Scottie objects right up to the very end to the increasingly desperate attempts of Judy to love and be loved by him, the attentive girl who throws herself at him, so too does L.B. Jefferies, expertly played by one of Hitchcock's favorite film stars, Jimmy Stewart remain highly ambivalent toward Lisa throughout most of their relationship.

Rear Window is one of Hitchcock's most subtle and intriguing and mysterious films, as it concentrates on the phobias and manias that bedevil most of its unforgettable characters. Similarly, "El amante del teatro" skillfully and subtly combines highly dramatic external action with intense exploration of the vagaries of he distressed, finally tormented mind of the protagonist.

CHAPTER IV: TORN CURTAIN—

HITCHCOCK, FUENTES AND

THE SUPERNATURAL

> "WALT DISNEY HAS THE IDEAL SITUATION: IF HE DOESN'T LIKE AN ACTOR, HE JUST TEARS HIM UP." (ALFRED HITCHCOCK)

The impact of the cinematic genius of Alfred Hitchcock on the narrative art of Carlos Fuentes is both extensive and profound. One of the many links between cinematic director and Latin American author is Hitchcock's appreciation of and constant employment of literary works upon which the film scripts to his major works were based: Bouleau and Narcejac's *D'entre les morts* (*The Living and the Dead*, 1958) was the literary inspiration for *Vertigo*, Hitchcock's outstanding films *Rebecca* and *The Birds* both are based on a novel and short story, respectively, by the English writer Daphnie DuMaurier with Hitchcock for the elegant creation *The Birds* again changing the locale—provincial rural England where a farmer and his wife are attacked mercilessly by a flock of birds, to Northern California, again to a beloved San Francisco, with Hitchcock initally envisioning the regal, glamorous Grace Kelly in the role of the rich, spoiled super-sophisticated Melanie Daniels, and the gallant, charming Cary Grant as her eagerly pursued romantic interest, Mitch Brenner. Apparently, according to Evan Hunter (*Me and Hitch*) the Director did not want to render half of the profits of *The Birds* to Grant, so a relatively unknown (and definitely less expensive), Australian male lead was hired. In any case, Hitchcock undoubtedly saw the true stars of the bizarre, terrifying film as the marauding birds—twentieth century descendants of the fierce, befowling Harpies of classical Greek and Roman literature, including Vergil's *The Aeneid*. Indeed, both Hitchcock and Fuentes are mythomaniacs. Birds do not in nature suddenly and fiercely and viciously attack and kill human beings, but they do attack humans and kill them in classic literature—and

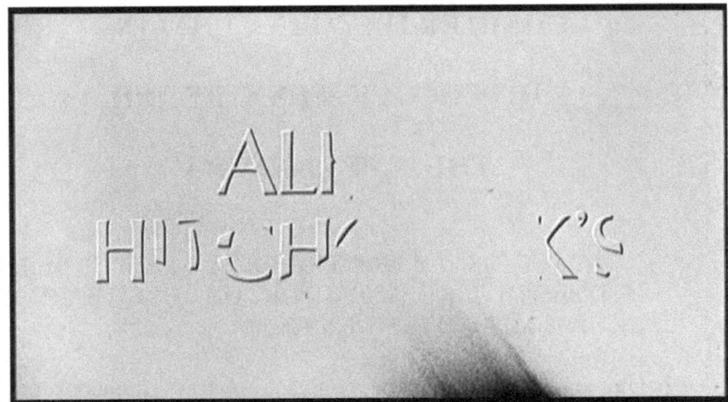

Figure 125. Ravaging, screeching birds tear to shreds even titles of film.

Figure 126. Birds as dark symbols of supernatural evil contrast with cerulean blue of lettering

Figure 127. Poised, self-confident Melanie responds delightedly to wolf whistle.

Figure 128. "Back in your gilded cage, Melanie Daniels!" Adumbration of Things to Come. Mitch as heroic façade. Rugged exterior but essentially helpess against bird onslaught.

surely the erudite Hitchcock knew the classical Greek and Roman literature and the screaming attacks on the men of Aeneas by the huge Harpies, half women, half birds. Similarly, "Vlad" demonstrates Fuentes's extensive delving into the many forms of the Vampire, not only the tuxedo-dressed, elegant Bela Lugosi and the bald-headed, misshapen Max Shreck in *Nosferatu* but the whole range of mythic monsters.

As McGilligan points out, Hitchcock sought out and collaborated with a whole series of eminent authors (*Alfred Hitchcock: A Life in Darkness and Light*, p. 625):

> Sean O'Casey, John Galsworthy, John Steinbeck, Thornton Wilder, Ben Hecht, James Bridie, Maxwell Anderson.

Rear Window was inspired by the short story "It Had to Be Murder," written by Cornell Woolrich under the pseudonym of William Irish. And the distinguished British scholar V.S. Pritchett contributed valuable suggestions to the filmscript of *The Birds*, written by Evan Hunter, the author of the best-selling novel *The Blackboard Jungle*. Irony, paradox, and ambiguity are hallmarks of both the cinema of Hitchcock and the narrative and dramatic production of Carlos Fuentes. One of the most ambiguous films of Hitchcock, *The Birds* (1963) stars Hitchcock's vaunted discovery after the great disappointment of losing Grace Kelly, Tippi Hedren, as the slim, elegantly dressed in a sable mink coat, stunningly blonde Melanie Daniels, with a superb supporting cast including the Australian actor Rod Taylor as Mitch Brenner, the distinguished stage and screen actress Jessica Tandy as the aloof and hypercritical but extremely insecure and ultimately terrified mother of Mitch, and the captivating, smoldering Suzanne Pleshette as Annie Hayworth, former love interest of—and still in love with—the criminal lawyer who initially chides Melanie for her antics and practical jokes, including the smashing of a plate glass window—an ominous adumbration of the voracious flock of birds that smash the walls of the glass telephone booth in which Melanie is entrapped in Bodega Bay—handsome and dapper Mitch Brenner. The feelings of Annie toward the rich, beautiful, stylish Melanie Daniels are decidedly ambivalent. Although Annie is superficially cordial toward Melanie, whom Annie from the start

Figure 129. Glamorous, super-sophisticated Melanie anticipates easy capture of her prey: a willing Mitch. Note once again Hitchcock's red and green insistence.

Figure 130. Alluring, serene goddess, swathed in mink elegance and in anticipation.

Figure 131. Sudden intrusion of the demonic. First blood drawn.

Figure 132. Melanie quickly regains composure and deftly spins web of amorous intrigue.

recognizes as Mitch's new, splendidly attractive interest and therefore the woman who will undoubtedly succeed where she herself has failed. Indeed, an initially reluctant Annie ultimately welcomes Melanie to her home and even consents to Melanie's staying the night, all the while brooding over this new—and, underneath—highly unwelcome intrusion into her private life, which up to this point is ironically satisfying to Annie because although Mitch is no longer in love with her, at least he is attracted to no other woman and Annie can play the role of a surrogate—and sexually frustrated—big sister to the almost teenager Cathy. Indeed, Melanie's dramatic and permanent intrusion into Annie's *detente* with Mitch parallels the sudden intrusion of the malefic birds into isolated Bodega Bay. That Annie is slated for attack by the birds and brutal death is adumbrated by the loud thump of a seagull against the closed door of her house, which is suddenly converted from sanctuary to death cell. As in "Vlad," Fuentes's masterful short story that is decisively influenced by the demonic film of Hitchcock which rapidly turns from romantic comedy to horror film, the supernatural emerges suddenly, mysteriously, and overwhelmingly. The extreme agitation of the only human being left at the end of "Vlad," the terrified husband Navarro—is paralleled by the victimized Brenner family and the dazed Melanie at the end of *The Birds*, as their fragile vehicle fades into the distance, leaving behind thousands of massing birds, relentless, screeching, waiting to attack again.

The Birds is one of the most supernatural of Hitchcock's works—the strange massing of seagulls, crows, blackbirds, and even seemingly harmless finches, whose veritable army does not diminish after their attacks are temporarily suspended, but monstrously increases, constitutes an inexplicable, demonic force unleashed primarily on the California coastal town of Bodega Bay then on Santa Rosa, by demon birds that are not only victorious but never even counterattacked by a helpless population that remains stunned and divided—one anguished resident of Bodega Bay even heatedly blaming the intruder—Melanie Daniels—for unleashing the invasion. Ironically, the one occasion in which Mitch picks up a rock to hurl at the attacking birds, Melanie warns him against provoking them. And in the terrifying conclusion of *The Birds*, a solitary and unarmed Melanie opens the door to Cathy's bedroom

Figure 133. Helpless birds in permanent cages to delight human captors.

Figure 134. Errant Melanie as determined exploiter of birds: first talking mynah then cooing lovebirds.

Figure 135. Melanie symbolically imprisoned from start, surrounded by innocent-appearing but fatalistic bird cages.

Figure 136. Two beautiful rivals, fixated on ominous birds and also targeting Mitch Brenner.

and steps into a hellworld of attacking birds who despite being unprovoked, relentlessly attack and nearly kill her, as they have her rival for Mitch's love.

Hitchcock satirizes small town, provincial mentality in the hypnotic *The Birds*, initially underappreciated but now regarded as one of his finest films—the towns-people run the gamut in their responses to the bird invasion—one drunken denizen even seeing the ever more frequent and violent attacks as the End of the World, while an amateur, pseudo-authoritative ornithologist Mrs. Bundy eloquently, passionately defends the creatures as innocent, and, in any case, destructive or not, invincible.

There are three centers of ambiguity in *The Birds* which are countered by the myriad centers of ambiguity in Fuentes's story of mystery and horror, "Vlad," from the same superb collection as "El amante del teatro." Just as Hitchcock's thriller combines supernatural domination with psychological and emotional struggles, just as the initial hatred and jealousy of Mitch's cold and controlling mother Lydia toward the super cool blonde goddess whom Lydia sees as a threat, as the person who will take from her the last protector she has, now that her husband has suddenly passed away, and seen by Lydia as much more capable of protecting her than her only son, the ineffectual Mitch. Indeed, all through the suspenseful Hitchcock thriller run deep undercurrents of rivalry. Rivalry is a major theme in both *The Birds* and "Vlad." Hitchcock's highly suspenseful film traces the increasing jealousy, envy, suspicion, and hatred among the three women who are all on distinct levels, fixated on Mitch and constantly pressuring him to gain his favor and his love. Indeed, paralleling the voracious attacking birds are the women who are constantly—albeit restrainedly—at each other's throats. So too does the main narrative of "Vlad" which focuses on Dracula—Count Vladimir Radu—and his invasion of Mexico, and his taking possession of both the unhappy wife of Navarro, Asunción, and her daughter Magda function on several levels—realistic and supernatural, bloodsucking vampires and tense, convoluted and finally disintegrating familial relationships. Demonic possession, as Magda is bitten by a vampire and thus turns into one along with her willing mother, who desperately pacts with the demonic as the means of acquiring immortality for her sole remaining child,

Figure 137. Birds calm, orderly but massed for vicious attack. Menacing sky augments terror.

Figure 138. Things to come. Dead seagull bangs ominously on Annie's door.

Figure 139. Seagull attacks innocent Cathy. Birthday party turns from tense celebration to horror show.

Figure 140. Birds attack relentlessly and inexplicably.

Magda, after her first, male child dies violently by drowning—and is perhaps brought back to life at the end by the demonic Vlad at the highly ambiguous ending of Fuentes's story of mystery and terror.

Both Hitchcock's terrifying film and Fuentes's mystery-enshrouded short story are filled with gruesome and inexplicable deaths. In *The Birds, The* screaming birds viciously attack and maul and horrendously bite Annie Hayworth. In "Vlad," the death by drowning of Navarro's only son is but the prelude to the spiritual loss of Navarro's demon-afflicted wife and daughter. The initially romantic relationship between Annie and Mitch is over yet it isn't over, as a fanatic Annie who needs to keep Mitch in her life, moves from San Francisco to Bodega Bay to be near him, and who becomes part of the Brenner family, and, ironically, is finally accepted by Lydia now that Annie is no longer a threat to the suspicious and controlling Mother. The various planes of *The Birds*—on one level a story of romantic passion—Melanie is at first intrigued by Mitch, at first vexed by his bluntness as he flippantly states "See you in court!"—a harsh directness which contrasts with her demureness and evasiveness—and readily pursues him—eagerly driving sixty miles from San Francisco to Bodega Day, even renting a flimsy motor boat that she herself captains in order to surprise him with a birthday gift of two lovebirds—symbolizing Melanie and Mitch—calculatingly given to Cathy who is celebrating her eleventh birthday and who upon receiving the lovebirds instantly becomes Melanie's adoring ally.

In both *The Birds* and "Vlad" children are of major importance, and in both works, are violated repeatedly by demonic powers. Throughout the film, the huge ugly ravenous blackbirds and the aggressive swooping, biting sea gulls contrast with the two green gentle, cooing love birds—in one of the final scenes rescued from the destroyed house of the Brenner family by the terrified but protective Cathy, the only one who defends the harmless, innocent, affectionate lovebirds—despised by Lydia, since she perceives them as symbols of Mitch's romantic attraction to the aggressive , unstoppable Melanie. Indeed, for most of the film, the attacking birds are perceived by both an intensely frustrated Annie Hayworth and a domineering yet extremely fearful Lydia Brenner, as much less of a threat than the regal, intrusive, fashionable gorgeous

Figure 141. Effective contrast between reserved, supremely self-confident Melanie and open-mouthed but silent, anguished Annie.

Figure 142. Children surrounded by adults who strive but cannot protect them.

Figure 143. Dan Fawcett slain by marauding birds; police suspect deadly assault by human robber.

Figure 144. Corridors in Hitchcock are ominous and many times labyrinths of despair and death.

blonde Melanie.

Throughout Hitchcock's filmic art there is an obsessive emphasis on developing a story through visual action—in *The Birds*, the silver luxury car, Aston Martin of Melanie, the motorboat, the family truck driven by Lydia at breakneck speed away from the farmhouse where she has found the still bleeding cadaver of her friend Dan Fawcett, his eyes pecked out by ravenous birds. As a plotting Melanie, after surreptitiously depositing the lovebirds in the living room of the Brenner farmhouse—the first invasion of this sanctuary by birds—and then speeds away from the Brenner house, there is a highly effective contrast between a surprised Mitch, evoked only in distant shots, and a series of rapid jump cuts on Melanie, whose image grows larger and larger to underscore her importance, her seductive power. Indeed, the calm, intrepid heroine from the boat delights in her surprise of Mitch—Melanie who is stronger-willed and exceedingly more self-possessed than is her dark-haired rival, the attractive but very moody, too often melancholy Annie.

The color green is expertly utilized by Hitchcock, in both *Vertigo* and *Rear Window*, as we have seen, as well as in *The Birds*, where green is repeated over and over again. Melanie has now sought to dissociate herself from her scandal-ridden past life of dissipated socialite, jumping naked into a fountain in Rome—a scandalous newspaper article that she herself denies, referring to it as a plant by a newspaper that rivals the one owned by her powerful, wealthy but never seen father. Indeed the sensationalistic newspaper article constitutes the first attack on the poised, self-assured Melanie, who as soon as she encounters the handsome Mitch in the pet shop in downtown San Francisco knows what she wants and aggressively pursues him—despite the obsessed Annie, despite the initial opposition of Lydia, despite the constant and extreme danger of remaining in Bodega Bay, a town under relentless attack by the marauding birds, whose number geometrically increases as the fim progresses. The absent Father—the death of the husband that afflicted Lydia forever and drove her into a sick dependency on Mitch—is paralleled by the deserting of the mother of Melanie Daniels, to run off with another and permanently to disappear from her daughter's life. Similarly, in

Figure 145. Mitch can only swat furiously but futilely to resist invasion.

Figure 146. At first the aerial demonic is silent, subdued, and unnoticed by its future prey.

Figure 147. Rapid and inexorable massing of vicious invaders.

Figure 148. Orderly "Fire Drill" foolishly commanded by Annie quickly dissolves into terror and panic for schoolchildren.

"Vlad" the father figure again and again is reduced, rendered helpless, as is the stunned Navarro, and even the frightening Vlad himself is finally subordinate to his young daughter.

"Vlad" on the human level is also scarred by love—the tragic death of Navarro's only son, which deeply affects his grieving wife, Asunción, who longs for return of the boy from death and seems to get her wish fulfilled through her bizarre pact with the demonic, vampiric "Vlad." Destruction of the heavily and laboriously boarded up house of the Brenners on Bodega Bay in the horrific *The Birds* is paralled by the ultimate disintegration of the elaborate gloomy mansion that Vlad has constructed for himself in Mexico, complete with open sewer drains through which the blood of his myriad victims runs.

Both Fuentes and Hitchcock seem to demonstrate a compasssion for the strange and the monstrous. Several of Hitchcock's critics have commented on Hitchcock's apparent commiseration with the centuries long imprisonment—and killing and devouring of helpless birds who cannot strike back—until they do, for some critics in retribution, in *The Birds*. In one of the most crucial scenes in Hitchcock's bizarre ornithological thriller, the key, lengthy scene in the Bodega Bay Tides Restaurant there are strikingly evoked a cross-section of townspeople with various, highly contradictory reactions toward the bird attacks, ranging from an Act of Damnation to a War of the Birds, waged in retribution, to an impassioned defense of the Birds and their majesty—and how it would be impossible to eradicate them. Indeed, there is a sense of dark inevitability of disaster in both *The Birds* and "Vlad." The question arises as to whether it would have been better to have barricaded the Bodega Bay School, converting it into a defensive fortress, instead of sending out the children unprotected. Why doesn't Annie Hayworth summon the police to protect the children? Knowing their propensity to attack from the time of Cathy's birthday party, why does Annie send the unprotected children out in the guise of an orderly fire drill which quickly disintegrates into a scene of terror and blood? The mentally anguished mother of the children who rails against the essentially innocent Melanie as a source of evil and destruction is the only one to question why the police were not summoned to the Bodega Bay School. Indeed the helplessness of Annie Hayworth

Figure 149. Birds hunted down and caged now hunt down and cage their human captors. Poetic justice or supernatural devastation? Ambiguity is paramount.

Figure 150. Initial poise and captivating flair dissolve into bewilderment and anguish.

Figure 151. Ironic reversal. Melanie's pranks include breaking a glass window. Now birds repeat her prank viciously.

Figure 152. Hitchcock as master of incremental horror. Fire started by match tossed on river of gasoline converts placid Bodega Bay into inferno.

and Melanie and Mitch are reflected in the anguished helplessness of Navarro in "Vlad," who can only watch in horror as both his wife and daughter are converted into vampires—and maybe his dead son as well.

Both *The Birds* and "Vlad" are narratives of the rapid incrementing of the demonic, which at the end of both works remains supreme. Again and again in *The Birds* law enforcement, as it is in *Rear Window*, is evoked as skeptical and hesitant and, ultimately ineffective. The brutal slaying of Dan Fawcett, his eyes pecked out by the savage birds, is deemed by the police to be the result of a robbery and murder by human hands, with the bird attack as an incidental occurrence after the crime has been committed. Yet there is no evidence to suggest that a robbery had occurred. The sheriff summoned to the Brenner house after the first invasion of the countless sparrows and finches who suddenly, inexplicably pour out the chimney and attack the family, sees—incredibly—nothing unusual or threatening about the attack. Indeed the sheriff places the blame for the invasion on the occupants of the Brenner household—they have attracted the birds with their lights. And even the greatest attack which frighteningly concludes the horror film, results in no telephone calls to the police or to any other authority and no attempts to resist the murdereous flocks who have come close to killing Melanie—only an excruciatingly slow avoidance of provoking them. The ultimate feeling is that an ever greater force is, silent and threatening, ready to launch an even greater attack, as are the vampiric bats soaring skyward at the end of "Vlad." In both Fuentes and Hitchcock final scenes are powerful and determining and highly ambiguous.

Hitchcock apparently considered various endings to *The Birds*—the happily-ever-after Hollywood ending of humans triumphant, a violent ending with the birds once more and this time overwhelmingly attacking before Mitch and the family outspeed the ravenous flock and safely head toward San Francisco. The ending finally utilized by Hitchcock is not peaceful but eerily stunning, as is the end of Fuentes's macabre "Vlad." An eery quietude, with hundreds of thousands of birds waiting, poised, but not attacking—an ending that is paradoxical, although shot from the point of view of the commanding birds, leaving the ending in suspense—and for the audience to collaborate with the Director in

Figure 153. Double meaning: in Great Britain, a "Bird" is an attractive young woman.

Figure 154. Why is Melanie over and over again singled out for persecutorial attacks?

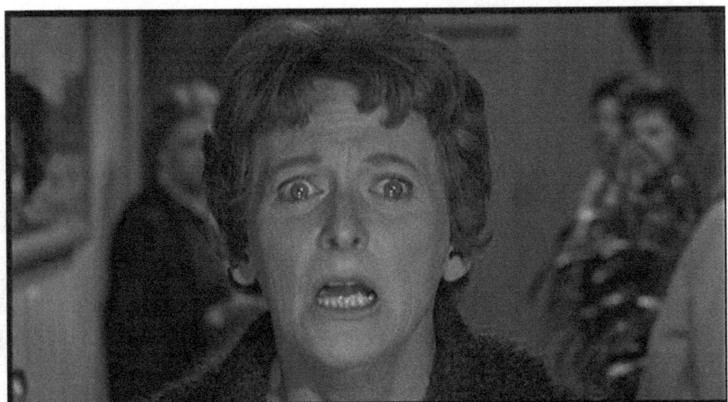

Figure 155. Over wrought Mother, protecting her brood, screams "You're evil!" at aiding and protecting Melanie, turning into scapegoat. Witch Hunt at Bodega Bay.

Figure 156. Annie attacked and slain while protecting Cathy. A persistent rival eliminated?

supplying their own ending, either saving or condemning the victimized Brenner family and the still shell-shocked Melanie. Similarly, the ending of "Vlad" is much more mysterious than is the beginning, as it evokes a shocked Navarro contemplating a horror scene the details of which are left by Fuentes to the imagination of the reader. As in Hitchcock, there is no happily-ever-after ending, no resolution to the dissolution of the family of the dismayed Navarro.

Hitchcock in his extensive focus on the seemingly authoritative disquisition of Mrs. Bundy again and again undercuts scientific reasoning—so eloquently and even defiantly articulated by the seemingly commanding Bundy—who nonetheless, after the horrendous attack on the center of Bodega Bay is reduced to a stunned silence. Bundy with pointed assurance rather pompously, with only pseudo-authority, declares that birds are incapable of mass attack because they have insufficent brain pans—yet Hitchcock's massing birds, with their sudden overwhelming attacks followed by equally sudden disappearances prove to be far more intelligent than the humans who can only react with words, or as Mitch does, with defensive reactions like frantically attempting to board up his house from first floor to attic—a laborious process that is totally ineffective against the marauding birds. Bundy's assertation "Birds are not aggressive" is proved totally wrong, even absurd, by the attack that Bundy herself remains shocked by—an invasion made even more horrifying by the torrent of leaking gasoline suddenly set afire by a carelessly thrown match and engulfing and killing the human victim as quickly as birds are trapped and slaughtered by their indifferent human predators. Once again attempts to warn the victim of the fire and explosions—Melanie's cry of shock and horror at what she knows will happen—prove totally useless, just as are the anguished Navarro's reactions at the end of "Vlad." A variety of extremely vocal townspeople blatantly express widely differing views, some defending the birds, as does the well-dressed, well-spoken amateur ornithologist, and in contrast another person is blatantly desirous of shooting them all. Indeed, the anonymous townsperson, who refuses to lead the way out of Bodega Bay for the increasingly frantic mother and her two children who cry that they will be eaten by the birds—an ironic circular process since they are dining on

Figure 157. What is relationship between bird assaults and raging but repressed conflict among three women protagonists?

Figure 158. Doorknob to Cathy's bedroom becomes a character in film. Entranceway to Hell.

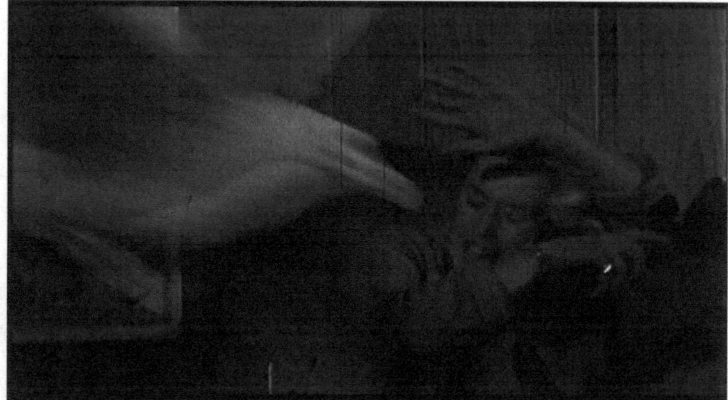

Figure 159. Bird species uncannily unite to wreak vengeance.

Figure 160. Doorknob subsumed by demonic: turns to entrap Melanie, whose body falls across doorway to impede rescue.

roast chicken—states remoreselessly: "Get yourselves guns and wipe them off the face of the Earth"—what no one in this terrifying film ever even attempts to do, for reasons that are never explained.

Perhaps Hitchcock seeks to reflect how the helplessness of *The Birds* against their voracious human predators is finally matched by the total helplessness of the humans once they are suddenly converted into desperate, panicked victims. But the unflappable Mrs. Bundy states calmly that 100 Billion Birds could never be exterminated. And the wide-eyed Mother, fiercely dedicated to protecting her young and in the exact same helpless situation that the mothers of defenseless birds face with deadly hunters with increasingly powerful and accurate weapons, lashes out against a highly concerned Melanie, who herself has been relentlessly attacked by the demonic birds and who has rescued several of the children, as the fierce Mother exclaims hysterically "*Who* are you? *What* are you? *Where* did you come from?" finishing her parody with the condemnatory "You're evil" before Melanie finally responds by slapping her attacker—detailing the Mother in a way that she never is capable of accomplishing against the vicious bird attacks as Hitchcock presents the other side of small town America, countering his initial evocation of the kindly and attentive shopkeeper who treats Melanie—the glamorous outsider —with respect and even tenderness. Ironically, the collaboration, the flocking and attacking in a combined force of various subspecies of birds—which the haughty ornithologist declares never occurs in nature—is countered by the human beings, who rapidly begin to attack one another not only in the highly dramatic *Tides Restaurant* scene but even in the house of Lydia Brenner, who remonstrates against her own son for his ineffectiveness, his failure to protect her—as her deceased husband would have done had he been alive.

And the difficulty that an obstinate Melanie encounters in prying Mitch away from his possessive mother is paralleled by the difficulty that she encounters in prying away Cathy from a possessive—and, parallel to the extremely possessive Lydia—equally frustrated and despondent Annie Hayworth.

The Birds, like Fuentes's "Vlad," is filled with ambiguity and constantly shifting perspectives. Hitchcock's marked

Figure 161. Close-up on beauty and horror. Symbolic light green suit of Melanie, reflected in green lovebirds, torn to shreds.

Figure 162. Tippi Hedren victimized both as Melanie and in reality, attacked not by mechanized but real birds primed for destruction.

Figure 163. Like everything utilized against bird assaults, huge flashlight is useless.

Figure 164. Initially antagonistic and highly possessive, Lydia turns, at least temporarily, sympathetic.

ambiguity toward the all powerful birds that he has created is paralleled by Fuentes's ambivalence toward the Monstrous as exemplified in his epic novel *Cambio de piel*, in which one of the characters plays the Devil's advocate in defending the monstrous as necessary to inspire artistic creation. We recall the savagery of duck hunting and partridge hunting as opposed to lion and tiger hunting where there is always some danger to the hunters. Birds can never strike back against their human predators. Is this why they suddenly mass and kill in the devastated world of *The Birds*, and at the end, instead of vanishing as they do after they suddenly, threateningly appear in the opening scene in downtown San Francisco, silently and stealthily mass until they fill the entire landscape, completely erasing the fragile vehicle containing a still dazed Melanie and a tortured Brenner family whose ultimate fate, like that of Navarro and his demonized family in "Vlad" is deliberately left open to the spectator/reader to decide. Indeed, the transformation of the sleek expensive Aston Martin from an initial symbol of feminine wealth and power to a fragile vessel tightly packed with stunned victims who are fleeing for their very lives, exemplifies the shocking reversals that so characterize *The Birds* as they do the enigmatic "Vlad."

In his piercingly illuminating *Me and Hitch*, the gifted writer Evan Hunter states that Hitchcock presumably under the influence of his good friend and fellow Englishman V.S. Pritchett, an eminent short story writer, imposed on *The Birds* a far more pessimistic ending than the one originally written by Hunter, who also worked on the filmscript for Hitchcock's subsequent film, also starring his prized discovery Tippi Hedren, *Marnie*, after Grace Kelly—now Princess Grace of Monaco—initially agreeing to return to Hollywood to star in *Marnie*, withdrew after strong objections from her subjects in Monaco over their Princess playing a thief and a mentally ill criminal character. As at the end of "Vlad" it is unclear whether the human protagonists will escape the silent, swarming, malefic forces. Neither Hitchcock nor Fuentes ever provides a happily-ever-after typical Hollywood ending to their bizarre masterworks. Hitchcock as always presents various perspectives on his characters, as he has done throughout his intriguing cinematic achievements, beginning with *The Lodger*, the compelling story of a victim almost executed before it is

Figure 165. Dazed Melanie, bloodied and rendered catatonic

Figure 166. Melanie never regains full consciousness; is *The Birds*, like Psycho, tinged with impossible exorcism?

Figure 167. Dark Apocalyptic sky spelling doom. Thousands of screeching birds poised for new assault, never shown in film without "The End"

Figure 168. As in Psycho and Vertigo, dwellings offer no protection. Attacks begin, mysteriously cease, then irremediably begin again.

revealed that he is completely innocent of murder.

Hitchcock includes in attempting to explain to the viewer the reason for the bird attacks, sociopolitical or even religious explanations—the allusion to Divine Judgment is made by the drunken resident of the town of Bodega Bay. It is chilling that even though the menace to the children at the Victorian Bodega School rapidly grows—with a solitary and increasingly agitated Melanie on a mission to protect Cathy, rapidly becoming more and more impatient, even though Daniels has apprised the school teacher Annie of the need to take Cathy back immediately to her family, the somewhat sadistic—and secretly vengeful—Annie seems deliberately to prolong the chanting of the song—by the children totally under her control, exercising her authority over the children but also at least temporarily thwarting her beautiful rival for Mitch's love—a game that the incorrigible Annie knows that she has lost long ago but refuses to admit defeat as she utilizes the school children as pawns in her desire to thwart her stunning blonde rival for the only man she is ever capable of loving—a parallel to the perverse love that Scottie Ferguson fanatically nurtures for Madeleine Elster.

Indeed, the pent-up emotions in the scenes between the two beautiful rivals—the splendidly coifed Madeleine and the dark-tressed, brooding Annie Hayworth far more subtle—and searing—than the much more evident open hostility of the increasingly hysteric Lydia towards her unwanted rival—the rich, glamorous, aggressive, young, self-confident woman whom Lydia knows will take Mitch —her last bastion of strength and support—permanently away from her. A startling scene of short duration is Lydia's straightening of the imposing portrait of the recently deceased father of Mitch—and being shocked by a bird still behind it—another indication of the awesome power of the incessantly massing birds, including those that in nature are most helpless, the most innocent of creatures—the soft and gentle finches. The birds are evoked as a supernatural, overpowering and indeed indestructible force—the attack of the finches that come roaring down the chimney—prompting Mitch to keep a fire burning when another attack is imminent, this time by larger, much more vicious birds.

Hitchcock, like Fuentes, is a master of irony—the gentle

Figure 169. Final escape, redemption for casualties left problematic; ending is eerily unsettling.

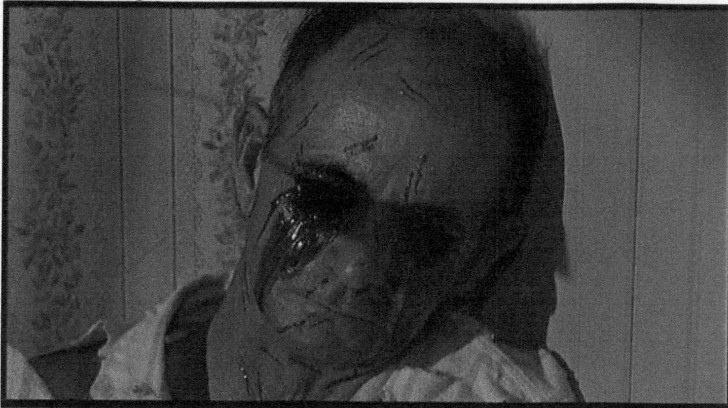

Figure 170. Shockingly dramatic jump cut to pecked out eye sockets of Dan Fawcett.

Figure 171. Up until the very end, the most fearful--and, paradoxically, the most powerful human presence in Hitchcock's film.

Figure 172. Gentle, cooing lovebirds symbols of amatory relationship between Melanie and new catch, Mitch.

cooing of the two charming lovebirds, symbolic of Melanie and Mitch—who on Melanie's accelerated drive from San Francisco to Bodega Bay through winding, precipitous roads even sway gently —together—into the curves, contrasts with the reiterated clawing, biting, and screeching of the huge, savage crows and black birds. Unlike cats and dogs, animals trained for the benefit of their owners yet allowed freedom to roam, at least in limited spaces, birds are incessantly caged by their human owners. Indeed the escaping of even a harmless bird from its endless captivity—as evoked in the initial scene of *The Birds*, is a cause for consternation and panic by the human bird keepers—until a masterful Mitch deftly traps the escaped canary by throwing his hat over it—the only victory over the birds that Mitch will ever enjoy. Indeed, an embittered Annie utters a harsh judgment against the seagulls, whom she nervously watches massing in the sky over her house, stating: "will they ever stop migrating?" even though she herself has determinedly migrated from San Francisco to spend the rest of her life close to her former lover with little hope of his ever returning her love. Annie is content to spend the rest of her life in a state of suspended animation, just as is a superficially contented Scottie Ferguson at the Empire Hotel with what he believes triumphantly is his perfect re-creation.

Indeed there is a marked parallel between the existential self-castration of the darkly beautiful but somber, melancholy, lost-in-a-trance Annie Hayworth and the intensely self-absorbed, panic-stricken, highly insecure Lydia, who paralleling Annie also continues to be obsessed by her attachment to a lost male—her strong-willed yet empathetic deceased husband. Ironically Annie shows the same insensitivity toward birds as do many of the townspeople, because she herself has permanently migrated from San Francisco to Bodega Bay, unwilling ever to end her relationship with Mitch, who significantly spends much more time in San Francisco more than he ever does in the initially pastoral Bodega Bay. It seems as of Annie seeks to be a permanent part of Mitch's entire family, indeed she is proud of the fact that Lydia now accepts her, since she is no longer a threat, and when Melanie states to her the marital cliché of the mother *not* losing a son but gaining a daughter, Annie responds dismissively that Lydia already has a daughter—one toward whom Lydia seems as cold and loveless as she is toward Mitch, whom she seeks to convert into a surrogate husband-protector. Symbolic action is predominant in both Fuentes and Hitchcock—that both Annie and Melanie are marked for destruction is indicated in the seagull that suddenly swoops down on Annie's front door—and kills itself, falling on the porch dropping down to the front porch with the weight of Doom.

How utterly helpless are the flocks of birds shot down by gleeful and trimphant hunters throughout the world is completely reversed in *The Birds*, as Hitchcock in a savage depicion focuses on two attacks of the birds on the most helpless of human beings—the innocent, totally defenseless school children—who nonetheless can be protected by the adults in the way that young birds cannot by their parents—the way that a mother bear, for example, can lunge at a human attacker to protect her young, while a mother bird can only cry out in helpless agitation. The extreme vulnerability of birds in the natural world contrasts with their ominousness and never thwarted power in Hitchcock's terrifying fantasy. *The Birds* is one of his most fascinating and least appreciated films, a masterwork from the height of Hitchcock's career—his Hollywood epoch. The harsh cry of the waitress in the crowded restaurant yelling out "Sam! Three southern fried chicken, baked potatoes on all of them" to indicate that the fryers are ready for consumption provides a harsh indication of how mercilessly and thoroughly humans have devastated the bird population down through the centuries. Yet Melanie gives a chilling explanation of why the vicious birds have mercilessly attacked the children: "To kill them" and almost suffers the same fate as Annie Hayworth, until Melanie is finally rescued by Mitch and even comforted at the end of the film by a Lydia who, like Melanie herself, has become more human, more humane, countering the increasing ferocity and monstrousness of *The Birds*, whose relentless demonism is brilliantly foreshadowed at the very outset of *The Birds* in the masterful credits, which are bitten and torn apart by a flock of screeching ravens from Hell.

Both Fuentes and Hitchcock are painstaking, exacting masters of their respective crafts. When Hitchcock attempts to reassure a doubting and querulous Kim Novak, who objected to wearing a grey dress and black pumps, in her role as the stricken Madeleine in *Vertigo* he stated to her paternally, reassuringly,

"Kim, it's only a movie." But films, on the contrary, were life itself for this brilliant director, who would, as he did in the unforgettable shower scene in *Psycho* with Janet Leigh, spend weeks filming a single scene that would last for only seconds or minutes on the screen. Similarly, Fuentes has explicitly, in *Diana or the Goddess Who Hunts Alone*, declared that everything in his life—love, politics, family, friends—is subordinate to writing, and has insisted that he will continue to write until his dying day—just as Hitchcock continued to make films almost to the end of his life, until he died at age eighty-one, leaving his last work, *The Short Night*, unfinished. And Evan Hunter has documented Hitchcock's desire, after his brilliant film *Psycho* failed to gain even a single Academy Award, when Hitch sought to create a deeply philosophical, deeply meaningful film, perhaps even in a sociopolitical sense as a plea for compassion toward birds which in the millions have been slain by human beings, consumed by the millions, trapped and shot down and caged to delight their human captors—Hitchcock who apparently sought to break through his image as a slick director pandering to the lurid and the sensational to make a serious film that would constitute high art—and gain for him the coveted Academy Award as Best Director. Whether Hitchcock succeeded in his lofty goals without achieving recognition in his lifetime for *The Birds* or not is up to the viewer to decide.

Fuentes is a master of words; Hitchcock a master of visuals, yet Fuentes's art is strikingly permeated—implicitly and explicitly—by the visual—embellished by architecture and paintings, sculpture, and, above all, film, just as Hitchcock's art reveals his mastery of words, of dialogue, of a precise balance between expressive utterances and deeply significant silence. Indeed Hitchcock hired many of his writers from the staff of the *New Yorker* magazine, world renowned for its prose mastery. Both Hitchcock and Fuentes have a flair for the dramatic, for the sensational—evinced in Hitchcock's films, from the gruesome and morbid *Psycho* to the corpse-scattered *The Birds* and from the ever-shifting luminous and ominous images of *Rear Window* to the savage images of violation and murder characterisitic of *Frenzy* (1972), in which women are raped then strangled to death. Indeed, moreso than most film directors, Hitchcock has the dual capacity both to work with highly talented writers on his productions such as Michael Hayes, who worked on the filmscripts for Hitchcock masterpieces such as *The Man Who Knew Too Much* and *Rear Window* and then to take the verbal images that they have produced and convert them unerringly into bold, poetic, suspenseful, visual sequences. For example, Hitchcock deleted scenes of *The Birds* written by Hunter that included Melanie's search for a hotel room in Bodega Bay and the purchase of a night gown at the General Store and a romantic tryst with Mitch before a terrified Lydia drives back to the Brenner farm after her horrified reaction to the death of Dan Fawcett and is too horrified even to speak to the would-be lovers whom she still perceives as a dire threat to her well being. The purpose of Hitchcock is to remove all extraneous episodes in order to produce a tightly woven, intensely powerful film of incremental suspense—exactly as does Fuentes in *Aura* and "Vlad."

In the climactic scene of *The Birds*, in which Melanie is attacked and almost killed by a seemingly endless flock of voracious birds of many species, the bedroom door itself to Cathy's room becomes a key character in the episode. First, as Melanie attempts to waken an exhausted Mitch and is unsuccessful, she decides to investigate the cause of an ominous fluttering by herself alone. Here again we see the power of the Director to mold the scene to underscore the highest possible dramatic development and tension. Evan Hunter, the screenwriter of *The Birds*, had initially thought of the sound of falling plaster—but Hitchcock changed the noises to make them far more ominous —the intermittent sound of the fluttering of birds. Armed with only a huge flashlight—which Melanie attempts to use as a weapon but which proves to be totally ineffectual in halting the obsessive, high speed attack on her, Melanie has finally fallen from an initial pinnacle of elegance and authority and supreme self-confidence to the state of impotent and terrified victim. Melanie, who has decided to solve the problem by herself, first checks the kitchen of the Brenner house and finds the two lovebirds in a peaceful and even contented state—a seemingly reassuring sign that proves to be just the opposite. Melanie then slowly, cautiously ascends the stairwell to Cathy´s bedroom, and Hitchcock masterfully increases the tension by having her pause before she turns the door knob.

Her first astonished sight is of a huge hole in the roof through which the birds have entered the room. The fierce birds, kept away from the cameras by streams of air, are hurled directly at Tippi Hedren who apparently was surprised that real birds not mechanical ones were being used by a Hitchcock fanatically pursuing a brutal realism to make even more convincing his fantastic, macabre, tortured vision. The door acts almost as a living personage, as a bewildered Melanie turns the door the wrong way—and entraps herself. And when a frantic Mitch arrives to rescue her, he has great difficulty in entering the hellworld of the bedroom because Melanie´s unconscious body has fallen to block the doorway. Now the elegant green dress of the blonde goddess is in shreds and her face, arms, and legs are all bloodied. Finally the initially hostile then cold then ambivalent Lydia reacts to the person whom she knows will be victorious in claiming Mitch by aiding her son in fighting off the birds and even crying out "Poor thing" to mark the final emergence of a maternal attitude free of condescension toward Melanie.

Both Hitchcock and Fuentes are masters of tension, masters of mystery and suspense. We never know the outcome of Felipe's rapid descent into the maelstrom in *Aura*, just as we never know what will happen either to the caring Midge or the increasingly judgmental, sadistic Scottie Ferguson in *Vertigo* or to L.B. Jefferies with his adoring Lisa Fremont in *Rear Window* or to Mitch Brenner and the ever relucant perhaps even misogynistic Lydia Brenner at the grim and spectral finale of *The Birds*. Similarly, we have to speculate on the horrific scene that a stunned and terrified Navarro witnesses at the end of "Vlad"—some unspeakable horror—perhaps newly invigorated Vlad seducing Navarro's revenant son or sucking his blood—a scene that Fuentes deliberately leaves to the imagination of the reader, just as Hitchcock deliberately leaves the fate of an anguished, crucified Scottie up to the spectator of *Vertigo*—in which, ironically, the only certainty is that the arch plotter Gavin Elster gets off entirely free. And what does the quiet but lethal massing of *The Birds* at the end of Hitchcock's shocking thriller portend? Have Mitch and Melanie and Cathy finally escaped their vicious predators or will the silver Aston Martin of Melanie—now a cramped, fragile vehicle that can be easily attacked and by the predatory, avenging birds, be pursued invaded, and demolished. Indeed, the geometrically increasing mass of patient, expectant birds who, strangely, randomly, viciously peck at Mitch over and over again as he takes the car out of the garage but refrain—at least temporarily—from attacking and killing him as they have so many others provides a highly disturbing ending to *The Birds*. Why are Mitch and Melanie and the rest of the Brenner family finally allowed to escape the house that becomes a hellworld apparently even literally for the victimized actress Tippi Hedren herself, who at the end almost loses an eye to the pecking birds, as Hitchcock decided to scrap mechanical birds because their artificiality was readily apparent to the viewer for the real things—countless birds hurled at Hedren by assistants with lengthy and protective leather gloves—before the now ramshackle Aston Martin can break through the road blocks and reach the safety of San Francisco?

The sudden and silent massing of the black birds at the Bodega School is a prelude to the attack which brutally kills Annie Hayworth—does the final massing of a much greater force adumbrate a similar disaster for the protagonists? It is left for the audience to decide. Another ambiguity to decipher is why is Melanie Daniels singled out for *repeated* attacks by the marauding birds, assaults that grow ever more vicious? It is clear that unlike the extremely authoritative and imposing Mrs. Bundy—expertly played by Ethel Griffies, a character actress whose experience began in silent films—a highly experienced eighty-year-old who speaks extensively and eloquently to her rapt audience in *The Tides Restaurant*, defending the Birds, which Mrs. Bundy masterfully played by the English character actress, with whom Hedren herself was in awe, views as both age-old, innocent victims of mankind, and because they number in the billions, if they were to wage war, they would be unbeatable—a verbal evocation of the Apocalypse that is reiterated visually at the chilling end of Hitchcock's suspense-filled film.

Melanie Daniels coyly and very shrewedly—and again and again—uses birds to her personal advantage, both as part of her life as flamboyant and devil-may-care heiress and to ensnare the man whom she is determined to catch as a lover—Mitch Brenner.Yet Melanie has little or no knowledge of birds—just the opposite of the precise knowledge imparted in the crucial *Tides Restaurant* scene by a forceful and very eloquent Mrs. Bundy. Indeed, in the sparkling, light-hearted, initial “meet cute” scene at the outset of *The Birds,* sizing up the ruggedly handsome and dapper Mitch as a suitable romantic interest. Melanie pretends to be a saleswoman of the Pet Shop, but makes mistake after mistake in identifying species of birds and characterizing their mating habits. She declares that the Pet Shop has love birds and even points them out to Mitch but in reality the store has none and the birds have to be specially ordered. Melanie has swept regally into the Pet Store to pick up a mynah bird that constitutes another example of her insensitivity to both birds and human beings—she wants to play one of her many practical jokes —this time on a prudish aunt, by teaching the mynah bird a stream of obscenities that will shock her straitlaced relative. And Melanie’s insensitivity to birds is futher exemplified by her initial desire just to drop the pair of lovebirds off at Mitch’s apartment and run—abandoning them until she is apprised that Mitch has left San Francisco to spend the weekend at Bodega Bay. The two lovebirds that she purchases, ostensibly as a birthday gift for Mitch’s eleven-year old sister Cathy, are really to ingratiate herself with her fiercely targetted romantic lover. The crabbed and tormented and highly vulnerable Lydia, the domineering mother of Mitch is even more hateful of birds; she cannot stand even the innocent, often cooing love birds and demands that they be quarantined in the kitchen of the Brenner household. Indeed, the only person in the Brenner family to evince the slightest compassion toward the innocuous—and endearing—lovebirds is the innocent Cathy. It is Cathy at the end, after the brutal attack on Melanie, who entreats an initially hostile Mitch to take the lovebirds in the car with them as they all attempt to escape *The Birds* by fleeing to the haven of San Francisco. The sensitive Cathy exclaims that as opposed to the vicious and devastating birds that still encircle the entire Brenner house, the lovebirds have not harmed anyone. This time Mitch, who has previously sided with Lydia in her condemnation of the lovebirds, relents. Intense family friction characterizes both the compact Brenner family and the three person, severely divided family of Navarro in “Vlad.”

Significant honors have been heaped on both Hitchcock and Fuentes. Did Hitchcock ever achieve an Academy Award? He was knighted—Sir Alfred Hitchcock—by Queen Elizabeth II of

England in 1979 for his outstanding accomplishments, and he received the American Film Institute's Distinguished Achievement Award near the end of his brilliant career. Similarly, Fuentes has received myriad honors, including the Cervantes Prize, bestowed on him by Juan Carlos, King of Spain, who also awarded Fuentes the prestigious Príncipe de Asturias Award. And Fuentes received the Gallegos Prize for the distinguished Mexican author's epic masterpiece of Habsburg Spain and the Discovery and Conquest of the New World, *Terra nostra* (1978). Yet although two of his fellow Latin American Boom Authors—Gabriel García Márquez and, in 2010, Mario Vargas Llosa, have received the greatest literary prize of all—the Nobel Prize in Literature, an award which the Argentine short story masters Jorge Luis Borges and his disciple Julio Cortázar greatly deserved but failed to obtain—Fuentes for decades now has been a leading candidate for the Nobel Prize, which has thus far eluded him but which he most definitely deserves.

Extraordinary talent—in the case of both Alfred Hitchcock and Carlos Fuentes—genius—is often not recognized at the highest levels. Although *Rebecca* won an academy award for Best Picture, Hitchcock, unlike Billy Wilder, whose films also significantly influenced Fuentes, never received an Academy Award for Best Director, despite his many stunning, profound achievements, paralleled by Fuentes's to this day not receiving the Prize that he at one point in his career in the 1990s almost received—the Nobel Prize for Literature.

Both Hitchcock and Fuentes are masters of symbolism. Indeed, Fuentes himself has characterized his complex, paradoxical art as one of Symbolic Realism—not Surrealism or Magical Realism, the latter term that can best be applied to the narratives of one of Fuentes's closest friends, Gabriel García Márquez. Objects in *Aura* and "El amante del teatro" and "Vlad" colors and buildings and geographcial settings, all are imbued with symbolic import. Similarly, symbolism—color symbolism, architectural monuments, seemingly deserted and shadow-infested crumbling Victorian mansions, doorways and corridors and sinuous streets and alleyways, bridges and bays, bluffs and towering forests, all have psychological and metaphysical significance in Hitchcock's dense, convoluted, highly Romantic vision. As we have seen, green is an eery, mystifying color in so many of Hitchcock's masterpiece films. In the malevolent *The Birds*, Melanie is dressed in a stylish two piece light green suit; the two love birds symbolizing her eagerly hoped for relationship with Mitch, are bright green crowned with a blood-red patch, which is subsequently reflected in the circle of blood that stains one of Melanie's gloves after her first attack by a lone seagull. And the Deere tractor on the farm of Lydia's neighbor and Lydia's own speeding truck are green—all signifying ominousness, just as the color does throughout *Vertigo* and throughout *Aura* as well, as we have seen. Even the telephone that Melanie uses to call her father at the outset is ominous green—telephone connections will finally be severed as the voracious birds tear the wires apart.

At the terrifying ending to *The Birds*, the visual economy of Hitchcock again is stressed. Hunter had written an ending in which a vigilant Melanie patiently searches a number of rooms, to be certain that the attack of the birds is over, before she ascends to the attic floor and opens the door of Cathy's room to be rapidly entrapped and almost devoured by the screaming birds. The dramatic mastery of Hitchcock is especially evident in his stark condensation of Melanie's investigation to the slow, suspenseful climbing of the darkened staircase—the birds have severed the electrical wiring—and the equally slow, suspenseful twisting of the doorknob to Cathy's room.

Both Fuentes and Hitchcock are compulsive artists, both are fanatic perfectionists—but they contrast in one significant aspect—the slim and regally appearing Fuentes has never been preoccupied with his weight—a constant problem for Hitchcock, whose weight varied between 349 pounds and for him, a slim 189, and who, apparently, because Tippi Hedren had made disparaging remarks concerning his rotundity, after *Marnie*, never starred her again in any of his films, yet refused to release her from her contract with him—thus ending the cinematic stardom of the actress whom Hitchcock discovered after seeing her in a television commercial, a poised, melodically voiced, statuesque, breathtakingly beautiful actress, with whom the apparently possessive Hitchcock reputedly had fallen in love. Rivalry between the stunning blonde Tippi Hedren—obviously Hitchcock's favorite—and the sultry Suzanne Pleshette, assigned to play a definitely less glamorous role as a beleagured school teacher, seems to have spilled onto the set. As Hunter states, quoting Pleshette's pointedly jealous remarks concerning Tippi Hedren, who paralleling Hitchcock's disdainfully referring to Hedren again again as "the girl" Pleshette refers to Hedren not by name but only as "the blonde."

> The blonde, he gives a mink coat. Me, he gives wedgies and a house dress (MH, 27)

Fuentes's writing is highly cinematic, intensely visual; Hitchcock's dialogue is crisp and clear and vivid, as he has employed master screenwriters and, as in *Vertigo*, has not hesitated to replace them as he did Evan Hunter who worked on the filmscript of *Marnie*, and was replaced by Jay Presson Allen. When Hitchcock found their contributions unsatisfactory, the always demanding director apparently was merciless with his actors and writers, just as Cecil B. DeMille taunted actors and actresses under his commanding directorship for their lack of courage on the set, as he did with Victor Mature, the star of *Demetrius and the Gladiators* when the muscle man actor refused to wrestle even with an old and toothless lion—in Hitchcock's unswerving quest for visual perfection and that all important Box Office appeal, which parallels Fuentes's ardent quest for linguistic perfection and a wide audience of appreciative readers.

Both *Aura* and *Vertigo* are permeated by a dark, NeoGothic Vision, which Hitchcock also develops in *Psycho* in the eery, imposing Victorian mansion of the mentally disturbed killer Norman Bates—the greatest role in the film career of Anthony Perkins, which ironically type casted him for the remainder of his career. The huge foreboding mansion, significantly, an ominous character itself in *Psycho*, just as Consuelo's mansion is a leading character in *Aura* down to its fatalistic thirteen steps that Felipe must traverse—towering above the characters with its stairways above which Norman lies in wait and its basement containing the gruesome cadaver of Bates´s mother, stuffed with sawdust just like Norman´s collection of predatory birds. Fuentes too is submerged in the Gothic, creating huge lugubrious mansions in *Aura*, Fuentes´s *Una familia lejana* and his collection of short stories, in particular the one which focuses on the gloomy mansion of Dracula, a Gothic mausoleum transported to Mexico City. Dracula, reborn, not in the Carpathian Mountains but in contemporary Mexico. Fuentes's hideous Dracula is also reminiscent of Murnau's grotesque monster Nosferatu, in addition acquiring a comic appearance in an ill-fitting wig. In *Vertigo* the eery Hotel McKittrick in which Madeleine disappears, looms threateningly above an increasingly mystified who at this point is evoked in a distant shot that dramatically reduces him in size and significance, as it accentuates the mansion, which appears as threatening. Scottie Ferguson. As Kraft and Leventhal perceptively state (*Footsteps in the Fog,* p. 405):

> The two-story road building, with its tall narrow windows and eerie ornamental façade, and short black spiked fence, creates a sense of unnerving mystery. Scottie's cautious facial expression adds to this feeling.

The rambling, labyrinthine Portman Mansion in the spellbinding *Vertigo* is exactly paralleled by the Neo Gothic domain of the sorceress Consuelo in *Aura*—also a realm of impenetrable mystery and incessant deception, of characters that suddenly appear and then mysteriously disappear, of flickering lights alternating with sudden plunges into darkness.

Both Fuentes and Hitchcock are masters of the techniques of unreality. Moreso than most Hollywood directors, Hitchcock is fond of using back projection, as he does in the scene in *Vertigo* where the two supposedly illicit lovers Scottie and Madeleine passionately kiss against the backdrop of an extremely agitated Pacific Ocean to underscore their emotional distress. Here Hitchcock turns what could have been a romantic cliché into an intense, brooding, passionate but ultimately tragic encounter between the two doomed lovers, a poignant scene that adumbrates the final, seemingly redemptive but tragic embrace of Judy and Scottie right before her accidental death. In *The Birds,* back projection is again utilized in the significant scene where Melanie singlehandedly crosses Bodega Bay in a flimsy outboard motor boat to surprise Mitch with the gift of the love birds. Melanie/Tippi Hedren in actuality is probably rowing a boat on a studio floor against a blue screen, with Bodega Bay subsequently matted in with extensive back projection. The effect is to give a decidedly unnatural appearance to the rowing, which underscores the absolute—and highly unreal—tranquility that Hitchcock sought deliberately to project. Not a breeze nor a wave disturbs Melanie's perfectly smooth boat or ruffles a single hair of her classically molded hairdo until the sudden, excruciating and completely unexpected moment that marks the emergence of a vicious seagull that attacks her, drawing blood from her forehead, just as she enticingly and with *exultant flair* approaches her would-be lover who has rushed to meet her as she docks. The effect—similar to the startlingly brutal but sudden attack by Antony Perkins/Norman Bates on the private investigator Arbogast, expertly played by Martin Balsam as he climbs the stairs of the eery mansion in *Psycho*, is all the more powerful because of the extreme placidity of the moments that precede the attack. Markedly increasing the unreality of the scene is the circumstance that Melanie alone is piloting the flimsy outboard motor boat dressed in a full length sable mink coat. Not a breeze ruffles her shimmering Grecian molded hairdo, not an errant wave dampens her mink. Inspiration for this highly unrealistic setting comes from the classic Renaissance painting by Botticelli, *Venus Emerging From the Waves* and provides the viewer with an idyllic scene—the more to increase the shock when a potentially rabid sea gull attacks and wounds her, just as she is excitedly looking forward to a romantic interlude with the San Francisco lawyer whom she is pursuing and has quickly found again. The artistic dimensions of the motor boat crossing of Bodega Bay have been emphasized by Camille Paglia (*The Birds:* BFI Publishing, 1998, pp. 33-34): "it could be a Surrealist painting by Dali or Magritte...On the smooth waters, Melanie is like the Lady of the Lake or those sinister, self-contained femmes fatales who so love boating—Spenser's Acraeia, Shelley's Witch of Atlas... Hedren at the helm exudes an airy, affable elitism, a noble, relaxed power, like the banqueting Olympians of the Elgin marbles."

Adumbrated by the sudden and eery massing of the seagulls in the early scene in downtown San Francisco in *The Birds*, the attack by a single seagull on the smooth waters of Bodega Bay is unexpected and comes as a shock both to the flirtatious Melanie, as she confidently moves in on her male prize and to the viewers of *The Birds*. And, as occurs so often in the Theatre of the Absurd which has definitely influenced Hitchcock, objects rapidly multiply. Indeed, this single attack foreshadows the devastating attack on Melanie several times more at the Bodega School, at the burning gas station in the center of town and finally, overwhelmingly, on the second floor of the house of Mitch, where the voracious birds have broken through the rafters of the ceiling and are quietly waiting for their prey—the Melanie who initially hears no outcry from the huge mass of birds, only a menacing fluttering which fails to deter her investigation. Why Melanie decides to ascend the staircase to open the bedroom door on her own without summoning help, can be explained by her apparent need to prove her mettle, her worth both to the Mitch who has previously chided her for her scandalous behavior and especially to her crusty, forbidding future mother-in-law, Lydia, as well as to underscore how definite is her break with her scandalous and partygoing and frivolous past—to a Mitch who has condemned it and yet is greatly attracted to the beautiful and self-possessed and intriguing socialite.

Both Hitchcock and Fuentes are masters of the thriller genre—Hitchcock in films like *Psycho* and *The Birds* and Fuentes in his spy thriller, filled with throat cuttings, shootouts, jungle chases, forced plastic surgery on the face of the protagonist, kidnappings, defenestrations, *La cabeza de la hidra* and in his short story of vampirism, death, and immortality, "Vlad." Throughout *The Birds* is evident a repeated and incremental pattern of ominousness and terror, from the eery start, when the glamorous, fashionable protagonist, the wealthy and impetuous Melanie Daniels, faces a flock of sea gulls eerily massing outside of the pet store in downtown San Francisco, to the repeated and vicious bird attacks that she suffers in *The Birds*—attacks that kill her rival for Mitch's affections Annie Hayworth and threaten the lives of Lydia, Cathy and Mitch who are all powerless to stop their attacks—just as is the hapless and helpless narrator of "Vlad," who can only watch in horror as the flock of vicious bats encircles him at the end of Fuentes's shocker.

Just as in *Vertigo*, where an initially "Happily-ever-after" ending is scrapped for a pessimistic, anguished, crucifixion dominated finale, so too is *The Birds*, originally was characterized by a finale written by Evan Hunter that was never filmed by Hitchcock—Hunter's positive ending with an ultimately triumphant Brenner family eluding their voracious predators. Paglia summarizes the original Evan Hunter script, detailed in Hunterr's *Me and Hitch*. As Paglia states in her incisive summary of the ending envisioned by Hunter:

> A still resentful Evan Hunter revealed that as the characters drove away, they passed through Bodega Bay in 'absolute chaos,' with victims in 'open shopdoors;' 'an overturned school bus;' a dead policeman draped over a roadblock, and a male corpse covered with birds on a beach. Attacked by *Birds, The* car sped along the winding road, by which Melanie arrived. Catching up because they travel 'as the crow flies,' the birds tore through the convertible roof, with the women 'huddled inside crying,' seen from above. When the road straightened out, the sports car could go faster than the birds and so escaped. The script ended optimistically, with the passengers spotting the clear, dawn sky in the distance. (*The Birds*, 86-87)

Hitchcock, true to his attachment to ambiguous endings, scrapped Hunter's Hollywood ending, with its clear affirmation of the power of human fortitude and technology to thwart the marauding birds, which would have been highly inconsistent with the pitiful, indecisive, never utilized power either of the police force nor of the military, which had contemplated an intervention. Indeed, even the slightest attempts to attack the birds, such as Mitch's desire to stone them, are nullified. Instead, Hitchcock abruptly ends his masterpiece without even the conventional Hollywood closure "The End," and instead focuses on the geometrically incremental flocks of birds—even though still on the ground, nervous and fluttering—an echo of a spectacularly enormous scale of the menacing fluttering Melanie hears issuing from Cathy's room in the attic of the Brenner house prior to the unleashing of a torrent of screaming, voracious birds that terrifyingly assault her. And Hitchcock increases the screeching of *The Birds* at the very end, another indication of their imminent mass attack. The sky is ominous, dominated by apocalyptic black clouds, and even the piercing ray of sunlight seems more like a symbol of a gigantic piercing beak of monstrous birds ready to again pluck out the eyes of its victims, as the vicious birds have done with the surprised and totally helpless Dan Fawcett.

Paralleling Hitchcock's decidedly open, ambiguous, but menacing ending is Fuentes's climax to "Vlad," in which a horrified Navarro is as helpless to save either his loving family, now adjuncts of the demonic Vlad and his daughter Minea, or to rescue his beloved son, now in the grasp of the blood-sucking vampire.

Even the purpose of the powerful, intricate, creative works of both Carlos Fuentes and Alfred Hitchcock is the same—Fuentes has remarked on the necessity to *epater les bourgeoisie,* radically to unsettle *las buenas conciencias*, to agitate and even infuriate the self-satisfied, closed-in, smugly sanctimonious reader nestled in his or her intellectual cocoon. Similarly, Hitchcock has conceived of his function as Director as not only providing superb entertainment but administering "healthy mental shake-ups" to the spectators of his films whom he perceives, paralleling the iconoclastic Fuentes, as the perpetual "Angry Young Man," as "sluggish and jellified" (Consult Gottlieb, *Hitchcock on Hitchcock*). Thus both the British-American director and the Latin-American writer so enamoured of film that he wanted to be a movie star, share the desire to form and re-form and re-create the reader/spectator and to jolt him or her out of indolence and complacency. Hitchcock himself, like Fuentes, who so often assumes the role of commentator on his own narrative production and even on individual characters and scenes, has stated that Melanie Daniels in *The Birds* is too complacent—implying that she needs something to shake her out of her pampered, cosseted existence. At the end of *The Birds*, her stylish green ensemble torn to shreds, her legs and face bloodied by the attack, the jolt that alters Melanie's "Wild child" existence has been horrifyingly delivered.

Indeed, the audience—either filmic or literary—is paramount for both Fuentes and Hitchcock, both of whom incessantly play to that audience, and who are iconized by their myriad fans, and have both been transmuted into larger-than-life figures. Indeed, Hunter comments that every time Hitchcock left the Fairmont Hotel in his chauffered limousine for the Bodega Bay location of *The Birds*, swarms of school children lined the roads with signs stating "MR. HITCHCOCK PLEASE STOP!" (MH, 58-59). And Hitchcock always did, to sign countless autographs every day. Hitchcock, who has influenced numerous directors both in Great Britain, and even more so, in the United States, is now universally celebrated for his raising film from a popular expression to High Art. Fuentes, whose impact both on the stellar Latin American Boom and now on the generations of the successors to the Boom, eloquent and authoritative, strident, towers above Latin American literature and for decades has been the clamorous, eloquent sociopolitical voice of Latin America.

CONCLUSION: HITCHCOCK AND FUENTES—TWIN MASTERS OF MYSTERY AND THE MACABRE

The geographical trajectories of Alfred Hitchcock and Carlos Fuentes trace a full circle that undoubtedly would delight both masterful creators. Born in Great Britain, Hitchcock achieved his greatest success in Hollywood, fell in love with America, particularly Northern California, dwelled on Bellagio Road in Los Angeles where he lavishly entertained countless movie stars and business associates, and instead of being buried in Great Britain, requested that his ashes be strewn over the Pacific Ocean. Fuentes, born in Panama City, where his father, a career diplomat was stationed, in 1928, was brought to Mexico City to consolidate his citizenship but, like Hitchcock, has spent many years, both of his formative youth—as a young, pampered child schooled in exclusive MacLean, Virginia, while his father was a diplomatic attaché in Washington, D.C. and returning again and again both to lecture at Universities across the United States, from Connecticut to California, and from Yale University to UCLA, to assume a Visiting Professorship at Harvard University as Professor of Comparative Literature and to teach at Princeton and Brown Universities. Hitchcock is a British film director who has admitted that he is an Americanophile; Fuentes is a Mexican author who is decidedly ambivalent toward the United States but who without a doubt is an Anglophile, one who for many years now for the greater part of each year resides in his beloved London, in Kensington Gardens, like Hitchcock preferring the fog and dampness and cold—what drew the master English craftsman to chilly Northern California, where for many years he resided in the hills outside of San Francisco.

Both Fuentes and Hitchcock are fiercely devoted to their

art, so much so that their artistic carerers are equivalent to life itself. Indeed, when questioned by a student abroad from Mexico at a lecture at Cambridge University when Fuentes would stop writing, the octogenarian abruptly shot back "And when, sir, will you stop breathing?" indicating that only death would halt his writing. Similarly, when Hitchcock, suffering debilitating illnesses finally gave up filmmaking, according to McGilligan (*Alfred Hitchcock: A Life in Darkness and Light*, p. 745):

> …his constitution was strong and he was not dying. He could have lived out months, even years, with care and comfort, said Dr. Flieg. Yet always a man of tremendous willpower, now the director willed himself to die. A man who loved food and drink, now he refused either, taking only sips of water. He stopped getting out of bed; he refused to see or talk to friends: he stared coldly at the few who braved a visit, and more than once confronted them with irrational anger and epithets.

Both Carlos Fuentes and Alfred Hitchcock are masters of illusion, dream and nightmare. Both have the magic capability of constructing scenes that are apparently realistic because of masterful, exquisite detail and yet are ultimately symbolic and fantastic worlds. For example, San Francisco, evoked in excruciating detail by Hitchcock, who over and over again re-created San Francisco locations down to the minutest detail—lavish department stores like *Ransohoff's*, plush restaurants like *Ernie's*, elaborate historical mansions like the haunting, majestic Portman Mansion, quiet zones of spiritual transport like the Mission Dolores and the Convent at San Juan Bautista—places caught so exquisitely that they are seared on the imaginations and memories of the spectators of *Vertigo*. Similarly, throughout Fuentes's vast, epic vision of Mexico City, palaces and monuments, castles and museums, statues and plazas of Fuentes's beloved Mexico City—which corresponds to Alfred Hitchcock's beloved, fog-enshrowded San Francisco—hold the reader spellbound, as Fuentes with consummate artistry evokes a Mexico of both history and imagination, archaelogical mystery and wonder and of illusion and dream. Both *Vertigo* and *Aura*, *Rear Window* and "The Theatre Lover," *The Birds* and "Vlad" envelop the spectator/reader in concentric worlds of past, present, remote epochs and of mysteries and ever captivating timelessness.

Hitchcock and Fuentes are highly prolific artists. Alfred Hitchcock directed fifty-four films, from the silent to the sound era, from black and white to dazzling color. Fuentes is the author of over twenty novels and five collections of short stories, beginning in 1954 with the expressionistic collection of short stories *Los días enmascarados* ("The Masked Days") and encompassing *Cantar de ciegos* ("Songs of the Blind") *Agua quemada* (*Burnt Water*), *Inquieta compañía* ("Disquieting Company") and *Carolina Grau* (2010). In addition, he has collaborated on several filmscripts, including *Tiempo de morir* ("A Time to Die") with Gabriel García Márquez and *Los caifanes*, and is the author of three dramatic works and even an opera, dedicated to the controversial Mexican President whose forces successfully attacked the Alamo fortress in San Antonio but who eventually was defeated and forced to surrender huge portions of Mexican territory to the United States, including what is now California, Texas, New Mexico and Arizona, *Santa Ana* (2010). Indeed, in the year before his death, Hithcock was struggling to complete the film "A Short Night" and the act of closing down his studio probably hastened his demise, for the primary purpose of his life was gone.

Hunter comments on the spectacular visibility of Alfred Hitchcock—which is paralleled in the literary world by the extraordinary attention given to and insistently sought by—Carlos Fuentes, who cultivates a literary star ethos. Hunter alludes to Hitchcock's *Alfred Hitchcock Presents*, an enormously successful 372 episode television show, in which Hitchcock himself appeared to introduce each episode in his characteristically witty and mordant style:

> These monologues, coupled with the short cameo appearances he made in all of his films, resulted in his becoming the most highly visible director in the world. I sincerely doubt that many movie-goers today would recognize Steven Spielberg if he walked into a restaurant unannounced. When *Hitch* walked in, *everyone* knew who he was. (MH, 5)

Both Fuentes and Hitchcock fully enjoy the high life that fame and money bring. Hitch and his wife Alma regularly vacationed during the Christmas holidays on St. Moritz. When he is in New York, Fuentes at times resides in the plush Regis Hotel in exclusive Manhattan, the same hotel in which Hitchcock stayed before the premiere of *The Birds* at the Museum of Modern Art Theatre in an exclusive black-tie showing. Both director and writer own marvellous collections of paintings, which Hitchcock displayed at his home in Bel-Air, California on Bellagio Road, and Fuentes, who does not own property, states are his only possessions.

Both Carlos Fuentes and Alfred Hitchcock are disciplined perfectionists. Both are extraordinarily dedicated to their respective crafts, down to the minutest details. Hitchcock even selected the details of costuming and jewelry for his female stars, as he did for Tippi Hedren in *The Birds*. And Hitchcock was so entranced by his new found discovery that even before the filming of *The Birds* began he presented Hedren with three gold pins of birds filled with seed pearls. Fuentes is an avid reader and devours works from medieval times to the epoch of the Spanish Golden Age, including Miguel de Cervantes's *Don Quixote* and Tirso de Molina's *El burlador de Sevilla* to construct his voluminous epic masterpiece of the caticlysmic encounter of the Wold World and New World civilizations, *Terra nostra*. Asked at McGill University in April of 2011 what makes a good writer, Fuentes responded bluntly and enthusiastically: "Diligence. I get up at 6:30 or seven and start writing at eight. I work from eight to twelve, read all afternoon, then go to the movies…I don't wait for inspiration from the heavens." Yet without a doubt, inspiration frequently comes to Fuentes from the many films—Hollywood and European, Japanese and Indian, silent era and sound films, that he as an inveterate cinephile constantly watches.

Both Fuentes and Hitchcock, as we have seen, are devoted to public appearances, both dress elegantly and to sartorial perfection. Fuentes is always attired in elegant suits and ties when he lectures or grants interviews, which he has done myriad times. Hitchcock's standard, courtly attire was a Mariani suit, formal white shirt and tie, and members of his film crew—including scriptwriters, as Evan Hunter attests, were encouraged—even pressured—to dress formally on the set.

Sir Alfred Hitchcock fell permanently in love with the United States, particularly San Francisco. Hitchcock died in the United States, in California, far from his native land. In contrast, the Mexican Carlos Fuentes has consistently identified himself with Great Britain. Fuentes, appearing while at Harvard in an English trench coat jauntily striding across historic Harvard Yard on his way to instructing hundreds of undergraduates in a course on Latin American fiction and history, has carefully cultivated the appearance of a dapper English gentleman. In a highly formative period in his life, as a youth in Chile, he was educated in the English Grange School along with his classmate José Donoso, who throughout his life spoke with an English accent, and Fuentes has praised the high quality of English schools in both Chile and Argentina (consult his interview in *Paris Review*). For many years he has resided contentedly, exuberantly, in London, even donating many volumes of his private collection to Emmanuel College at Cambridge University and no doubt thoroughly enjoying his walks around Trafalgar Square, just as years ago, as Fuentes has stated, he delighted in his daily walks, while he was a Visiting Professor at Princeton University, past the house where once dwelled Albert Einstein, the house of Thomas Mann, and finally that of Herman Broch—an artistic pilgrimage. And, in a final parallel between Americanophile Hitchcock and Anglophile Fuentes, Fuentes dwelled in a huge Victorian mansion while teaching at Princeton that no doubt echoes the stately Portman Mansion of *Vertigo*, Hitchcock's spellbinding work so elaborately mirrored in Fuentes's mesmerizing novella *Aura*.

Robin Wood, one of the first and most eminent critics and interpreters of the films of Alfred Hitchcock, has commented in an interview included at the end of the DVD version of *Marnie*, deemed to be the last great picture of Alfred Hitchcock, that Hitch's art is one characterized by artifice and by his desire for a purely cinematic expression of his material. Similarly, the art of Carlos Fuentes is artificial, in the sense that its style is one of the most unreal and illusory of literary styles: The Baroque.

Like the formalistic, highly artificial worlds meticulously constructed by Alfred Hitchcock, in all of Fuentes's literary works there are layers and layers of meanings, so that every reading yields new wonders. In *Aura* the density of the narrative is reinforced by backdrops that are not real but pictorial, illusory, like the mesmeric backdrops in Hitchcock's convoluted art. Thus for example when Felipe in *Aura* discovers a moldering photograph of Consuelo as a young, ravishingly beautiful girl, she is posed against a Doric column—like the nineteenth century painting of the beautiful, enigmatic Carlotta in *Vertigo*—with a background not of reality but of a painting—yet another highly disturbing unreality—of the fascinating but deadly Lorelei on the Rhine.

An intricate baroque, highly symbolic style characterizes Fuentes's work from his initial narratives *La region más transparente* and *La muerte de Artemio Cruz* to his gigantic *Terra nostra* and New World epic *Cristóbal nonato*, to one of his most recent works, *El destino y la fortuna*. And Fuentes and Hitchcock are united in the deep influence that one of the key currents in world film history has exerted on their art—German Expressionist films of the 1920s. Hitchcock began his career in this period, in the silent era of the 1920s, and Wood has depicted even a much later work like *Marnie* (1964) as an expressionist film. Similarly, Carlos Fuentes has been decisively impacted by the expressionist art of Robert Wiene and Fritz Lang, as well as the expressionism of Welles's *Citizen Kane*. A critic has pointed out that Hitchcock preferred studio made films. Here again Hitchcock coincides with the art of one of the film directors he has most admired, Fritz Lang. We may speculate that the root of this preference is in the much greater control that a studio made film gives to the Director, as well as the conveying with much greater immediacy of the key phenomenon of unreality.

SELECTED BIBLIOGRAPHY

CRITICAL STUDIES ON ALFRED HITCHCOCK

Allen, Richard. *Hitchcock's Romantic Irony*. New York: Columbia University Press, 2007.

—. and Sam Ishii-Gonzáles, editors. *Hitchcock: Past and Future*. London and New York: Routledge, 2004.

—. and Sam Ishii-Gonzáles, editors. *Alfred Hitchcock: Centenary Essays*. London: British Film Institute, 1999.

Auiler, Dan. *Vertigo: The Making of a Hitchcock Classic*. New York. St. Martin's Press, 1998.

—. *Hitchcock's Notebooks: An Authorized and Illustrated Look Inside the Creative Mind of Alfred Hitchcock*. New York: Avon Books, 1999.

Belton, John, Editor. *Alfred Hitchcock's Rear Window*. Cambridge and New York: Cambridge University Press, 2000.

Bordwell, David. *On the History of Film Style*. Cambridge: Harvard University Press, 1997.

Brill, Lesley. *The Hitchcock Romance: Love and Irony in Hitchcock's Films*. Princeton, New Jersey: Princeton University Press, 1988.

Chabrol, Claude, and Eric Rohmer. *Hitchcock: The First Forty-Four Films*, translated by Stanley Hickman. New York: Ungar, 1979.

Chandler, Charlotte. *It's Only a Movie: Alfred Hitchcock, a Personal Biography*. New York: Applause Books, 2005.

Cohen, Paulo Marantz. *Alfred Hitchcock: The Legacy of Victorianism*. Lexington: University of Kentucky Press, 1995.

Deutelbaum, Marshall and Leland Poague, Editors. *A Hitchcock Reader*. Ames, Iowa: Iowa State University Press. 1986.

Durgnat, Raymond. *The Strange Case of Alfred Hitchcock*. Cambridge: MIT Press, 1978.

Ebert, Roger. *The Great Movies*. New York: Broadway Books, 2002.

Falk, Quentin. *Mr. Hitchcock*. London.: Haus Publishing, 2007.

Freedman, Jonathan and Richard Millington, editors. *Hitchcock's America*. New York: Oxford University Press, 1999.

Gottlieb, Sydney, Editor. *Hitchcock on Hitchcock*.. Berkeley: University of California Press, 1995.

Hill, John and Pamela Church Gibson, Editors. *Oxford Guide to Film Studies*. Oxford and New York: Limelight Editions, 1997.

Hunter, Evan. *Me and Hitch*. London and Boston: Faber and Faber, 1997.

Hurley, Neil P. *Soul in Suspense: Hitchcock's Fright and Delight*. Metuchen, New Jersey: Scarecrow Press, 1993.

Kapsis, Robert. *Hitchcock: The Making of a Reputation*. Chicago: University of Chicago Press, 1992.

Kraft, Jeff, and Aaron Leventhal. *Footsteps in the Fog: Alfred Hitchcock's San Francisco*. Santa Monica: Santa Monica Press, 2003.

LaValley, Albert J., editor *Focus on Hitchcock*. Englewood Cliffs, New Jersey: Prentice Hall, 1972.

Leitch, Thomas and Leland Poague, Editors. *A Companion to Alfred Hitchcock*, Malden, Massachusetts: Wiley Blackwell, 2011.

Maxford, Howard. *The A-Z of Hitchcock*. London: B.T. Batsford, 2002.

McDewitt, Jim, and Eric San Juan. *A Year of Hitchcock: 52 Weeks with the Master of Suspense*. Lanham Maryland: The Scarecrow Press, 2009.

McGilligan, Patrick. *Alfred Hitchcock: A Life in Darkness and Light.* New York: Harper Collins, 2003.

Modleski, Tania. *The Women Who Knew Too Much: Hitchcock and Feminist Theory*. New York: Routledge, 1989.

Mogg, Ken. *The Alfred Hitchcock Story.* Titan, 1999.

Morris, Christopher D. *The Hanging Figure: On Suspense and the Films of Alfred Hitchcock.* Westport, Connecticut: Praeger, 2002.

—. *The Hanging Figure: On Suspense and the Films of Alfred Hitchcock*. Westport, Connecticut: Praeger, 2002.

Mulvey, Laura. *Visual and Other Pleasures*. Bloomington, Indiana: Indiana University Press, 1989.

Nourmand, Tony and Mark Wolff. *Hitchcock Poster Art*. Aurum, 1999.

Orr, John. *Hitchcock and Twentieth Century Cinema.* London and New York: Wallflower Press, 2005.

Paglia, Camille. *The Birds*. British Film Institute, 1998.

Perry, Dennis R. *Hitchcock and Poe: The Legacy of Delight and Terror*. Lanham, Maryland: The Scarecrow Press, 2003.

Raubichek, Walter and Walter Srebnick, editors. *Hitchcock's Rereleased Films: From "Vertigo" to "Rope."* Detroit, Michigan: Wayne State University Press. 1991.

Rothman, William. *Hitchcock: The Murderous Gaze*. Cambridge: Harvard University Press, 1982.

—. *The "I" of the Camera: Essays in Film Criticism, History and Aesthetics*. Cambridge and New York: Cambridge University Press, 1988.

Sharff, Stefan. *The Art of Looking in Hitchcock's Rear Window.* New York: Limelight Editions, 1997.

Sloan, Jane E. *Alfred Hitchcock: The Definitive Filmograpy.* Los Angeles: University of California Press, 1993.

—. *Alfred Hitchcock: A Guide to References and Resources*. Berkeley and Los Angeles: University of California Press, 1995.

Smith, Susan. *Hitchcock: Suspense, Humour and Tone*. London: British Film Institute, 1999.

Spoto, Donald. *The Dark Side of Genius: The Life of Alfred Hitchcock*. New York: Da Capo Press, 1999.

—. *The Art of Alfred Hitchcock: Fifty Years of His Motion Pictures*. New York: Anchor Books, 1992.

Sterritt, David. *The Films of Alfred Hitchcock*. New York: Cambridge University Press, 1993.

Taylor, John Russell. *Hitch: The Life and Times of Alfred Hitchcock*. New York: Da Capo, 1996.

Truffaut, François (with Helen Scott). *Hitchcock*, revised edition. New York: Simon and Schuster, 1984.

Walker, Michael. *Hitchcock's Motifs*. Amsterdam: University of Amsterdam Press, 2005.

Weis, Elisabeth. *The Silent Scream: Alfred Hitchcock's Sound Track*. Rutherford, NJ: Farleigh Dickinson Press, 1982.

Wood, Robin. *Hitchcock's Films Revisited*. New York: Columbia University Press, 1989.

—. *Hitchcock's Films*. New York: A.S. Barnes, 1977.

Zizek, Slavoj, ed. *Everything You Always Wanted to Know About Lacan (But Were Afraid to Ask Hitchcock)*. London: Verso, 1992.

CARLOS FUENTES: WORKS

Fuentes, Carlos. *Los días enmascarados*. México, D.F.: Ediciones Era, 1954.
—. *La región más transparente*. México, D.F.: Fondo de Cultura Económica, 1958.
—. *Las buenas conciencias*. México, D.F.: Fondo de Cultura Económica, 1959.
—. *Aura*. México, D.F.: Ediciones Era, 1962.
—. *La muerte de Artemio Cruz*. México, D.F.: Fondo de Cultura Económica, 1962.
—. *Cambio de piel*. México, D.F.: Joaquín Mortiz, 1967.
—. *Zona sagrada*. México, D.F: Siglo XXI Editores, 1967.
—. *La cabeza de la hidra*. Barcelona: Argos, 1978.
—. *Orquídeas a la luz de la luna*. Barcelona: Seix Barral, 1982.
—. *Gringo viejo*. México, D.F.: Fondo de Cultura Económica, 1985.
—. *Cristóbal nonato*. México, D.F.: Fondo de Cultura Económica, 1987.
—. *Diana o la cazadora solitaria*. México, D.F.: Alfaguara, 1994.
—. *La frontera de cristal: Una novela en nueve cuentos*. México, D.F.: Alfaguara, 1996.
—. *Instinto de Inez*. México, D.F.: Alfaguara, 2001.
—. *En esto creo*. Barcelona: Seix Barral, 2002.
—. *La Silla del Águila*. México, D.F.: Alfaguara, 2003.
—. *Inquieta compañía*. México, D.F.: Alfaguara, 2004.
—. *Todas las familias felices*. México, D.F.: Alfaguara, 2006.
—. *La voluntad y la fortuna*. México, D.F.: Alfaguara, 2008.
—. *Adán en Edén*. México, D.F.: Alfaguara, 2010.
—. *Carolina Grau*. México, D.F. Alfaguara, 2010.
—. *La gran novela latinoamericana*. México, D.F.: Alfaguara, 2011.

Translations to English

—. *Aura*. Translated by Lysander Kemp. New York: Farrar, Straus and Giroux, 1968.
—. *Burnt Water*. Translated by Margaret Sayers Peden. New York: Farrar, Straus and Giroux, 1980. [Contains selected stories from *Los días enmascarados, Cantar de ciegos, Agua quemada*]
—. *A Change of Skin*. Translated by Sam Hileman. New York: Farrar, Straus and Giroux,1991.
—. *Christopher Unborn*. Translated by Alfred J. Mac Adam and Carlos Fuentes. New York: Farrar, Straus and Giroux, 1991.
—. *The Crystal Frontier: A Novel in Nine Stories*. Translated by Alfred J. Mac Adam. New York: Farrar, Straus and Giroux, 1997.
—. *The Death of Artemio Cruz*. Translated by Sam Hileman. New York: Farrar, Straus and Giroux, 1964. Re-translated by Alfred J. Mac Adam. New York: Farrar, Straus and Giroux, 1991.
—. *Destiny and Desire*. Translated by Edith Grossman. New York: Random House, 2010.
—. *Diana, or the Goddess Who Hunts Alone*. Translated by Alfred J. Mac Adam. New York: Farrar, Straus and Giroux, 1995.
—. *Distant Relations*. Translated by Margaret Sayers Peden. New York: Farrar, Straus and Giroux, 1982.
—. *Don Quijote, or the Critique of Reading*. Austin: Institute of Latin American Studies, University of Texas 1976.
—. *The Eagle's Throne*. Translated by Kristina Cordero. New York: Random House, 2006.
—. *The Good Conscience*. Translated by Sam Hileman. New York: Farrar, Straus, and

Giroux, 1961.
—. *Happy Families*. Translated by Edith Grossman. New York: Random House, 2009.
—. *Holy Place*. Translated by Suzanne Jill Levine. In *Triple Cross*. New York: E.P. Dutton, 1972.
—. *The Hydra Head.* Translated by Margaret Sayers Peden. New York: Farrar, Straus and Giroux, 1978.
—. *Inez.* Translated by Margaret Sayers Peden. New York: Harcourt, 2003.
—. *Myself with Others: Selected Essays* [written in English by Fuentes]. New York: Farrar, Straus, and Giroux, 1988.
—. *The Old Gringo.* Translated by Margaret Sayers Peden and Carlos Fuentes. New York: Farrar, Straus and Giroux, 1985.
—. *Orchids in the Moonlight*. Translated by Carlos Fuentes. Included in *Drama Contemporary: Latin America*, edited by Marion Peter Holt and George W. Woodyard. New York: PAJ Publications, 1986, 143-186.
—. *Terra nostra.* Translated by Margaret Sayers Peden. New York: Farrar, Straus and Giroux, 1976.
—. *This I Believe*. Translated by Kristina Cordero. New York: Random House, 2005.

CARLOS FUENTES: CRITICAL STUDIES

Bloom, Harold, editor. *Carlos Fuentes' The Death of Artemio Cruz*. Philadelphia: Chelsea House, 2000.
Brody, Robert, and Charles Rossman, Editors. *Carlos Fuentes: A Critical View.* Austin: University of Texas Press, 1982, 2011.
Duran, Gloria. *The Archetypes of Carlos Fuentes: From Witch to Androgyne*. New Haven, Connecticut: Archon, 1980.
González, Alfonso. *Carlos Fuentes: Life, Work, and Criticism.* York Press: 1967.
Gyurko, Lanin A. *Magic Lens: The Transformation of the Visual Arts in the Narrative World of Carlos Fuentes*. New Orleans: University Press of the South, 2010. [550 pp.]
—. *The Shattered Screen: Myth and Demythification in the Art of Carlos Fuentes and Billy Wilder*. New Orleans: University Press of the South, 2009 . 450 pp.
—. *Lifting the Obsidian Mask: The Artistic Vision of Carlos Fuentes*. Potomac, Maryland: Scripta Humanistica, 2007. 433 pp.
Sommers, Joseph. *Landmarks of the Modern Mexican Novel.* Albequerque: University of New Mexico Press, 1968.
Van Delden, Maarten. *Carlos Fuentes, Mexico and Modernity*. Nashville, Tennessee: Vanderbilt University Press, 1998.

LIST OF ILLUSTRATIONS

INDEX

Zeitfracht Medien GmbH
Ferdinand-Jühlke-Straße 7
99095 Erfurt, Deutschland
produktsicherheit@kolibri360.de